Ethics in Action

Making Ethical Decisions in Your Daily Life

Jane Ann McLachlan

Conestoga College

Pearson Canada
Toronto

DEDICATION

This textbook is dedicated to my daughter Tamara.

If everyone was as kind, loving and intuitively fair as you are, there would be fewer ethical issues to resolve. Thank you, Tamara, for your sound insights and helpful suggestions concerning this text.

"Put all things to the test; keep that which is good."
—*(I Thessalonians 5:21)*

Library and Archives Canada Cataloguing in Publication

McLachlan, Jane Ann

Ethics in action: making ethical decisions in your daily life / Jane Ann McLachlan.

Includes bibliographical references and index.
ISBN 978-0-13-504140-6

1. Ethics--Textbooks. I. Title.

BJ1521.M345 2009   170   C2008-907530-7

Vice President, Editorial Director: Gary Bennett
Editor-in-Chief: Ky Pruesse
Acquisitions Editor: Joel Gladstone
Executive Marketing Manager: Judith Allen
Associate Editor: Megan Burns
Production Editor: Avivah Wargon
Copy Editor: Gex Publishing Services
Proofreader: Gex Publishing Services

Production Coordinator: Avinash Chandra
Composition: Gex Publishing Services
Permissions Research: The Editing Company
Art Director: Julia Hall
Cover Design: Anthony Leung
Interior Design: Anthony Leung
Cover Image: Veer Inc.

1 2 3 4 5   13 12 11 10 09

Printed and bound in the United States of America.

ISBN-13: 978-0-13-504140-6
ISBN-10: 0-13-504140-6

CONTENTS

College textbooks on ethics generally fall into two categories: academic textbooks on ethical philosophy, or workbooks with exercises geared to practical application, but very little theory. The college students and corporate employees that I teach expect the stimulation of learning new material, but it must be offered in an interesting, interactive format that will engage them and it must be clearly relevant to their lives.

This textbook, therefore, offers a combination of ethical theory and practical application. My goal has been to make it reader-friendly and interactive, in order to engage college students and adult learners who would not want to read a heavy academic textbook on ethical philosophy. It offers an entry-level study of ethics, and does not require any prerequisites. Furthermore, this is a Canadian textbook. Students will relate to it because it explores ethical issues facing Canadians, gives Canadian information, and the examples and case studies are part of their experience as Canadians.

Ethics in Action: Making Ethical Decisions in Your Daily Life provides an overview of ethical philosophy meant for general learners, not philosophy majors, as well as practical application in the form of discussions and exercises geared to a number of major ethical issues facing Canadians today. It has a basic three-part structure consisting of ethical theory, ethical issues and Canadian cases for consideration and discussion, and applied ethics techniques such as writing a personal code of ethics and using different methods to resolve ethical dilemmas.

Part I: Understanding the Foundations of Ethics This section begins with self-reflection intended to encourage the student to examine what he or she already knows about ethics and where his or her personal morals and beliefs came from. As with any subject, it is important to build on the student's current knowledge and also to uncover any biases or misunderstandings. Some instructors prefer to teach a course heavier in ethical theory; Chapters 2, 3, and 4 are geared to do this. Excerpts from the original writings of the major western philosophers follow each of these chapters, although some instructors may choose not to use them due to time constraints or to the nature of their course. For teachers interested in having students read the original works, these are significant excerpts and are accompanied by focus questions and by a brief synopsis of the philosopher's life and circumstances.

Part II: Current Issues for Canadians This section begins with the study of the principles of sound reasoning. While students are usually taught how to write an essay, they are seldom taught how to structure an argument and prove their points using logic and the techniques of persuasion. Chapter 5 shows students how to use the ethical theories presented in Chapters 2–4 and the principles of sound reasoning to create valid arguments to support their opinions, and how to avoid logical and emotional fallacies. Chapters 6 and 7 examine a number of modern ethical issues in the context of Canadian society and global responsibilities, with specific references to Canadian cases and examples. Students are asked to examine, evaluate and develop ethical arguments for the issues in these chapters.

Part III: Developing an Ethical Lifestyle The final section deals with applying ethics in our daily lives. It briefly examines the influence of laws and culture on our ethical decisions, and provides practical tools for leading an ethical life, such as writing a personal code of ethics and using a variety of methods to identify and resolve ethical problems and dilemmas that confront us. Eight case studies of ethical dilemmas are included for students to practice resolving.

A textbook is a teaching tool, so reflective questions and worksheets are included throughout the text for students to fill out. Students are thus asked to think about and respond to the content as they are reading it, for a deeper learning experience. There are also numerous exercises in each chapter, which promote higher-order learning through applying the new ideas to realistic case studies or published articles. Some of the exercises are meant for students' personal use, to help them understand an idea, or for self-examination; others are intended as in-class exercises. There are many exercises geared to this so that teachers can choose which are most useful for their program goals. There are also exercises which can be used for evaluation purposes, and teachers can choose those best suited to their instruction style and program goals. Many of the exercises are designed to allow students to research issues directly relevant to their course of study. The exercises which can be used for evaluation will be indicated in the teacher's manual that accompanies the text, along with marking rubrics for each exercise and some examples of responses. The teacher's manual also includes additional quizzes similar to those embedded in the text, with answers and suggestions for using and for altering the exercises in the text.

Each chapter begins with a list of contents and clear learning objectives. The list of contents clarifies the structure of the chapter for the student and the learning objectives will be useful to students for measuring their achievement. Both contents and objectives are useful to the instructor for evaluation purposes and for matching the chapters to a course outline.

Like any tool, this textbook has been designed to be used in many different situations. The amount of material an instructor can cover in the time given is often an issue. Therefore, the chapters can be used independently. Topics such as writing a code of ethics, or reading excerpts of original writings, or any of the issues covered in Chapters 6 and 7, which may not be relevant to a particular group, can easily be omitted to allow more time for other sections. College professors generally teach courses of approximately 15–16 weeks, continuing education instructors often have only 12-week courses, and corporate trainers have two- to five-day sessions. They all teach to very different audiences. However, I have used the material in this text to deliver instruction in professional ethics to all three of these groups, with very positive feedback from students.

A textbook is a starting point that is meant to be supplemented with lectures and discussions geared to the instructor's expertise and teaching style and to the students' program of study. This Canadian textbook offers a combination of ethical theory and practical application in the form of discussions and exercises geared to the major social and global ethical issues facing Canadians. It encourages self-reflection by asking questions and leaving space for answers within the text, and through worksheets for students to fill out. Because it is a combination textbook-workbook, it is especially suited to college, where most of the students are hands-on learners and simply will not read densely written texts. I have attempted to make its exercises and writing style flexible in order to accommodate different teaching styles, areas of expertise and different students' program needs.

JANE ANN MCLACHLAN

INSTRUCTOR SUPPLEMENTS

The following instructor supplements are available for this textbook:

- **Instructor's Manual.** Includes a brief topic outline as well as learning objectives and how they can be met for each chapter, with detailed lecture outlines with teaching tips, discussion questions, evaluation methods and marking rubrics. This supplement can be downloaded by instructors from a password-protected location on Pearson Education Canada's online catalogue (vig.pearsoned.ca). Simply search for the text, then click on "Instructor" under "Resources" in the left-hand menu. Contact your local sales representative for further information.
- **PowerPoint Presentation.** Includes slide shows for each chapter which highlight and summarize the main ideas along with questions for class discussion. These helpful presentations are also located on the online catalogue.
- **CourseSmart.** A new way for instructors and students to access textbooks online anytime from anywhere. With thousands of titles across hundreds of courses, CourseSmart helps instructors choose the best textbook for their class and give their students a new option of buying the assigned textbook as a lower-cost eTextbook. For more information, visit **www.coursesmart.com.**

ACKNOWLEDGEMENTS

I wish to acknowledge my family, Ian, Amanda, John, Tamara, Steve and Caroline for their invaluable encouragement and assistance while I worked on this textbook. I am also indebted to my team at Pearson Education, Christine Cozens, Kathleen McGill, Megan Burns, Avivah Wargon, and Avinash Chandra, as well as Marisa Taylor and all the copy editors, formatters and proofreaders who have made this textbook better than I could ever have made it alone.

AUTHOR BIOGRAPHY

Jane Ann McLachlan is a professor at Conestoga College in Kitchener, Ontario. She has been teaching Communications and Professional Ethics for eight years. She has a B.A. from York University, an M.A. from Carleton University and a certificate in Adult Education from Conestoga College. *Ethics In Action: Making Ethical Decisions In Your Daily Life* is her second textbook on ethics. She has also written a textbook on business and health-care applied ethics entitled, *The Right Choice: Making Ethical Decisions on the Job.* Her academic email address is jmclachlan@conestogac.on.ca.

Introduction

> "Morality, like art, means drawing a line someplace."
>
> —OSCAR WILDE (1854–1900)

An individual living alone on an island would have no need to concern himself with ethics. He would have no one but himself to consider, and if his decisions all revolved around his own desires, there would be no one to complain that he was not acting ethically. If he cut down trees on the island and burned out the undergrowth, we would probably consider him stupid rather than unethical, as he would have destroyed important food sources as well as his protection against the weather. In fact, he would likely die and the trees and vegetation would soon come back as robust as ever.

Most of us would die fairly quickly if we had to be entirely self-sufficient, even if we didn't destroy our food sources and burn off our habitat. We are too accustomed to our interdependent lifestyle, where some people provide the goods they can produce and others provide the services they are skilled at doing. We all benefit from the daily exchange of goods and services in Canada, but benefits are always accompanied by obligations. Along with the pleasures and advantages of living among other people come responsibilities and obligations.

The study of ethics concerns the way we deal with others and uphold the obligations of our various roles. We all play a number of roles in our lives: parent, partner, son or daughter, brother or sister, friend, student, employee, customer, neighbour, citizen, and so on. Each of these roles places expectations on us and obligations toward those who relate to us in that role. A student has an obligation to attend class, to study, not to cheat; an employee has an obligation to do her job well, to take direction from her boss, to show up regularly and on time for work; a spouse or partner has an obligation to be loyal and supportive and to be there when his partner needs him; a citizen of a country has an obligation to obey its laws and to be a productive participant in that society.

Most of the time our moral path is clear-cut and straightforward, but sometimes situations occur which cause conflicts between our different obligations. When this happens it is sometimes hard to determine what the right thing to do is. For example, a student is expected to attend classes and hand in assignments on time, but if a family emergency comes up, that student may also have an obligation to help and support the family member in need. If she cannot do both at the same time, how should she decide which has priority? Sometimes the conflict is not between different roles, but between different expectations in the same role. A friend or a spouse is expected to be honest and to be supportive. What if someone's friend or partner asks for an opinion on something he's done, which the friend or partner thinks has not been done well at all, even though she knows he put a lot of effort and time into it, and there is no time to redo or improve it? Is honesty or encouragement more important in a case like this? In the first case, two different roles were in conflict; in the second case, two principles, honesty and supportiveness, were in conflict. Sometimes another kind of conflict arises, between principles and outcomes. For example, what if someone knows his best friend's car accident was actually suicide? If he tells them, his friend's wife and little daughter will be emotionally deeply hurt and the insurance company won't pay the claim, so they'll also be left with debts and no money. On the other hand, not telling is the same as helping his friend to commit insurance fraud. What if this is the same insurance company that wriggled out of paying his friend an honest claim because of some technicality in small print on the document and that's what put his friend in debt in the first place?

In all of the above situations, only two things are in conflict, but in fact, everyone has many obligations to many different people, and many moral principles they believe in living up to. Sorting through those obligations and principles of behaviour and determining which ones are more important when they are in conflict can be extremely time-consuming and difficult. During a busy day or in a crisis situation it is not always possible to evaluate each principle and obligation. Therefore, people often rely on rules to help them make these decisions. There are three levels of rules.

First there are the laws of the province and country where a person lives. Anyone who does not abide by those laws can be charged and brought to civil court. Next there are rules of behaviour set down by specific professions and companies. These can be written as a code of ethics or as standards of practice. Professionals and employees who fail to live up to these standards of practice and codes of conduct face disciplinary actions from their licensing body or the company they work for, which can include losing their licence to practice or being fired. These two levels of rules and the obligations they impose upon us provide guidelines for many aspects of our lives. The third level is not written anywhere. It is composed of the social, cultural and family expectations that a person is expected to know and follow. Failing to live up to those expectations can result in criticism, physical punishments or withdrawal of financial support, or even being ostracized from the family or cultural group.

Where, in all this, do personal ethics come in? If we blindly obey all these rules, does that make us ethical? In the sense that abiding by ethical rules is the ethical thing to do, perhaps. But being an ethical person is much more complicated than that.

First, rules, policies and standards of practice need to be interpreted. What exactly is harassment? When does joking with someone become harassment? When is it necessary to keep a client's or friend's information confidential and when is it important to disclose a dangerous situation? When is it important to live by family and cultural expectations and when is it important to set your own standards? Without a personal understanding of the intent or moral basis behind these rules we will sometimes have trouble using them to establish appropriate ethical behaviours.

Second, rules often need to be prioritized. How does a person choose between conflicting obligations or principles, as in the above examples? Is respect for honesty and justice more important than achieving the best for one's client or family, or vice versa? Are the needs of the student who repeatedly disrupts class more or less important than the rest of the students' need for a positive learning environment? Should the person who is having trouble adjusting to an accident that has left him disabled be forced to accept life-saving measures or should his right to refuse them be respected? These are difficult questions, especially if all we have to resort to are the seemingly conflicting rules.

Finally, ethical individuals have a duty to examine the rules for themselves and decide whether they are relevant and morally acceptable. If they are not, the issue of disobeying the rules or attempting to change them comes up. Canada is currently wrestling with a number of ethical areas in its social customs and its laws. Even those which have been resolved by recent laws are still often disputed. Should the use of marijuana be decriminalized? Should same-sex marriages and abortion be legal? Should physician-assisted suicide be available on demand? Should businesses be allowed to pollute the environment, and if not, what restrictions should be placed on them? As members of our society, what obligation do we have to participate in the ethical discussions that create and change our laws?

The same kind of discussions can take place within a company regarding its policies. Some organizations refuse to hire relatives of current employees. Is this discrimination or protection against nepotism? What if the company is the largest source of employment in a community? This company's refusal to hire employees' children could mean that many or even most of the young people in the community will be forced to move away to find work. Should the employees of the organization accept this policy or lobby for change?

What are some rules in your family or your culture that you live by?

_____

_____

_____

What are some rules in your family or your culture that you disagree with?

_____

_____

_____

Rules in themselves cannot ensure ethical practices. People need to be able to apply ethical guidelines to actual situations, to analyze and resolve ethical conflicts and to recognize ethical and unethical rules. To do so, they must be educated in applied ethics. And to understand applied ethics, it is necessary to have at least a basic grasp of ethical theories.

What standards should we use to measure whether a rule is ethical or whether we are interpreting it in an ethical manner? Often the answer we are given is something like, "Use your common sense." But what is common sense? Is it the sum of our own personal beliefs and past experiences? If we go by this, the result could be totally different interpretations of the same rule. For example, a person who grew up in an affectionate family, where the members constantly teased each other, might consider joking in the workplace to be an expression of friendship or affection. Another person who grew up in a family where sarcasm and insults were actually intended to control or put a person "in his place," might consider the same teasing remark to be harassment.

Should we use the measure of common opinion? Until two centuries ago, slavery was common practice and not considered unethical. Did common opinion make it ethical for one person to own another? At one time, common opinion also considered it ethical to deny women the vote or the right to hold property, but very few Canadians consider this to be ethical today. Should we instead use the law of our country as a measure of ethical behaviour? But the law, at its best, is not a much better measure of ethical behaviour than common opinion—our laws are only a reflection of our current understanding of justice as a society. And if we wish to examine our laws to determine whether they are ethical, we cannot use the laws themselves as the measuring rod.

So neither individual common sense nor the common opinion of our colleagues and compatriots can be used with confidence to interpret and assess whether an action, a policy or a law is ethical. We may be able to judge these subjectively—that is, based on our personal beliefs and values—but can we justify these criteria to others? We would be arguing endlessly over whose personal opinion should have the final say. So we are left with the question: Are there any objective ethical truths? And if there are, what criteria are they based on?

This is the study of ethics. Just as the study of science results in scientific theories, the study of ethics leads to ethical theories—that is to say, theories about what our ethics should be. There are many scientific theories which cannot be proven true or false because of our limited knowledge, such as the existence of wormholes or alien intelligence, but that doesn't mean that these things do not exist. In the same way, we may not know whether capital punishment is objectively ethical or unethical, but that doesn't mean that there isn't an objective truth about it.

We can use ethical theories, as we use known scientific facts, to get at these truths. Ethical theories justify certain behaviours and refute others. They provide us with a degree of objectivity in measuring the moral worth of the rules we live by. They provide us, in our daily lives as well as in times of confusion and crisis, with the confidence of knowing that our choices and behaviours are based on the best knowledge and carefully considered use of ethical reasoning available to us. They enable us to justify our behaviour to ourselves and to others, both at the time and after the fact, in a way that our subjective common sense or the prevailing common opinion of our colleagues or society cannot. Although all ethical theories have their weaknesses and shortcomings, well-reasoned arguments based on sound ethical theories will get us much closer to ethical truths than our subjective opinions will.

This text cannot tell readers what the ultimate right and wrong or good and bad is. Its intent is to make the readers' own ethical judgments more conscious, more broadly considered and more ethically informed.

> "The truth is that there is nothing noble in being superior to somebody else. The only real nobility is in being superior to your former self."
>
> —WHITNEY YOUNG (1921–1971)

1 Personal Ethics

CONTENTS

- Understanding the Language of Ethics
- External Forces That Shape Our Ethics
- Theories of Moral Development
- Self-Reflection

> "I think that somehow we learn who we really are, and then live with that decision."
>
> —ELEANOR ROOSEVELT (1884–1962)

How many decisions have you already made today? Perhaps you considered whether to walk, bike, drive or take public transit to work or to school. If driving, you decided whether to go above the speed limit. Perhaps you had to choose between supporting a friend or colleague's charity by sponsoring him in a walkathon or buying raffle tickets; whether to be helpful and courteous or brisk and cool in interacting with strangers; whether to toss your empty pop can into a wastebasket or carry it home to recycle.

All of these decisions affect the people around us or the environment that we all share. Because they affect others, we can say that our choices are ethical choices, even though they may appear to be small events in our lives. The decision to act ethically or unethically is one that we make every day. But do we always make these decisions consciously? Are we acting out of habit, because of attitudes and experiences from our past and maybe even beliefs that we no longer hold? Do our choices really reflect how we want to behave, or are they the result of pressure from others or how we have been taught we should behave?

Some people never question their actions or their motives, while others second-guess every decision they make. Both of these situations result from people being unclear about what they believe, what they value and what they should base their actions and their choices on. Even those individuals who have strong and clear beliefs need to take time to consider how these beliefs translate into everyday behaviours in modern life.

It is important to take time to reflect on this, because behaving well is not the same thing as behaving ethically. It is quite likely that doing what we are expected or have been taught to do will result in doing the right thing, but being unconsciously well-behaved is very different from being consciously ethical. First of all, unconscious ethical behaviour cannot be relied upon in new situations or situations where there is no external pressure. Second, it will not offer any guidance when the right thing to do is unclear or in conflict with another right thing.

If a person tells the truth because she has been taught from childhood that it's the right thing to do and that she will be punished if she's caught lying, is she being ethical or just careful to protect herself? If she tells the truth even when it is difficult and causes her some personal sacrifice, and even when she would not be found out if she didn't, because she believes that honesty is important, is she then being ethical? If she lies because she knows telling the truth in this situation will have harmful consequences for others, is she being ethical? The difference between the first situation and the second and third situation is that in the second and third situations she is making a personal choice. Behaving ethically must first of all be a conscious choice that comes from inside a person.

Growing up, as the previous quote by Eleanor Roosevelt suggests, is a process of learning "who we really are." What we believe in, what we value and how we behave are part of that equation, as are all the influences that shape those beliefs, values and behaviours. We expect the quote to end, "and then live with that." But it doesn't. It says, "with that decision." As thinking human beings, we make decisions. Consciously or unconsciously, we choose who we will be. If we accept (or "come to terms with") what we have learned about ourselves as being the final definition of who we are, we are choosing to be that person. It may be an unconscious decision. We may feel we have no choice in the matter, that our attitudes and actions have defined us. But we have chosen to accept that definition. Or we may take the next step. We may say to ourselves, "This is who I want to be," and then act accordingly. We can decide not to be governed by instinct or habit or emotion, but to decide what sort of person we want to be. And then we can live with that decision.

Before we can do this, however, we have to find out who we are.

UNDERSTANDING THE LANGUAGE OF ETHICS

Ethics comes from the Greek word *ethos*, which means character in conjunction with custom. Character is a complex word. It can be described as the attitudes, values and beliefs that determine a person's behaviour. Obviously these will be related to the customs of a person's culture or time period. A person's character, or ethics, will largely determine which choice he or she makes when faced with a moral decision.

Understanding ethics begins with understanding the language of ethics. We use words like *morals*, *values* and *beliefs* all the time, but few of us spend much time thinking about what they really mean. Furthermore, in order that the words we use actually communicate what we mean, we must have a shared understanding of their meaning. This is difficult enough in a multicultural society like Canada when dealing with English as a second language and different cultural attitudes, but it is even more difficult with nebulous words such as morals and values. To complicate matters further, these particular words often elicit strong opinions and emotions, which makes it hard to discuss them.

EXERCISE 1.1

Understanding the Language of Ethics

In a group of four to five students, discuss the meaning of the following words and how they differ from one another. Write down a definition for each of them.

Ethics:

_____

_____

_____

Code of ethics:

_____

_____

_____

Morals:

_____

_____

_____

Duties:

_____

_____

_____

Values:

_____

_____

_____

Beliefs:

_____

_____

_____

Assumptions:

_____

_____

_____

Did your group have any disagreement over the meaning of these words?
Were you surprised by how others understood any of them? Did others
add some meaning to the words that you had not considered?

English is a complex language in which one word often has several meanings. "Home" can mean a building, but it can also mean a place where we feel welcome and appreciated. Moreover, English is a living language. In a living language, the meaning of a word can change with repeated use over time. Thus, the word "gay" is now a synonym for "homosexual" and is seldom, if ever, used in its original meaning, "happy." Because English is a complex and changing language, and because of the cultural differences among Canadians, it is important when discussing ethical issues and decisions to make sure that the words being used mean the same thing to everyone. Therefore, for the purpose of this course, let us consider each of the words in Exercise 1.1.

Ethics

The study of ethics is the study of the process of determining moral conduct through reflection and analysis. Ethics converts values, morals and beliefs into actions. Ethics is primarily concerned with the end of the process: our conduct or behaviour. A code of ethics, therefore, is a verbal or written set of guidelines for moral behaviour. A code of ethics often is a written record that sets the boundaries of acceptable moral conduct for an organization or a group of people.

Morals

The basis of ethics are the morals, duties, values and beliefs that determine correct or acceptable behaviours. Morals are concerned with what is good or bad, right or wrong. They are ideals for behaviour, rather than actual behaviours. For example, consider a mechanic, Tom, whose customer has asked him to check the brakes on his car. Tom finds that the car needs brake fluid, but the brakes are fine. His customer knows nothing about cars and will believe whatever Tom tells him. Tom believes that it is moral to tell the truth rather than to lie (ideal behaviour = morals). Therefore, Tom tells his customer that he does not need to have his brakes replaced yet (actual behaviour = ethics).

List some of your morals (the things you believe are right and wrong).

It is moral to:

_____

_____

It is not moral to:

_____

_____

There is often some confusion about the difference between ethics and morals, because we tend to use the two words interchangeably. This is normally the case when we use them as adjectives or adverbs. We say "an ethical issue" or "a moral issue" and mean the same thing. We say, "he's behaving ethically," or "he's behaving morally," and once again, we mean the same thing. In this text, when the terms are used as adjectives or adverbs, they are used to mean essentially the same thing. However, when we discuss morals, used as a noun, what we are discussing is ideas of what is right and wrong; when we discuss ethics, as a noun, we are referring to actions or behaviours.

Duties

The sense of duty or obligation is closely related to morals. Duties are claims upon us that are either self-imposed or imposed by others. They refer to the attitudes and behaviours we feel that others have a right to expect of us because of their relationship to us, be it personal, professional or societal. We understand these duties even though they are not written down anywhere, and even though we may not always act in accordance with them. Children have a duty to obey their parents and parents have a duty to protect and provide for their children. Professionals have a duty to deliver goods or services that will fulfill their customers' expectations. Customers have a duty to reimburse the professional fairly and promptly. Like morals, these duties or obligations are ideal concepts which determine actual behaviours in a given situation.

What are some of the roles that you play in your life?

_____

_____

_____

Circle the five roles in your list which you consider to be the most important.

Now record what obligations come with each of them.

1. _____

2. _____

3. _____

4. _____

5. _____

Finally, record some actions or choices you might make which would violate the expectations of each role.

1. _____

_____

2. _____

_____

3. _____

_____

4. _____

_____

5. _____

_____

Values

Our concept of what is right and wrong or good and bad is based upon our values. Values are clear and uncompromising statements about what is important to us. They are the abstract principles that we believe in and upon which we base our morals and ethics. The terms "values" and "morals" are often used interchangeably because we can value a moral. "Tell the truth" states a moral, while "honesty" is something we value. A person who values honesty will believe that it is morally right to tell the truth and morally wrong to lie, and will, therefore, in a given situation, tell the truth.

What are some of your personal values?

_____

_____

_____

_____

Beliefs

Our values, in turn, are based upon our beliefs. A belief is a personal and subjective conviction in an absolute truth or in the existence of a higher being or deity. Beliefs have to do with the higher meaning or purpose of our lives. An individual's values, morals and sense of duty all stem from his or her beliefs. For example, "Thou shalt not bear false witness (lie)" is one of the commandments in the Old Testament. Therefore, an individual who believed in Christianity or Judaism, or whose own holy book contained a similar command (the Quran, for example, states "They invoke a curse of God if they lie" (24:7)), would value the ideal of honesty and would think that it was morally wrong to lie; therefore, he or she would tell the truth in a given situation. Non-religious people may value honesty just as much, but they would believe in it as a moral truth that we should aspire to, not as a religious commandment. Beliefs go beyond the way we behave to define our overall attitude toward life. A person whose beliefs included a belief in an afterlife would presumably react to the news that he was dying differently from someone who believed that death was the end of his existence. And what a person believed about the means of achieving that afterlife would have a great effect upon her actions.

What are your beliefs about the meaning of life?

_____

_____

_____

It should be apparent that as we move from ethics to morals, duties, values and beliefs, we are moving deeper and deeper into the core of what determines how a person responds to other people and to situations requiring a choice of action. The more conscious and clear people are about their morals, sense of duty and personal values and beliefs, and how these translate into ethics, the more they will be able to take conscious control over their behaviour.

Assumptions

At the very deepest level of what motivates our actions are our assumptions about life. Assumptions are the underlying basis of our values, morals and sense of duty. They are usually unconscious, and are taken for granted as self-evident truths. Because they are to a large extent formed in our childhood, they are often outdated or irrelevant to situations which we face as adults. And yet, because they are unconscious, they are very difficult to examine and change. An individual growing up in a dysfunctional family and a rough neighbour-hood may learn to assume that people have to take care of themselves, that they cannot rely on others and that the world is a dangerous place. Another individual growing up in a supportive family in a friendly neighbourhood might make very different assumptions about people and the way they relate to each other. In other words, we unconsciously draw conclusions that the world works in a certain way, that "that's just the way things are," based on our experiences and observations. And often those experiences and observa-tions were made when we were much too young to examine their accuracy. Even when we are older, it is not easy or it makes us uncomfortable to decide that the world does not work the way we have always assumed it did, or that people can be different than our own experience has led us to believe.

What are some of your assumptions about the way things really are?

Family is

_____

Men are

_____

Women are

_____

People are

_____

Government is

_____

Life is

_____

You have to

_____

The total process, from assumptions to ethics, would look something like this:

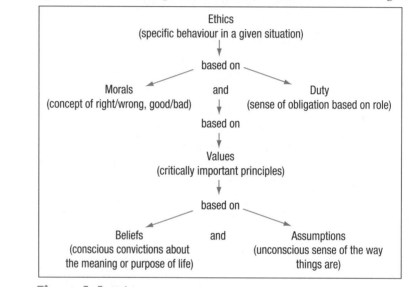

Figure1.1 Ethics

The following scenario offers a concrete example of this process. Bob, a human resources manager at a large welding shop, has just hired a female welder, Heather, because she was better qualified than any of the other applicants, even though there are no other female welders in the shop. What morals, values, beliefs and assumptions led Bob to this decision?

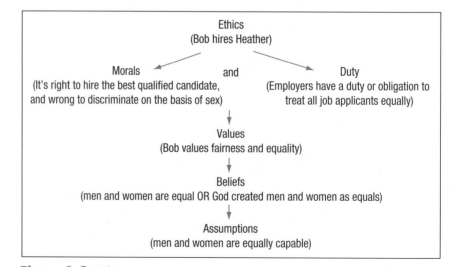

Figure1.2 Ethics

If, at the deepest level, Bob's observations and experience caused him to assume that women are not as capable as men, he would probably not have hired Heather. He might still consciously value fairness, but argue that it isn't fair to make the other welders carry some of Heather's workload. He might still feel morally obligated to hire the best candidate, but not believe that the best candidate is Heather. He might still believe that he is treating all job applicants equally because he also disqualified a male applicant who came across in the interview as being less capable than the other applicants. It is possible that this assumption about men and women was formed during childhood based on his observations and early experiences. But the childhood experiences that formed this assumption are totally irrelevant to the current situation and the people in this situation—the job candidates. Nevertheless, if this is one of Bob's most basic assumptions about people, he will be inclined to consider it obviously true, and will not question whether it is accurate or appropriate in this situation.

Ironically, during World War II, when women went to work welding in factories because the men were fighting, women turned out to be better welders than men. Women, in general, have steadier hands. However, this reality is not reflected in most welding shops, where there are few, if any, female welders. Obviously there are some assumptions in our society that are still barring women from equal consideration for work in certain fields, and that are not based on actual job performance.

If an individual's ethics come from his morals, values, beliefs and assumptions, the next question is, where do those come from? For most of us, there is no point during our formative years when we say to ourselves, "this is what I am going to value," or "this is what I'm going to believe." Our morals, values and beliefs come to us gradually based on what we are told, what we observe and what we personally experience. Unfortunately, we are not in control of any of those three things. From the beginning, other people tell us what to believe and how to behave, particularly the authority figures in our lives. What we observe and what we directly experience are both dependent partly upon the circumstances in our lives and partly upon our ability to correctly interpret our observations and experiences. We seldom, if ever, pause to question and reconsider our interpretations of events, particularly in childhood and youth. Therefore, unless we decide at some point to try to objectively examine our morals, values, beliefs and assumptions, they will remain extremely subjective, mostly a mixture of habit and reaction, and more in control of us than we are rationally in control of them.

This course offers an opportunity to do exactly that. It is a period of time set aside from the hectic pace of living for reflection and self-evaluation. The discussions with other students will provide an opportunity to listen to other points of view and to hear your own opinions more objectively. Examine your beliefs, values, morals and basic assumptions by the measure of the ethical theories you will learn. Whether this process serves to change or to confirm your current ethics, either way it will make you more conscious of your morals, assumptions, values and beliefs, and therefore, more in control of your ethics. This self-reflection offers you a chance to decide what you will live with, as Eleanor Roosevelt put it. It is an essential part of the process of becoming a more consciously ethical person.

EXTERNAL FORCES THAT SHAPE OUR ETHICS

Family

Our earliest experiences come from within our family. This is where we form our most basic assumptions about human nature and the way people relate to each other. Parents and siblings influence our values, morals and beliefs. They have the strongest impact on our character because theirs is the first influence and this influence is exerted over us at a time when we are too young to do anything but accept what we are told and what we observe and experience. Whether as adults we accept our family's values, morals and beliefs or reject them, or respond with a combination of acceptance and rejection, they still form the foundation from which we build our own values, morals and beliefs.

> When Chandra was six, she told her eight-year-old brother, Sing, that she hated him because he was teasing her. That afternoon, while swimming in the river with his friends, Sing drowned. Chandra always remembered that the last thing she had said to Sing was that she hated him. When Chandra had her own children, she would not allow them to express anger toward one another. She told them the story of her brother and warned them never to say anything they would regret. Chandra's daughter, Deep, grew up feeling that she was not allowed to express her true feelings in her family, and that she was not as close to them as she might have been because of it. When she became a mother, she encouraged her children to express their feelings to one another and work out their differences.

This story, told by a student taking an ethics course, shows how a childhood experience can form the values and morals of two generations within a family. Of course, other influences were probably at work also. Chandra's parents might have reprimanded her for her fight with her brother. Their reprimand would have reinforced her feeling of guilt later when her brother drowned. Her family might also have discouraged her from expressing and resolving her feelings of guilt, perhaps because they were unable to deal with it in the midst of their own grief. Deep's father quite likely shared his wife, Chandra's, aversion to hearing the children argue, and later, Deep's husband probably shared her opinion that it is better to express negative emotions than to keep them bottled up inside. In other words, the experience, combined with the observed family culture and expressed opinions of both parents, all worked together to reinforce a behaviour pattern.

Within a family the same values, beliefs and morals are usually reinforced by observations, experiences and direct statements, not only once but over and over. For example, a child might be told, "Never take what isn't yours." She might observe her parents returning an item they hadn't paid for that was put into their shopping bag by mistake. She might also experience pleasure when something she thought she had lost is returned to her. These and similar recurring experiences and observations all reinforce the same moral statement. When parents' statements are contradicted by observations and experience, as when parents do one thing and say the opposite, repeated contradictions either reinforce the real moral or cause a direct reaction. The following example demonstrates this:

> Pavel's parents always told him, "Don't tell lies." However, Pavel sometimes witnessed his parents lying to extended family members when they wanted to avoid a family obligation, and often caught them lying to his younger brother or to him. The real moral statement he observed from them was to lie when it is expedient to do so. Either Pavel will accept the moral he experienced, and lie when it is useful to do so, or he will react against it. In this case, Pavel never lies, not even when the truth will cause pain to himself or others, because he resented being lied to when he was a child.

Use the following charts to reflect upon some of the morals and values learned from your family, following the example in the first square. In the second column write what you observed, experienced or were told to make you learn these morals and values. An example has been given to start each chart.

EXERCISE 1.2

Family Influence on Morals and Values

Morals:	Learned through:
Good = telling the truth	Was told: "Always tell the truth"
	Observed: Parents telling the truth to children and others
	Older sibling owning up to doing something wrong
Bad = lying	Experienced: A situation when you were praised or rewarded by a teacher or parent for being honest
Good =	Was told:
	Observed:
Bad =	Experienced:
Good =	Was told:
	Observed:
Bad =	Experienced:
Good =	Was told:
	Observed:
Bad =	Experienced:

(Continued)

(Continued)

Values:	Learned through:
Family connections are important	Was told: "Family comes first." Observed: Parents making time to help grandparents/their siblings/me and my siblings when they/we needed help Experienced: Family time and outings with our family and family get-togethers with extended family
	Was told: Observed: Experienced:
	Was told: Observed: Experienced:
	Was told: Observed: Experienced:

Understanding where your assumptions about life came from and how your morals and values were taught to you is the first step to becoming a consciously ethical person. It is how you learn who you are. Now you have the opportunity to decide who you will be.

EXERCISE 1.3

Uncovering Your Basic Assumptions

Consider some of your basic assumptions about human nature and the way people relate to one another; not the way they should, but the way you assume people actually do relate to each other. Write down three of these assumptions (the ones you consider most important) here.

1. _____

2. _____

3. _____

How were these assumptions formed in your childhood?

Was told:

1. _____

2. _____

3. _____

Observed:

1. _____

2. _____

3. _____

Experienced:

1. _____

2. _____

3. _____

What observations or experiences have you had as an adult that either confirm or contradict these assumptions?

Confirm:

1. _____

2. _____

3. _____

Contradict:

1. _____

2. _____

3. _____

(Continued)

(Continued)

Do you think your childhood assumptions are accurate? To what extent?

1. _____

2. _____

3. _____

Religion

Our beliefs about the meaning of life are formed not only by our family but also by whatever religious upbringing we received. These beliefs are passed on to us in written form (the scriptures or holy book of a religion), through formal teaching (Sunday school, religious classes) and through the worship services we attend and hymns we are taught to sing. These beliefs are either reinforced or contradicted by parental teachings and by the examples set by the religious authorities in our lives at the time. Often children are taught or take in a more simplified, literal version of their religion, which they later adjust to accommodate a more complex understanding of life.

What religious precepts were you taught as a child?

_____

_____

How did these beliefs affect your values and morals at the time?

_____

_____

How have your religious beliefs changed in adulthood?

_____

_____

What changed them?

_____

_____

Has this change affected your values and morals, and if so, in what way?

_____

_____

Education

Our educational experiences also exert an early influence over our values and morals. This is particularly true for those in the separate school system in Canada or those who are sent to a private religious school. However, there are many morals and values taught in the public system that are not directly related to a particular religion, such as not taking another child's possession, not cheating on assignments and tests, not lying about homework and so on.

The content of the courses students must take is also value-laden. The themes of the stories and novels studied in English, the teachings about different cultures in geography and social studies, the interpretations of who is a hero and who a villain in history, all contain hidden moral lessons. In Canadian history, for example, Laura Secord warning British troops about an American invasion is taught as an example of courage and loyalty. The hidden moral is that we should be willing to risk our lives to protect our country. This may or may not be a value we want to retain in adulthood.

If the values taught in school are in agreement with the values in the child's home, they serve to reinforce one another. If they are in conflict, they may open a child's eyes to another way of thinking and behaving, but will likely have less effect in the long run unless the child is already questioning her home values. In Canada, for example, public schools warn children of the health dangers of smoking, drinking, taking drugs and unprotected sex. But if a child goes home to parents who indulge in any or all of these activities and appear to suffer no negative effects, the child is unlikely to believe what he has been told in school. If, however, there are conflicts between the parent and the child that cause the child to question the parent's example and there is a close, more supportive relationship between the child and the teacher, then the child may consider the school's values more seriously. There are too many factors involved to say definitively that any one of them is a deciding factor, but none of them can be totally discounted, either.

Friends and Colleagues

In late childhood and adolescence, peer groups usually begin to exert a stronger influence over people's values and morals than their family does. In the workplace this can also translate into role-modelling of a successful or admired colleague. In both instances, there are three methods by which friends and colleagues influence our values and morals. We are influenced by direct comments made to us, by shared activities and by our internal perception of our friends and colleagues.

The first way that they exert an influence over us is by direct comments or indirect taunts, such as "Don't be a baby," or "He's afraid." Friends and colleagues often try to tell us what is or isn't fun and exciting to do. These statements may take the form of a challenge, as in the following example:

> Although Jillian was raised in a home where stealing was considered wrong, in Grade 9 she joined a group of girls whose values were very different. They challenged each other to shoplift. When it was Jillian's turn, she took a lipstick. Despite her friends' admiration, Jillian felt so bad about it that the next day she sneaked the unopened lipstick back onto the store rack she had taken it from. She was even more nervous returning it than she had been while stealing it the day before, and when she left the store she vowed that she'd never shoplift again.

While direct statements are an effective influence, particularly when they are delivered in a group setting, the activities undertaken with a friend or colleague exert an equally strong influence. We might learn that winning fights is valued by the peer group; later, actually fighting another person and being admired by the group for winning the fight might reinforce that value. However, there is the possibility that the activity itself can activate opposing values learned at home, in church or at school, and cause a backlash, as in the following example:

> Mike's grandmother died of emphysema. His family did not approve of smoking. But at Mike's first job away from home, he found that most of his colleagues smoked. Although they didn't pressure him to smoke, he wanted to fit in. Later, when he lit up a cigarette on a visit home, his family was so disappointed and worried about his health that he soon decided to quit.

Not all external influences are negative. Some have a broadening effect beyond our learned values.

> Ruth was raised in a traditional Jewish home. Her parents emigrated from Israel when she was nine, and brought with them a strong distrust of Palestinians. As an adult, Ruth was upset when she was transferred into a department to work under the supervision of a Palestinian. When an important project she was working on failed, Ruth expected that she would be blamed. Instead, her supervisor recognized the effort Ruth had put into the project, acknowledged that the failure was not Ruth's fault, and backed her up in his report to management. As a result, Ruth no longer believes all Palestinians are untrustworthy.

Consider some of your own attitudes that friends or colleagues encouraged with their words or by example, which conflicted with values or morals you learned at home. They may be negative experiences which you now regret or positive experiences which broadened your outlook. By reflecting on how others influence you or have influenced you, you will be better able to consciously control influences outside yourself now.

1. The attitude or activity:

   _____

   _____

   The home values in conflict with it:

   _____

   _____

   The outcome for you:

   _____

   _____

2. The attitude or activity:

   _____

   _____

   The home values in conflict with it:

   _____

   _____

   The outcome for you:

   _____

   _____

A third and more subtle method by which friends and colleagues influence us is through our perception of them. This is our internalized assessment of their values and morals. The swaggering boss who appears to us to be an egotistical buffoon does not make us want to emulate him. However, if we perceive him instead to be successful and powerful within the organization, we may want to adopt his values and behaviours. The friend whose fearless defiance of school authority we admire may not seem so admirable when she betrays our confidence as easily as she rebels against her teacher. In this case, nothing has changed about the friend except for our perception of her, but she has become the person we don't want to be like rather than the one we want to imitate. Instead of adopting our former friend's values and morals, we will now be more inclined to use them as an example of what to avoid.

Social Culture

As we grow older, we are influenced by the values of our society through newspaper and magazine articles, television and movies, radio newscasts and public discussions. We can become aware of these values by considering who the heroes and villains in our society are and how they are portrayed. The rewards and punishments that a society metes out also shape our perception of right and wrong. Finally, the laws and policies of our society influence our values and morals because we must abide by them. The following is an example of this influence:

> We read in the newspaper that police have discovered another marijuana harvesting operation and are shocked that it is in our neighbourhood. The facts of the case are that it is illegal in Canada to grow, sell or use marijuana without a permit for health reasons, and the punishment is a fine or a jail term. We may conclude that at the current time, in Canadian culture, marijuana use is considered morally wrong except in certain circumstances related to health issues. Both the fact that there is a law against it and the punishment for being caught indicates this. We may or may not share this opinion, but we cannot help being influenced by it. Even if we have smoked marijuana on occasion, we do not view a marijuana harvesting operator the same way we view a local farmer. We tend to view those who break the law as generally having low moral standards, especially if they do so for no better reason than personal profit.

Our analysis of the values and morals of our society is filtered through our personal perception or interpretation of what we are observing. Different people may examine the law to determine the moral stance behind it and come to completely different conclusions about what is being valued. In the previous example, we concluded that the moral stance behind the law is that growing, selling and using recreational marijuana is morally wrong. But what can we conclude about the social values driving that social moral stance? One person might say that in Canada a high value is placed on protecting citizens from the dangers of addictive drugs. Another might say that in Canada freedom of choice is not highly valued. A third might conclude that Canada is a very hypocritical place because alcohol and tobacco, both very addictive and dangerous to users, are legal while marijuana isn't.

This example is meant only to show how laws portray social morals and how the values behind those morals can be interpreted differently depending on our own opinion of the issue. The influence of our social culture and the relationship between culture, laws and ethics is very complex and will be discussed further in Chapter 8.

EXERCISE 1.4

Analyzing Societal Standards in Canada

Answer the following questions individually. For the questions where there is a blank, you may choose to write in names or issues that are meaningful to you.

Societal Heroes and Villains:

What are the values that make Terry Fox a hero?

_____

_____

Why do you think this?

_____

_____

What are the values that make Paul Bernardo a villain?

_____

_____

Why do you think this?

_____

_____

What are the values that make _____ a hero?

_____

_____

Why do you think this?

_____

_____

What are the values that make _____ a villain?

_____

_____

Why do you think this?

_____

_____

Societal Laws, Rewards and Punishments:

What are the values of a society that does not live up to the Kyoto Accord?

_____

_____

Why do you think this?

_____

_____

What are the values of a society that does not allow capital punishment?

_____

_____

Why do you think this?

_____

_____

What are the values of a society that sends soldiers to Afghanistan?

_____

_____

Why do you think this?

_____

_____

What are the values of a society that _____?
(Choose a current law or significant social issue in Canada.)

_____

_____

Why do you think this?

_____

_____

Now, in small groups or with the class as a whole, share your answers and your reasons for them. Notice how different people's evaluation of Canada's values and morals depends upon their personal opinions about the issues.

THEORIES OF MORAL DEVELOPMENT

Often we read about events in the newspaper involving clearly unethical practices and wonder why no one did anything to stop or expose the perpetrators. A Canadian example is the physical, emotional and cultural abuse endured by Native children across the country who were taken from their families and sent away to strict, church-run residential schools, from the late 1800s to the mid-1970s. Even when the government took over the schools in 1970, stories of abuse continued. Not everyone involved with these children was corrupt or unethical. Abuse did not take place at all of the residential schools, and not all of the teachers and caregivers at schools where abuse did take place were active participants. But no one exposed the cruel punishments, the pervasive belittling of Native culture and the restrictions imposed on the children against using their native languages.

Why do good people do bad things or fail to act to prevent them? Of course the answer is very complex and the situation and characters of the people involved plays a large role, but there is another aspect of moral development that is important in determining how an individual will act in a situation requiring a moral choice. It is called locus of control. Locus of control refers to an individual's perception of how much control he has over the situation. In other words, does he perceive himself as being able to stop, prevent, improve or change what is happening? Whether it is perceived or real, a person's sense of having control over the events of her life (internal locus of control) will encourage action. Conversely, a sense of not having control over what happens (external locus of control) will inhibit action. We might see hundreds of homeless, suffering people on the streets of Calcutta and be overwhelmed by our inability to help them all. Mother Teresa perceived herself as being able to help.

Locus of control in itself does not explain a situation as complex as the residential schools fiasco mentioned previously. Cultural beliefs about natives, child-rearing and strict education practices, and religious beliefs including vows of obedience, all played a part along with other influences; but locus of control was most likely one of those influences. Perceiving ourselves to have some control over the events around us and accepting responsibility to act ethically upon that assumption is a mark of moral maturity.

Consider a situation from your childhood in which you felt that you had very little control over the outcome. How did you behave? Would you have behaved differently if you believed that your actions would make a real difference?

_____

_____

_____

_____

_____

One of the most important tasks of growing up is to take the external moral lessons imposed upon us in childhood and personalize them. This is also referred to as internalizing, because when we have done this, our morals and values are no longer external to us—that is to say, imposed upon us by others—but have become internal. When morals are internal, they become the behaviour we expect of ourselves. Psychologists refer to this process as "moral development." It is important to know a little about the work of Lawrence Kohlberg and Carol Gilligan in this area.

Lawrence Kohlberg was a developmental psychologist at Harvard University. In the early 1870s he developed a theory that children go through progressive stages of moral development similar to the stages of cognitive development. He believed that as we mature, we become more independent in making our moral choices. Kohlberg's studies demonstrated a progression through six identifiable stages of moral development. This progression, he believed, had to be made one stage at a time, and was usually prompted by social interaction which included moral conflict and discussion with others who had reached the next stage.

Kohlberg called the first two stages of moral development level one, the pre-conventional period. It is characterized by the type of moral thinking found in elementary school, because it is essentially a response to authority. At stage one, the motivating force for moral choices is obedience in order to avoid punishment. Stage two introduces more individualism and egoism, as the motivation for moral decisions is one's own best interests. This includes but goes beyond merely avoiding punishment.

Stages three and four are characterized by the type of moral thinking usually found within society; therefore, Kohlberg referred to these stages as level two, the conventional period of moral development. He referred to stage three as "good boy/girl," because the motivating force for decisions is gaining the approval of others. Stage four includes the desire for approval, but is further oriented to conforming to societal laws and the obligations of duty.

The final level, which includes stages five and six, Kohlberg called post-conventional. He did not believe that the majority of people ever reached this level. He referred to stage five as a social contract, which included an understanding of our social interdependency and a concern for the welfare of others. The final stage he referred to as principled conscience. This stage, stage six, is oriented toward universal principles and is motivated by the demands of the individual's conscience. According to Kohlberg's theory, moral development is therefore, a progression toward making more independent, objective and rational responses in situations which involve ethical considerations.

In the 1980s, Carol Gilligan noted that Kohlberg's studies involved only boys and young men. She repeated his experiments using girls, and her results were very different. Her book, *In a Different Voice: Psychological Theory and Women's Development*, postulates that females make moral decisions based on how their choices will affect their relationships with other people, such as parents, friends, teachers, siblings and other authority figures. Their moral growth is a growth in understanding the effect certain behaviours will have on their relationships. Unlike Kohlberg, Gilligan did not see moral maturity as being the individual's growth toward moral autonomy or independence from others, but instead as the individual's ability to make decisions that would result in deeper connections and would nurture relationships with the significant people in her life, as well as to the larger community as a whole. Gilligan wrote that girls' "awareness of the connections between people gives rise to a recognition of responsibility for another." (Gilligan, C., 1982)

So what is moral development? What should we be moving toward? Is it an increasing ability to make objective choices based on rational consideration and independent of the need for others' approval, or the ability to make choices that increase our connections with others? If the purpose of ethics is to enable people to live together harmoniously, then an emphasis on relationship makes sense. However, objective principles of behaviour and doing the right thing regardless of others' approval is also important for maintaining moral standards and behaviour. When we vote, when we invest our money, when we donate to worthy causes, even when we choose which products to buy in our local stores, our choices have an effect all over the world. In many situations, relationship can be hard to define, and our values and principles, or our consideration of consequences, can help us determine the ethical choice. Is it more ethical to donate to Foster Parents Plan, which includes personal correspondence with a Third World child, or to give money to the Red Cross to provide relief to tsunami or hurricane victims? Undoubtedly, the relationship as a benefactor is less close when the donation is for anonymous assistance, but that doesn't make one cause less worthy than the other. Other things such as the extent of the need and the amount of ongoing help we can provide come into consideration.

SELF-REFLECTION

Despite our best intentions as ethical human beings, from time to time we all make compromises in thought or action. The danger is that these compromises can easily become habit, and escape our notice until something causes our behaviour to be scrutinized, either by ourselves or by others. Perfection is not possible, but accepting responsibility to change and to improve is the mark of an ethically mature person.

The following task is a good tool for self-reflection. Here is an example of how to fill it out. Self-reflection: "I recognize that I often lie to make my friends feel better." Analysis: "I do this so they will be happy, they will like me and they will be my friends. I noticed it when a friend challenged the truth of what I said. It isn't good to continually adjust the truth to suit circumstances."

EXERCISE 1.5

Analyzing Personal Compromises

Self-Reflection	Analysis
I recognize that I ... (Complete this sentence about yourself.)	Why do you do it? What made you notice it? How does it undermine your overall ethics?
1. _____ _____ _____	1. _____ _____ _____
2. _____ _____ _____	2. _____ _____ _____
3. _____ _____ _____	3. _____ _____ _____

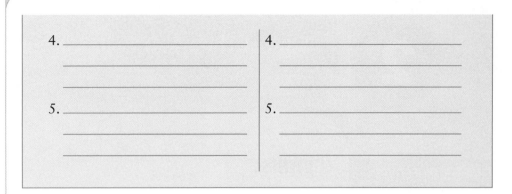

4. _____   4. _____
   _____   _____
   _____   _____
5. _____   5. _____
   _____   _____
   _____   _____

Recognizing compromises and our reasons for them is the first step toward becoming a more consciously ethical person. Of course, the next step is doing something about them. Begin with a statement of intent. This should be a general statement that indicates your goal for change. It should also be something you can do realistically.

Tom, on reflection, recognized that he sometimes makes belittling comments to others about people who have done or said something that bothered him. He knows that there are better, more honest ways to deal with conflicts. His statement of intent is "I want to deal with behaviours that annoy me in others in a productive and positive way. I can do this by talking to them about what they said or did in private."

Write a statement of intent for each of the compromises you noticed you were making.

1. _____
   _____
2. _____
   _____
3. _____
   _____
4. _____
   _____
5. _____
   _____

"The strongest principle of growth lies in human choice."

—GEORGE ELIOT (1819–1880)

Ethical Theories: Religion and Reason

By the end of this chapter the student should be able to:

- Appreciate the historical origins of ethical philosophy
- Compare and evaluate various models of ethical reasoning
- Recognize the basis of moral argument
- Understand the "Socratic method" of questioning
- Discuss divine command theory and virtue ethics
- Apply divine command theory and virtue ethics to current ethical issues

CONTENTS

- Introduction to Ethical Theories
- Divine Command Theory
- Socrates and Plato—The Healthy Soul
- Aristotle—Virtue Ethics

SELECTED READINGS

- Socrates and Plato, selections from *Crito* and *The Republic*
- Aristotle, selections from *Nicomachean Ethics*

> *"The wise are instructed by reason; ordinary minds by experience; the stupid, by necessity; brutes, by instinct."*
>
> —CICERO (106 BC–43 BC)

The study of ethics is beneficial to everyone because it has immediate relevance in our everyday lives. The ancient Greek philosophers called ethics "practical philosophy." It is practical because it is necessary and useful to us. We all have to make ethical choices and, as discussed in Chapter 1, we have to live with the decisions that we make. In order to make good decisions we can live with, we must first of all know ourselves and know what kind of person we want to be, and be honest with ourselves about that. Second, we need to decide what the ethical decision we make will be based on. This is where an understanding of the various ethical theories comes in.

We want to do the right thing, to behave ethically, but how do we determine what the right thing to do is? Should we all decide for ourselves, or should we follow the dictates of our society? The dictates of God? Should we act on principle, and if so, which principles are important? Why are they important? Are our intentions important? Are they more important than the consequences of our actions? Should we take into account only the consequences of our actions, and if so, the consequences to whom? Are we permitted to act in our own best interests, or should we consider only what is best for others? Is there some higher "good" to which we should aspire, or is human happiness an acceptable goal, and if so, how do we define happiness?

INTRODUCTION TO ETHICAL THEORIES

The various ethical theories discussed in the next three chapters are all concerned with finding answers to the previous questions. Different philosophers have responded in different ways, but all were trying to answer the same question: What is the basis on which we should form our decisions in order to be ethical human beings? Ethical theories are essentially an attempt to uncover the basis or foundation that will create a set of ethics people can live by. In other words, an ethical theory must not only describe good and bad, moral and immoral behaviours; it must also rationally justify, or prove, why certain behaviours are good and others are bad. As any parent knows, laying out rules of behaviour is much easier than justifying them, or than convincing someone else to follow them.

Consider the first exercise in Chapter 1. In defining the terms "ethics," "morals," "duties," "values" and "beliefs," we saw how our beliefs determined what we would value, and our beliefs and values together determined what our morals, our sense of duty and our ethics would all be. Therefore, a theory of ethics must first address belief. The definition of belief, as we saw in that first exercise, is not limited to religion. Although it could mean religious faith, in its broader sense belief refers to our understanding of the meaning or purpose of human life. That meaning or purpose is the motivation behind everything we do. An ethical theory must address that. It must be based on a convincing view of the meaning of human life in order to persuade us of its authority to dictate our ethics.

Therefore, when discussing ethical theories, we should also closely examine the rationale or authority on which the ethics are based. To do this, we can ask three questions:

1. What is the theory's basis or source of authority?
2. Does it convince us? Is the basis arrived at through sound reasoning?
3. Do the ethics proposed follow logically from that basis?

These questions will be referred to following the discussion of each of the major ethical philosophies introduced in Chapters 2, 3 and 4.

This text cannot deal with the contributions of every moral philosopher, and therefore only the major theories are included. Many of these philosophical stances are now part of our everyday language. When we talk about being "outcome-based" or considering the consequences, we are speaking from a utilitarian perspective; when we say "my handshake is as good as a contract" or talk about personal integrity, we are using virtue-based ethics; when we talk about basic rights or universal principles of behaviour, such as freedom to make decisions about ourselves (autonomy) or honesty, we are using a principle-based or Kantian focus; when we talk about limiting our freedom to not harming others or reaching agreements, we are referring to social contract theories.

Although we are already familiar with many of these concepts, it is still necessary to study the theories themselves. In fact, it is necessary to study the theories because we are so familiar with some of the concepts. Familiarity may lead us to simplify a theory or to generalize it to fit all situations. When we think we are familiar with a concept, we tend to take it out of context and use it to justify a decision we have already made, rather than using it as a basis for making the decision. By studying each theory more completely, we can come to understand not only the original concept but also if and how it should be applied. We can recognize whether a concept has been applied incorrectly or incompletely, by ourselves or by others.

Everyone has a "moral vision." This concept refers to an individual's way of seeing the world in terms of what he thinks, feels or believes is right or wrong. Terry Fox had a moral vision about helping to cure cancer, and he ran across Canada to raise funds to do so. Rene Levesque had a moral vision about a separate, sovereign Quebec, and he started the Parti Quebecois to achieve it. Henry Morgentaler had a moral vision about the right of women to obtain abortions, and he dedicated himself to giving them that choice even when it meant going to jail. Karla Homolka and Paul Bernardo apparently had a moral vision of self-gratification that included rape, torture and murder, a vision that horrifies most of us. A person's moral vision is subjective and not necessarily accurate or even what anyone else would call "moral."

In Chapter 1 we examined our own moral vision. We also tried to determine where this vision came from, and whether it reflects what we still believe and who we want to be. By studying each of the major ethical theories, we have an opportunity to choose our own moral vision. We can decide which theory or theories, or which parts of each theory, we think would serve us best in making our own ethical decisions. We can better understand the arguments and point of view of those who differ from us when we understand the different basis on which their decisions are made. We can respect others as ethical people, even though we may disagree with them. Most important of all, we can learn to examine our opinions on ethical issues from many different angles, and in the end, feel more confident about the stand we take.

Complete the following exercise before reading any further in this chapter. It is a good way to start the process of ethical reasoning.

EXERCISE 2.1

Personal Opinion Paper #1

Tracy Latimer was a 12-year-old girl living on a farm in Saskatchewan. She was severely disabled with cerebral palsy, was confined to a wheelchair and had to undergo multiple operations. She could not walk, talk or feed herself and suffered great pain constantly. Because of her illness she couldn't take anything stronger than Tylenol for her pain. Cerebral palsy is incurable, and Tracy's life expectancy was unknown.

In October, 1993, Tracy was scheduled for another round of surgery. Instead of taking her into town for treatment, Tracy's father, Robert Latimer, carried her out to the family truck in the garage. He started the engine and left it running, circulating the exhaust back into the cabin where his daughter sat. Tracy died of carbon monoxide poisoning.

Robert Latimer was tried for first-degree murder. His defence was that he acted out of love, trying to end his daughter's unbearable suffering. Every neighbour who knew the family testified to Latimer's gentle nature and his love for Tracy. Robert Latimer was convicted of second-degree murder, but he was released when the Supreme Court declared that the jurors had not been questioned properly about their opinions on euthanasia, or mercy killing. He was tried again in December, 1997, and was once again convicted of second-degree murder. Ordinarily, the guilty verdict for this charge is a mandatory life sentence with eligibility for parole in ten years. However, the judge, stating that Latimer didn't need rehabilitation and was no threat to society, gave him a special exemption and his sentence was reduced to one year in jail. The Council of Canadians with Disabilities and two other groups for the disabled were bitterly opposed to the reduced sentence, and objected to it, claiming that the rights and safety of people with disabilities would be compromised by the decision. In January 2001, the Supreme Court of Canada upheld Robert Latimer's conviction of second-degree murder and gave him a mandatory life sentence with eligibility for parole in ten years.

Write a brief, one- or two-page comment on this case. What was morally right and what was morally wrong? Why do you think so? Give reasons for your opinions. Talk about this case specifically and also about euthanasia in general. Can you imagine someone else thinking differently? What reasons might they give for their position? What would you say in response to their reasons for taking a different position from yours?

In this chapter, we will look at the earliest prototypes of ethical philosophy for the Western world—those based on faith (divine command theory) and those based on reason (the philosophies of Socrates, Plato and Aristotle). Although faith and reason are often viewed as being in conflict with one another, not everyone holds this opinion. Faith does not necessarily exclude the use of reason, and reason does not need to deny faith. Socrates, Plato and Aristotle were all devout believers in the religion of their culture, as were most of the philosophers we will study. However, there are distinct differences between ethical theories that are based on religion and those that are based on reason, and therefore in this text they will be examined separately.

DIVINE COMMAND THEORY

Divine command theory refers to all ethical systems that claim that ethical imperatives originate from a supreme being or God, or several gods or spirits. Followers of such a system, commonly called religion, are told in a holy book or in stories that are passed on orally, what they should value, which behaviours they should consider moral and good, and which they should consider immoral and unacceptable.

It is interesting to note that most of the original writings or oral teachings in religions were passed on through parables or myths. The depth and complexity of these stories usually produce as many questions as answers. Consider the ancient Greek myths, the stories in the Old Testament, the parables of Jesus, the stories told by the Islamic Sufi masters (mystics) and North American Native legends. The messages in these stories are subtle and require interpretation.

Consider, as one example, the ancient Greek story of Orpheus and Eurydice.

Orpheus was the son of the god Apollo and Calliope, the Muse of Poetry. He became the most famous musician among gods and mortals alike, and his music brought peace and harmony wherever he went. He settled down in Thrace, where he met and married the lovely nymph Eurydice. For a while they were very happy, but one day Eurydice stepped on a snake. It turned and bit her. When Orpheus found her, she was dying, and nothing he could do could save her. Eurydice passed down into Pluto's dark realm, Hades. Orpheus was so heart-broken, he took his lyre and went to Mount Olympus, the home of the gods. There he kneeled before Zeus and begged the god to give him back his beloved Eurydice. Zeus had no power over Pluto's realm, but he gave Orpheus the ability to go down to Hades where he might try to win her back. He warned Orpheus that it would be very dangerous, but Orpheus replied that he would rather stay in Hades with Eurydice than remain on Earth without her. He saw terrible things on his way down, but at last came to where Pluto sat on his throne. Orpheus made his plea into a song, accompanied by his lyre. The music was so beautiful and so sad that everyone in Hades heard it and wept. Pluto demanded that Eurydice be brought and she appeared, pale and shadowy, but smiled with joy to see her husband. "Take her," said Pluto, "and lead her forth from Hades, if indeed your music has power to draw her to the upper air. But look always before you, for if you so much as glance behind the spell will be broken, and your wife will pass back again to dwell forever with the shades." Orpheus and Eurydice joyously turned toward the gate of Hades, Orpheus playing such wonderful music Eurydice had to follow. They climbed the steep, dark ascent till they were only moments from the upper air. Then Orpheus felt a sudden fear that he might pass through and leave Eurydice behind. He glanced back to make sure she was still following. In that second, he heard a cry and his wife disappeared back down to Hades.

(Cruse, Amy [1957]. *The Book of Myths*. Toronto: Clarke, Irwin & Company Limited.)

Religious stories are meant to give direction, but what directions are being given here? Orpheus lost his wife because he looked back, but to understand the message of the story, we need to know why looking back was wrong. Was it because Orpheus disobeyed Pluto's command? If that is the only reason looking back was wrong, then are the gods' commands arbitrary whims? Was Orpheus being tested to see if he was worthy of the gods' favour, and he failed the test? It seems unfair that Eurydice paid the price for Orpheus' disobedience. True, the story was written at a time when women and children were considered possessions, less important than men, which is a value we no longer hold in our culture. Nevertheless, if there is a moral lesson here that goes beyond mere historical documentation, why wasn't Eurydice freed and Orpheus sent to Hades? Did Orpheus look back because he doubted that Pluto would keep his promise? In that case it is lack of faith that Orpheus is guilty of, not just disobedience. Did he look back because he doubted the power of his music to draw Eurydice after him? Is self-doubt our downfall? Or because he doubted that his wife had the strength or courage or faithfulness to follow him? Is the story saying that he didn't have faith in her, therefore he didn't deserve her? In order to get at the moral teaching of the story, these are questions we have to ask.

Greek religious myths are not alone in being subtle, as this example from the Old Testament shows.

Lot is a righteous man living in the city of Sodom. Two angels are sent from God to determine whether Sodom should be destroyed, and Lot takes them in and protects them from the wicked citizens of Sodom. The text continues: "And when the morning arose, then the angels hastened Lot, saying, 'Arise, take thy wife and thy two daughters which are here, lest thou be consumed in the iniquity of the city.' And while he lingered, the (angels) laid hold upon his hand and upon the hand of his wife and of his two daughters, the Lord being merciful unto him, and they brought him forth and set him without the city. And (they said), 'Escape for thy life; look not behind thee, neither stay thou in all the plain; escape up the mountain, lest thou be consumed.'" (Genesis 19:15–17) After Lot and his family escape, God destroys the city. But then the text reads, "But his wife looked back from behind him, and she became a pillar of salt." (Genesis 19:26)

What is being condemned in this story? We learn nothing more about Lot's wife, other than this terse statement. Is the moral, as we asked previously, that God's commandments must not be disobeyed? Or is it something less obvious, something related to why Lot's wife looked back? Did she regret leaving Sodom? Was she, unlike her husband, addicted to its wicked ways? She had no choice about leaving; again, the story was written when women and children were possessions. Did she look back out of concern for friends and family left behind, and if so, is that wrong? The text does not say why they were commanded not to look back, or why Lot's wife did. It is richer and more ambiguous than a simple moral commandment, and requires our interpretation. In other words, thinking and evaluation on our part is required, even in a divine command philosophy.

Unquestioning obedience to any religion can result in unconsciously ethical behaviour, but it can just as easily result in unconsciously unethical behaviour. A lot of good has been accomplished by religious orders and their followers. But a lot of evil has also been done by devoutly faithful people who accept without independent thought a religious leader's (or leaders') interpretation of their holy book. Life is complex. The difference between good and evil/right and wrong behaviour is sometimes obvious and sometimes subtle and ambiguous. Perhaps religious instruction was deliberately couched in complex and ambiguous stories in order to encourage the complex moral thinking and subtle interpretation that creates a consciously ethical human being. The following exercise is aimed at helping students to consider the complexity of determining ethical teachings from religious stories.

EXERCISE 2.2

Examining Religious Stories and Myths

Choose three stories, parables or myths from different religions. Compare their similarities and differences, considering the following aspects of each story:

1. Who is the righteous person in the story?
2. Why is he or she righteous?
3. Who are the unrighteous or evil people in the story?
4. What do they do that is unrighteous or evil?
5. What is the moral teaching of the story?

For each story, consider as many alternative answers for questions 2, 4 and 5 as you can. Which interpretation do you think best fits the story? If you did this as a group, did members of your group agree or disagree on the best interpretation? Do the different stories from different religions seem to promote the same values, or do they appear to be preaching conflicting values? Share your results with the class, first presenting the details of the stories and then explaining your interpretations. If time permits, a class discussion could follow each presentation.

There is a second issue to consider in divine command theory that also points to the need for independent thought and interpretation within a religion. Philosophically we could ask, are good things good because a deity says so, or does he say they are good because they are? Is God defining for us what is inherently good, or dictating to us what we shall consider good? The more traditional definition of divine command theory suggests that God's word defines goodness; a thing is good because a deity says so. Although this sounds like it should simplify things, it raises some difficult questions. What if instead of commanding us not to kill or not to tell untruths, our religion commanded us to do these things? If God's commandments define goodness, this would make murder and lying good, and refraining from murder or telling the truth bad. But this defies logic. We all inherently know that murder and lying are wrong and that not taking another life and telling the truth are both good. On the other hand, if we conclude that God says certain things are good because they are inherently good, are we saying that goodness is something independent of God? If this is the case, religious faith is more than deferring to divine commands; it involves thinking and evaluation on our part. It involves interpreting the stories and commandments in our religion.

Most religions offer a combination of direct commands and parables or teaching stories. Although acceptance of a religion is usually based on faith rather than on reasoning, the values and ethics within a religion should flow logically from the alleged relationship between God (or the gods) and humankind, and from God's (or the gods') intent toward his followers. If they do, the religion is cohesive and has internal rational integrity. In other words, the values and behaviours God demands should be in keeping with his relationship with humans, regardless of how that relationship is perceived in any particular religion.

In ancient Greek and Native North American religions, and many other religions which encompass multiple gods, the gods often possess many human characteristics, including human weaknesses. The gods may take the form of humans or animals and natural elements (tree spirits, the ocean, etc.). They are often indifferent to human suffering, and can be portrayed as jealous lovers, demanding tyrants or even capricious tricksters. Humans attempt to mollify the gods through worship and sacrifice or endure the misfortunes caused by the gods' displeasure. Occasionally humans try to outwit the gods. Some of the values and ethics which would logically follow from gods like these would be blind obedience, sacrifice (possibly human sacrifice), seeking revenge (consider the gods of Voodoo), a measure of deceit, and cleverness (in outwitting them). Religions that include animal and nature spirits would also logically value respect and caring for animals and nature.

Monotheistic religions tend to represent God as a caring and benevolent deity, concerned with helping humans individually and with improving the relationships between humans in order to create a strong, cohesive culture of followers. Some of the values and ethics which would logically follow from gods like these would be showing compassion and courtesy toward others, and the values that enable people to live together harmoniously, such as not lying, stealing or killing. If the religion identifies a "chosen people," then racial integrity is a value, and xenophobia might be encouraged. If the religion promotes the conversion of outsiders, then benevolence across cultural boundaries would likely be a value. These are only some examples of how the values and ethics a religion promotes flow logically from the nature of the god or gods at its head in divine command theory.

Applying Divine Command Theory to Modern Life

The moral values taught by different religions apply not only to being a good follower of that religion, but also to the kind of dealings people should have with one another in general. This includes the professional life of religious followers. The Bible, for one example, talks about forgiving debt (in a story about a businessman who asks his superior to forgive his debt, but refuses to forgive the debt his servant owes him); about paying taxes honestly (in Jesus' quote, "Render unto Caesar that which is Caesar's and unto God that which is God's); about returning good for ill (Jesus' advice to his followers to "turn the other cheek" if someone slaps them); about how to deal with customers and competition alike (the Golden Rule, "Do unto others as you would have them do unto you"). Other religions have similar statements which can be applied to modern life. The same directions that tell people how to be good human beings also tell them how to be ethical professionals.

Can you think of a statement made by someone you know based on divine command theory?

_____

_____

Do you agree with his/her comment? Why or why not?

_____

_____

Proponents' View

Proponents of divine command theory are, of course, those who believe in a supreme being or beings. They point out the beneficial and civilizing influence of religion. From religion we have received positive concepts such as brotherly love, helping those in need and a concern for non-material things. Religious leaders such as the Dalai Lama, Dr. Martin Luther King, Jr., Mother Teresa, and the Pope often act as the voices of our social conscience. They speak out (or spoke out while alive) against injustice, poverty and prejudice and voice their concerns about countless ethical issues that face us, such as abortion, suicide, Third World debt and capital punishment, to name a few. Whether we agree or disagree with their arguments, they help bring to the foreground important ethical issues for public debate and political consideration.

Critics' View

Critics of divine command theory point to the wars and other terrible injustices that have been committed in the name of religion. Canadian examples include the treatment of Native Canadians, Prime Minister Mackenzie King's refusal to accept Jewish refugees escaping Germany just before WWII, and the current backlash against Muslims, particularly since 9/11. Critics also claim that it is not religion but human compassion that has been and is still a civilizing and benevolent influence. They point to the many secular figures like Terry Fox, Rick Hansen, and others like them who volunteer their time and energy for good causes, or to common people who have spoken or acted to relieve suffering, such as the men and women who assisted slaves in their escape to freedom on the underground railway to Canada.

In summary, consider the three questions used in this chapter to analyze each theory.

1. What is the basis or source of authority in divine command theory?

_____

_____

_____

2. Does it convince us? Is the basis arrived at through sound reasoning?

_____

_____

_____

3. Do the ethics proposed follow logically from that basis?

_____

_____

_____

SOCRATES AND PLATO—THE HEALTHY SOUL

Socrates was the first philosopher to be interested in examining human nature rather than trying to determine the nature of the universe. He was also the first to claim that ethical behaviour could be determined through reason rather than faith. He invented a method of examining, through a series of probing questions, the traditional beliefs about the meaning of life and accepted notions of good and bad. He claimed to have no wisdom except the wisdom to know that he knew nothing, and his keen questioning soon pointed out the fallacy of those who did claim to be wise. We call this type of rather relentless questioning to get at the truth of something the "Socratic method" or the "dialectic method." Using this method, Socrates would begin a conversation as though he knew nothing, but through careful questioning he would get his opponents to clarify their ideas and recognize, and hopefully eventually to resolve, any logical contradictions. It is important to note that Socrates did not question others merely to make them look foolish. He used his questioning method as a way of searching for the truth, and believed that he was called to expose human frailties and wrong thinking in order to influence others to live more virtuous lives. The beginning of wisdom, according to Socrates, is recognizing our own ignorance.

Through his questioning, Socrates first pointed out the problem with divine command theory, mentioned in the previous section. Socrates believed that there were ideal principles of goodness that humans could perceive dimly, like shadows on a wall, and that could be determined by careful reasoning. He believed that humans are born with innate reason, and that by searching inside ourselves and examining our lives, beliefs and behaviours, we can find the truth.

Socrates looked inward, to the human soul, to define the just and virtuous man. The ancient Greeks did not use the word "soul" in a religious sense, however. Socrates was referring to the essence of a person, the core of our personality or character, which defines who we really are. He identified three distinct principles of the soul. The first he called the rational element. This is the part of a person that reflects or reasons. He called the second principle or part of the soul the irrational appetites. These are our physical impulses, such as hunger, thirst and sexual desire. The third principle he called the spirited element. These are our feelings or emotions, which Socrates referred to as our passions. For Socrates, the virtuous person was one in whom these three elements were balanced. By "balanced," Socrates meant that an individual's appetites and emotions should be governed by his reason.

But isn't it natural to wish to indulge our physical needs and our emotions? Why should we always be governed by reason? Wouldn't we miss a lot of enjoyable experiences if we always were? In other words, why should we be any more ethical than we have to be? This question was just as relevant in Athens in the fifth century BC as it is today. Plato addresses this question several times in his work, *The Republic*.

In Book II of *The Republic*, a man named Glaucon approaches Socrates. Glaucon states that people are good only out of fear of punishment if caught doing wrong, or out of a desire for the social benefits of having a reputation as someone who is honest, trustworthy and who keeps his commitments. These benefits are that people will like or admire us, do business with us or perhaps elect us to office. If it weren't for these punishments and rewards, Glaucon says, no one would choose to live ethically. To prove his point, Glaucon tells a story of a man named Gyges, who finds a ring that makes him invisible when he turns it a certain way on his finger. When he realizes the ring's power, he arranges to become one of the king's messengers. In this position, with the help of the ring, he is able to seduce the queen, murder the king and take over the kingdom. Glaucon claims that if the opportunity presented itself to us, and we had the power to act as we wished with impunity, we would all act the way Gyges did.

Is this true? Is it only public opinion and the fear of being caught and punished that keeps us from behaving unethically?

_____

_____

_____

Plato's response, also in Book II, is to propose the most extreme examples imaginable of a just (ethical) person and an equally unjust (unethical) person. In order to avoid the influence of any tangible rewards or punishments, he has his readers imagine that the unjust person is so good at being unethical that he knows exactly how to get away with it, and if he makes any slips, he is such a persuasive speaker, and has so many important friends and so much wealth, that he can talk his way out of the problem. On the other hand, the just person is one who wants to be truly good, not just to appear to be good. In order to be certain that the just person is ethical for the sake of being ethical, and not to gain the rewards that come with having a good reputation, Plato proposes that he be given the reputation of being unethical, even though it is false, since he has never behaved unethically. The point that Plato is making is that most of the reasons people are given for behaving ethically have to do with the external benefits that come with a good reputation—the friendship, admiration and trust of others, and all that can result from these.

Here, Plato is really asking, is moral virtue valuable in itself? Would it be worthwhile to be ethical even if there were no external benefits or rewards for being so? Would there be any reason to resist unethical behaviour if there was no likelihood of punishment?

Which would be better, to be an unethical person with a good reputation, or an ethical person with a bad reputation? Why?

_____

_____

_____

In order to answer this question, Plato returns to Socrates' concept of the balanced soul, which he describes in Book IV of *The Republic*. He compares a soul in which the three elements are out of balance—one in which the rational or reasoning element is not in control—to illness in the body. Everyone has some experience of illness. When we are ill, we experience physical pain and weakness that prevents us from doing the things we want. We may miss a party or an outing we had planned to attend, we may be unable to talk because of laryngitis, or our illness may even prevent us from walking or doing other necessary things. Illness also affects our ability to think and concentrate, so that we may be unable to study or to work. It makes us irritable and short-tempered, so that we may say or do things that we'll later regret. In total, illness in our bodies causes us to lose a certain amount of freedom and control over our lives, and the amount lost depends on the extent of our illness.

Plato claims that when our soul, the essential core of who we are, is out of balance, we also lose a measure of control of our lives, depending on the extent of the imbalance. In this way, a soul can be ill just as a body can be ill. To understand this, we must first know what Plato means by a "balanced soul."

A balanced soul is one in which the physical appetites and the emotions are ruled by reason. This is not to say that physical appetites or emotions are bad. They each serve a purpose and are necessary. It is only when they are not under the control of reason that they are harmful to the individual. When all three elements are in harmony, the individual will have the four key virtues: courage, wisdom, temperance and justice. He will be brave because he is not ruled by fear but by reason; he will act wisely because his rational element will consider the good of his entire being; he will be temperate because his appetites and emotions are controlled by his reason; and he will be just because each of the three elements of his soul are fulfilling their duties. All other virtues flow from these four.

A soul that is not in balance, on the other hand, is one in which the rational element is not in control. Plato noted that the three elements of the soul are often in conflict with one another. For example, the irrational appetite part of our soul may tempt us to eat or drink something that our rational mind knows is not good for us. Or we may be caught in the grip of an emotion, such as fear, jealousy or even extreme enthusiasm for a hobby or project, which causes us to say things or to behave in a way we will later regret. We all know people who have let their physical appetites get out of control. They may be obese, addicted to nicotine, drugs, sex or alcohol. We also know people whose emotions are out of control. Their anger may lead to violence, or their greed may lead to theft, deception or an addiction to gambling, or their fears or insecurities may cause them to limit their activities or fall in with a bad group. Even love, or an overwhelming enthusiasm for something, may lead people to ignore all other aspects of their lives. Today we call a person who is controlled by her appetites an addict. Theft, dishonesty, violence, greed, selfishness—all human vices are the result of a soul that is governed by the appetites and the emotions, rather than by reason.

Socrates and Plato ask, are these people happy? It is interesting to note that they do not ask if they are "good" or "religious" people. The basis or authority behind Socrates' teaching is not whether a certain type of behaviour is acceptable to the gods, but whether it causes more or less personal happiness. Happiness, as Plato defines it, is more like peace of mind and contentment. It is the lack of inner turmoil that results when the three elements of the soul are in harmony.

Personal happiness is not the only thing at stake, however. Socrates believed that doing wrong harmed the wrongdoer even more than the victim. Each time a person acts unethically, it becomes easier to do so again, and harder to resist. And when the rational element loses control over the appetites and emotions, these elements begin to gain control. In other words, physical desires and emotions subvert the mind to serving them. People in the grip of their appetites and emotions use their reasoning mind to justify their behaviours. They deceive themselves in order to continue with their self-destructive behaviours. They distort their moral vision in order to accommodate their addictions. All of this weakens their powers of reason and their grip on reality. This is how clever, even brilliant, people who cheat or break the law are eventually caught. They come to believe their own distorted vision of reality. They think they are above the laws of ordinary people and believe themselves to be invincible. They are no longer able to think objectively and to assess a situation accurately. If they are addicted to one or several physical appetites, they are unable to see the physical damage they are doing to themselves. If they are prey to certain overwhelming emotions, they distort reality by blowing up situations to give them an excuse to indulge the emotion and in so doing destroy the important relationships in their lives. In the end, they destroy their own personality, or soul.

Socrates believed so strongly that vice harms the doer that he sacrificed his own life to avoid the personal harm of acting unethically. Socrates' relentless questioning, particularly of those who thought they had all the answers, made him unpopular among many important people in Athens. At the age of seventy-one, he was brought before council on charges of corrupting the youth by making them question their faith in the gods. It was a trumped-up charge, but he was nevertheless convicted and sentenced to death by drinking hemlock. On the night before his sentence was to be carried out, one of his young followers, Crito, came to his cell. Crito and other friends of Socrates had arranged an escape plan. Socrates makes the same comparison between a healthy or balanced soul and a healthy body in Crito, which is deemed to be a faithful account of Socrates' own words, as Plato later made in his *The Republic*.

Socrates: Is life worth living with the body corrupted and crippled?

Crito: No, certainly not.

Socrates: Then is life worth living when that part of us which is maimed by injustice and benefited by justice is corrupt? Or do we consider that part of us, whatever it is, which has to do with justice and injustice to be of less consequence than our body?

Crito: No, certainly not.

Socrates: But more valuable?

Crito: Yes, much more so.

Socrates and Crito then debate the ethics of making an escape, and Socrates concludes that it is unethical for many reasons. Rather than behave unethically and allow the emotional fear of death and the physical appetite for life to gain control of his reason, Socrates refuses to escape. The next morning he drinks hemlock and dies.

Applying Socrates' Ethics to Modern Life

The key concepts that Socrates introduced are so deeply entrenched in Western philosophy that it is impossible to consider ethics without them. In fact, they are part of our everyday thinking, as individuals and in our professional dealings. When we say, "I have to be able to look myself in the mirror," we are using Socrates' idea of examining ourselves and our lives to evaluate our moral worth. We are implying that what others think of us—our reputation—is not as important as knowing within ourselves that we have behaved ethically. When we say, "How can he live with himself?" we are referring to the concept that vice harms the doer, and that being virtuous brings us peace of mind and happiness. When we believe that immoral behaviour eventually will come to light, we are counting on the harm that unethical behaviour does to a person's powers of reason to trip that person up. When we praise moderation and self-control, we are implying that we can and should rationally control our appetites and emotions in order to be ethical people. We are implying that we can consciously choose our behaviour, and that maintaining this control over ourselves is important. All of these concepts came from Socrates' and Plato's philosophies.

The four key components of the ethical beliefs of anyone who follows Socrates' and Plato's ethics today are:

- There are universal principles or ideals of good and bad.
- People all innately know good from bad and right from wrong.
- It is our ultimate goal, or duty, to make ourselves (our souls) as good as possible.
- Behaviours that hurt us or deter us from this goal are wrong because they hurt us—in other words, we should always act in our own self-interest, and it is our highest self-interest to make ourselves as good as possible, because this leads to inner peace and happiness.

Can you think of a statement made by someone you know based on the healthy soul theory?

_____

_____

Do you agree with his/her comment? Why or why not?

_____

_____

_____

Proponents' View

Proponents of Socrates' and Plato's ethics like this system because it does not rely on a complex formula to identify right and wrong behaviours. Right and wrong are internal—we all innately know what is ethical, if we think about it, and don't need anyone else to tell us. This also eliminates the need to convince others about what's right and wrong, either by the use of a complex, logical argument or by referring to a divine authority. They already know what's ethical, if they listen to their "soul" or inner wisdom. Furthermore, this system addresses head-on the question, "Why be ethical?" and answers it in terms no one can dispute—because it is in our own best interest to be so. Finally, this ethical theory or system can work for everyone, because it simply requires exercising self-control over our appetites and emotions, and letting reason, or common sense, guide our behaviour. Not that Socrates or Plato would say this is a simple thing to do—but it is something anyone can do, with careful thought and willpower.

Critics' View

Critics of Socrates' and Plato's ethics claim that this system does not take different cultural values and beliefs into account when claiming that there are universal principles of good and bad. They also believe that it is too individualistic. Not everyone knows good from bad, and in cases where there is a dispute about moral behaviour, this system leaves it up to each individual to decide. This leads to moral relativism, which will be discussed later. Another complaint is that not everyone has the foresight to determine his or her best interest in the higher sense of what is good for the soul, or has the kind of willpower to control appetites and desires. Critics also claim that our inner wisdom may not always be able to tell us what is the best course of action when we are faced with a conflict of principles, such as in a situation where we must choose between honesty and compassion, or when we are faced with a conflict between our own highest best interest and that of another person's—for example, when we must make a decision for someone else.

In summary, consider the three questions used in this chapter to analyze each theory.

1. What is the theory's basis or source of authority?

_____

_____

_____

2. Does it convince us? Is the basis arrived at through sound reasoning?

_____

_____

_____

3. Do the ethics proposed follow logically from that basis?

_____

_____

_____

VIRTUE ETHICS

Virtue ethics focuses on the moral character of each individual, rather than on rules or principles of behaviour. It originated in the philosophy of Aristotle, an ancient Greek philosopher who studied under Plato. Although Aristotle's approach has been added to and adapted to different times, the basic system he laid out has not changed. Therefore any study of virtue ethics must begin with Aristotle.

In Aristotle's famous work, _Nicomachean Ethics_, he states that the end or goal of every action is some good, and the end of all actions is happiness. "Happiness is of all things the one most desirable, and it is not counted as one good thing among many others. ...We see then that happiness is something final and self-sufficient and the end of our actions."

This sounds a bit like utilitarianism; however, Aristotle, like Plato, defines happiness very differently than we do. He also defines it differently than Plato did. Plato and Socrates defined happiness as a balanced soul controlled by reason, as a lack of inner turmoil. For Aristotle, happiness is acting in conformity to one's function. Another way of putting this would be to say that we are happy when we are behaving in accordance with what we are meant to be.

According to Aristotle, everything has a distinct and essential function, or purpose. Anything that is judged to be good is considered good because it is serving its function well. Performing well means performing to high standards. A good pen is one that performs its function well (presumably to write). Within the professional life, a good businessman, journalist, teacher, healthcare worker, etc. is one who performs the duties of his profession well, or to high standards of excellence. A good person is one who performs her function as a person well. But what are humans meant to be? What is our distinct and essential human function?

The distinct and essential function of humankind, not shared by animals, plants or objects, is our ability to reason. We are, in Aristotle's famous definition, "rational animals." For Aristotle, being rational means having the ability—the wisdom and the judgment—to make important decisions rationally and to act in accordance with reason and virtue. Therefore, the good person is one who performs his function as a human being by using his reason to act in a virtuous manner. The more we do this, the closer we come to excellence as human beings. In other words, we must continuously improve our characters throughout our lives by using our reason to act virtuously. Happiness is the result of achieving this balanced self-actualization.

By pursuing this essentially human function or activity we will acquire admirable, or "excellent," character traits, which Aristotle called moral virtues. That is to say, by acting virtuously, we become virtuous. It is important to note that we must pursue virtue with actions. Although Aristotle acknowledged the importance of intentions and motives, it was actions or behaviours he considered excellent and praiseworthy. The intention alone is not enough. However, unlike Socrates and Plato, Aristotle did consider our intentions to be of some importance, particularly when we fail to meet the standards of virtuous action.

Since being a good person means developing a good moral character by acting in accordance with reason and virtue, it is necessary to understand what virtue is. Aristotle answered this question by explaining that virtue is a way of acting. But it is not an instinctive behaviour, the way a rabbit runs from a shadow or a bird flies south before winter. It is also not something that can be taught, like mathematics or geography or keyboarding, because it is not external, like knowledge. Instead, virtue is an internal disposition, or inclination. We are either inclined to act virtuously, or inclined to not act virtuously. Virtue is a habit. For example, honesty is a virtue, and a person who acts in accordance with the virtue of honesty is a person who has developed the habit of being honest. In order to be an honest person, someone must act honestly until she gets to the point where being honest is a habit. According to Aristotle, when a person has achieved the habit of always acting virtuously, it will be easy and natural for him to resolve any ethical dilemmas that come up. He will not have to weigh principles or measure consequences. A person of good character will automatically do the right thing—out of habit. But virtuous habits are not something others impose upon us, as we mentioned in Chapter 1 when we discussed unconsciously ethical behaviours; they are behaviours that we have deliberately chosen to make a habit of.

This leads to the important question: What are the virtues that we should develop in ourselves to the point of becoming habits? Moral virtues are habits, but more importantly, they are the right kind of habits. But who is to say which are the right kind of habits? The ancient Athenians believed in temperance; therefore, being virtuous meant acting in moderation. Aristotle created a method of distinguishing between good and bad habits by looking for the median between two extremes. He called this his "doctrine of means." Virtues are habits that fall in the middle between the two extremes of excess (too much of a trait) and deficiency (too little of it). In *Nichomachean Ethics*, Aristotle uses the example of courage. Courage is the mean—the appropriate middle point—between cowardice, which is too much fear or too little confidence, and foolhardiness, which is too little fear or too much confidence. Generosity is also a virtue, because it is the mean between stinginess and extravagance. Stinginess is too little generosity; extravagance is too much.

In order to decide which habits we should develop in ourselves to achieve a virtuous character, we must use our reason to decide which characteristics are moderate, or which are the middle point between traits that are too little or too much of something. Not every action has a mean; some, such as adultery, theft and murder, are so immoral, according to Aristotle, that it is not their excess or deficiency that makes them wrong but the acts themselves that are always wrong. However, in most cases, by striving for the mean between excess and deficiency, with practice a person can develop the habit of acting in virtuous moderation and become a morally good person.

What are some other examples of the mean? In the first example, which is written on the following page, self-confidence is given as the mean between self-effacement and arrogance. Record other examples on the following page.

Aristotle did not make a formal list of the virtues a morally good person should have. To a certain extent, he assumed that most virtues are self-evident and he simply instructed followers of virtue ethics to refrain from excess. Like Plato and Socrates, he believed in the Athenian virtues of justice, temperance, courage and wisdom. He also shared with Plato and Socrates the belief that reason, or the rational faculty, must be in control in order for a person to behave ethically.

Aristotle's virtue ethics deeply influenced medieval Christian thinkers. Saint Thomas Aquinas (1224–1274) borrowed Aristotle's concept of virtue as people performing their essential function, but he redefined the purpose or function of humans to mean being in communion with God. Reason became a means of better knowing, or communing with, God, rather than of personal self-actualization. In keeping with this religious definition of the purpose or function of humans, the medieval Church added the virtues of faith, hope and charity to the Greek virtues of wisdom, courage, justice and temperance. They also redefined the Greek virtue of temperance to include humility, patience and chastity. These became known as the "cardinal virtues." On the other hand, the deadly sins were those that opposed spiritual development. Pride, lust and avarice, for example, prevent people from communing with God.

The Protestants, particularly the Puritans, later added industriousness and a strong work ethic to the virtues a person must develop in order to have an excellent character. As we see through these examples, each community or culture adapts virtue ethics to conform to its values.

<u>self-effacement</u> (too little <u>self-esteem</u>)	<u>self-confidence</u>	<u>arrogance</u> (too much <u>self-esteem</u>)
_____ (too little _____)	_____	_____(too much _____)
_____ (too little _____)	_____	_____(too much _____)
_____ (too little _____)	_____	_____(too much _____)

Applying Virtue Ethics to Modern Life

Virtue ethics can be applied to our professional life as well as to our personal character. Aristotle defined good professionals as having the traits and skills that make them good at their professions. He gave the example of a doctor. A doctor's function is to heal; therefore, a good doctor is one who possesses the skills and character traits necessary to heal patients and utilizes them to a high standard. The knowledge of human illness and medications, the skill in diagnosing and performing current medical procedures, the characteristics of patience, attention to detail, and good listening and communication skills are all examples of virtues necessary to be a good doctor. Every work function, from office manager to marketing consultant to childcare worker, has its own internal virtues. An office manager, for example, must be organized and courteous; a marketing consultant must be creative and understand human nature; a childcare worker must be gentle and patient. These traits, or habitual virtues, are necessary to enable the professional to fulfill his work function to a standard of excellence.

Within personal relationships, such as being a mother, father, son, daughter, sister, brother, friend or neighbour, different virtues are required. Our function in these roles is to relate to each other, to strengthen and deepen our connectedness, not only with family, but with friends, neighbours, co-workers, members of our church, community, and the world. The connections between people require such virtues as understanding, sensitivity, acceptance, empathy and caring. Carol Gilligan's "ethics of care" and sustaining relationship is relevant here, and will be discussed further under feminist ethics. A virtuous person would develop the caring virtues into habits in order to perform well the functions of the relationships in her life.

Can you think of a statement made by someone you know based on virtue ethics?

_____

_____

Do you agree with his/her comment? Why or why not?

_____

_____

_____

Ethics of Purpose

Organizations have also adapted Aristotle's concepts to create an "ethics of purpose" philosophy. An organization or business is ethical if it is fulfilling its purpose, or function. For example, the function of a hospital is to heal. Therefore, a hospital is fulfilling its function and acting ethically whenever it is engaged in practices (performed to a high standard of excellence) that contribute to healing. On the other hand, a hospital is not fulfilling its purpose if it is acting in a way that does not promote healing or that does not display a high standard of practice.

Complete the following statement to give another example similar to that of the hospital:

The function of an educational institute (college, university, corporate training program) is to

_____

Therefore, it is fulfilling its function when

_____

It is not fulfilling its function when

_____

The significant issue here is to correctly define the function of the organization, and to define it in terms that are in accordance with reason and virtue. For example, the purpose of a hospital is not to balance its budget, although that is an important and necessary task.

Consider this: Is the purpose of a business to make a profit, or to understand and satisfy customer needs? Explain your response.

_____

_____

If the purpose of a business is to make a profit, then any activity that fulfills that purpose is morally acceptable. On the other hand, if the purpose of a business is to understand and satisfy customer needs, that includes such things as developing new products that satisfy unmet needs, producing those products in a way that is acceptable to the consumers, marketing those products honestly so customers are aware of their features and of which needs the products will and will not meet, selling the products at the cost and quality level that customers want, and doing it all to a high standard of professionalism. Making a profit, like the hospital balancing a budget, is a necessary and important aspect of business, but is it the main purpose of business? Is it sustainable as a main purpose? In Aristotle's words, is it rational and virtuous? Making a profit alone will not necessarily lead to virtuous behaviour or high standards of performance, and rationally, it will not lead to long-term customer satisfaction; therefore it will not sustain the organization. Satisfying customer needs, on the other hand, is more likely to lead to virtuous choices (habits), high standards of performance and sustainable long-range profits.

Proponents' View

Proponents of virtue ethics consider it to be superior to other ethical theories for a number of reasons. First, virtue ethics acknowledges the importance of motivation, while also holding a person accountable for his actions. Motivation does not have to be as grandiose as communing with God or dedicating one's life to lofty principles; it can be as simple as natural desires and emotions, satisfied in moderation. A natural feeling of compassion can motivate a person to volunteer or donate funds for a good cause, as long as it is done in moderation. And motivation can be taken into account if an action does not turn out well; however, Aristotle writes that if the result of a person's actions is repeatedly bad or harmful, that person cannot be considered to be good.

Virtue ethics maintains that good character and personal integrity are central not only to our personal lives but also to our professional lives and business relations. This theory holds people accountable for their actions even in the most complex situations, because people are responsible for forming their own characters. If someone behaves unethically, no matter how difficult the situation, she is responsible for allowing herself to be put in that situation. The person should have established very different habits and character traits long before this particular situation occurred. Proponents of virtue ethics also insist that moral choices can't be made by following rigid rules or calculations. They don't trust simple, rigid formulas, like utilitarianism's "the greatest good for the greatest number" (to be discussed under teleology) or Kant's universal rule (to be discussed under deontology) to guide us unerringly to make moral choices. Proponents of virtue ethics believe that such rules cannot possibly take the specific circumstances of each situation into account. They say that what is essential is good judgment, and that virtue ethics promotes the development of good moral judgment through practice and habit.

EXERCISE 2.3

Developing Habits of Virtuous Behaviour

Consider your own character traits from the point of view of virtue ethics. List three traits or habits of virtue that you are proud of. How did you develop these into habits? When you are listing these habits, keep in mind Aristotle's emphasis on action. Write the habits as actions or behaviours, not as morals. You can do this by starting with "I do (this or that)" instead of "I am (this or that)." For example, rather than "I am supportive," you might write, "I verbally support and actively assist my friends and family when they need encouragement or help."

I

_____

How I developed this into a habit of behaviour

_____

_____

I

_____

How I developed this into a habit of behaviour

_____

_____

I

_____

How I developed this into a habit of behaviour

_____

_____

Now list three traits or habits that you are not so proud of. Be honest with yourself. Focus on ethical habits. Being late for work or school may be an annoying habit, but it is not an ethical issue. Failing to keep your word is an ethical issue.

1. _____

2. _____

3. _____

Look at the three traits that you consider "bad character habits" rather than "good character habits." How can you change them into good habits? It may be tempting to say, "I will stop doing this," but that isn't the same as developing good habits. It also isn't a very effective way to break a habit. Instead, you will need to develop in yourself a habit of doing the opposite of the bad habit. If, for example, you wrote, "I tend to criticize and find fault with other people, even those I love," you might now write, "I will actively look for and verbally praise the good qualities in others, especially when I am feeling critical."

(Continued)

(Continued)

Describe a positive habit you will substitute for each negative habit you listed.

1. _____

2. _____

3. _____

Critics' View

Critics of virtue ethics are mainly concerned that the theory does not provide a reliable tool to guide behaviour. A good ethical theory, they argue, should provide clear direction about what to do in difficult situations. For example, in a situation in which different virtues are in conflict, virtue ethics does not provide a method of choosing which virtue to uphold. If you knew that your friend had broken a just law, perhaps by stealing something, but he said that it was a one-time-only occurrence and he had learned his lesson, should you support your friend and not betray his confidence, or support the law and report his crime to the police? Should a sales clerk follow her supervisor's order and exaggerate the quality of the product for sale, or tell the truth and drive away some of her boss's potential customers? In either case, should a person practice the virtue of loyalty or the virtue of honesty? Virtue ethics does not provide a method of weighing different virtues against each other.

Followers of virtue ethics might respond by quoting the concept of the "unity of virtues." The unity of virtues theory claims that virtues cannot truly conflict. When they appear to be in conflict, there is still always a virtuous way out of the situation, and truly virtuous people will know it, or they would not be in such situations in the first place because of their virtuous habits. Critics, however, claim that "good judgment" is too individualistic and relative. One person's judgment of a situation may be very different from another's, and who can say which is more virtuous? Another criticism is that virtues are defined by our community, which makes them dated in time and dependent on the culture's values. We saw this in the way virtue theory was adapted to a religious focus in the Middle Ages. If virtues are dictated by our culture, this implies that obeying the law and following cultural customs are all that is needed. Any number of activities that we no longer believe are (or ever were) virtuous, such as keeping slaves and punishing Native Canadian children for speaking their own language, would have been considered virtuous at the time. But does that really make such actions virtuous? Followers of virtue ethics from Aristotle to modern times might not agree with this conclusion, but at the same time they cannot deny that individual good judgment is greatly affected by the age and culture in which the individual lives.

In summary, consider the three questions used to analyze each theory.

1. What is the theory's basis or source of authority?

_____

_____

2. Does it convince us? Is the basis arrived at through sound reasoning?

_____

_____

3. Do the ethics proposed follow logically from that basis?

_____

_____

> "If you think that a man of any worth at all ought to [consider] the chances of life and death when he acts, or that he ought to think of anything but whether he is acting justly or unjustly, and as a good or a bad man would act, you are mistaken."
>
> —SOCRATES (470–399 BC)

Answers

ANSWERS TO THE THREE QUESTIONS ABOUT EACH THEORY.

1. What is the theory's basis or source of authority?
2. Does it convince us? Is the basis arrived at through sound reasoning?
3. Do the ethics proposed follow logically from that basis?

DIVINE COMMAND THEORY

1. In divine command theory, the basis, or authority, for the distinctions between good and bad is that God has said so, and God is omniscient (all-knowing).

2. Most religions require faith rather than reason to convince their followers. However, a careful consideration and interpretation of its ethical teachings could be a way of convincing a person of the values and ethics espoused by the religion.

3. First examine the nature of God and his intent toward humanity, as laid out in the religion. Then compare whether the values and ethics taught by the religious stories and direct commandments would logically achieve that intent.

SOCRATES AND PLATO—THE HEALTHY SOUL

1. The reason given for behaving ethically is to achieve personal health (physical and mental health) and happiness, where happiness is defined as inner harmony.

(Continued)

(Continued)

2. Yes, if we accept Socrates' arguments that vice harms the doer and that every unethical act makes it harder to remain ethical, and his analogy between a healthy body and a healthy, balanced soul.

3. Courage, wisdom, temperance and justice are said to be the main virtues and Plato shows how they naturally result from a soul in which reason is in control of the appetites. It is not so well explained how all other virtues flow from these four.

ARISTOTLE—VIRTUE ETHICS

1. Aristotle believed that the individual's happiness was the goal or end of ethical behaviour. He defined happiness as fulfilling our human function as rational creatures by becoming virtuous by habit.

2. Yes, if one accepts the definition of man's function as being self-actualization through reason and through developing the habit of acting virtuously.

3. The definition of virtue flows logically from the definition of what the function of a human being is. Therefore, virtuous behaviour is the moderate action between extremes and is defined by the values of our community or culture.

SELECTED READINGS

Ethics, or moral philosophy, is one of the most complex subjects of study, because it is interwoven with the religion, culture, scientific understanding and social attitudes and expectations of the country and historical period in which each philosopher lived. Moral philosophers, just like scientists, build upon the concepts of earlier philosophers. However, their own insights are influenced by their personal experiences and the times they live in. The ideas and concepts in moral philosophy progress less like a ladder than like a jigsaw puzzle, where the different pieces must be fitted into the picture in a way that ultimately makes the whole more comprehensible. Therefore, it is important to know at least a little about the philosophers and their times in order to understand their contribution to moral philosophy.

Socrates (470–399 BC)

Socrates, sometimes called the father of ethical philosophy, has influenced Western philosophy for over two thousand years. Athens at the time of Socrates was a thriving city that encouraged artists and playwrights and the exploration of new ideas. It was the first city ruled by democracy and served as a prototype for future democracies.

Socrates was the son of a sculptor and a midwife. Growing up, he was educated in music, language studies and gymnastics, and through apprenticeship he became a sculptor like his father. He married and had three children. Like all Athenians, he served his city for a time during his young adulthood in the army, and as a mature adult he served as a city councilor. He did not continue in politics after his required service. As a philosopher he is best known for his method of questioning or "examining" people for their ideas. His questions usually exposed them as less knowledgeable and more hypocritical than the way in which they saw themselves.

Socrates did not officially take on students or write down anything himself. The young men of Athens enjoyed witnessing his intense questioning of vain and purportedly wise men, however, and followed him around, often practicing his method themselves. Most of what we know of Socrates is from the writings of one of his young followers, Plato.

At the age of seventy-six, Socrates was brought before the Council and accused of corrupting the young men of Athens with his ideas. The charges were false; in fact, Socrates' questioning was aimed at encouraging people to follow higher standards of just behaviour that they were following at the time. But because his questioning had embarrassed so many of the most influential men in Athens, Socrates was convicted and sentenced to death by drinking hemlock. The night before his sentence was to be carried out, Crito, one of Socrates' young followers, came to his prison cell to tell Socrates of an escape plan his friends had arranged and to urge him to accept it. The first excerpt here is from Plato's *Crito*, which is believed to be an accurate recounting of a conversation between Socrates and Crito, in which Socrates gives his reasons for refusing to escape.

**Plato
(428–347 BC)**

Plato was the youngest child of a family distinguished in politics in Athens. Socrates' death when Plato was twenty-eight had a huge impact on Plato, and was probably the reason he became a philosopher rather than follow his family into politics. After Socrates' death, Plato travelled and wrote his early dialogues of Socrates, including *Apology of Socrates and Crito*

When he returned to Athens, Plato founded a school of philosophy, which he called the Academy. It is generally thought to be the world's first university, and it continued for nearly one thousand years.

Since Plato's writings are conducted in the style of Socrates' questionings, using Socrates' name as the questioner, it is difficult to say for sure which of the writings contain Socrates' ideas and which are Plato's. However, the earliest of his writings, including *Euthyphro*, *Apology of Socrates*, *Crito* and *Phaedo* are generally considered to be Socrates' views. Those written later, after Plato founded the Academy, are considered to be Plato's own ideas. The most famous of these is *The Republic*, in which Plato describes his ideal of the "just state" and clarifies his views on justice and ethics. The final excerpts in this section are from Book I and Book IV of Plato's *The Republic*.

Excerpts from *Crito*

Socrates: Now consider whether we still hold to the belief that we should set the highest value, not on living, but on living well?

Crito: Yes, we do.

Socrates: And living well and honourably and justly mean the same thing: do we hold to that or not?

Crito: We do.

Socrates: Then, starting from these premises, we have to consider whether it is just or not for me to try to escape from prison, without the consent of the Athenians. If we find that it is just, we will try; if not, we will give up the idea.

Socrates: Then, my next point, or rather my next question, is this: Ought a man to carry out his just agreements, or may he shuffle out of them?

Crito: He ought to carry them out.

Socrates: Then consider. If I escape without the state's consent, shall I be injuring those whom I ought least to injure, or not? Shall I be abiding by my just agreements or not?

Crito: I cannot answer your question, Socrates. I do not understand it.

Socrates: Consider it in this way. Suppose the laws and the commonwealth were to come and appear to me as I was preparing to run away (if that is the right phrase to describe my escape) and were to ask, "Tell us, Socrates, what have you in your mind to do? What do you mean by trying to escape but to destroy us, the laws and the whole state, so far as you are able? Do you think that a state can exist and not be overthrown, in which the decisions of law are of no force, and are disregarded and undermined by private individuals?" How shall we answer questions like that, Crito? Much might be said, especially by an orator, in defense of the law which makes judicial decisions supreme. Shall I reply, "But the state has injured me by judging my case unjustly?" Shall we say that?

Crito: Certainly we will, Socrates.

Socrates: And suppose the laws were to reply, "Was that our agreement? Or was it that you would abide by whatever judgments the state should pronounce?" And if we were surprised by their words, perhaps they would say, "Socrates, don't be surprised by our words, but answer us; you yourself are accustomed to ask questions and to answer them. What complaint have you against us and the state, that you are trying to destroy us? Are we not, first of all, your parents? Through us your father took your mother and brought you into the world. Tell us, have you any fault to find with those of us that are the laws of marriage?" "I have none," I should reply. "Or have you any fault to find with those of us that regulate the raising of the child and the education which you, like others, received? Did we not do well in telling your father to educate you in music and athletics?" "You did," I should say.

Socrates: "Then consider, Socrates," perhaps they would say, "if we are right in saying that by attempting to escape you are attempting an injustice. We brought you into the world, we raised you, we educated you, we gave you and every other citizen a share of all the good things we could. Yet we proclaim that if any man of the Athenians is dissatisfied with us, he may take his goods and go away wherever he pleases; we give that privilege to every man who chooses to avail himself of it, so soon as he has reached manhood, and sees us, the laws, and the administration of our state. No one of us stands in his way or forbids him to take his goods and go wherever he likes, whether it be to an Athenian colony or to any foreign country, if he is dissatisfied with us and with the state. But we say that every man of you who remains here, seeing how we administer justice, and how we govern the state in other matters, has agreed, by the very fact of remaining here, to do whatsoever we tell him. And, we say, he who disobeys us acts unjustly on three counts: he disobeys us who are his parents, and he disobeys us who reared him, and he disobeys us after he has agreed to obey us, without persuading us that we are wrong. Yet we did not tell him sternly to do whatever we told him. We offered him an alternative; we gave him his choice either to obey us or to convince us that we were wrong; but he does neither.

Socrates: They would say, "Socrates, we have very strong evidence that you were satisfied with us and with the state. You would not have been content to stay at home in it more than other Athenians unless you had been satisfied with it more than they. You never went away from Athens to the festivals, nor elsewhere except on military service; you never made other journeys like other men; you had no desire to see other states or other laws; you were contented with us and our state; so strongly did you prefer us, and agree to be governed by us. And what is more, you had children in this city, you found it so satisfactory. Besides, if you had wished, you might at your trial have offered to go into exile. At that time you could have done with the state's consent what you are trying now to do without it. But then you gloried in being willing to die. You said that you preferred death to exile. And now you do not honour those words: you do not respect us, the laws, for you are trying to destroy us; and you are acting just as a miserable slave would act, trying to run away, and breaking the contracts and agreement which you made to live as our citizen. First, therefore, answer this question. Are we right, or are we wrong, in saying that you have agreed not in mere words, but in your actions, to live under our government?" What are we to say, Crito? Must we not admit that it is true?

Crito: We must, Socrates.

FOCUS QUESTIONS

1. What personal reasons (having to do with his own well-being) does Socrates give for refusing to escape his death by accepting Crito's escape plan?

2. What societal reasons (having to do with his obligations to his city-state) does Socrates give for refusing Crito's escape plan?

Excerpt from *The Republic*: Book I

Has the soul a function that can be performed by nothing else? Take for example such actions as deliberating or taking charge and exercising control: is not the soul the only thing of which you can say that these are its proper and peculiar work?

That is so.

And again, living—is not that above all the function of the soul?

No doubt.

And we also speak of the soul as having a certain specific excellence or virtue?

Yes.

Then, Thrasymachus, if the soul is robbed of its peculiar virtue, it cannot possibly do its work well. It must exercise its power of controlling and taking charge well or ill according as it is itself in a good or a bad state.

That follows.

And did we not agree that the virtue of the south is justice, and injustice its defect?

We did.

So it follows that a just soul, or in other words a just man, will live well; the unjust will not.

Apparently, according to your argument.

But living well involves well-being and happiness.

Naturally.

Then only the just man is happy; injustice will involve unhappiness.

Be it so.

But you cannot say it pays better to be unhappy.

Of course not.

Injustice then, my dear Thrasymachus, can never pay better than justice.

Excerpts from *The Republic*: Book IV

Now, is it sometimes true that people are thirsty and yet unwilling to drink?

Yes, often.

What, then, can one say of them, if not that their soul contains something which urges them to drink and something which holds them back, and that this latter is a distinct thing and overpowers the other?

I agree.

And is it not true that the intervention of this inhibiting principle in such cases always has its origin in reflection; whereas the impulses driving and dragging the soul are engendered by external influences and abnormal conditions?

Evidently.

We shall have good reason, then, to assert that they are two distinct principles. We may call that part of the soul whereby it reflects, rational; and the other, with which it feels hunger and thirst and is distracted by sexual passion and all the other desires, we will call irrational appetite, associated with pleasure in the replenishment of certain wants.

Yes, there is good ground for that view.

Let us take it, then, that we have now distinguished two elements in the soul. What of that passionate element which makes us feel angry and indignant? Is that a third, or identical in nature with one of those two?

It might perhaps be identified with appetite.

I am more inclined to put my faith in a story I once heard about Leontius, son of Aglaion. On his way up from the Piraeus outside the north wall, he noticed the bodies of some criminals lying on the ground, with the executioner standing by them. He wanted to go and look at them, but at the same time he was disgusted and tried to turn away. He struggled for some time and covered his eyes, but at last the desire was too much for him. Opening his eyes wide, he ran up to the bodies and cried, "There you are, curse you; feast yourselves on this lovely sight!"

Yes, I have heard that story too.

The point of it surely is that anger is sometimes in conflict with appetite, as if they were two distinct principles. Do we not often find a man whose desires would force him to go against his reason, reviling himself and indignant with this part of his nature which is trying to put constraint on him? It is like a struggle between two factions, in which indignation takes the side of reason. But I believe you have never observed, in yourself or anyone else, indignation make common cause with appetite in behaviour which reason decides to be wrong.

No, I am sure I have not.

Again, take a man who feels he is in the wrong. The more generous his nature, the less can he be indignant at any suffering, such as hunger and cold, inflicted by the man he has injured. He recognizes such treatment as just, and, as I say, his spirit refuses to be roused against it.

That is true.

But now contrast one who thinks it is he that is being wronged. His spirit boils with resentment and sides with the right as he conceives it. Persevering all the more for the hunger and cold and other pains he suffers, it triumphs and will not give in until its gallant struggle has ended in success or death; or until the restraining voice of reason, like a shepherd calling off his dog, makes it relent.

An apt comparison, and in fact it fits the relation of our Auxiliaries to the Rulers: they were to be like watch-dogs obeying the shepherds of the commonwealth.

Yes, you understand very well what I have in mind. But do you see how we have changed our view? A moment ago we were supposing this spirited element to be something of the nature of appetite; but now it appears that, when the soul is divided into factions, it is far more ready to be up in arms on the side of reason.

Quite true.

Is it, then, distinct from the rational element or only a particular form of it, so that the soul will contain no more than two elements, reason and appetite? Or is the soul like the state, which had three orders to hold it together, traders, Auxiliaries, and counsellors? Does the spirited element make a third, the natural auxiliary of reason, when not corrupted by bad upbringing?

It must be a third.

Yes, provided it can be shown to be distinct from reason, as we saw it was from appetite.

That is easily proved. You can see that much in children: they are full of passionate feelings from their very birth; but some, I should say, never become rational, and most of them only late in life.

And we have surely not forgotten that justice in the state meant that each of the three orders in it was doing its own proper work. So we may henceforth bear in mind that each one of us likewise will be a just person, fulfilling his proper function, only if the several parts of our nature fulfill theirs.

Certainly.

And it will be the business of reason to rule with wisdom and forethought on behalf of the entire soul; while the spirited element ought to act as its subordinate and ally. The two will be brought into accord, as we said earlier, by that combination of mental and bodily training which will tune up one string of the instrument and relax the other, nourishing the reasoning part on the study of noble literature and allaying the other's wildness by harmony and rhythm. When both have been thus nurtured and trained to know their own true functions, they must be set in command over the appetites, which form the greater part of each man's soul and are by nature insatiably covetous. They must keep watch lest this part, by battening on the pleasures that are called bodily, should grow so great and powerful that it will no longer keep to its own work, but will try to enslave the others and usurp a dominion to which it has no right, thus turning the whole of life upside down. At the same time, those two together will be the best of guardians for the entire soul and for the body against all enemies from without: the one will take counsel, while the other will do battle, following its ruler's commands and by its own bravery giving effect to the ruler's designs.

Yes, that is all true.

And so we call an individual brave in virtue of this spirited part of his nature, when, in spite of pain or pleasure, it holds fast to the injunctions of reason about what he ought or ought not to be afraid of.

True.

And wise in virtue of that small part which rules and issues these injunctions, possessing as it does the knowledge of what is good for each of the three elements and for all of them in common.

Certainly.

And, again, temperate by reason of the unanimity and concord of all three, when there is no internal conflict between the ruling element and its two subjects, but all are agreed that reason should be ruler.

Yes, that is an exact account of temperance, whether in the state or in the individual.

Finally, a man will be just by observing the principle we have so often stated.

Necessarily.

The just man does not allow the several elements in his soul to usurp one another's functions; he is indeed one who sets his house in order, by self-mastery and discipline coming to be at peace with himself, and bringing into tune those three parts, like the terms in the proportion of a musical scale, the highest and lowest notes and the mean between them, with all the intermediate intervals. Only when he has linked these parts together in well-tempered harmony and has made himself one man instead of many, will he be ready to go about whatever he may have to do, whether it be making money and satisfying bodily wants, or business transactions, or the affairs of state. In all these fields when he speaks of just and honourable conduct, he will mean the behaviour that helps to produce and to preserve this habit of mind; and by wisdom he will mean the knowledge which presides over such conduct. Any action which tends to break down this habit will be for him unjust; and the notions governing it he will call ignorance and folly.

That is perfectly true, Socrates.

So be it, Next, I suppose, we have to consider injustice.

Evidently.

This must surely be a sort of civil strife among the three elements, whereby they usurp and encroach upon one another's functions and some one part of the soul rises up in rebellion against the whole, claiming a supremacy to which it has no right because its nature fits it only to be the servant of the ruling principle. Such turmoil and aberration we shall, I think, identify with injustice, intemperance, cowardice, ignorance, and in a word with all wickedness.

Exactly.

And now that we know the nature of justice and injustice, we can be equally clear about what is meant by acting justly and again by unjust action and wrongdoing.

How do you mean?

Plainly, they are exactly analogous to those wholesome and unwholesome activities which respectively produce a healthy or unhealthy condition in the body; in the same way just and unjust conduct produce a just or unjust character. Justice is produced in the soul, like health in the body, by establishing the elements concerned in their natural relations of control and subordination, whereas injustice is like disease and means that this natural order is inverted.

Quite so.

It appears, then, that virtue is as it were the health and comeliness and well-being of the soul, as wickedness is disease, deformity, and weakness.

True.

And also that virtue and wickedness are brought about by one's way of life, honourable or disgraceful.

That follows.

So now it only remains to consider which is the more profitable course: to do right and live honourably and be just, whether or not anyone knows what manner of man you are, or to do wrong and be unjust, provided that you can escape the chastisement which might make you a better man.

But really, Socrates, it seems to me ridiculous to ask that question now that the nature of justice and injustice has been brought to light. People think that all the luxury and wealth and power in the world cannot make life worth living when the bodily constitution is going to rack and ruin; and are we to believe that, when the very principle whereby we live is deranged and corrupted, life will be worth living so long as a man can do as he will, and wills to do anything rather than to free himself from vice and wrong doing and to win justice and virtue?

Yes, it is a ridiculous question.

FOCUS QUESTIONS

1. What does Socrates believe to be the function of the soul?
2. What are the three distinct principles of the soul, according to Socrates?
3. Why does Socrates conclude that it is better to be just (ethical) than unjust?

**Aristotle
(384–322 BC)**

The families on both sides of Aristotle's parentage were physicians. His father was the court physician to the King of Macedonia. At seventeen, Aristotle was sent to Athens to study in Plato's Academy. He stayed for nearly twenty years, until Plato's death in 347. After a few years of travel, Aristotle returned to Macedonia to tutor the young Alexander the Great for seven years. When Alexander ascended to the throne, Aristotle returned to Athens and opened his own school, which he called Lyceum. Under Alexander's patronage, it flourished. However, when Alexander died in 323 BC, the Athenians turned against everyone associated with him, and Aristotle was forced to flee Athens. He died a year later.

Aristotle's writings and ideas dominated medieval philosophy, and many of his carefully defined terms and arguments are still used in philosophical and legal debates today. His work, *Nicomachean Ethics*, named for his son and his father, who were both called Nicomachus, is considered one of the greatest works on ethics.

The following excerpts from *Nicomachean Ethics* introduce Aristotle's theory of what has become known as "virtue ethics."

Excerpts from *Nicomachean Ethics*: Book I

Moreover, happiness is of all things the one most desirable, and it is not counted as one good thing among many others.

We see then that happiness is something final and self-sufficient and the end of our actions.

To call happiness the highest good is perhaps a little trite, and a clearer account of what it is, is still required. Perhaps this is best done by first ascertaining the proper function of man. For just as the goodness and performance of a flute player, a sculptor, or any kind of expert, and generally of anyone who fulfills some function or performs some action, are thought to reside in his proper function, so the goodness and performance of man would seem to reside in whatever is his proper function. Is it then possible that while a carpenter and a shoemaker have their own proper functions and spheres of action, man as man has none, but was left by nature a good-for-nothing without a function? Should we not assume that just as the eye, the hand, the foot, and in general each part of the body clearly has its own proper function, so man too has some function over and above the functions of his parts? What can this function possibly be? Simply living? He shares that even with plants, but we are now looking for something peculiar to man. Accordingly, the life of nutrition and growth must be excluded. Next in line there is a life of sense perception. But this, too, man has in common with the horse, the ox, and every animal. There remains then an active life of the rational element. The rational element has two parts: one is rational in that it obeys the rule of reason, the other in that it possesses and conceives rational rules. Since the expression "life of the rational element" also can be used in two senses, we must make it clear that we mean a life determined by the activity, as opposed to the mere possession, of the rational element. For the activity, it seems, has a greater claim to be the function of man.

The proper function of man, then, consists in an activity of the soul in conformity with a rational principle or, at least, not without it. In speaking of the proper function of a given individual we mean that it is the same in kind as the function of an individual who sets high standards for himself: the proper function of a harpist, for example, is the same as the function of a harpist who has set high standards for himself. The same applies to any and every group of individuals: the full attainment of excellence must be added to the mere function. In other words, the function of the harpist is to play the harp; the function of the harpist who has high standards is to play it well. On these assumptions, if we take the proper function of man to be a certain kind of life, and if this kind of life is an activity of the soul and consists in actions performed in conjunction with the rational element, and if a man of high standards is he who performs these actions well and properly, and if a function is well performed when it is performed in accordance with the excellence appropriate to it; we reach the conclusion that the good of man is an activity of the soul in conformity with excellence or virtue, and if there are several virtues, in conformity with the best and most complete.

Now, in our definition we are in agreement with those who describe happiness as virtue or as some particular virtue, for our term "activity in conformity with virtue" implies virtue. But it does doubtless make a considerable difference whether we think of the highest good as consisting in the possession or in the practice of virtue, viz., as being a characteristic or an activity. For a characteristic may exist without producing any good result, as for example, in a man who is asleep or incapacitated in some other respect. An activity, on the other hand, must produce a result: [an active person] will necessarily act and act well. Just as the crown at the Olympic Games is not awarded to the most beautiful and the strongest but to the participants in the contests—for it is among them that the victors are found—so the good and noble things in life are won by those who act rightly.

The life of men active in this sense is also pleasant in itself. For the sensation of pleasure belongs to the soul, and each man derives pleasure from what he is said to love: a lover of horses from horses, a lover of the theatre from plays, and in the same way a lover of justice from just acts, and a lover of virtue in general from virtuous acts. In most men, pleasant acts conflict with one another because they are not pleasant by nature, but men who love what is noble derive pleasure from what is naturally pleasant. Actions which conform to virtue are naturally pleasant, and, as a result, such actions are not only pleasant for those who love the noble but also pleasant in themselves. The life of such men has no further need of pleasure as an added attraction, but it contains pleasure within itself. We may even go so far as to state that the man who does not enjoy performing noble actions is not a good man at all. Nobody would call a man just who does not enjoy acting justly, nor generous who does not enjoy generous actions, and so on. If this is true, actions performed in conformity with virtue are in themselves pleasant.

FOCUS QUESTIONS

1. How does Aristotle define happiness?

2. What does he consider to be unique about man?

3. What does he determine to be the proper function of man?

Excerpts from *Nicomachean Ethics*: Book II

Virtue, as we have seen, consists of two kinds, intellectual virtue and moral virtue. Intellectual virtue or excellence owes its origin and development chiefly to teaching, and for that reason requires experience and time. Moral virtue, on the other hand, is formed by habit, *ethos*, and its name, *ethike*, is therefore derived, by a slight variation, from *ethos*. This shows, too, that none of the moral virtues is implanted in us by nature, for nothing which exists by nature can be changed by habit. For example, it is impossible for a stone, which has a natural downward movement, to become habituated to moving upward, even if one should try ten thousand times to inculcate the habit by throwing it in the air; nor can fire be made to move downward, nor can the direction of any nature-given tendency be changed by habituation. Thus, the virtues are implanted in us neither by nature nor contrary to nature: we are by nature equipped with the ability to receive them, and habit brings this ability to completion and fulfillment.

Furthermore, of all the qualities with which we are endowed by nature, we are provided with the capacity first, and display the activity afterward. That this is true is shown by the senses: it is not by frequent seeing or frequent hearing that we acquired our senses, but on the contrary we first possess and then use them; we do not acquire them by use. The virtues, on the other hand, we acquire by first having put them into action, and the same is also true of the arts. For the things which we have to learn before we can do them we learn by doing: men become builders by building houses, and harpists by playing the harp. Similarly, we become just by the practice of just actions, self-controlled by exercising self-control, and courageous by performing acts of courage.

This is corroborated by what happens in states. Lawgivers make the citizens good by inculcating [good] habits in them, and this is the aim of every lawgiver; if he does not succeed in doing that, his legislation is a failure. It is in this that a good constitution differs from a bad one.

Moreover, the same causes and the same means that produce any excellence or virtue can also destroy it, and this is also true of every art. It is by playing the harp that men become both good and bad harpists, and correspondingly with builders and all the other craftsmen: a man who builds well will be a good builder, one who builds badly a bad one. For if this were not so, there would be no need for an instructor, but everybody would be born as a good or a bad craftsman. The same holds true of the virtues: in our transactions with other men it is by action that some become just and others unjust, and it is by acting in the face of danger and by developing the habit of feeling fear or confidence that some become brave men and others cowards. The same applies to the appetites and feelings of anger: by reacting in one way or in another to given circumstances some people become self-controlled and gentle, and others self-indulgent and short-tempered. In a word, characteristics develop from corresponding activities. For that reason, we must see to it that our activities are of a certain kind, since any variations in them will be reflected in our characteristics. Hence it is no small matter whether one habit or another is inculcated in us from early childhood; on the contrary, it makes a considerable difference, or, rather, all the difference.

However, the question may be raised what we mean by saying that men become just by performing just actions and self-controlled by practicing self-control. For if they perform just actions and exercise self-control, they are already just and self-controlled, in the same way as they are literate and musical if they write correctly and practice music.

But is this objection really valid, even as regards the arts? No, for it is possible for a man to write a piece correctly by chance or at the prompting of another: but he will be literate only if he produces a piece of writing in a literate way, and that means doing it in accordance with the skill of literate composition which he has in himself.

Moreover, the factors involved in the arts and in the virtues are not the same. In the arts, excellence lies in the result itself, so that it is sufficient if it is of a certain kind. But in the case of the virtues an act is not performed justly or with self-control if the act itself is of a certain kind, but only if in addition the agent has certain characteristics as he performs it: first of all, he must know what he is doing; secondly, he must choose to act the way he does, and he must choose it for its own sake; and in the third place, the act must spring from a firm and unchangeable character. With the exception of knowing what one is about, these considerations do not enter into the mastery of the arts; for the mastery of the virtues, however, knowledge is of little or no importance, whereas the other two conditions count not for a little but are all-decisive, since repeated acts of justice and self-control result in the possession of these virtues. In other words, acts are called just and self-controlled when they are the kind of acts which a just or self-controlled man would perform; but the just and self-controlled man is not he who performs these acts, but he who also performs them in the way just and self-controlled men do.

Thus our assertion that a man becomes just by performing just acts and self-controlled by performing acts of self-control is correct; without performing them, nobody could even be on the way to becoming good. Yet most men do not perform such acts, but by taking refuge in argument they think that they are engaged in philosophy and that they will become good in this way. In so doing, they act like sick men who listen attentively to what the doctor says, but fail to do any of the things he prescribes. That kind of philosophical activity will not bring health to the soul any more than this sort of treatment will produce a healthy body.

... and if virtue, like nature, is more precise and better than any art, we must conclude that virtue aims at the median. I am referring to moral virtue: for it is moral virtue that is concerned with emotions and actions, and it is in emotions and actions that excess, deficiency, and the median are found. Thus we can experience fear, confidence, desire, anger, pity, and generally any kind of pleasure and pain either too much or too little, and in either case not properly. But to experience all this at the right time, toward the right objects, toward the right people, for the right reason, and in the right manner—that is the median and the best course, the course that is a mark of virtue.

We may thus conclude that virtue or excellence is a characteristic involving choice, and that it consists in observing the mean relative to us, a mean which is defined by a rational principle, such as a man of practical wisdom would use to determine it. It is the mean by reference to two vices: the one of excess and the other of deficiency.

A mean can also be found in our emotional experiences and in our emotions. Thus, while a sense of shame is not a virtue, a bashful or modest man is praised. For even in these matters we speak of one kind of person as intermediate and of another as exceeding if he is terror-stricken and abashed at everything. On the other hand, a man who is deficient in shame or has none at all is called shameless, whereas the intermediate man is bashful or modest.

Righteous indignation is the mean between envy and spite, all of these being concerned with the pain and pleasure which we feel in regard to the fortunes of our neighbours. The righteously indignant man feels pain when someone prospers undeservedly; an envious man exceeds him in that he is pained when he sees anyone prosper; and a spiteful man is so deficient in feeling pain that he even rejoices [when someone suffers undeservedly].

FOCUS QUESTIONS

1. How does Aristotle believe an individual can achieve moral virtue?

2. What are the three prerequisites that make an action just?

3. What does Aristotle mean by the "median"?

4. Give two examples of the mean in particular virtues, and explain why they are the mean.

Excerpts from *Nicomachean Ethics*: Book III

Virtue or excellence is, as we have seen, concerned with emotions and actions. When these are voluntary we receive praise and blame; when involuntary, we are pardoned and sometimes even pitied. Therefore, it is, I daresay, indispensable for a student of virtue to differentiate between voluntary and involuntary actions, and useful also for lawyers to help them in meting out honours and punishments.

It is of course generally recognized that actions done under constraint or due to ignorance are involuntary. An act is done under constraint when the initiative or source of motion comes from without. It is the kind of act in which the agent or the person acted upon contributes nothing. For example, a wind might carry a person somewhere he did not want to go, or men may do so who have him in their power. But a problem arises in regard to actions that are done through fear of a greater evil or for some noble purpose, for instance, if a tyrant were to use a man's parents or children as hostages in ordering him to commit a base deed, making their survival or death depend on his compliance or refusal. Are actions of this kind voluntary or involuntary? A similar problem also arises when a cargo is jettisoned in a storm. Considering the action itself, nobody would voluntarily throw away property; but when it is a matter of saving one's own life and that of his fellow passengers, any sensible man would do so. Actions of this kind are, then, of a mixed nature, although they come closer to being voluntary than to being involuntary actions. For they are desirable at the moment of action; and the end for which an action is performed depends on the time at which it is done. Thus the terms "voluntary" and "involuntary" are to be used with reference to the moment of action. In the cases just mentioned, the agent acts voluntarily, because the initiative in moving the parts of the body which act as instruments rests with the agent himself; and when the source of motion is within oneself, it is in one's power to act or not to act. Such actions, then, are voluntary, although in themselves they are perhaps involuntary, since nobody would choose to do any one of them for its own sake.

Ignorance in moral choice does not make an act involuntary—it makes it wicked; nor does ignorance of the universal, for that invites reproach; rather, it is ignorance of the particulars which constitute the circumstances and the issues involved in the action. It is on these that pity and pardon depend, for a person who acts in ignorance of a particular circumstance acts involuntarily.

It might, therefore, not be a bad idea to distinguish and enumerate these circumstances. They are: ignorance of (1) who the agent is, (2) what he is doing, (3) what thing or person is affected, and sometimes also (4) the means he is using, e.g., some tool, (5) the result intended by his action, e.g., saving a life, and (6) the manner in which he acts, e.g., gently or violently.

Now no one except a madman would be ignorant of all these factors, nor can he obviously be ignorant of (1) the agent; for how could a man not know his own identity? But a person might be ignorant of (2) what he is doing. For example, he might plead that something slipped out of his mouth, or that he did not know that he was divulging a secret, as Aeschylus said when he was accused of divulging the Mysteries: or again, as a man might do who discharges a catapult, he might allege that it went off accidentally while he only wanted to show it. Moreover, (3) someone might, like Merope, mistake a son for an enemy; or (4) he might mistake a pointed spear for a foil, or a heavy stone for a pumice stone. Again, (5) someone might, in trying to save a man by giving him something to drink, in fact kill him; or, (6) as in sparring, a man might intend merely to touch, and actually strike a blow.

As ignorance is possible with regard to all these factors which constitute an action, a man who acts in ignorance of any one of them is considered as acting involuntarily, especially if he is ignorant of the most important factors. The most important factors are the thing or person affected by the action and the result. An action upon this kind of ignorance is called involuntary, provided that it brings also sorrow and regret in its train.

Since an action is involuntary when it is performed under constraint or through ignorance, a voluntary action would seem to be one in which the initiative lies with the agent who knows the particular circumstances in which the action is performed.

Even ignorance is in itself no protection against punishment if a person is thought to be responsible for his ignorance. For example, the penalty is twice as high if the offender acted in a state of drunkenness, because the initiative is his own: he had the power not to get drunk, and drunkenness was responsible for his ignorance. Moreover, punishment is inflicted for offenses committed in ignorance of such provisions of the law as the offender ought to have known or easily might have known. It is also inflicted in other cases in which ignorance seems to be due to negligence: it was in the offender's power not to be ignorant, it is argued, and he could have made sure had he wanted to.

But, it might be objected, carelessness may be part of a man's character. We counter, however, by asserting that a man is himself responsible for becoming careless, because he lives in a loose and carefree manner; he is likewise responsible for being unjust or self-indulgent, if he keeps on doing mischief or spending his time in drinking and the like. For a given kind of activity produces a corresponding character. This is shown by the way in which people train themselves for any kind of contest or performance: they keep on practicing for it. Thus, only a man who is utterly insensitive can be ignorant of the fact that moral characteristics are formed by actively engaging in particular actions.

Moreover, it is unreasonable to maintain that a man who acts unjustly or self-indulgently does not wish to be unjust or self-indulgent. If a man is not ignorant of what he is doing when he performs acts which will make him unjust, he will of course become unjust voluntarily; nor again, can wishing any more make him stop being unjust and become just than it can make a sick man healthy. Let us assume the case of a man who becomes ill voluntarily through living a dissolute life and disobeying doctors' orders. In the beginning, before he let his health slip away, he could have avoided becoming ill; but once you have thrown a stone and let it go, you can no longer recall it, even though the power to throw it was yours, for the initiative was within you. Similarly, since an unjust or a self-indulgent man initially had the possibility not to become unjust or self-indulgent, he has acquired these traits voluntarily; but once he has acquired them it is no longer possible for him not to be what he is.

FOCUS QUESTIONS

1. How does Aristotle define voluntary actions? Give an example.

2. How does Aristotle define involuntary actions? Give an example.

3. What is the difference between ignorance for which a man is not responsible and ignorance for which he is responsible?

Ethical Theories: Deontology and Teleology

CONTENTS

- Deontology—Immanuel Kant, Kantian Ethics
- Teleology—John Stuart Mill, Utilitarianism
- Balancing Deontology and Teleology

SELECTED READINGS

- Immanuel Kant, selections from *Fundamental Principles of the Metaphysic of Morals*
- John Stuart Mill, selections from *Utilitarianism*

> *"The only thing necessary for the triumph of evil is for good men to do nothing."*
>
> —EDMUND BURKE (1729–1797)

One of the fundamental issues in ethics is whether an action is good because it is based on a good moral principle or because it has good consequences. Should we tell the truth because honesty is a good moral principle, or because lying is likely to have negative consequences for us and for those to whom we lie? In many situations we are faced with, the resulting action—telling the truth—is the right choice whether the moral decision is based on a principle (honesty) or on the likely consequences of the behaviour. In other situations, however, the result will be different.

Describe a situation in which upholding a principle such as telling the truth would have a more negative consequence than lying would:

_____

_____

_____

Should you tell a person bent on violence where his or her intended victim could be found alone, or should you lie and say you didn't know? Should you keep a promise to a friend even if you realize later that keeping that promise will harm other people? In many situations like the ones just described, we have to choose between upholding a principle we believe in or behaving in a way that will produce the best outcome for everyone concerned. These are the most difficult issues to resolve, and it is often tempting to procrastinate or not to act at all. But as the above quote points out, not acting has ethical consequences also. For this reason, we will examine in a little more depth the ways that considering principles and consequences affect our ethical decisions. In this chapter we will consider deontological (principle-based) ethics and teleological (consequence-based) ethics.

DEONTOLOGY

The term "deontology" comes from the Greek word *deos*, meaning duty. Deontological theories, therefore, refer to all ethical theories that are based on the concept of duties or principles. Deontology considers duties, rights and principles the correct measuring rods—in fact the only measurements—for evaluating actions. This means that certain actions are intrinsically right, or morally good, even if they result in negative consequences; and other actions are wrong, or unethical, no matter how beneficial their consequences may be. Therefore, telling the truth, keeping promises and respecting the rights of others are actions that are good in themselves, while dishonesty, theft and cruelty are always wrong. No matter how much good could come from telling a lie, a deontologist would argue that lying would always be wrong. The following example will demonstrate deontology.

> While a man is out driving he passes the scene of an accident. He is the only one present, and he sees a woman lying on the road beside her car, which is smashed against a tree. He drives past without stopping. The next car to come by is driven by a doctor, who administers CPR and revives the woman. Regardless of the eventual positive result—the woman's life is saved—most of us would consider that the first man's behaviour in ignoring her need for help is morally wrong. On the other hand, imagine the same scenario again, but this time the man stops to help the injured woman. He administers CPR, but she is too badly injured and dies anyway. The outcome in this case would have been no different than if he had not stopped at all. Nevertheless, the act of trying to help a person in need is still intrinsically good, so his behaviour is morally right regardless of the consequences.

As this example shows, according to deontological theories, a person's intentions matter more than the consequences of his actions. But how do we determine which actions and intentions are right and which are wrong? The purpose of a moral theory, as we have discussed, is not merely to identify good and bad behaviours, but to provide a method of justifying, or proving, that certain actions are morally right and others are morally wrong. Consider the situation above, of the man who drove past an accident. Our moral vision might make us feel intuitively that it was wrong of the man to drive by and right or good of him to stop and help the unconscious woman. Most of us would agree that if he didn't know CPR, the least he could do was phone 911. But how do we know that our intuition is right? How do we know if our moral vision is accurate?

Deontology does not depend upon individual virtues, as virtue ethics does, but on a careful evaluation of what our duties or responsibilities are in each situation. Divine command theory is in some ways an example of a deontological theory, because broad, universal principles and duties are expected to be followed regardless of the particular situation or the probable consequences. Many deontological theorists rely on reason rather than religion to determine the duties and principles we should follow. The best known deontological theorist is Immanuel Kant (1724–1804), a German philosopher of ethics.

Immanuel Kant and Kantian Ethics

Immanuel Kant played such an important role in developing deontological ethics that the theory is often referred to as "Kantian ethics." Like Socrates, Kant believed that principles or duties are universal (the same for everyone) and absolute (true in every situation); that they can be discovered through human reason; and that they are good for their own sake, not because they were ordained by God.

Kant set about proving his theory with a series of questions. He called the answer to each question a "proposition of morality," and his propositions, taken together, form the justification of his belief in certain principles of behaviour. First he asks, What makes a person morally good? Kant claims that when we judge people as good or bad, we don't look at their achievements. People often don't accomplish what they set out to do, through no fault of their own. In the previous scenario, the man was unable to save the injured woman even though he stopped and did his best to help her. Nevertheless, we would consider him morally good because his intention was to help her. Therefore, Kant concluded, it is our intention, or our will, that makes us morally good.

This leads to his second question, What sorts of intentions make a person morally good? Aristotle might say, those intentions that lead to happiness. It's human nature to do things that will increase our own happiness. A student might intend to do well in school because she intends afterwards to get a well-paying job so she can help support her family. There is nothing wrong with these intentions. Kant, however, pointed out that being happy is not the same thing as being a morally good person; therefore, the intention of achieving happiness doesn't make us morally good. Acting with the intention of doing our duty is what makes us morally good. In the example of the man who stopped to help the injured woman, his action didn't increase his personal happiness. In fact, when the woman died anyway, the man was probably even more unhappy than if he hadn't tried to save her. However, he did try, because he felt it was his duty to try to help someone in need. Acting out of good intentions is the same as acting from the motive of doing our duty. Therefore, Kant's second proposition is that morally good people are motivated to do the right thing because it is their duty.

Kant's third moral proposition is an extension of this concept. He states that acting out of an intention to do our moral duty means respecting the "moral law." To clarify his concept of the moral law, Kant uses the example of a nation's law. Federal law is what the government demands of us, and we are required to act according to that law, simply because it is the law. Kant's moral law is the embodiment of objective moral truth, a concept similar to Socrates' ideal of goodness. Acting out of respect for that moral law means not allowing anything—not personal happiness, not love, not fear, not even the government's laws—to get in the way of doing what is morally right.

These are Kant's three propositions of morality:

1. A person is morally good if her intention (her will) is good.
2. An intention is good if it is based on the motive of doing our duty.
3. Being motivated by duty means respecting the moral law.

Some Kantians believe that acting from the right motive is a necessary aspect of doing the right thing—that an action isn't morally good unless it is done out of duty, in respect for the moral law. Others believe that the two notions are separate, that one should do the right thing *and* do it for the right motive, which is respect for the moral law. In this case, it is possible to do the right thing without doing it for the right reason—out of duty and respect for the moral law. Either way, however, Kant clearly made motive and intentions the basis of his moral theory. He also clearly put no importance on the consequences of action, and believed that all motivations other than duty or moral law should be ignored. When a person is trying to determine the ethical course of action, motivations such as personal inclination, happiness, emotions and desires only get in the way of doing the right thing. A rational consideration of our moral duty is the only appropriate tool for making ethical decisions. Like Socrates, Kant believed that people should be ruled solely by reason in conformity with what Socrates called virtue, but Kant called the moral law. Unlike Socrates, however, he did not believe that the goal was personal happiness under any definition of happiness.

We are still left with the question, How do we rationally determine what our duty is? What is the basis of the moral law that is to be our ultimate motivation? Kant's three propositions don't answer this question. Instead, Kant answers it with what he calls his "categorical imperative." An imperative is a command, so Kant's moral imperative is meant to tell us what we must do in order to act ethically. In doing this, he is telling us what the "moral law" actually is. Kant's categorical imperative is:

> *"Act only according to that maxim by which you can at the same time will that it should become a universal law."*

This is the fundamental moral law which determines the moral worth of any action, no matter what the circumstances or the outcomes may be. By "maxim" Kant meant the rule a person proposes to himself when trying to decide what to do; the principle on which the action he is considering is based. By "will" he means want or wish. The categorical imperative is a test to determine whether that rule or principle is moral. The test is, would you want it to be a rule that everyone follows all the time?

There are four steps required in order to use the categorical imperative correctly. These steps take the form of questions we should ask ourselves when considering a particular course of action.

1. What is my motive for doing this?
2. What is my maxim (the general rule or principle involved) for this behaviour?
3. What is the universal form of this maxim?
4. Can this universalized maxim be made a moral law?

To show how this would work, consider the following situation:

> Jim is a college student near the end of his final year. He recently found out that his best friend has been seeing his girlfriend and as a result he has fallen out with both of them. He's been so upset over this that it's been hard to study, and now he's facing a final exam worth fifty percent of his grade. He wonders if just this once he should sneak some crib notes into the test.

Now work through Kant's four questions with Jim.

1. Jim's motive for cheating is that he is not well enough prepared to pass the test and cheating will enable him to pass it.
2. The general maxim or principle that Jim is proposing to himself is: should he cheat on a test whenever he is not adequately prepared to pass it? The categorical imperative states that cheating is moral only if Jim can say that he would want it to be a universal rule that everyone should follow all the time.

3. The universal form of Jim's maxim in step 2 is: should all students cheat on every test that they are not adequately prepared to pass?
4. Jim must decide whether the universal maxim is consistent. In other words, would it accomplish what it's meant to accomplish, or would it be self-defeating? By self-defeating, Kant means that it would negate the very goal it is trying to accomplish. If the maxim is consistent and not self-defeating, then it can be made into a moral law. When Jim thinks about this universal maxim seriously, he realizes that if every student cheated on every test, then test marks would have no value and college degrees would be meaningless. The goal he is trying to achieve by cheating—to get a good grade so he will receive a diploma that will help him get a good job—will be defeated if college diplomas become meaningless. All the hard work he's put in these past two years would be worthless. Even if the maxim were limited to this test, he wouldn't want it to be universal. If every student taking this test cheated, it wouldn't matter if Jim passed or failed this test because the professor would be sure to notice that the test results were off and would probably make everyone take a replacement test. The only way Jim can benefit by cheating on this test is if other students don't cheat. Since the maxim of the behaviour Jim is considering cannot be made into a universal law and still achieve its goal, it does not have internal consistency, and therefore is not a moral action.

Kant believed that since ethics is basically an exercise of reason, ethical principles or maxims should have the same qualities as other rational subjects, such as logic and mathematics—they must be internally consistent and universally valid. If a person can wish the principle on which her action is based to be a universal law, then that principle meets these requirements. Principles or maxims that fail this test—i.e., those that we would not want to become universal laws—are contradictory and self-defeating. As Jim realized in the previous scenario, if cheating on tests became a universal rule, the whole purpose of cheating would be lost because marks would be meaningless. Therefore, the rule of universal cheating does not have internal consistency—it is self-defeating and contradictory.

It may appear that Kant is concerned with consequences, since the last part of the process of using the categorical imperative does consider the universal consequences if everyone behaved in the manner being questioned. However, Kant is not considering the actual, natural consequences of a proposed action. He is analyzing idealized consequences, or he might say, the logical, universal consequences of a moral law, to decide whether a course of action is internally self-defeating, not actually self-defeating. In Jim's situation, for example, a Kantian deontologist would not say, "If I get caught using my crib notes, I will be given a failing grade regardless of how I do on this test." This is a possible natural consequence of the specific action of Jim taking crib notes into the test. This argument does not consider maxims or a moral law; it is concerned only with a possible real outcome of a specific behaviour. Kant, on the other hand, is not concerned with real outcomes, because he did not consider them important. He is interested only in finding out whether a principle or maxim has internal consistency or is self-defeating in logical, theoretical terms. In short, Kant is asking us to examine our behaviour and ask ourselves the theoretical question, What if everyone did that?

EXERCISE 3.1

Applying Kant's Categorical Imperative

Apply the four steps of Kant's categorical imperative to the following situation to determine whether the behaviour Joan is considering is consistent with moral law.

Joan works part-time at Tim Hortons to help pay for her college education. She is scheduled to work on Thursday, but some friends have asked her to go clubbing with them. One of the guys in the group is some-one Joan has wanted to get to know better, and this would be a perfect chance. She knows she won't be able to trade her shift with anyone—none of the part-timers like working Thursdays—so she is thinking about calling in sick, even though she's perfectly well and just wants to go out. It's not like this is a prestigious, high-paying job, so what's the harm?

1. Joan's motive is:

_____

_____

2. The general maxim she is considering is:

_____

_____

3. The universal maxim would be:

_____

_____

4. The universal maxim can/cannot be made a moral law because:

_____

_____

The categorical imperative, used this way, will show whether an action is morally wrong. This isn't the same as saying that it is morally required, however. An action can be morally wrong, morally right or simply permissible. If the owner of the Tim Hortons store where Joan works decided to close his store at 9 p.m. on Thursdays instead of keeping it open until midnight, the categorical imperative would not show any internal inconsistency. It could be a universal law that all Tim Hortons close at 9 on Thursdays. If the owner reversed the categorical imperative and considered staying open on Thursday evenings, there still wouldn't be any internal inconsistency. It could also be a universal law that all Tim Hortons stay open on Thursdays. Neither of these laws is self-defeating; therefore, both behaviours are morally permissible. But consider the earlier example of the driver who stopped to help the injured woman. If everyone always offered help to people in need, everyone would receive help when they needed it in turn. There is no inconsistency here. But turned around, the maxim asks, suppose no one ever stopped to help or report an injured person? In that case, we would never receive help, either. In this way the maxim of not offering help is self-defeating. Since the categorical imperative only works one way, helping those in need is not a morally permissible behaviour, but a morally required behaviour. It is our duty to help those in need, Kant would say. In other words, if behaving in a certain way is wrong, then behaving in the opposite way is required. If failing to keep a promise is wrong, then honouring a promise is morally required.

Rephrasing the Categorical Imperative

There is some question as to whether the following maxim is a second categorical imperative or a rephrasing of the first, but either way it is central to Kant's moral philosophy. This second categorical imperative is:

> *"Act so that you treat humanity, whether in your own person or in the person of any other, always as an end and never as a means only."*

A "means" is a way of getting something. Money is a means of buying what we want; a car is a means of travelling somewhere; a computer is a means of communication, among other things. When we talk about means we are referring to things, to objects that we can use to achieve some other goal. An object is only valuable to us as long as it is useful to us; it has no inherent value in itself. For this reason, it's perfectly acceptable to use an object as we wish. We can kick our car when it runs out of gas or throw our computer out the window, if there's no one outside who could be hurt.

People, however, have an inherent value in themselves because they are rational beings. In his second phrasing of the categorical imperative, Kant is saying that people are "ends in themselves," as real and as valuable as we are. They are not means, and should not be treated as merely objects we can use to achieve some goal. Of course, to some extent we are means to each other. A mechanic is a means of getting our car repaired, a waitress is a means of getting our food, and a pharmacist is a means of getting our prescriptions filled. But that is not all they are, and they shouldn't be treated only as objects with the sole purpose of being useful to us. There are many examples of people who do this: the salesperson who acts like your best friend and then leaves you in mid-sentence when she realizes you're not going to buy anything, the manager who walks past his office staff without even seeing them, the friend who drops you when you won't lend him any more money. These are all examples of people who treat others as means, or objects they can make use of.

This is the reason why anything we choose to do should apply universally, to everyone. We should grant everyone the same freedom to act as we grant ourselves, and we should be prepared to limit our actions as much as we wish to limit theirs. This is how we show our respect for others. Any behaviour that attempts to deceive, coerce or manipulate others as means to achieve our ends is not moral because it fails to recognize the dignity and worth of all human beings. If Jim had cheated on his test, he would have been trying to deceive and manipulate his teacher into giving him a mark he didn't deserve. He would have been treating her as a means to achieve good grades, and not as a person worthy of respect. He would also have been considering himself different and more special than his classmates because he would be making himself the exception to the rule against cheating—it's all right for him to cheat, but not for others. Kant insisted that we recognize the equal dignity and equal standing of every person, ourselves no more and no less than anyone else.

Thus the two ways of phrasing the categorical imperative both amount to the same thing: We are no more special and worthy of respect than anyone else is; people are all ends, not means, and any rule that applies to us should apply equally to everyone else. Either phrasing of the categorical imperative should, therefore, reach the same conclusion about a course of action. If it is not moral because it cannot be made a universal law, it is also not moral because it treats people as means, not as ends. In the case of Jim, we have seen in the previous paragraph that this is true.

Applying Deontology/Kantian Ethics to Modern Life

Kantian ethics helps people act ethically in their professional and their personal lives. By using the two forms of the categorical imperative, we will be able to make ethical decisions on any aspect of our lives. Take, for example, a company that decides to relocate its Canadian branch in the U.S. Its managers are morally free to do whatever they want with the building they are vacating and any furniture or machinery that they will not need in the new location. This may mean selling some items, discarding others, donating some to charity for a tax write-off, and so on. However, the maxim, treat other people as ends, not means, requires that the company managers consider the employees in the branch as fellow human beings with lives and goals worthy of consideration and respect. They are not simply a means for the company to achieve its goal of making a profit. They cannot simply be "discarded" because they are no longer of use to the company. In this situation, treating the employees with respect means recognizing their intrinsic value as human beings and their right to fair treatment and autonomy. Autonomy means having the right to make decisions over our own lives. Thus the managers might offer the employees the choice of relocating, at the company's expense, and keeping their same jobs in the new location, or of accepting a fair buy-out package. Or they might even ask themselves whether the increase in profit is a valid reason, ethically, to disrupt so many people's lives, and reconsider their decision to relocate.

Some modern followers of deontology have moved away from Kant's position that moral rules are absolute, in order to deal with the problem of what to do when there is a conflict between two moral principles. The most notable of these followers is Sir W. D. Ross (Scotland, 1877–1971). Ross proposed that moral rules can have exceptions, and that some moral rules, such as honesty and promise-keeping, may be broken in certain situations. He called these rules *prima facie* moral rules, which simply means rules that are not absolute. To give an example of this, if an angry husband comes to a women's shelter waving a gun in the air, demanding to know whether his wife is there, the manager of the shelter may make an exception of the moral rule not to lie, and is not required to tell the husband whether his wife is in the shelter. In contrast, under strict Kantian deontology, the manager would be morally obligated to tell the husband the truth, regardless of the consequences.

Ross lists seven prima facie duties, although he does not say that this list is complete. These are:

1. Fidelity—this includes honesty and promise-keeping
2. Reparation—this means "putting right" any harm we may cause another person

3. Gratitude—this is used in a general sense
4. Distributive justice—this means ensuring that benefits and material goods are distributed fairly
5. Beneficence—this refers to our duty to help or improve the conditions of others in need
6. Self-improvement—this means we have a duty to continually improve ourselves in a moral sense
7. Nonmaleficence—this means we are not in any way to cause harm to others

When prima facie duties are in conflict, they can be set aside. For example, imagine that a person—we'll call him Roger—has promised to drive a friend to buy groceries at 2 p.m. On the way over to his friend's apartment, Roger passes a car broken down at the side of the road. The driver of the car waves him down and asks for a ride to a mechanic shop. Should Roger uphold the duty of keeping a promise (fidelity) and continue to his friend's house, or uphold the duty to help others in need (beneficence) and give the driver of the broken-down car a lift? Under Kant's deontology there is no way to resolve this conflict. But Ross's more moderate deontology allows a person in a situation like this to decide which is the more pressing duty and to make an exception of this situation to set aside the lesser one. However, Ross does not propose a clear way to determine which prima facie duty is less important in a given situation.

Can you think of a statement made by someone you know based on deontology or principles and duties?

_____

_____

Do you agree with his/her comment? Why or why not?

_____

_____

Proponents' View

Proponents of Kantian deontology claim that it upholds the dignity and worth of every human being. This is the basic premise of the concept of fundamental human rights—that we are all entitled to be treated equally and fairly, with respect and dignity, for the very reason that we are human beings. Legal rights are sanctioned by governments, but fundamental human rights are simply recognized, not granted by a country or a written law. A deontological approach to ethics recognizes these rights as duties that we owe to one another. Proponents also prefer the straightforward focus on the moral worth of the act itself, rather than trying to uncover and weigh all possible short- and long-term consequences of an action in order to decide whether it is ethical. In deontology, ethical behaviour is simply and always behaviour that treats people fairly and equally, respects the rights of everyone involved and avoids deceiving or manipulating others. Another positive aspect of deontology is that it takes a person's motives and intentions into account. Proponents of Ross's moderate deontology say that it is more flexible than Kant's and that it solves the problem of how to decide between conflicting principles.

Critics' View

Critics of Kantian deontology point out that no direction is given in situations where duties or rights are in conflict. There is no method of weighing conflicting duties to determine which should be upheld at the cost of not upholding others. This is a serious shortcoming, as we saw in the previous example of Roger's dilemma between keeping his promise and helping someone in need. Because Kant's rules or duties are absolute, they are also inflexible. They can never be put aside, and therefore there is no method of determining what to do when a conflict between them arises. The same problem is apparent when using the alternate form of the categorical imperative, to treat people as means, not ends. Whose rights take precedence, for example, in the case of abortion? If the rights of the fetus are more important, does that mean that a pregnant woman is simply a means of incubating a fetus? If the rights of the woman are more important, does that mean that a baby is only a means of achieving parenthood, and if parenthood is not a desirable goal for the woman, then the baby is disposable? Kant does not provide a method of deciding whose rights should prevail when people's rights are in conflict.

Another problem with Kantian deontology is the difficulty of putting aside our emotions and inclinations and acting out of cold reason and duty. Most people would rather receive assistance from someone who enjoys helping others, rather than from someone who does it without any pleasure, out of a sense of duty; yet that cold duty is, in Kant's opinion, the more moral motive. Asking people to put aside fundamental human emotions and inclinations, particularly the good ones, does not seem to be the way to make them better people. Furthermore, are people really capable of doing this? Kant's philosophy is more concerned with identifying and defining ethical behaviour than with giving a reason to adhere to it. We are to act out of a sense of duty because a fundamental moral law requires us to do so. His logic may be sound, but his understanding of human nature and motivation is lacking.

Critics of Ross's moderate deontology say that it does not offer a good, clear method of how to decide when a prima facie moral principle can be ethically set aside, or how to decide which principle to uphold when two are in conflict. In the example on page 72, of the manager of the woman's shelter, the answer seems fairly obvious, but what if the husband has no weapon, and claims that his wife has lost custody of their children because she was mentally unstable, and he is able to show a doctor's certificate proving his claim? Then deciding between the duty of honesty to the husband and the duty of protecting the wife's privacy becomes more difficult.

In summary, consider the three questions used to analyze each theory.

1. What is the theory's basis or source of authority?

_____

_____

2. Does it convince us? Is the basis arrived at through sound reasoning?

_____

_____

3. Do the ethics proposed follow logically from that basis?

_____

_____

TELEOLOGY

The term "teleology" comes from the Greek word *telos*, meaning end or goal. Teleological theories, therefore, refer to all ethical theories that focus on the end goals or consequences of actions. Teleological theories are concerned with acting to achieve an outcome that is in keeping with the chosen goal, or that produces the best consequences overall.

First, all teleological theories must have a specific goal, which must be clearly stated and be morally worthy of being pursued. This goal is called the "good." Any actions that achieve this goal are then considered morally right, and any actions that prevent its achievement or achieve the opposite of the goal are considered morally wrong. For example, a liberty-based teleological theory would describe the "good" as freedom. Any action that achieves or increases freedom is ethical, and any action that prevents or limits freedom, or promotes oppression, is unethical. During World War II, Japanese Canadians were put into internment camps for the duration of the war. This action would be unethical because it limited the personal freedom of a large number of people, it lowered the overall quality of freedom in Canada and it contributed to oppression, which is the opposite of freedom. Interestingly, this action would also be unethical according to Kantian deontology, although for a different reason. In Kantian theory, it would be unethical because it failed to respect the dignity and value of some individuals, and could not be made a universal law (otherwise all Canadians would have been placed in internment camps). In the study of ethics, there is often less disagreement over *what* behaviours are ethical or unethical than over *why* a behaviour is unethical.

The second critical aspect of teleological or consequence-oriented theories is the degree to which the good must be achieved. The issue here is whether it is necessary to maximize the good or just to sufficiently reach it. When teleologists talk about maximizing the good, they mean that there is no limit to achieving the good. If freedom is the good, the more freedom there is, the better. It is not enough, for example, to say, "We won't intern Japanese Canadians, but we won't let them into the military." If maximization is the standard, then we are morally required to act in whatever way produces the maximum amount of the good—in this case, freedom—that it is possible to achieve, and not to do so is morally wrong. On the other hand, when teleologists talk about a sufficient achievement of the good, they mean that the good must be achieved only to a satisfactory degree. Not interning or in any other way oppressing Japanese Canadians during World War II might be considered a satisfactory degree of freedom. Allowing them to apply for military jobs, which would give them access to military plans and strategies, may not be necessary. In a satisfying or sufficiency version of teleology, it would be morally permissible to stop when a satisfactory level of the good was achieved.

The most famous of the teleological theories is utilitarianism. Most people associate utilitarianism with John Stuart Mill (1806–1873). Although Mill was the most prolific defender of this theory, and in fact coined the phrase "utilitarianism," the basic theory was first developed by an English philosopher, Jeremy Bentham (1748–1832) and later refined by Mill.

John Stuart Mill and Utilitarianism

Original, or classical, utilitarianism claims that the ultimate goal of human action is happiness. Bentham and Mill defined happiness as pleasure and well-being, and the opposite of pain, suffering and deprivation. Bentham began his theory with what he called the self-evident observation that pleasure and pain govern people's lives and all their actions. Therefore, he reasoned, pleasure and pain must be the prime consideration when we are determining what we ought or ought not to do. Pleasure, or happiness, is the "good," which we must pursue, and pain is the opposite, which we must diminish or decrease as much as possible. Classical utilitarianism, as developed by Bentham and Mill, takes the maximizing approach. In other words, the more happiness that is achieved, the better. Therefore, ethical behaviour is behaviour that creates as much happiness as possible and causes as little pain and suffering as possible.

We could say that this is just what most of us do anyway. Even when we are willing to suffer some unpleasantness or even pain in the present, it is usually with the intention of getting more overall happiness and less pain in the future. Some people get vaccinations and flu shots to avoid future illness. Students sacrifice their time and money to earn a post-secondary degree in order to secure a better-paying and more satisfying job after graduation. Workers sacrifice a little of their present earnings to build an RRSP for their retirement. These are all ways we try to minimize personal suffering and maximize our overall happiness.

At this point, it may sound like we are talking about a kind of rational or reasoned self-interest. But Bentham and Mill go on to say that it is necessary to maximize everyone's happiness, not just our own. One person's happiness, even if it is our own, must not be considered more important than everyone else's happiness—or even than anyone else's happiness. By the same token, one group of people's happiness (our own family, the people in our community) is not more important than the happiness of any other group of people, or of society as a whole. Instead of asking us to consider only our individual happiness, utilitarianism requires a moral commitment to the happiness of all people. It promotes "the greatest good (happiness) for the greatest number." An action, therefore, is ethical if it will result in the greatest amount of overall happiness possible for the greatest number of people who will be affected by it. In order to determine who will be affected by an action and how, we must consider every possible effect that the action or behaviour might have on every person who might be affected by it, and even on society in general.

Bentham wanted to make ethics simple and practical, so he developed a system for measuring the amount of pleasure and pain that an action would produce. His system, which he called the "hedonistic calculus," identifies seven aspects of an action's consequence. These can be measured and used to compare the results of different actions in order to choose the one that will produce the most happiness and least pain for the most people. The seven aspects to consider are:

1. The intensity of the pleasure or the pain produced
2. The duration or length of the pleasure or pain
3. The likelihood of these sensations being produced (degree of certainty or uncertainty)
4. How soon they will be felt (propinquity or remoteness)
5. Whether they will lead to future happiness (fecundity)
6. Whether they will lead to future pain (purity)
7. The number of people who will be affected (extent)

Bentham's system of measurement ensures that everyone's happiness counts, but no one's counts more than anyone else's. It is important to note that no importance is placed on principles, rights, intentions, motives, personal attitudes or religious precepts. All that is necessary is an honest, thorough and fair analysis of the happiness to be created by the action, balanced against any harm that will result.

John Stuart Mill revised utilitarianism, adding the idea that happiness could be measured according to its quality, as well as by its amount. Some pleasures are of a higher quality, and therefore more valuable than others, according to Mill. Like Socrates and Plato, Mill considered those pleasures that appeal to our senses or appetites, such as food, drink and sexual gratification, to be inferior to the pleasures that appeal to our reason, education, creativity and sense of morality. He also included in the higher-order pleasures sensitivity to and concern for others. This could mean concern for others individually and concern for other people in general. Thus, helping someone in need is a higher-order pleasure, and working to improve society as a whole, or the lot of certain groups, such as the poor, or inner-city children, is also a higher-order pleasure. Because a higher-order pleasure brings a greater degree of happiness, a smaller amount of the higher-order pleasures outweighs a larger amount of the lesser pleasures. Even if the higher-quality pleasures are accompanied by substantial amounts of unhappiness, they count as more pleasure than a larger amount of lower pleasures not accompanied by as much unhappiness. "It is better to be a human being dissatisfied, than a pig satisfied," Mill wrote.

Mill also added to Bentham's ethics a concern for the long-term and far-reaching effects of wrongdoing. This means that the immediate benefits to individuals of an action such as lying would be outweighed by the long-range damage done to society as a whole if people could not trust one another, even though the particular lie being considered might not cause very much immediate harm to anyone. This is similar to the universal law argument (don't lie in this situation because if everyone lied all the time it would defeat the purpose of lying), but it is actually what we call the "slippery slope" argument.

The slippery slope argument, put briefly, goes like this: If we start doing a particular thing, it is likely we will do it again, then more and more often, and it will be done by more and more people, until who knows where it will end. The analogy is that of starting down a slippery slope, and because it is slippery, losing more and more control until you are tumbling helplessly down the slope. Mill argued that although an individual lie may cause more immediate happiness than harm to those directly affected by it, the long-range consequence will be more overall harm than there was immediate happiness. If lying is deemed morally acceptable in one situation, people will be more likely to lie in future situations, and will lie more and more often until it leads to a society in which lying is common and no one can trust each other. That far-range consequence is harmful to society as a whole, and does not promote the greatest happiness for the most people.

A thorough analysis of the consequences of an action is crucial to using utilitarian ethics. This means gathering a lot of information, such as

- A careful analysis of the immediate consequences for everyone directly involved
- A sensitive assessment of the quality, quantity and comparative value of the sensations experienced by everyone as a result of the action
- An insightful uncovering of the subtle, indirect and far-reaching results of the action

To do this requires patience, detailed research, careful observation and an understanding of how people actually respond to certain situations and experiences. This may not be required for every moral decision, but certainly for complex ones with potentially serious results.

So far we have examined teleology and the origins and general aspects of utilitarianism. After Mill, utilitarianism split into two different versions, act-utilitarianism and rule-utilitarianism. These two main versions will be examined separately.

Act-utilitarianism

Act-utilitarianism is a branch of utilitarian ethics that focuses on judging specific actions as being ethical or unethical based on their immediate consequences to all the individuals involved. More specifically, act-utilitarianism holds that the morally right act is the one that causes at least as much overall happiness to everyone affected by that act as any alternative act will cause. In other words, a person must consider all the foreseeable outcomes of every course of action to determine which one will produce the best outcomes in the circumstances for everyone involved. The act that would produce the most overall happiness must be carried out. If there are two or more actions that would produce equal amounts of overall happiness, either course of action may be carried out. Either action would be morally permissible. However, if there is a third alternative which would produce less overall happiness, then one of the two equal courses of action must be taken.

Act-utilitarians use an informal numbering system to measure the overall happiness of a course of action. This can be demonstrated with a simple example.

Janice is one of two dental hygienists who work in a dentist's office. The office is open on Saturdays until 12 p.m., and the hygienists take turns working the Saturday shift. This Saturday it is the turn of the other dental hygienist, Kyle, to work, and Janice is planning to spend the day at the beach. The beach is several hours' drive from town, so it's too far for Janice to go when she doesn't have the morning off. Janice visits her mother on Sundays, so she can go to the beach only on Saturdays when she doesn't work. On Friday afternoon, Kyle gets a phone call in the office. His sister, Elaine, whom he hasn't seen for at least a year, is in town. Elaine's supervisor was booked to attend a sales meeting in town but couldn't make it at the last moment so the company sent Elaine in her place. The meeting runs into the evening and she's expected to attend every minute, so the only time she can see Kyle is Saturday morning. Kyle asks Janice to take his Saturday shift. If Janice says yes, she'll be very disappointed at not going to the beach. On the other hand, Kyle and his sister will be very happy to see each other, and very unhappy if they can't. If she doesn't go to the beach, Janice could go to the park after work and read her book. At least she'll be outside in the afternoon sun. If she does go to the beach she'll be happy to be there, but she'll feel a little guilty about Kyle and Elaine not seeing each other. But if she stays home and takes Kyle's shift, she'll feel good about helping Kyle and Elaine, so she'll feel a little less unhappiness about not getting to the beach.

Act-utilitarians analyze the happiness and unhappiness caused by each course of action, taking into account the different quantity and quality of the happiness or unhappiness for each person involved. Unless the strength of each person's response is taken into account, it's not a true reflection of the total overall happiness gained or lost by the action. The following chart captures these calculations.

Table 3.1

Course of Action	Janice	Kyle	Elaine	Total
Go to the beach	+ 8	–10	–10	–12
Take Kyle's Saturday shift	– 5	+10	+10	+15

As this chart shows, Kyle and Elaine would get more happiness from seeing each other than Janice would by going to the beach. And they would be much more unhappy if they couldn't see each other than Janice will be if she can't go to the beach, because Janice's unhappiness will be a little balanced by feeling good about letting the siblings see each other. The chart indicates that the world would be happier by 15 "units" if Janice takes Kyle's shift, and unhappier by 12 "units" if she goes to the beach. This is because Kyle and Elaine have more happiness or unhappiness at stake than Janice does. So the act-utilitarian would say it is Janice's moral duty to take Kyle's shift. This example is somewhat over-simplified—it would also be necessary, for example, to consider if there were any other alternatives—but it shows the act-utilitarian method of determining the morally right action. If, however, Kyle and Elaine weren't particularly close, and were only getting together to be polite, the chart might look like this:

Table 3.2

Course of Action	Janice	Kyle	Elaine	Total
Go to the beach	+ 8	– 3	– 3	+ 2
Take Kyle's Saturday shift	– 4	+3	+ 3	+ 2

In this case the overall happiness produced by each alternative is the same, so it is morally permissible for Janice to choose either alternative.

EXERCISE 3.2

Using Act-utilitarianism to Decide a Course of Action

Put yourself in the following situation: Your parents want you to attend a family gathering. It is the thirtieth anniversary of your grand-parents' immigration to Canada. It is an important date to them, and your

(Continued)

(Continued)

family, along with your aunt and uncle and cousins, are all taking your grandparents out to dinner to celebrate. You knew about this, but you'd forgotten it was this weekend, and three friends have asked you to go with them to a movie you've been wanting to see. You enjoy time with your grandparents, but you just saw them last weekend, and you don't particularly like spending time with your aunt and uncle, who are always complaining about something, and their three noisy little kids. However, they all seem to like spending time with you, especially the kids, who are always excited to see you. Your parents and grandparents will be very disappointed if you don't go, and very happy if you do. However, you'll miss the movie, which will cause you some unhappiness, and your friends will be unhappy not to have you join them, though they will still go without you. Should you go to the family event or to the movie?

Use the following chart to figure out the total happiness each course of action will cause.

Table 3.3

Course of Action	Grandparents (x2)	Aunt & Uncle (x2)	Cousins (x3)	Parents (x2)	You	Your Friends (x3)	Total
Go to movie							
Attend family event							

What are you morally obligated to do in this situation?

_____

_____

Rule-utilitarianism

Rule-utilitarianism focuses on formulating rules for ethical and unethical ways of acting, based on the long-range consequences to society of those rules. The rules are generated by considering what the long-term consequences for the overall happiness of the society would be if that particular act or behaviour were performed in all similar situations. In other words, the right course of action is to follow the rule that, in this type of situation, causes at least as much overall happiness as any alternative rule. Mill's concern for long-range consequences is captured in this version of utilitarianism.

An example was given earlier showing that telling a lie is wrong, even if it causes more immediate happiness to the individuals involved, because of the long-range damage done to society as a whole if people could not trust one another. Rule-utilitarianism would use this as the basis or justification, in terms of overall consequences, for an ethical rule against lying.

Applying Teleology/Utilitarianism to Modern Life

Utilitarianism, with its focus on accomplishing the greatest good for the most people, is well suited to making ethical decisions in personal and professional dealings. Its fair and equal consideration of everyone's best interest makes it particularly useful when dealing with large numbers of people, and with people who have very different interests at stake. Under utilitarianism, a company that is considering downsizing, for example, would need to consider the interests and well-being, or overall happiness, of the following people:

■ employees and their families (How will those who stay and those who leave be affected?)
■ customers (Will they receive poorer service because of the downsizing?)
■ the board of directors (What do they stand to gain or lose by the downsizing?)
■ shareholders (How will their investments be affected by downsizing? By not downsizing?)
■ the community in which the company is located (How will it be affected?)

Utilitarian ethics guarantees fairness to everyone in a decision like this, because it insists on considering everyone's happiness, but puts no one's happiness above anyone else's. It does, however, consider the quality and quantity (which includes the intensity) of each person's happiness. Therefore, an employee's loss of a job and subsequent inability to support his family would count as a greater unhappiness than a shareholder's slight dip in profits. However, suppose the employees are given good settlements and have a strong likelihood of securing other jobs, but the shareholder's whole retirement savings are tied up in the company and she will not be able to rebuild them. In this case, the shareholder might suffer a greater quantity of unhappiness if the downsizing doesn't take place than the employees will if it does.

Rule-utilitarianism, with its focus on rules that are based on long-term and general consequences, is a particularly useful tool for creating company policies and codes of conduct.

Can you think of a statement made by someone you know based on teleology or consequences?

_____

_____

Do you agree with his/her comment? Why or why not?

_____

_____

Proponents' View

Proponents of utilitarianism claim that it forces people to consider the consequences of their behaviour to others and that it focuses on what is actually good or harmful to people, rather than on abstract rules and idealized principles of behaviour. Proponents of act-utilitarianism claim that it is a simple and easy tool for deciding what is morally right or wrong: if an action would promote the social good, and thus increase the general happiness of the greatest number of people, then it should be allowed. Because it is simple and based on common sense, it is accessible to more people than more complex ethical theories. It is also a useful tool for business people and professionals because it can be applied to real-life cases and it is fair and impartial.

Proponents of rule-utilitarianism claim that since rules play such an important role in guiding conduct in the workplace or within a profession, it is very important to make sure that those rules are morally justified. It is easy and ethical to justify workplace rules by using rule-utilitarianism to assess whether the current rules promote the well-being and overall happiness of those who must follow them. Proponents also claim that rule-utilitarianism resolves the problems of act-utilitarianism while still providing a consequence-based ethical framework. This will be discussed in the section that follows.

Critics' View

Critics of act-utilitarianism point out several problems with the theory. One problem is that it is not really possible to measure happiness. It is hard enough to measure the amount of happiness we ourselves may get from different things. Does receiving a good grade in a difficult subject make us happier than a night out with our friends? How do we compare such different things? And if we can't objectively measure the happiness we feel, how can we ever presume to decide how much happiness or unhappiness someone else feels over something? There is no way we can make a reliable estimation of other people's happiness. And yet if we don't quantify happiness in ourselves and others, we can't determine which course of action will produce the most overall happiness. Mill's reliance on personal experience when he says that anyone who has felt the higher pleasures is more qualified to judge them than someone who has not is only a partial answer. We ask our mechanic to give us his opinion about the value of a car, so why shouldn't we ask someone who's experienced a pleasure to rate the happiness it brings? However, this means that only certain people will be entitled to make moral judgments about certain issues and could undermine the fair and objective method of assessing consequences that is crucial to utilitarianism. Many groups and individuals, such as missionaries and dictators, have claimed that they have a special moral insight to achieve ethical aims.

Another criticism is that it is often difficult and sometimes impossible to obtain all the information necessary to evaluate all the consequences of a course of action for all individuals. Determining the long-term harms and benefits to individuals and even more, to society as a whole, enters the realm of speculation. How can we predict the future with any degree of certainty?

The most serious criticism of act-utilitarianism is that it does not always lead to an ethically acceptable course of action. If, for example, more happiness for more people can be achieved by murdering someone, let's say a member of the Rock Machine, the Quebec-based criminal biker gang that causes a great deal of grief in Montreal, would that make the cold-blooded, premeditated murder of that person morally acceptable? According to act-utilitarianism, if the action increases overall happiness it is not only acceptable but morally required. What about murdering all the members of the Rock Machine? What about murdering all bikers? This is the way vigilantes think. A vigilante is someone who takes the law into his own hands. Morally responsible people do not go about murdering, even if some people are causing harm to others. What if doctors experimented with patients, using untested procedures or medications without obtaining the patients' consent? If new cures were found in this way, which would increase the happiness of thousands of people, would it be morally acceptable? Act-utilitarianism says yes. If we were one of the patients experimented on without our consent, we would likely say no.

Here is a less dramatic example of this same criticism.

Chris and Sandra are both child-care workers at Bumblebee Nursery School. They both have their early childhood education certificates and are both good at their job. Chris is a recent college graduate who is engaged to be married next year and who lives with her parents. She has worked at the school for one year now. Sandra is a single mom with three young children to support. She has been employed at Bumblebee Nursery School for eight months. Recently, a number of new families have moved into the area, and the school has grown. Robin, the owner and manager of Bumblebee, realizes that she can afford to offer a pay raise. She can either offer one dollar an hour more to both Chris and Sandra, or two dollars an hour to one of them. Chris would be happy to get a pay raise, but she doesn't really need one. Sandra, on the other hand, is struggling to pay her bills and would be ecstatic to be given a raise. Not only would her own happiness be increased, but her children would benefit, also. Chris would be disappointed not to get a raise if Sandra does, especially since she has been there longer, but because she doesn't need the extra money as badly as Sandra does, her disappointment will not be as great as Sandra's happiness will be.

This is how the calculation would work out:

Table 3.4

Course of Action	Chris	Sandra	Sandra's kids (×3)	Total
$1.00/hr raise for both Chris and Sandra	+4	+6	$+4 \times 3 = 12$	+22
$2.00/hr raise for Sandra	−4	+10	$+6 \times 3 = 18$	+24

Most of us would agree that the fair and ethical thing to do would be to give the two women each a dollar an hour raise, but according to act-utilitarianism, more overall happiness will be generated by giving the entire raise to Sandra. This example shows that act-utilitarianism does not always lead to the course of action that we intuitively feel is the ethical choice.

Proponents of rule-utilitarianism claim that their theory resolves this problem. In the example of vigilante justice, a moral rule prohibiting people from killing (which is, of course, the law) will, in the long run, maximize happiness for society as a whole. Without such a rule, we would live in fear of one another. However flawed we may think our justice system is, most of us are happier living by it than under vigilante justice. In the case of the doctor experimenting on patients without their consent, a rule could be made (as it has been) requiring that patients consent to care. This is justified by the need to avoid the long-range negative consequences if we did not believe we could trust our doctors. In the case of Bumblebee Nursery School, a moral rule stating that salary increases should be applied fairly and shared equally by everyone would, in the long run, maximize everyone's overall happiness.

Critics of rule-utilitarianism point out that this theory is likely to pose the same problem as Kant's moral principles. That is, do the rules always have to be followed, or can we make exceptions? If they must always be followed, without exception, then we no longer have utilitarianism because there will be times when following a rule will cause more unhappiness than breaking it. Consider the earlier example we looked at when discussing Kantian ethics, of Roger, who promised to take his friend to buy groceries, but came across a man whose car had broken down on the way to pick up his friend. If Roger follows a rule that says, always keep your promises, he would cause more unhappiness to the man who needs his help than he would cause happiness to his friend by arriving on time for a trip to the grocery store. By following the rule, he would not be maximizing happiness and therefore not be practicing utilitarianism. On the other hand, if rules can be set aside in order to achieve the greatest happiness for the greatest number, then we are not really following rule-utilitarianism; we are back to act-utilitarianism, deciding what to do to maximize happiness in each situation.

In summary, consider the three questions used to analyze each theory.

1. What is utilitarianism's basis or source of authority?

   _____

   _____

2. Does it convince us? Is the basis arrived at through sound reasoning?

   _____

   _____

3. Do the ethics proposed follow logically from that basis?

   _____

   _____

BALANCING DEONTOLOGY AND TELEOLOGY

Some people are comfortable acting on principles, regardless of the consequences. Others think that each situation should be judged and acted upon in terms of the likely consequences of the available courses of action. Both of these positions have sound ethical reasoning behind them, as we have learned in this chapter. Most people, however, consider both the principles they value and the consequences of their actions when they are trying to decide what to do in a situation. When upholding a principle we believe in will have harmful consequences for us or for others, how do we decide which is more important? Balancing principles against consequences is a central problem in ethics, as we noted at the start of this chapter. The following exercise will illustrate this problem.

EXERCISE 3.3

Balancing Principles Against Consequences

Jane Doe is the pseudonym of a young woman living alone in Toronto. She was attacked in her apartment by Paul Callow, a serial rapist, in July 1986. After her attack, it became known that the Toronto police had worked up a profile of Callow's victims and the type of locations and geographical area where he attacked women. Jane Doe was one of several women who fit that profile, but the police did not release this information to her or to the general public. After her attack, Jane Doe sued the police for withholding information that would have alerted her to danger. If she had known that she fit the profile of the rapist's previous victims and lived in the same area and type of accommodation he chose for his attacks, this information would have enabled her to take precautions that could have prevented her rape. The police response was that their responsibility was to capture Callow and prevent him from continuing to be a danger. If they had released the information, Callow would have been aware that police were watching a certain area of Toronto and a particular type of woman. It is most likely that he would have either changed his pattern or gone elsewhere; in either case he would still be violating women and the police would have to start all over again in their attempt to capture and convict him. They chose instead to watch the area and the potential victims in it closely in hopes of catching Callow on the way to or during his next attack.

Give a Kantian or principle-based argument in support of Jane Doe's position.

_____

_____

Give a utilitarian or consequence-based argument in support of Jane Doe's position.

_____

_____

Give a Kantian or principle-based argument in support of the Toronto police's position.

_____

_____

Give a utilitarian or consequence-based argument in support of the Toronto police's position.

_____

_____

Whose position do you think is more ethically justifiable, and why?

_____

_____

_____

(Continued)

(Continued)

Are the arguments concerning principles and the arguments concerning consequences in this issue in conflict? How would you balance them in order to make a decision (for example, in cases where breaking a moral principle seems to lead to the best outcome)?

_____

_____

_____

_____

_____

_____

EXERCISE 3.4

Personal Opinion Paper #2

Reread the information on the Tracy Latimer case in Exercise 2.1, on page 30. Without looking at your original opinion paper, write a second two-page paper on the issue of euthanasia. Make several carefully reasoned arguments for and against euthanasia, using the Latimer case as an example to illustrate your points. Make sure to include arguments based on principles and arguments based on consequences. What would a virtue ethicist say, and why? What would a religious argument be on this issue?

"Aim above morality. Be not simply good; be good for something."

—HENRY DAVID THOREAU (1817–1862)

Answers

ANSWERS TO THE THREE QUESTIONS ASKED OF EACH THEORY:

1. *What is the theory's basis or source of authority?*
2. *Does it convince us? Is the basis arrived at through sound reasoning?*
3. *Do the ethics proposed follow logically from that basis?*

KANT—DEONTOLOGY

1. There is no reason given for behaving ethically as the consequences of ethical behaviour are not considered important. The authority behind Kant's model of ethical behaviour is the moral law, as stated in his categorical imperative.

2. Kant's philosophy is a model of logical thinking. In order to be convinced, we must accept the ideal concept of an absolute moral law and his categorical imperative as the expression of that moral law.

3. All ethical behaviours follow logically from Kant's categorical imperative.

MILL—TELEOLOGY

1. The basis of utilitarianism is that the goal of all human action is to increase our happiness and decrease our pain and suffering. To do this ethically, we must be concerned not just with our own happiness but with everyone's.

2. The basis is arrived at through observation of human nature and through our instinctive need to socialize and identify with others.

3. If the goal of human activity is happiness, then acting to achieve the greatest amount of happiness for the most people logically follows.

SELECTED READINGS

Immanuel Kant (1724–1804)

Immanuel Kant's life was as dull and stable as Hobbes' life was dangerous and uncertain. Kant spent his entire life in the city where he was born, Konigsberg, East Prussia. He came from a lower-middle-class, devout Lutheran family and remained deeply religious all his life. Kant studied philosophy at the University of Konigsberg, and then tutored the children of wealthy families. He never married. In 1755, he began lecturing at the University and in 1770 he was given the chair of logic and metaphysics. It was after this that he began writing his philosophy.

Kant's major work on ethics, *Foundation for the Metaphysics of Morals*, was published in 1785, when he was sixty. Kant gave so little care to his writing style that his works were almost unintelligible to most readers. Despite this drawback, his ideas revolutionized philosophical thought. Kant's deontological or "duty-based" theory of moral philosophy directly repudiates the goal of personal happiness that earlier philosophers endorsed, and probably originates in part from his strict Lutheran Pietist upbringing, which endorsed hard work and high moral standards.

The following excerpts from *Foundation for the Metaphysics of Morals* introduces Kant's theory of one moral principle, which he called the categorical imperative, as binding on all rational beings.

Excerpts from *Fundamental Principles of the Metaphysics of Morals*—Section 1

Nothing in the world—indeed nothing even beyond the world—can possibly be conceived which could be called good without qualification except a GOOD WILL. Intelligence, wit, judgment, and other talents of the mind however they may be named, or courage, resoluteness, and perseverance as qualities of temperament, are doubtless in many respects good and desirable; but they can become extremely bad and harmful if the will, which is to make use of these gifts of nature and which in its special constitution is called character, is not good.

Moderation in emotions and passions, self-control, and calm deliberation not only are good in many respects but seem even to constitute part of the inner worth of the person. But however unconditionally they were esteemed by the ancients, they are far from being good without qualification, for without the principles of a good will they can become extremely bad, and the coolness of a villain makes him not only far more dangerous but also more directly abominable in our eyes than he would have seemed without it.

The good will is not good because of what it effects or accomplishes or because of its competence to achieve some intended end; it is good only because of its willing (i.e., it is good in itself). And, regarded for itself, it is to be esteemed as incomparably higher than anything which could be brought about by it in favour of any inclination or even of the sum total of all inclinations. Even if it should happen that, by a particularly unfortunate fate or by the niggardly provision of a step-motherly nature, this will should be wholly lacking in power to accomplish its purpose, and if even the greatest effort should not avail it to achieve anything of its end, and if there remained only the good will—not as a mere wish, but as the summoning of all the means in our power—it would sparkle like a jewel all by itself, as something that had its full worth in itself. Usefulness or fruitlessness can neither diminish nor augment this worth.

(R)eason is given to us as a practical faculty (i.e., one which is meant to have an influence on the will). As nature has elsewhere distributed capacities suitable to the functions they are to perform, reason's proper function must be to produce a will good in itself and not one good merely as a means, since for the former, reason is absolutely essential. This will need not be the sole and complete good, yet it must be the condition of all others, even of the desire for happiness. In this case it is entirely compatible with the wisdom of nature that the cultivation of reason, which is required for the former unconditional purpose, at least in this life restricts in many ways—indeed, can reduce to nothing—the achievement of the latter unconditional purpose, happiness. For one perceives that nature here does not proceed unsuitably to its purpose, because reason, which recognizes its highest practical vocation in the establishment of a good will, is capable of a contentment of its own kind (i.e., one that springs from the attainment of a purpose determined by reason), even though this injures the ends of inclination.

We have, then, to develop the concept of a will which is to be esteemed as good in itself without regard to anything else. It dwells already in the natural and sound understanding and does not need so much to be taught as only to be brought to light. In the estimation of the total worth of our actions it always takes first place and is the condition of everything else. In order to show this, we shall take the concept of duty.

(I)t is easily decided whether an action in accord with duty is done from duty or for some selfish purpose. It is far more difficult to note this difference when the action is in accord with duty and, in addition, the subject has a direct inclination to do it. For example, it is in accord with duty that a dealer should not overcharge an inexperienced customer, and wherever there is much trade the prudent merchant does not do so, but has a fixed price for everyone so that a child may buy from him as cheaply as any other. Thus the customer is honestly served, but this is far from sufficient to warrant the belief that the merchant has behaved in this way from duty and principles of honesty. His own advantage required this behaviour, but it cannot be assumed that over and above that he had a direct inclination to his customers and that, out of love, as it were, he gave none an advantage in price over another. The action was done neither from duty nor from direct inclination but only for a selfish purpose.

On the other hand, it is a duty to preserve one's life, and moreover everyone has a direct inclination to do so. But for that reason, the often anxious care which most men take of it has no intrinsic worth, and the maxim of doing so has no moral import. They preserve their lives according to duty, but not from duty. But if adversities and hopeless sorrow completely take away the relish for life; if an unfortunate man, strong in soul, is indignant rather than despondent or dejected over his fate and wishes for death, and yet preserves his life without loving it and from neither inclination nor fear but from duty—then his maxim has moral merit.

To be kind where one can is a duty, and there are, moreover, many persons so sympathetically constituted that without any motive of vanity or selfishness they find an inner satisfaction in spreading joy and rejoice in the contentment of others which they have made possible. But I say that, however dutiful and however amiable it may be, that kind of action has no true moral worth. For the maxim lacks the moral import of an action done not from inclination but from duty.

Thus the first proposition of morality is that to have genuine moral worth, an action must be done from duty. The second proposition is: An action done from duty does not have its moral worth in the purpose which is to be achieved through it but in the maxim whereby it is determined. Its moral value, therefore, does not depend upon the realization of the object of the action but merely on the principle of the volition by which the action is done irrespective of the objects of the faculty or desire. From the preceding discussion it is clear that the purposes we may have for our actions and their effects as ends and incentives of the will cannot give the actions any unconditional and moral worth. Wherein, then, can this worth lie, if it is not in the will in its relation to its hoped-for effect? It can lie nowhere else than in the principle of the will irrespective of the ends which can be realized by such action.

The third principle, as a consequence of the two preceding, I would express as follows: Duty is the necessity to do an action from respect for law.

Now as an act from duty wholly excludes the influence of inclination and therewith every object of the will, nothing remains which can determine the will objectively except law and subjectively except pure respect for this practical law. This subjective element is the maxim that I should follow such a law even if it thwarts all my inclinations.

But what kind of law can that be, the conception of which must determine the will without reference to the expected result? Under this condition alone can the will be called absolutely good without qualification. Since I have robbed the will of all impulses which could come to it from obedience to any law, nothing remains to serve as a principle of the will except universal conformity to law as such. That is, I ought never to act in such a way that I could not also will that my maxim should be a universal law. Strict conformity to law as such (without assuming any particular law applicable to certain actions) serves as the principle of the will, and it must serve as such a principle if duty is not to be a vain delusion and chimerical concept. The common sense of mankind (*gemeine Menschenvernunft*) in its practical judgments is in perfect agreement with this and has this principle constantly in view.

Let the question, for example, be: May I, when in distress, make a promise with the intention not to keep it? I easily distinguish the two meanings which the question can have, viz., whether it is prudent to make a false promise, or whether it conforms to duty. The former can undoubtedly be often the case, though I do see clearly that it is not sufficient merely to escape from the present difficulty by this expedient, but that I must consider whether inconveniences much greater than the present one may not later spring from this lie. Even with all my supposed cunning, the consequences cannot be so easily foreseen. Loss of credit might be far more disadvantageous than the misfortune I am now seeking to avoid, and it is hard to tell whether it might not be more prudent to act according to a universal maxim and to make it a habit not to promise anything without intending to fulfill it. But it is soon clear to me that such a maxim is based only on an apprehensive concern with consequences.

To be truthful from duty, however, is an entirely different thing from being truthful out of fear of untoward consequences, for in the former case the concept of the action itself contains a law for me, while in the latter I must first look about to see what results for me nay be connected with it. To deviate from the principle of duty is certainly bad, but to be unfaithful to my maxim of prudence can sometimes be very advantageous to me, though it is certainly safer to abide by it. The shortest but most infallible way to find the answer to the question as to whether a deceitful promise is consistent with duty is to ask myself: Would I be content that my maxim of extricating myself from difficulty by a false promise should hold as a universal law for myself as well as others? And could I say to myself that everyone may make a false promise when he is in a difficulty from which he otherwise cannot escape? Immediately I see that I could will the lie but not a universal law to lie. For with such a law there would be no promises at all, inasmuch as it would be futile to make a pretense of my intention in regard to future actions to those who would not believe this pretense or—if they overhastily did so—would pay me back in my own coin. Thus my maxim would necessarily destroy itself as soon as it was made a universal law.

I do not, therefore, need any penetrating acuteness to discern what I have to do in order that my volition may be morally good. Inexperienced in the course of the world, incapable of being prepared for all its contingencies, I only ask myself: Can I will that my maxim become a universal law? If not, it must be rejected, not because of any disadvantage accruing to myself or even to others, but because it cannot enter as a principle into a possible enactment of universal law, and reason extorts from me an immediate respect for such legislation.

FOCUS QUESTIONS

1. Why does Kant believe that a good will is the only morally good quality?

2. What is the purpose of human reason?

3. Describe Kant's concept of duty. How does it differ from inclination? Give an example that shows the difference.

4. What are Kant's three propositions of morality?

5. What is Kant's law that determines the moral worth of an action and serves as the principle of the will?

6. What example does he give to show how this law works?

Excerpts from *Fundamental Principles of the Metaphysics of Morals*—Section 2

Everything in nature works according to laws. Only a rational being has the capacity of acting according to the *conception* of laws (i.e., according to principles). This capacity is the will. Since reason is required for the derivation of actions from laws, will is nothing less than practical reason.

The conception of an objective principle, so far as it constrains a will, is a command (of reason), and the formula of this command is called an *imperative*.

All imperatives are expressed by an "ought" and thereby indicate the relation of an objective law of reason to a will which is not in its subjective constitution necessarily determined by this law. This relation is that of constraint. Imperatives say that it would be good to do or to refrain from doing something, but they say it to a will which does not always do something simply because the thing is presented to it as good to do. Practical good is what determines the will by means of the conception of reason and hence not by subjective causes but objectively, on grounds which are valid for every rational being as such. It is distinguished from the pleasant, as that which has an influence on the will only by means of a sensation from purely subjective causes, which hold for the senses only of this or that person and not as a principle of reason which holds for everyone.

A perfectly good will, therefore, would be equally subject to objective laws of the good, but it could not be conceived as constrained by them to accord with them, because it can be determined to act by its own subjective constitution only through the conception of the good. Thus no imperatives hold for the divine will or, more generally, for a holy will. The "ought" here is out of place, for the volition of itself is necessarily in unison with the law. Therefore imperatives are only formulas expressing the relation of objective laws of volition in general to the subjective imperfection of the will of this or that rational being, for example, the human will.

All imperatives command either *hypothetically* or *categorically*. The former present the practical necessity of a possible action as a means to achieving something else which one desires (or which one may possibly desire). The categorical imperative would be one which presented an action as of itself objectively necessary, without regard to any other end.

Since every practical law presents a possible action as good and thus as necessary for a subject practically determinable by reason, all imperatives are formulas of the determination of action which is necessary by the principle of a will which is in any way good. If the action is good only as a means to something else, the imperative is hypothetical; but if it is thought of as good in itself, and hence as necessary in a will which of itself conforms to reason as the principle of this will, the imperative is categorical.

(I)t is to be suspected that all imperatives which appear to be categorical are tacitly hypothetical. For instance, when it is said, "Thou shalt not make a false promise," we assume that the necessity of this prohibition is not a mere counsel for the sake of escaping some other evil, so that it would read: "Thou shalt not make a false promise, lest, if it comes to light, thou ruinest thy credit." [In so doing] we assume that an action of this kind must be regarded as in itself bad and that the imperative prohibiting it is categorical, but we cannot show with certainty by any example that the will is here determined by the law alone without any other incentives, although it appears to be so. For it is always possible that secretly fear of disgrace, and perhaps also obscure apprehension of other dangers, may have had an influence on the will. Who can prove by experience the nonexistence of a cause when experience shows us only that we do not perceive the cause? In such a case the so-called moral imperative, which as such appears to be categorical and unconditional, would be actually only a pragmatic precept which makes us attentive to our own advantage and teaches us to consider it.

Thus we shall have to investigate purely *a priori* the possibility of a categorical imperative, for we do not have the advantage that experience would show us the reality of this imperative so that the [demonstration of its] possibility would be necessary only for its explanation, and not for its establishment. In the meantime, this much at least may be seen; the categorical imperative alone can be taken as a practical law, while all other imperatives may be called principles of the will but not laws. This is because what is necessary merely for the attainment of some chosen end can be regarded as itself contingent and we get rid of the precept once we give up the end in view, whereas the unconditional command leaves the will no freedom to choose the opposite. Thus it alone implies the necessity which we require of a law.

There is, therefore, only one categorical imperative. It is: Act only according to that maxim by which you can at the same time will that it should become a universal law. Now if all imperatives of duty can be derived from this one imperative as a principle, we can at least show what we understand by the concept of duty and what it means...

We shall now enumerate some duties, adopting the usual division of them into duties to ourselves and to others.

[A] man finds himself forced by need to borrow money. He well knows that he will not be able to repay it, but he also sees that nothing will be lent him if he does not firmly promise to repay it at a certain time. He desires to make such a promise, but he has enough conscience to ask himself whether it is not improper and opposed to duty to relieve his distress in such a way. Now, assuming he does decide to do so, the maxim of his action would be as follows: When I believe myself to be in need of money, I will borrow money and promise to repay it, although I know I shall never be able to do so. Now this principle of self-love or of his own benefit may very well be compatible with his whole future welfare, but the question is whether it is right. He changes the pretension of self-love into a universal law and then puts the question: How would it be if my maxim became a universal law? He immediately sees that it could never hold as a universal law of nature and be consistent with itself; rather it must necessarily contradict itself. For the universality of a law which says that anyone who believes himself to be in need could promise what he pleased with the intention of not fulfilling it would make the promise itself and the end to be accomplished by it impossible; no one would believe what was promised to him but would only laugh at any such assertion as vain pretense.

[Another] man, for whom things are going well, sees that others (whom he could help) have to struggle with great hardships, and he asks, "What concern of mine is it? Let each one be as happy as heaven wills, or as he can make himself; I will not take anything from him or even envy him; but to his welfare or to his assistance in time of need I have no desire to contribute." If such a way of thinking were a universal law of nature, certainly the human race could exist, and without doubt even better than in a state where everyone talks of sympathy and good will or even exerts himself occasionally to practice them while, on the other hand, he cheats when he can and betrays or otherwise violates the right of man. Now although it is possible that a universal law of nature according to that maxim could exist, it is nevertheless impossible to will that such a principle should hold everywhere as a law of nature. For a will which resolved this would conflict with itself, since instances can often arise in which he would need the love and sympathy of others, and in which he would have robbed himself, by such a law of nature springing from his own will, of all hope of the aid he desires.

When we observe ourselves in any transgression of a duty, we find that we do not actually will that our maxim should become a universal law. That is impossible for us; rather, the contrary of this maxim should remain as a law generally, and we only take the liberty of making an exception to it for ourselves or for the sake of our inclination, and for this one occasion. Consequently, if we weighed everything from one and the same standpoint, namely, reason, we would come upon a contradiction in our own will, viz., that a certain principle is objectively necessary as a universal law and yet subjectively does not hold universally but rather admits exceptions. However, since we regard our action at one time from the point of view of a will wholly conformable to reason and then from that of a will affected by inclinations, there is actually no contradiction, but rather an opposition of inclination to the precept of reason....

FOCUS QUESTIONS

1. Why does Kant consider it important that reason be in control of our actions?

2. What are the two types of imperatives? How does Kant define each of them?

3. What is Kant's categorical imperative?

4. Describe an example Kant gives that shows how the categorical imperative works.

Now, I say, man and, in general, every rational being exists as an end in himself and not merely as a means to be arbitrarily used by this or that will. In all his actions, whether they are directed toward himself or toward other rational beings, he must always be regarded at the same time as an end...

Such a being is thus an object of respect, and as such restricts all [arbitrary] choice. Such beings are not merely subjective ends whose existence as a result of our action has a worth for us, but are objective ends (i.e., beings whose existence is an end in itself). Such an end is one in the place of which no other end, to which these beings should serve merely as means, can be put. Without them, nothing of absolute worth could be found, and if all worth is conditional and thus contingent, no supreme practical principle for reason could be found anywhere.

The practical imperative, therefore, is the following: Act so that you treat humanity, whether in your own person or in that of another, always as an end and never as a means only.

FOCUS QUESTIONS

1. What does Kant's practical imperative mean?

2. Can you think of an example of it in use?

John Stuart Mill (1806–1873)

John Stuart Mill was an English philosopher and the eldest son of a well-known philosopher. He was home-tutored by his father, a strict, cold and intellectually demanding figure. Both father and son were followers of Jeremy Bentham, whose philosophy of utility was the basis of Mill's utilitarianism. At the age of twenty, Mill suffered a nervous breakdown and depression. This incident forced him to realize that he had never learned to respect emotions or allow himself to enjoy them, and he began to teach himself to feel his emotions. This may be why emotion, as well as reason, plays an important part in his philosophy.

John Stuart Mill is best known for his defense of utilitarianism and individual liberty, and for the social changes he promoted as part of his greatest happiness theory. Although Mill did not invent utilitarianism, he coined the name and contributed important concepts to the theory. The following excerpts introduce the reader to Mill's focus on the quality of different pleasures, the need for people's proper education in and appreciation of the higher pleasures, and the fact that individual rights are crucial to utilitarian morality.

Excerpts from *Utilitarianism*—Chapter 2

The creed which accepts as the foundation of morals Utility or the Greatest Happiness Principle holds that actions are right in proportion as they tend to promote happiness, wrong as they tend to produce the reverse of happiness. By happiness is intended pleasure, and the absence of pain; by unhappiness, pain, and the privation of pleasure. To give a clear view of the moral standard set up by the theory, much more requires to be said; in particular, what things it includes in the ideas of pain and pleasure; and to what extent this is left an open question. But these supplementary explanations do not affect the theory of life on which this theory of morality is grounded—namely, that pleasure, and freedom from pain, are the only things desirable as ends; and that all desirable things (which are as numerous in the utilitarian as in any other scheme) are desirable either for the pleasure inherent in themselves, or as means to the promotion of pleasure and the prevention of pain.

Now, such a theory of life excites in many minds, and among them in some of the most estimable in feeling and purpose, inveterate dislike. To suppose that life has (as they express it) no higher end than pleasure—no better and nobler object of desire and pursuit—they designate as utterly mean and grovelling; as a doctrine worthy only of swine, to whom the followers of Epicurus were, at a very early period, contemptuously likened; and modern holders of the doctrine are occasionally made the subject of equally polite comparisons by its German, French, and English assailants.

When thus attacked, the Epicureans have always answered, that it is not they, but their accusers, who represent human nature in a degrading light; since the accusation supposes human beings to be capable of no pleasures except those of which swine are capable. If this supposition were true, the charge could not be gainsaid, but would then be no longer an imputation; for if the sources of pleasure were precisely the same to human beings and to swine, the rule of life which is good enough for the one would be good enough for the other. The comparison of the Epicurean life to that of beasts is felt as degrading, precisely because a beast's pleasures do not satisfy a human being's conceptions of happiness. Human beings have faculties more elevated than the animal appetites, and when once made conscious of them, do not regard anything as happiness which does not include their gratification.

It is quite compatible with the principle of utility to recognise the fact, that some kinds of pleasure are more desirable and more valuable than others. It would be absurd that while, in estimating all other things, quality is considered as well as quantity, the estimation of pleasures should be supposed to depend on quantity alone.

If I am asked, what I mean by difference of quality in pleasures, or what makes one pleasure more valuable than another, merely as a pleasure, except its being greater in amount, there is but one possible answer. Of two pleasures, if there be one to which all or almost all who have experience of both give a decided preference, irrespective of any feeling of moral obligation to prefer it, that is the more desirable pleasure. If one of the two is, by those who are competently acquainted with both, placed so far above the other that they prefer it, even though knowing it to be attended with a greater amount of discontent, and would not resign it for any quantity of the other pleasure which their nature is capable of, we are justified in ascribing to the preferred enjoyment a superiority in quality, so far outweighing quantity as to render it, in comparison, of small account.

Now it is an unquestionable fact that those who are equally acquainted with, and equally capable of appreciating and enjoying, both, do give almost marked preference to the manner of existence which employs their higher faculties. Few human creatures would consent to be changed into any of the lower animals, for a promise of the fullest allowance of a beast's pleasures; no intelligent human being would consent to be a fool, no instructed person would be an ignoramus, no person of feeling and conscience would be selfish and base, even though they should be persuaded that the fool, the dunce, or the rascal is better satisfied with his lot than they are with theirs. They would not resign what they possess more than he for the most complete satisfaction of all the desires which they have in common with him.

Whoever supposes that this preference takes place at a sacrifice of happiness—that the superior being, in anything like equal circumstances, is not happier than the inferior—confounds the two very different ideas, of happiness, and content. It is indisputable that the being whose capacities of enjoyment are low, has the greatest chance of having them fully satisfied; and a highly endowed being will always feel that any happiness which he can look for, as the world is constituted, is imperfect. But he can learn to bear its imperfections, if they are at all bearable; and they will not make him envy the being who is indeed unconscious of the imperfections, but only because he feels not at all the good which those imperfections qualify. It is better to be a human being dissatisfied than a pig satisfied; better to be Socrates dissatisfied than a fool satisfied. And if the fool, or the pig, are of a different opinion, it is because they only know their own side of the question. The other party to the comparison knows both sides.

...According to the Greatest Happiness Principle, as above explained, the ultimate end, with reference to and for the sake of which all other things are desirable (whether we are considering our own good or that of other people), is an existence exempt as far as possible from pain, and as rich as possible in enjoyments, both in point of quantity and quality; the test of quality, and the rule for measuring it against quantity, being the preference felt by those who in their opportunities of experience, to which must be added their habits of self-consciousness and self-observation, are best furnished with the means of comparison. This, being, according to the utilitarian opinion, the end of human action, is necessarily also the standard of morality; which may accordingly be defined "the rules and precepts for human conduct" by the observance of which an existence such as has been described might be, to the greatest extent possible, secured to all mankind; and not to them only, but, so far as the nature of things admits, to the whole sentient creation.

The utilitarian morality does recognise in human beings the power of sacrificing their own greatest good for the good of others. It only refuses to admit that the sacrifice is itself a good. A sacrifice which does not increase, or tend to increase, the sum total of happiness, it considers as wasted. The only self-renunciation which it applauds, is devotion to the happiness, or to some of the means of happiness, of others; either of mankind collectively, or of individuals within the limits imposed by the collective interests of mankind.

I must again repeat, what the assailants of utilitarianism seldom have the justice to acknowledge, that the happiness which forms the utilitarian standard of what is right in conduct, is not the agent's own happiness, but that of all concerned. As between his own happiness and that of others, utilitarianism requires him to be as strictly impartial as a disinterested and benevolent spectator. In the golden rule of Jesus of Nazareth, we read the complete spirit of the ethics of utility. "To do as you would be done by," and "to love your neighbour as yourself," constitute the ideal perfection of utilitarian morality. As the means of making the nearest approach to this ideal, utility would enjoin, first, that laws and social arrangements should place the happiness, or (as speaking practically it may be called) the interest, of every individual, as nearly as possible in harmony with the interest of the whole; and secondly, that education and opinion, which have so vast a power over human character, should so use that power as to establish in the mind of every individual an indissoluble association between his own happiness and the good of the whole; especially between his own happiness and the practice of such modes of conduct, negative and positive, as regard for the universal happiness prescribes; so that not only he may be unable to conceive the possibility of happiness to himself, consistently with conduct opposed to the general good, but also that a direct impulse to promote the general good may be in every individual one of the habitual motives of action, and the sentiments connected therewith may fill a large and prominent place in every human being's sentient existence.

Utilitarians are quite aware that there are other desirable possessions and qualities besides virtue, and are perfectly willing to allow to all of them their full worth. They are also aware that a right action does not necessarily indicate a virtuous character, and that actions which are blamable, often proceed from qualities entitled to praise. When this is apparent in any particular case, it modifies their estimation, not certainly of the act, but of the agent. I grant that they are, notwithstanding, of opinion, that in the long run the best proof of a good character is good actions: and resolutely refuse to consider any mental disposition as good, of which the predominant tendency is to produce bad conduct.

FOCUS QUESTIONS

1. What does Mill consider the only desirable end or goal?

2. How does Mill justify his claim that some pleasures are superior to others?

3. What are the two measurements of happiness?

4. What social improvements does Mill call for in law and in education?

5. What does utilitarianism have to say about self-sacrifice? What makes it a virtue?

6. What is the best proof of good character?

Excerpts from *Utilitarianism*—Chapter 3

Society between equals can only exist on the understanding that the interests of all are to be regarded equally. And since in all states of civilisation, every person, except an absolute monarch, has equals, every one is obliged to live on these terms with somebody; and in every age some advance is made towards a state in which it will be impossible to live permanently on other terms with anybody. In this way people grow up unable to conceive as possible to them a state of total disregard of other people's interests: They are under a necessity of conceiving themselves as at least abstaining from all the grosser injuries, and (if only for their own protection) living in a state of constant protest against them. They are also familiar with the fact of cooperating with others and proposing to themselves a collective, not an individual interest as the aim (at least for the time being) of their actions. So long as they are cooperating, their ends are identified with those of others; there is at least a temporary feeling that the interests of others are their own interests. Not only does all strengthening of social ties, and all healthy growth of society, give to each individual a stronger personal interest in practically consulting the welfare of others; it also leads him to identify his *feelings* more and more with their good, or at least with an even greater degree of practical consideration for it. He comes, as though instinctively, to be conscious of himself as a being who *of course* pays regard to others. The good of others becomes to him a thing naturally and necessarily to be attended to, like any of the physical conditions of our existence. Now, whatever amount of this feeling a person has, he is urged by the strongest motives both of interest and of sympathy to demonstrate it, and to the utmost of his power encourage it in others; and even if he has none of it himself, he is as greatly interested as any one else that others should have it. Consequently the smallest germs of the feeling are laid hold of and nourished by the contagion of sympathy and the influences of education; and a complete web of corroborative association is woven round it, by the powerful agency of the external sanctions. This mode of conceiving ourselves and human life, as civilisation goes on, is felt to be more and more natural. Every step in political improvement renders it more so, by removing the sources of opposition of interest, and levelling those inequalities of legal privilege between individuals or classes, owing to which there are large portions of mankind whose happiness it is still practicable to disregard. In an improving state of the human mind, the influences are constantly on the increase, which tend to generate in each individual a feeling of unity with all the rest, which, if perfect, would make him never think of, or desire, any beneficial condition for himself, in the benefits of which they are not included.

...The deeply rooted conception which every individual even now has of himself as a social being, tends to make him feel it one of his natural wants that there should be harmony between his feelings and aims and those of his fellow-creatures. If differences of opinion and of mental culture make it impossible for him to share many of their actual feelings—perhaps make him denounce and defy those feelings—he still needs to be conscious that his real aim and theirs do not conflict; that he is not opposing himself to what they really wish for, namely their own good, but is, on the contrary, promoting it. This feeling in most individuals is much inferior in strength to their selfish feelings, and is often wanting altogether. But to those who have it, it possesses all the characters of a natural feeling. It does not present itself to their minds as a superstition of education, or a law despotically imposed by the power of society, but as an attribute which it would not be well for them to be without. This conviction is the ultimate sanction of the greatest happiness morality.

Excerpts from *Utilitarianism*—Chapter 4

Virtue, according to the utilitarian doctrine, is not naturally and originally part of the end, but it is capable of becoming so; and in those who love it disinterestedly it has become so, and is desired and cherished, not as a means to happiness, but as a part of their happiness.

Virtue, according to the utilitarian conception, is a good of this description. There was no original desire of it, or motive to it, save its conduciveness to pleasure, and especially to protection from pain. But through the association thus formed, it may be felt a good in itself, and desired as such with as great intensity as any other good; and with this difference between it and the love of money, of power, or of fame, that all of these may, and often do, render the individual noxious to the other members of the society to which he belongs, whereas there is nothing which makes him so much a blessing to them as the cultivation of the disinterested love of virtue. And consequently, the utilitarian standard, while it tolerates and approves those other acquired desires, up to the point beyond which they would be more injurious to the general happiness than promotive of it, enjoins and requires the cultivation of the love of virtue up to the greatest strength possible, as being above all things important to the general happiness.

It results from the preceding considerations, that there is in reality nothing desired except happiness. Whatever is desired otherwise than as a means to some end beyond itself, and ultimately to happiness, is desired as itself a part of happiness, and is not desired for itself until it has become so. Those who desire virtue for its own sake, desire it either because the consciousness of it is a pleasure, or because the consciousness of being without it is a pain, or for both reasons united; as in truth the pleasure and pain seldom exist separately, but almost always together, the same person feeling pleasure in the degree of virtue attained, and pain in not having attained more. If one of these gave him no pleasure, and the other no pain, he would not love or desire virtue, or would desire it only for the other benefits which it might produce to himself or to persons whom he cared for.

FOCUS QUESTIONS

1. What is the basis of a society of equals, and what should it lead to?

2. What makes virtue good, according to utilitarianism?

Excerpts from *Utilitarianism*—Chapter 5

...when we feel our sentiment of justice outraged, we are not thinking of society at large, or of any collective interest, but only of the individual case. It is common enough certainly, though the reverse of commendable, to feel resentment merely because we have suffered pain; but a person whose resentment is really a moral feeling, that is, who considers whether an act is blamable before he allows himself to resent it—such a person, though he may not say expressly to himself that he is standing up for the interest of society, certainly does feel that he is asserting a rule which is for the benefit of others as well as for his own. If he is not feeling this—if he is regarding the act solely as it affects him individually—he is not consciously just; he is not concerning himself about the justice of his actions. This is admitted even by anti-utilitarian moralists. When Kant (as before remarked) propounds as the fundamental principle of morals, "So act, that thy rule of conduct might be adopted as a law by all rational beings," he virtually acknowledges that the interest of mankind collectively, or at least of mankind indiscrimi-nately, must be in the mind of the agent when conscientiously deciding on the morality of the act.

...(T)he idea of justice supposes two things—a rule of conduct, and a sentiment which sanctions the rule. The first must be supposed common to all mankind, and intended for their good. The other (the sentiment) is a desire that punishment may be suffered by those who infringe the rule. There is involved, in addition, the conception of some definite person who suffers by the infringement; whose rights (to use the expression appropriated to the case) are violated by it. And the sentiment of justice appears to me to be, the animal desire to repel or retaliate a hurt or damage to oneself, or to those with whom one sympathises, widened so as to include all persons, by the human capacity of enlarged sympathy, and the human conception of intelligent self-interest. From the latter elements, the feeling derives its morality; from the former, its peculiar impressiveness, and energy of self-assertion.

FOCUS QUESTIONS

1. When is resentment a moral feeling?

2. How does Mill define justice?

Ethical Theories: Social Contracts, Feminist Ethics and Ethical Relativism

SELECTED READINGS

- Thomas Hobbes, selections from *Leviathan*
- John Rawls, selections from *A Theory of Justice*

> *"I think we ought always to entertain our opinions with some measure of doubt. I shouldn't wish people dogmatically to believe any philosophy, not even mine."*
>
> —BERTRAND RUSSELL (1872–1970)

The ethical theories we have examined so far include divine command theory, Socrates' healthy soul theory, virtue ethics, deontology (Kantian ethics) and teleology (utilitarianism). There are three other important ways of considering ethics, which will be discussed in this chapter. The first involves the concept of a social contract, which is an unstated but understood agreement between people in a society to abide by certain rules in order to live together peacefully. Thomas Hobbes first introduced this concept. His theory has evolved into what we today call enlightened self-interest. John Rawls also proposed a social contract view of ethics, which he called contractarianism. The second concept is ethics of care. It is often referred to as feminist ethics, because it claims to present the female approach to this subject.

Our modern view of the world as a global village has given rise to issues of cultural diversity in ethical approaches. This has led to a consideration of whether ethics are absolute or relative. This is a significant issue in ethics, so ethical absolutism and relativism will be examined at the end of this chapter.

It may seem by the end of this chapter that doing the right thing has been made more complicated, rather than easier, by the presentation of so many different theories on what the right way to behave is. That is because being an ethical person is about being consciously ethical, and for that you must have some understanding of the different ways of looking at ethics. As Bertrand Russell says in the previous quote, we must question our opinions in order to find the truth.

This chapter concludes our examination of ethical theories. Therefore, the exercises at the end of the chapter, on applying ethical reasoning, encompass all of the theories discussed in Chapters 2, 3 and 4.

SOCIAL CONTRACTS

Enlightened Self-interest

Enlightened self-interest, also known as ethical egoism, states that an action is morally permissible if it increases the benefits for the individual in a way that does not intentionally harm others, and if those benefits are believed to counterbalance any harm done. This philosophy is essentially concerned with deciding under what conditions individuals or organizations can pursue their own best interests and still act ethically. Unlike the earlier theories we examined, it is not concerned with finding the most ethical behaviour in a situation—only the behaviour that most closely achieves the goal and is still morally acceptable. Notice that the outcome of behaviour—achieving the self-interested goal—is the most important consideration. Intentions are slightly less important but still matter, particularly the lack of maleficence, or desire to harm anyone. Principles are not necessarily taken into account at all.

Enlightened self-interest originated from the "state of nature" philosophy of Thomas Hobbes, an English philosopher writing in the first half of the 1600s.

Thomas Hobbes (1588–1679)

Thomas Hobbes was primarily concerned with political structures, like most philosophers before him. His book, *Leviathan*, describes the perfect state. However, we shall examine his philosophy only as it relates to ethics.

Hobbes begins by describing the natural condition of man. Human beings living in a natural state would be no different from animals—constantly at war with one another to gain as much land and goods as they can, and to keep what they have secure from everyone who would try to take it away. Thus, the goal of all humans is to get and keep as much power over others as possible. This is a natural desire based on the fear and lack of security that would exist in a natural world, where it is each man for himself. According to Hobbes, the quarrel, or conflict, that arises between people in a natural state is caused by three things:

1. Competition, which puts people at war with each other to gain each other's possessions
2. Diffidence, or fear, which puts people at war with each other to defend their own territory and possessions
3. Glory, or pride, which puts people at war with each other to maintain other people's respect

In such a state, there is no such thing as justice or injustice, no concept of right and wrong, no law, no pleasure or leisure to pursue the arts. People are free to look after their own interests with no regard for anyone else, but violence is common and the interests of the strongest prevail. Therefore, people live in "continual fear and danger of violent death, and the life of man (is) solitary, poor, nasty, brutish and short." In order to escape this state of violence and insecurity, and to enjoy the benefits and pleasures of peace, humans are drawn by their reason toward peace. And in order to secure peace, people must sacrifice much of their "liberty to act," as Hobbes puts it, on the condition that everyone else will do the same. In other words, we have to give up our right to do whatever we wish in order to demand the same sacrifice from others. This right or liberty to act as we wish can either be renounced or transferred to another. To transfer our rights means to give someone else, such as a benevolent sovereign or dictator, the power to act on our behalf. This is Hobbes' preferred social order. To renounce our rights means to enter into an agreement with other equals whereby we accept the same constraints upon our actions as we demand that they accept upon theirs. This mutual renunciation or transferral of rights is what Hobbes calls a "contract." Having entered into such a contract, our greatest moral obligation is to keep our promise to abide by it, because the peace we sought to gain, and the very existence of our society, depends upon people doing so.

The restraints Hobbes claimed we must agree to put on our behaviour in order to live together peacefully in society are the tenets of enlightened self-interest. They include:

- Claim as much liberty as we are willing to grant to others.
- Keep promises and perform contracts to which we have agreed.
- Acknowledge the equality of all.
- Do not demand of others things we are unwilling to do ourselves.
- Things that cannot be divided should be shared in common.
- People who disagree should submit their dispute to arbitrators.
- Judges should be impartial.
- We should not do to others what we don't want them to do to us.

This agreement, or social contract, is called enlightened self-interest because, although we are agreeing to consider others and avoid doing any harm to them even when our interests are in conflict with theirs, we are still acting out of self-interest. The peace and security we gain through this contract is worth more to us than the amount of liberty we sacrifice for it. In the long run we will benefit more by it. Therefore, living by a social contract is intelligent self-interest, or enlightened self-interest.

Enlightened self-interest is unique among the other theories we have discussed because of its outlook that people adopt moral behaviours only in order to escape anarchy and they agree to be only as ethical as is necessary to live at peace with each other. In other words, we are no better than we need to be, and only because we need to be. Where this theory is similar to the others is in its belief that human reason is what causes us to apply morals to our behaviour.

Applying Enlightened Self-interest to Modern Life

Enlightened self-interest means limiting our behaviour to the same extent that we want others to limit theirs. Abiding by the eight tenets above will accomplish that. Consider Robin, the manager of Bumblebee Nursery School, and her decision to give a raise to Chris and/or Sandra in Chapter 3. Giving any employee a raise is not in Robin's own best interest, as the money will come from her profits on the school. However, from the point of view of the statement, We should not do to others what we don't want done to us, Robin could ask herself if she would want a raise if she were an employee at Bumblebee, and the school was growing. Obviously the answer is yes, she would. If she doesn't give her employees the raise they want, then they might seek work elsewhere, and she would have the problem of finding and training new employees. So it is ultimately in Robin's own best interest to give her employees a raise. Now she has to ask, if she were in Chris's place, would she want the entire raise given to Sandra? If the answer is no, she should give both women an equal raise. To do this isn't a moral obligation so much as it is in Robin's own best interest, in order to keep both employees. It's not necessarily in Robin's best interests to help Sandra, unless that means that Sandra, who is a good employee, will be more likely to stay. If Chris is moving away when she marries anyway, there is no advantage to Robin in keeping her happy. However, if both employees are likely to stay, then it is in Robin's best interest to keep them both contented so that the school will run harmoniously and she won't have to seek a replacement for either Chris or Sandra. In this case, it is in Robin's best interest to give each employee a one-dollar raise. Since Robin can honestly answer that this is what she would want done to her if she were Chris, she is morally permitted to do this.

It is not always possible to act without harming anybody—people's interests do conflict, and the best course of action must be found. This is when intention comes into play. Consider the original definition of enlightened self-interest: "An action is morally permissible if it increases the benefits for the individual in a way that does not intentionally harm others, and if those benefits are believed to counterbalance any harm done." What if Chris is planning to leave when she gets married? Then it is in Robin's best interest to act in a way that will at least keep Sandra at Bumblebee. Robin knows giving Sandra a two-dollar raise will benefit Sandra, and Robin has no intention of deliberately harming Chris. If Robin decides that the benefit to Sandra outweighs the harm to Chris, the action is morally permissible.

This example shows that under enlightened self-interest the person making the decision has more freedom of choice in his actions than under any other theory. The limitations involve preventing harm, rather than any obligation to do good to others.

Can you think of a statement made by someone you know based on enlightened self-interest?

_____

_____

Do you agree with his/her comment? Why or why not?

_____

_____

Proponents' View

Proponents of enlightened self-interest claim that the theory is realistic about human motivation and that it treats all people equally. Moreover, it does not rely on faith in a supreme being or in the existence of ideal, universal principles to make it credible. It is also very compatible with a multicultural society because it does not require that everyone believe the same thing, or find happiness in the same ways or to measurably equal degrees. The theory relies on only two things: that everyone will give up the same amount of liberty in pursuing their own interests at the expense of others, and that those who do not will be dealt with by the law. A strong advantage of this theory for business is that enlightened self-interest allows more freedom of choice to the person or organization in making business decisions and takes the interests of the person or organization into account more fully.

Critics' View

Critics of enlightened self-interest claim that it promotes personal egoism and self-centredness in individuals as well as organizations and businesses. They also point out that the egoism of individuals, no matter how enlightened in their self-interest, prevents the resolution of moral conflicts unless a standard of evaluating decisions other than self-interest is in place. In order to resolve conflicts of interest, we must look for a "higher" point of view than self-interest. In other words, we have to look outside the theory to find a way of resolving ethical issues or conflicts. Another problem (and this is a problem for all ethical theories, not just this one), is the difficulty of being honest with ourselves. In following the rule, We should not do to others what we don't want them to do to us, it is important to answer honestly whether we would want the action being considered to be done to us.

In summary, consider the three questions used to analyze each theory.

1. What is the theory's basis or source of authority?

   _____

   _____

2. Does it convince us? Is the basis arrived at through sound reasoning?

   _____

   _____

3. Do the ethics proposed follow logically from that basis?

   _____

   _____

Contractarianism

Contractarian ethics is similar to enlightened self-interest in that it is based on the idea of everyone agreeing to a theoretical social contract in order to live together. In both enlightened self-interest and contractarian ethics, the social contract is theoretical—it is an implied agreement; we don't actually sign a contract. The main difference in the two theories is the goal and terms of the contract and the human state from which it is envisioned. These are the issues we will explore in contractarian ethics.

Contractarianism is generally associated with John Rawls, a philosopher at Harvard University who developed the theory in his book, *A Theory of Justice*. Rawls was primarily concerned with economic justice, or distributive justice, which refers to the fair distribution of wealth and economic opportunity, but we will focus on how his theory applies to ethics.

The goal of the social contract in contractarian ethics is not to escape a state of violence and chaos, as is the goal of enlightened self-interest, but to create a state of equality and justice for all. Although this state may ultimately be as theoretical as the contract is, the moral rules which would generate such a state form the principles of contractarian ethics. Rawls, like Kant, believed that it is necessary to ignore or overcome personal inclinations, desires and interests in order to be able to recognize, and to do, the morally right thing. He believed that this required not so much an act of will, as an act of imagination. Imagine that we are all free and equal, is his beginning point. This is an act of imagination because, of course, we are not all free and equal. Consider this statement for a moment.

List the things in your personal life and situation that restrict your freedom and others that give you advantages and disadvantages (inequalities) over other people both here in Canada and in the world.

_____

_____

_____

We all have personal attributes—physical, psychological, intellectual and visual (which includes our gender and our physical appearance)—that give us advantages and disadvantages over others. Some of these individual characteristics, such as a health problem, limit our freedom, and all of them affect the equality between people. Add to this the fact that we come from different cultures, races, religions and family backgrounds, and the disparity and inequality between people is increased. Children born into poverty or into dysfunctional families face barriers that children born into middle- or upper-middle-class families or into supportive families never have to confront. Rawls calls these aspects of our lives "contingent attributes." They are matters involving luck, or what he refers to as "the natural lottery."

These natural inequalities, according to Rawls, cause most of the disagreement among people regarding the moral rules in our society. We cannot help but consider social issues and questions of personal freedom from inside the biases of our own situation. As we discussed in Chapter 1, our intuitive sense of right and wrong is very much a product of our background, upbringing and personal experiences. It is very difficult to step outside our background or our personal stake in something. Union disputes, for example, are a conflict between the goals and personal biases of plant workers and those of managers. Rawls claims that we must get beyond these contingent attributes in order to agree upon ethical truths.

Therefore, in order to formulate the principles of contractarianism, Rawls asks us to imagine ourselves without any of these contingent attributes. In other words, imagine ourselves just before birth, before we know anything about ourselves or our circumstances or even our personal inclinations and preferences. We don't yet know our family circumstances, race, gender or anything about our interests, talents or abilities. Rawls refers to this as our "original position." We are hidden from our future selves behind a theoretical "veil of ignorance" which keeps us from knowing anything about ourselves.

Although we are ignorant about our conditions of life behind this veil of ignorance, we are to imagine ourselves completely rational and able to consider, now free from any biases, the ethical rules which we would agree to abide by. Rawls assumes that we are still motivated by self-interest, and therefore we will formulate moral rules that will protect our interests. But because we don't know our situation in life, those rules will not be biased in favour of certain groups or interests. For example, we would not agree to moral rules that give preference to one gender or particular race, because for all we know, we may well end up being the other gender, or of another race.

From this theoretical position, in which we are ignorant of our personal situation but are still rational and self-interested, we would be able to come to agreement about the moral rules which should govern all of us. In this position we are truly free and equal and without biases, and so we would create rules that are fair. Rawls believes these rules represent true morality. As any child would say, you can't make up the rules while you play the game. You have to set the rules first, then play by them. This is what contractarian ethics attempts to do.

Rawls believes that in such a situation, we would choose rules that protect what he calls the "primary goods" of the most disadvantaged—in case we turn out to be in that group. These primary goods are those items that any rational person would want, whatever her contingent attributes turned out to be. In other words, regardless of race, religion, economic status, personal values, abilities and goals, there are certain things that everyone considers vitally important. These include such things as:

- health, or at least access to health care
- liberty, or the freedom and autonomy to pursue our interests within acceptable bounds
- opportunity, or the ability to achieve secondary wants (wealth, etc.) through our own efforts

Rawls' greatest interest was in the primary good of liberty, since liberty is necessary first, in order to pursue anything else. He called this the "principle of maximum equal liberty," and assumed anyone behind the veil of ignorance would agree to a rule whereby everyone would have the maximum amount of liberty possible, as long as it was equally held by all. His second principle is called the "difference principle." This principle holds that it is sometimes necessary to accept inequalities in primary goods other than liberty, in order to improve everyone's situation. These inequalities are especially acceptable if they help those who are the worst off. An example of this rule might be that people with special abilities or talents should be given more or better opportunities than others in order to develop these abilities. The discovery of insulin has helped millions of people all over the world, especially those disadvantaged by illness. Anyone behind the veil of ignorance, not knowing whether or not he will develop diabetes, would agree to a rule that increased the opportunity of someone like Dr. Frederick Banting, the Canadian who discovered insulin, to develop his talent in science. He would agree to such a rule even if it meant that other people didn't have equal opportunities for education, because Banting's discovery might some day save this person's life. This type of unequal opportunity might take the form of a scholarship or research grant. We can't all get scholarships or grants, so it's an inequality that some people do and others don't; but we all benefit when talented people in our society get to develop their talents. That doesn't mean that we would agree to a rule stating that other people wouldn't get any opportunity to have an education—we would agree only that there could be some inequality in order to benefit everyone.

Rawls was mainly concerned with distributive justice (the fair distribution of wealth in a society). This is a fairly straightforward issue, and therefore not a lot of information is needed by those behind the veil of ignorance to formulate rules about it. As an ethical theory, however, contractarianism needs to be able to be applied to a wide variety of situations calling for ethical decision-making. Most situations require the rule-makers to have a certain amount of information in order to make a fair rule. Rawls did not take this into account, but other contractarian theorists have suggested adjustments to his theory in order to do so. They suggest that those behind the veil of ignorance should have only as much knowledge as is necessary to put the issue into context. This information includes knowing who will be affected by the proposed rule and how they will be affected, but still does not include knowing anything about their own contingent attributes. This broadens Rawls' theory of economic justice into a theory which can be used to make ethical decisions about any aspect of the personal or professional life.

Applying Contractarianism to Modern Life

In order to apply contractarian ethics, it is necessary to imagine ourselves behind the veil of ignorance, and determine what rule would fit this situation. This process can best be explained through an example. Consider the increase in security at Canadian airports since 9/11. Depending upon their situation, people will have different opinions about it, and may or may not agree to the measures that have been taken. Airport and airline operators may resent the added cost and may feel that the likelihood of terrorists repeating 9/11 is too small to warrant it. They may also be concerned about losing business because air travel has become such a hassle. Airport food vendors may be concerned about a significant loss of business since people can no longer buy food to take on board. Passengers may resent the added time spent in travel—they now have to arrive at the airport three hours in advance of any international flight instead of two hours in advance, as they did previously. The lengthy line-ups are tiring as well as time-consuming. The expense of greater security is also passed on to passengers in higher ticket prices. Being randomly chosen to have their bags searched involves another delay as well as an invasion of privacy. People of Middle Eastern descent may feel they are the victims of profiling if their bags are searched. On the other hand, passengers who are nervous flying or who have experienced terrorism will appreciate the added security despite the cost and inconvenience. Pilots and airline attendants, who fly constantly and therefore have a higher risk of being victims of terrorism in the air, and who are not subject to the same airport scrutiny, will likely be in favour of the increased security because it makes their workplace safer. However, if security results in fewer people flying, or flying less often, pilots and attendants may face some job losses. The Canadian military and everyone involved in national security would be clearly in favour of the measures because they increase their job opportunities and make protecting Canadians from terrorist attacks easier.

All of these people have their own bias. If the issue is considered from behind the veil of ignorance, however, those making the decision about security will not know which role they may end up in. They are free of bias because they don't know what they may have at stake. They can reach agreement about what the rule should be without being hampered by personal interests. The result would be an impartial agreement that is fair and ethically justified. Since their main concern would be to protect the primary goods of all concerned, those making the decision would evaluate the impact on each of the parties with regards to the relevant primary goods. How is the liberty of each group affected? How is their opportunity affected? How is their health (potentially) affected?

If the rule were not to increase security measures, how would each group be affected? Choose between somewhat negatively, very negatively, no effect, somewhat positively or very positively. If the effect is possible rather than certain, add the word "potentially." Use the following chart to give your answers.

Table 4.1

Affected group	Liberty/ autonomy	Health and safety	Opportunity
Airport/airline operators			
Airport food vendors			
General passengers			
Middle Eastern passengers			
Pilots and airline attendants			
Military/national security personnel			

If the rule were to increase security measures, how would each group be affected? Choose between somewhat negatively, very negatively, no effect, somewhat positively or very positively. If the effect is not very likely to happen, add the word "potentially." Use the following chart to give your answers.

Table 4.2

Affected group	Liberty/ autonomy	Health and safety	Opportunity
Airport/airline operators			
Airport food vendors			
General passengers			
Middle Eastern passengers			
Pilots and airline attendants			
Military/national security personnel			

There may be other primary goods not listed here which would be relevant in this situation or in another one. These are only some examples of primary goods, not a complete list. So the chart would be different for different ethical issues. The next step is to determine which of the primary goods is most important in a given situation, and therefore must be protected by the rule. This, too, must be decided without bias, and therefore considered from behind the veil of ignorance. If the primary good of health and safety, in this situation, is deemed most important, then some degree of liberty and opportunity should be sacrificed to achieve it. On the other hand, it has been argued (but not proved either way) that the current increased security measures would not stop a real terrorist. If that were proven true, then these measures' effect on health and safety will be lessened and may not warrant the sacrifice of liberty and opportunity. It is apparent from this that a lot depends on what level of risk the rule-makers are willing to accept concerning whether they might end up being the most disadvantaged group in the equation.

In effect, however, in contractarian ethics, an action is morally right if it is in accordance with a rule which applies to that situation and which impartial people would agree to from behind the veil of ignorance. Whatever rule those behind the veil of ignorance would agree to is the morally right thing to do, and what they would not agree to is morally wrong. The type of rules that Rawls envisioned being made behind the veil of ignorance would be rules that increased the liberty/autonomy of individuals in all socioeconomic groups and promoted the fair distribution of social benefits, including the means to guard one's health and increase personal wealth.

Can you think of a statement made by someone you know based on a contractarian outlook?

_____

_____

Do you agree with his/her comment? Why or why not?

_____

Proponents' View

Proponents of contractarianism say its major strength is that it is more likely than other theories to treat everyone fairly and equally. They also claim that it acknowledges self-interest but converts it into a tool for achieving justice and equality. The most significant advantage of contractarian ethics, however, is that it provides for the vast differences in the beliefs, goals, attributes and attitudes of a multicultural society—a multicultural world, in fact—and offers a means of making decisions and rules of conduct that are fair and equal for all.

Critics' View

Critics of contractarianism claim that the imagination required to put ourselves behind the veil of ignorance is unrealistic. All ethical theories exhort us to overcome our biases, and contractarian ethics is no more or less likely to help us succeed. Furthermore, they argue that contractarian ethics does not give clear direction concerning ethical behaviour. The framework for the theory is very general, and there are no guidelines for precisely how those behind the veil of ignorance are to reach agreement on social rules. Rawls assumed that "rational" rule-makers would be low risk takers who would therefore make rules that would protect at least the minimum interests of those who are worst off, in case they themselves turned out to be in this group. But there is nothing in the theory that requires them to do so. These theoretical rule-makers might choose the rule that averages the best outcome and hope to be lucky in the "natural lottery" in order to take advantage of the risk they took. Rawls does not define rationality; he simply assumes that rational rule-makers will not be risk-takers when the stakes are as high as a lifetime without liberty or equal opportunity to improve our lot. Others may define rationality differently; for example, a rule-maker might rationally evaluate the odds of not being in the most disadvantaged group as being very low. Defined this way, rational rule-makers would come up with very different rules. The criticism is: Without a clear definition of rationality, how can we determine what rules "rational" people behind the veil of ignorance would generate?

In summary, consider the three questions used to analyze each theory.

1. What is the theory's basis or source of authority?

_____

_____

2. Does it convince us? Is the basis arrived at through sound reasoning?

_____

_____

3. Do the ethics proposed follow logically from that basis?

_____

_____

EXERCISE 4.1

Identifying the Basis of Ethical Argument

Find two articles which argue opposing sides of a current social issue. Choose an issue that you have not used or discussed previously in this course. The articles can be opinion pieces, editorials, letters to the editor, journal articles, etc. Select a subject that is appropriate to your program. The controversies examined in Chapters 5, 6 and 7 over racial issues, minimum wage or the war in Afghanistan, can be used for this exercise.

1. Describe the factual information in each article. Are different facts given to support the different sides of the debate? Are any facts contradictory or one-sided?
2. Identify a teleological (consequence-based) argument used. Give an example, quoting from one of the articles, and explain why it is a teleological argument.
3. Identify a deontological (principle-based) argument used. Give an example, quoting from one of the articles, and explain why it is a deontological argument.
4. Identify an argument based on virtue ethics. Give an example, quoting from one of the articles, and explain why it is virtue ethics.
5. Identify an argument based on enlightened self-interest. Give an example, quoting from one of the articles, and explain why it is enlightened self-interest.
6. Identify an argument based on contractarianism. Give an example, quoting from one of the articles, and explain why it is contractarianism.

If neither of the articles contains an argument based on virtue ethics, enlightened self-interest or conractarianism, make up arguments which are in keeping with each of these theories, supporting either side of the issue. Which argument(s) do you find more convincing? Why?

CURRENT ISSUES IN ETHICS

Feminist Ethics

All of the theories of ethics we have studied were developed by men. Each theory attempts, and claims, to treat people equally and to be gender-neutral, particularly contractarianism, which begins with the supposition of not knowing whether we will end up being male or female. But since they were created by men, feminists argue that this makes them male-biased on two counts. First, the theories approach the study of ethics from a male perspective, which is different from the female perspective. And second, the ethical rules and behaviours they generate may appear to be equal in the literal sense, but are in fact substantively unequal.

The first argument feminists make is based on the work of Carol Gilligan, as discussed in Chapter 1. Gilligan studied and compared the moral development of young boys and girls. Prior to Gilligan's work, studies of moral development, notably the work of Lawrence Kohlberg, focused on boys, and showed moral development as a progression toward rational, objective, independent ethical decision making. Gilligan studied the moral development of young girls and compared it to that of young boys. She found that, in brief, girls' moral development involved increasing their understanding of how their decisions affect others, and in particular how they affect the relationships in their lives. Female moral development is thus a progression toward making ethical decisions which will support and strengthen relationships with others. Based on this knowledge, Gilligan proposed her "ethics of care."

Ethics of care is very different from ethics of justice. As Gilligan states in her book, *A Different Voice*:

> [T]he "restorative activity of care" allows us to see the actors in (a moral) dilemma arrayed not as opponents in a contest of rights but as members of a network of relationships on whose continuation they all depend. Consequently (the) solution to the dilemma lies in...communication,... (in) strengthening rather than severing connections.

This is a very different concept of ethics from the ones we have studied, which all to a greater or lesser extent distrust emotions and sensitivity to others, but rely on objective reasoning to determine the moral rule or behaviour relevant to any situation. The emphasis on objectivity, which the previous theories claim makes them gender-neutral, is completely opposed to the female perspective of ethics, which emphasizes sensitivity, caring and our responsibility to others. Feminists also argue that it is not possible, given human nature, to be as objective and as rational in our decisions as the previous theories all exhort us to be. Furthermore, the emphasis in other theories is on individuality and individual decision-makers, rather than on community and relationships. Since female nature is not reflected in those theories, feminists argue, they are not truly gender-neutral.

The second argument feminists make is that the rules and behaviours these ethical theories generate are not substantively equal or fair for women and men. There are a number of issues which are particularly significant to women in society and in the workplace. Among these are abortion, child care, sexual harassment, equal hiring practices, equal compensation and equal opportunity for advancement. On the surface, the other theories do appear to deal with these issues fairly. Take, for example, the issue of discrimination against women in the workplace, specifically in such areas as hiring or promotions. Most reasonable people recognize that this is unfair and should be addressed, although there may be some disagreement as to how to do so. Feminists argue that women's issues cannot be addressed fairly by male-oriented theories of ethics. In order to test their claim, first we must ask, What would the moral theories we have discussed say about discrimination practices against women? Write down your own ideas before reading further.

Divine command theory

_____

_____

Virtue ethics

_____

_____

Deontology/Kantian ethics

_____

_____

Teleology/utilitarianism

_____

_____

Enlightened self-interest

_____

_____

Contractarianism

_____

_____

Divine command theory would require considering the commands and the meaning of the stories in each religion to ascertain God's dictate on this issue. Considering the attitude to women at the time most religions were formulated, most of them are likely to fail in promoting the fair and equal treatment of the sexes. However, rules such as "Do unto others as you would have them do unto you" could be used to argue that if an employer would not like to be discriminated against on the basis of gender, then he should not discriminate against others on that basis, either. Virtue ethics would likely find discrimination against women one extreme, with fairness as the mean, and over-compensation by discriminating in favour of women the opposite extreme. Virtue ethics would also likely consider discrimination a violation of the virtues of fairness and justice, and therefore not part of a virtuous character. Kant would consider discrimination against women, or any other group, to be a failure to respect people as ends in themselves. He would also find it illogical (irrational) to make discrimination a universal law, because then we would all be discriminated against and the benefit or goal of discrimination would not be achievable. According to utilitarianism, the rules adopted by any organization, including rules around hiring practices, should maximize overall happiness. The happiness gained by allowing gender discrimination would be much less than the happiness individuals and society in general would gain by not allowing it, since all or most of the significant contributions made by women in the professions would then be lost. Enlightened self-interest claims that we must restrict our freedom as much as we want others to restrict theirs, and that we should not do to others what we don't want them to do to us. Both of these restrictions on behaviour could be argued to reject gender discrimination. Contractarian ethics states that the ethically correct thing to do would be to abide by rules made behind the veil of ignorance, and since from that position we would not know whether we were male or female, the rules agreed to would probably prohibit gender discrimination.

All of the previously discussed theories appear to come to the same conclusion, a conclusion which feminists would surely approve, against discrimination of women in the workplace. Why, then, do feminists claim that these theories are not substantively equal or fair to women? To answer this, it is necessary to consider ethics from a female point of view—that of human relationships. Studies prove that even when wives and husbands both work full-time, the majority of household chores and childcare responsibilities are still borne by women. This means that when someone needs to stay home for a repairman's visit, the delivery and installation of an appliance, or to care for a sick child or an aging parent, it is far more likely to be the woman. Arriving home at a certain time to avoid leaving school-aged children unattended and getting them to appointments is also usually the woman's responsibility. So, of course, is pregnancy and childbirth.

Workplace rules which do not recognize the different roles men and women play outside of their role as employee may appear fair and equal, but they are not substantively fair. A policy of so many days of sick leave, or so many days of personal leave, that is the same for male and female employees may appear fair, because they apply equally to everyone. But in effect, women will likely need to take unpaid leave to fulfill their greater family responsibilities. So such a rule would effectively be unfair to women. Hiring practices that rely on word-of-mouth or networking, although not deliberately discriminatory against women, are also likely to be substantively unequal because there are fewer women in important positions to network with. Promotions, which are often based less on ability than dedication (as measured in overtime, etc.) are also unfair to women because they are the ones usually responsible for caring for their family after work hours and cannot put in the same overtime. Furthermore, time missed while on maternity leaves also counts against women when promotions are considered, or when their movement up the pay grid is counted in months of work accrued.

Feminist ethics proposes an ethics of care instead of the male-oriented theories that emphasize an unattainable level of objectivity and rationality and centre on the individual. There are variations of feminist ethics, but they all promote the idea that a good person will act in a caring manner that strengthens relationships. One proponent of feminist ethics is Nell Noddings, who in her book, *Caring*, proposed a framework of ethical decision-making which centres on two principles. The first is the principle of natural caring—our natural tendency to be concerned about those we know and are closest to. The second principle is one she calls a "vision of the best self." It is similar to virtue ethics except that it emphasizes qualities necessary to sustain relationships, such as sensitivity, empathy, understanding and reliability.

Applying Feminist Ethics to Modern Life

Applying an ethic of care involves considering people in terms of their total lives, not just their work lives. This means taking into account their roles and relationships and responsibilities outside of work, as well as their roles as employer, supervisor, co-worker or employee. It means breaking down the division between public and private lives. The ethical behaviour that would result from this approach would be that employers would consider offering employees flexible hours, on-site child care and time off for family responsibilities. Professional advances such as moving up the pay grid, achieving tenure in the academic field or partnership in law or business must make allowances for maternity leaves so women are not penalized in these areas. When considering specific issues, it is important to ask what the caring approach would be. For example, is refusing to allow gay marriages a caring approach toward others? Does it promote and strengthen relationships? If not, then it is not ethical according to the ethics of care.

An ethic of care is particularly applicable to the field of health and healing. In this field, clients are vulnerable and particularly in need of caring qualities in those who deal with them, from the office staff to practitioners in all areas of health care. In considering ethical issues around health care from this perspective, the two main questions are, What does my commitment to caring for this patient require me to do? What kind of a person must I become (what qualities or virtues should I develop) in order to show my caring? Ethics of care are also applicable to child care, for the same reasons.

Can you think of a statement made by someone you know based on feminist ethics?

_____

_____

Do you agree with his/her comment? Why or why not?

_____

_____

Proponents' View

Feminist ethics brings the female perspective into view in the ethical debate. It acknowledges that we are emotional, subjective beings and uses these attributes to support ethical decision-making instead of trying to suppress and deny these aspects of human nature. It also acknowledges the multifaceted nature of our lives, and encourages people to consider their various roles and relationships and the responsibilities that come with them when making ethical decisions.

Critics' View

Critics of feminist ethics claim that ethics of care theories do not offer a formal way of arriving at or assessing ethical behaviours or rules. They claim the theory is particularly unhelpful when deciding how to act ethically in situations where there are conflicting responsibilities of caring. For example, how should we divide our time between the needs of an elderly parent and a child? What if a person's own needs are in conflict with those of someone she cares about? What should a student do if a good friend needs a shoulder to cry on the night before the student has a major exam? General directions such as "be caring" and "act in ways that will support and strengthen relationships" do not give clear direction in many types of situation, and seem to imply that ethical people are never permitted to look after their own interests. This is similar to the criticism of virtue ethics, which directs people to "be virtuous."

Another criticism of feminist ethics is that, in criticizing the emphasis other theories place on objectivity, it seems to be implying that ethics is an entirely subjective study. This would mean that there are no objective moral truths. This sounds similar to ethical relativism. If ethical behaviour is subjective and based on relationships, then any behaviour that favours friends and relatives is morally acceptable. This could result in workplace nepotism, among other things.

A final criticism is that feminist ethics has the same problem of perspective as the other theories, only in reverse. The ethics of caring is more reflective of a female perspective, and therefore no more gender-neutral than those theories which may be more geared to the male perspective.

In summary, consider the three questions used to analyze each theory.

1. What is the theory's basis or source of authority?

_____

_____

2. Does it convince us? Is the basis arrived at through sound reasoning?

_____

_____

3. Do the ethics proposed follow logically from that basis?

_____

_____

Ethical Relativism Versus Absolutism

Relativism and absolutism are terms in ethics which indicate the nature of moral truths. If moral truths are considered absolute, then they are objective and external to, or separate from, the opinions and beliefs of the people involved, and not affected by the details of the situation. What is right is always right, and what is wrong is always wrong, for everyone, in all situations, in all cultures and all times. If moral truths are relative, however, then right and wrong are relative, which is to say their moral value depends upon either the details of the situation or who is involved, or the culture or time period. In other words, if moral truths such as "it is wrong to commit murder" or "it is right to be honest," are absolute, then it is always wrong to commit murder, no matter what the situation, and it is wrong for everyone, everywhere. If moral truths are relative, then committing murder or telling lies must be assessed subjectively by each individual for each situation (individual relativism), or determined by each culture, era or community (cultural relativism). Whether an action is good or bad depends upon the details of the situation and the personal, internal beliefs of the person deciding, or on the culture in which the action takes place. If moral truths are subjective and relative, then they can be morally right for some people and wrong for others, depending on the individual's thoughts and feelings. Or they can be right in some situations and wrong in others, depending on the situation. Or they can be right in some cultures and wrong in others.

The main types of relativism are cultural relativism and individual relativism. Cultural relativism comes out of the observation that different societies have different moral values. In some cultures, gender discrimination is not acceptable, while in others it is encouraged; some cultures condemn sex between unmarried young people, while others accept it. The relativist stand on this matter is that it is not possible for one culture to objectively judge another culture's moral values, because it is impossible to overcome the bias of our own cultural values. The saying, "When in Rome, do as the Romans do," is an expression of cultural relativism. However, in cultural relativism, the moral truths that are held by a society are considered absolute within that culture. If premarital sex is considered morally wrong by a society, then within that society it is always wrong, for everyone in that society, no matter what the situation. According to cultural relativism, then, moral truths are relative to each culture or society, but are absolute (binding for everyone) within the society. It would be wrong, for example, to visit another country and disobey its laws, which are the expression of that society's moral values, because they are not the same as the laws in our own country. Since culture changes over time, the same could be said about right and wrong in a previous era. Returning to the example of residential schools for Native children, referred to in Chapter 1, one of the criticisms we now make is that Native children were punished for using their own languages instead of speaking English. At the time it was thought to be in their best interests to make them forget their language and culture. An ethical absolutist would say that that was as wrong at the time it was done as it would be today. A cultural relativist might say that it was right for the culture of that era but would be wrong today.

What do you think?

_____

_____

How does this relate to immigrants coming into Canada and retaining their language, dress and culture here?

_____

_____

What are some behaviours that are morally acceptable in Canada but not morally acceptable in another culture?

_____

_____

What are some behaviours that are not morally acceptable in Canada but are acceptable in another culture?

_____

_____

Individual relativism is an extension of the observation that different individuals, even within the same country, have different beliefs, values and morals. To some extent this is a natural outcome of living in a multicultural country like Canada. In order to get along, we must respect the different beliefs and values that our fellow Canadians hold. Moral relativists claim that no one single standard of moral truth is right, because no one has a monopoly on virtue. Holding a position of cultural and/or individual relativism, therefore, sounds like simply being tolerant and open-minded. "Live and let live" is the relativist's ethic.

There are a number of arguments against relativism, however. The first objection critics of relativism make is that if moral truths are relative, then any behaviour is acceptable as long as an individual or a culture believes it is moral. If we accept cultural relativism, do we agree that suicide bombings, airplane hijackings and other terrorist activities are morally good for those involved in them because their culture—the Taliban culture, for example—believes them to be moral? If we accept individual relativism, are we saying that for Robert Picton, the British Columbia pig farmer charged with murdering forty-nine young women, killing young women is morally right? Does the fact that Picton believed it was right make it right for him? What about the 1989 murder of fourteen female students at the University of Montreal's engineering school by Marc Lepine because he felt that feminists were taking jobs away from men? Lepine believed he was morally justified. Does that make his actions morally right for him? Moral relativism would have us say that any group or individual's beliefs—no matter how racist, sexist or violent they may be—are morally acceptable just because they think so.

Another criticism of relativism is that it is not practical. Ethics often deals with issues that affect us all, and we need to come to an agreement about the right thing to do. For example, take the problem of alcohol or drug abuse. It doesn't affect only the alcoholic or addict. That person's family is affected. In the case of a pregnant woman there is serious harm done to her unborn children. If the individual drives or goes to work under the influence many other people may be put at risk. Pollution is another example. Factories that pollute the environment hurt us all; it can't be left up to the moral beliefs of the owner whether polluting is ethical or not. Furthermore, as citizens of Canada, we must all decide whether to spend our tax dollars on environmental projects and reducing greenhouse emissions. Cultural relativism can't solve this problem—what we do in Canada affects people in other countries and cultures, and vice versa.

While a person may believe moral truths are absolute, it is still possible to have some relativist leanings. Moral issues are very complex. Often, rather than a single right answer, there is moral truth on many sides of the issue. A person who believes that moral truths are the same for everyone might not believe that these truths are absolute in every situation. Indeed, this is the position that most of us take. We believe that it is morally wrong to kill another human being and that it is wrong for everyone, in every culture. But in some situations, such as self-defense or wartime, we consider it morally acceptable to kill. Or we may believe that some moral truths are absolute, while other truths that are less important are relative to the situation. A student may decide that cheating on a test is never acceptable. On the other hand, although he feels morally responsible for doing his share in a group project, there may be some situations, such as a family crisis, which make it morally permissible for him not to do his group work.

Most of the decisions professionals face in their day-to-day work can be made by referring to the written standards of practice for their profession or the code of conduct in their workplace. These could be considered absolute rules because they must be followed, just as provincial and federal laws governing our personal and professional activities must be followed. They apply to everyone under their jurisdiction, all of the time. The following chart shows the different positions that ethical absolutists and ethical relativists may take.

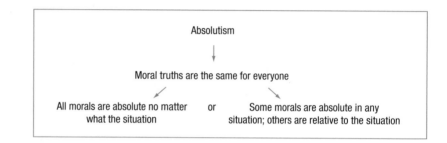

Figure 4.1 Absolutism

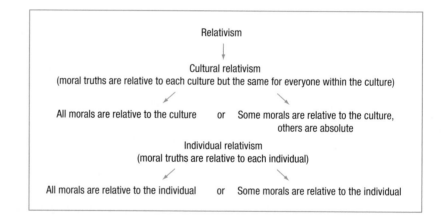

Figure 4.2 Relativism

Can you think of a statement made by someone you know based on individual relativism?

_____

_____

Do you agree with his/her comment? Why or why not?

_____

_____

Can you think of a statement made by someone you know based on cultural relativism?

_____

_____

Do you agree with his/her comment? Why or why not?

_____

_____

Can you think of a statement made by someone you know based on absolutism?

_____

_____

Do you agree with his/her comment? Why or why not?

_____

_____

EXERCISE 4.2

Identifying Relativism and Absolutism

Consider the different theories we have discussed so far. Which theories would you classify as being relativist and which as being absolutist?

Ethical Theory	Relativist or absolutist? Explain why you think so.
Divine command theory	
Socrates and Plato's healthy soul theory	
Virtue ethics	
Deontology/Kantian ethics	
Teleology/utilitarianism	
Enlightened self-interest	
Contractarianism	
Feminist ethics	

Normative and Descriptive Ethics

It is important to recognize that the major ethical theories will fall into one of two categories: normative ethics and descriptive ethics. Normative ethics means setting a norm, or standard, for ethical behaviour, and measuring people's behaviour against that standard. An ethical person meets or exceeds that standard expectation; an unethical person's behaviour falls below the ethical standard. In general terms, a normative ethical theory sets standards or expectations for behaviour. In other words, normative ethics is concerned with what our behaviour ought to be, and then justifies why it ought to be so. Descriptive ethics, on the other hand, describes people's actual behaviour and then explains why they behave in this way.

Table 4.3

Descriptive Ethics	Normative Ethics
Observes and describes people's actual behaviour	Sets a standard for how people ought to behave
Explains why people behave this way	Justifies why people ought to behave this way
The behaviour we exhibit defines us	Our conscious choices of action define us

EXERCISE 4.3

Recognizing Normative Ethics and Descriptive Ethics

Consider each of the ethical theories discussed so far. Which are normative, and which are descriptive? Fill in the following chart with your answers.

Ethical Theory	Normative or descriptive? Explain why you think so.
Divine command theory	
Socrates and Plato's healthy soul theory	
Virtue ethics	
Deontology/Kantian ethics	
Teleology/utilitarianism	
Enlightened self-interest	
Contractarianism	
Feminist ethics	
Relativism	
Absolutism	

APPLYING ETHICAL REASONING TO ETHICAL ISSUES

The theories we examined in Chapters 2, 3 and 4 are very complex. Each has its own strengths and weaknesses. All of them, if followed correctly, increase our ability to make consciously ethical decisions. Some people decide that one of these theories is better than the others, despite its flaws, and they have very good reasons for thinking so, as each theory also has strengths that others may lack. However, perhaps the best way to use these theories is to use them in combination. An individual might consider the kind of character she wants to develop in herself, the kind of person she wants to be (virtue ethics). That person might also, when faced with a difficult ethical choice, take into consideration the principles which are in question or in conflict, and how she would feel if everyone acted this way (Kantian ethics). Finally, she might also consider the short- and long-term consequences to the happiness and well-being of everyone involved, and to society as a whole, of the course of action she is contemplating (utilitarianism). Only after carefully considering all of these things, might she decide to act.

A business or organization might use a similar approach of incorporating many ethical considerations into its decision-making process. It might incorporate its ethical approach in a statement such as one of the following three:

- We should fulfill our purpose (virtue ethics—ethics of purpose) unless it treats people only as means (Kantian ethics) or unless the outcome is more harm than good (utilitarianism).
- We should act on principle (Kantian ethics) unless it causes more harm than good (utilitarianism) or unless it contradicts our purpose (ethics of virtue).
- We should do what causes the most good and least harm for all concerned (utilitarianism) unless it means treating some persons only as means and committing acts which cannot be universalized (Kantian ethics) or unless it prevents us from fulfilling our purpose (virtue ethics).

The same three theories are involved in each of the above statements, but are considered in a different order. In other words, these statements don't just combine the strengths of different theories; they also set priorities. They state which theory should be considered first and foremost, with the others having a sort of "veto power" in a descending order.

Write a statement of how to approach ethical issues that incorporate enlightened self-interest (or contractarianism) with utilitarianism and one other theory of your choice. Take time to consider which theory you want to place first, second and third.

_____

_____

_____

Now write another statement, this time a personal statement of ethical consideration or approach, which incorporates two or three of the theories that you consider most important, and prioritizes them.

_____

_____

_____

The following exercises will give students the opportunity to compare the different theories and to apply them to current social issues.

EXERCISE 4.4

Recognizing the Theoretical Basis of Ethical Arguments

Find three or more articles which present arguments for or against a current issue. The editorial section of a newspaper is a good place to find short opinion pieces.

For each article:

■ Determine the theoretical approach (or approaches) taken by the writer in making his/her arguments (e.g., deontological, teleological, virtue ethics, absolutist, relativist, divine command, etc.).

■ Write a five-to-ten sentence paragraph which identifies the approach and states why you think that is the approach taken. Use quotes to prove your point. For example, you might say, "This author uses a deontological approach because she bases her arguments on principles. An example of this in her article is when she says, 'People should be treated the same way regardless of their age or income level.' The principle here is fairness or equality. She is also taking an absolutist approach because she admits no exceptions and applies the principle universally. This is shown when she says, 'This is as true for Argentina as it is for North America, or anywhere else in the world.' She also later says, 'It is as true today as it was a hundred years ago,' which also shows that she is an absolutist."

After you have analyzed the approaches and arguments in each article, write a third short paragraph stating which article you find more convincing, and why. You might consider things such as the credentials of the author, the use of facts and statistics, sources of information (Are they given and are they good sources?), whether the approach is balanced or one-sided, or whether the arguments are reasonable or emotional.

Finally, write a short paragraph which examines your own opinion. Do you agree with the absolutist writer because you are an absolutist? Does the argument for consequences appeal to you because you believe that consequences are more important than principles or intentions?

"Believe those who are seeking the truth; doubt those who find it."

—ANDRÉ GIDE (1869–1951)

Answers

ANSWERS TO THE THREE QUESTIONS ASKED OF EACH THEORY.

1. *What is the theory's basis or source of authority?*
2. *Does it convince us? Is the basis arrived at through sound reasoning?*
3. *Do the ethics proposed follow logically from that basis?*

HOBBES — ENLIGHTENED SELF-INTEREST

1. The theory is based on Hobbes' observation about the natural state of humankind.
2. If we agree with the observation that people are motivated solely by the desire to promote their own self-interests, but that they must limit their freedom of action in order to gain peace and security from others, then the reasoning is convincing.
3. The limitations on personal freedom which Hobbes proposes are logical because they will allow people to live in peace and not fear violence or harm from one another, assuming that everyone honours the social contract. They also flow logically from the observation that people are motivated by self-interest because they only limit acting in our own self-interest to the degree that is necessary to live together peacefully.

JOHN RAWLS — CONTRACTARIANISM

1. Contractarianism is based on a theoretical social contract that everyone would agree to. This contract is created from an imagined position of ignorance of all the factors that create bias in decision-making.
2. The rules created from behind the veil of ignorance would be fair and equal for everyone if the rule-makers were rational and if rationality were clearly defined as low risk-taking. Low risk-takers would consider the interests of all groups equally, not just the interests of the largest, middle-range group, in which they would be most likely to end up.
3. No specific ethics are proposed, although "primary goods" are identified, which is logically in keeping with the concept of a social contract to which everyone would agree. However, a full list of these primary goods is never given.

FEMINIST ETHICS

1. Feminist ethics' source of authority is studies of the moral development of young girls. It is based on a branch of human psychology; in particular, female psychology.
2. The basis is scientifically accepted as coming from accurate studies of moral development in females. It was arrived at through experiment and observation rather than reasoning.
3. The ethics proposed, such as caring and strengthening relationships, although they are somewhat vague and general, do logically come from the observed development of moral awareness in young women. The fact that North American females develop their sense of morals this way does not prove that ethics of caring is either valid or not valid as a theory of ethics.

(Continued)

(Continued)

Table 4.1 How would a rule not to increase airport security affect the following groups?

Affected group	Liberty/ autonomy	Health and safety	Opportunity
Airport/airline operators	No effect	Potentially very negatively	Very positively
Airport food vendors	No effect	Potentially some-what negatively	Very positively
General passengers	No effect	Potentially very negatively	No effect
Middle Eastern passengers	No effect	Potentially very negatively	No effect
Pilots and airline attendants	No effect	Very negatively	No effect
Military/national security personnel	Very negatively	Potentially very negatively	No effect

Table 4.2 How would a rule to increase airport security affect the following groups?

Affected group	Liberty/ autonomy	Health and safety	Opportunity
Airport/airline operators	Very negatively	No effect	Very negatively
Airport food vendors	Very negatively	Potentially some-what positively	Very negatively
General passengers	Very negatively	Potentially very positively	No effect
Middle Eastern passengers	Very negatively	Potentially very positively	No effect
Pilots and airline attendants	Somewhat negatively	Potentially very positively	Somewhat negatively
Military/national security personnel	Very positively	Potentially very positively	Potentially very positively

EXERCISE 4.2

Ethical Theory	Relativist or Absolutist
Divine command theory	Absolutist
Socrates and Plato	Absolutist
Virtue Ethics	Relativist
Deontology/Kantian ethics	Absolutist

Teleology/utilitarianism	Absolutist
Enlightened self-interest	Relativist
Contractarianism	Relativist
Feminist Ethics	Relativist

EXERCISE 4.3

Ethical Theory	Normative or Descriptive
Divine command theory	Normative
Socrates and Plato	Normative
Virtue ethics	Normative
Deontology/Kantian ethics	Normative
Teleology/utilitarianism	Normative
Enlightened self-interest	Descriptive
Contractarianism	Descriptive
Feminist ethics	Descriptive
Relativism	Descriptive
Absolutism	Normative

SELECTED READINGS

Thomas Hobbes (1588–1679)

Thomas Hobbes lived in England during a time of great social upheaval. He lived through a civil war and the execution of Charles I, and on several occasions had to flee England for his life. As a child he was sent to live with a rich uncle when his father, a vicar, disgraced the family. He was a contemporary of Descartes, Galileo and Bacon, and his philosophy was influenced by their ideas. As a result of the tumult and uncertainty in his own life, his political and ethical philosophy focused on the darker side of human nature.

Hobbes wrote many books, but he is most famous for his work, *Leviathan, or the Matter, Form and Power of a Commonwealth, Ecclesiastical and Civil.* Hobbes was primarily interested in political philosophy, and believed the best rule was not a democracy but a sovereign with absolute power over the people. Although *Leviathan* mainly espouses Hobbes' political philosophy, it also deals with other philosophical studies such as religion and ethics.

The following excerpts introduce Hobbes' ethical theory of the state of nature and social contracts.

Excerpts from *Leviathan*—Chapter 6, "Of the Interior Beginnings of Voluntary Motions"

But whatsoever is the object of any man's appetite or desire, that is it which he for his part calls "good"; and the object of his hate and aversion, "evil"; and of his contempt "vile" and "inconsiderable." For these words of good, evil, and contemptible, are ever used with relation to the person that uses them, there being nothing simply and absolutely so; nor any common rule of good and evil, to be taken from the nature of the objects themselves; but from the person of the man, where there is no commonwealth, or, in a commonwealth, from the person that represents it; or from an arbitrator or judge, whom men disagreeing shall by consent set up, and make his sentence the rule thereof.

Excerpts from *Leviathan*—Chapter 11, "Of the Difference of Manners"

A restless desire of power in all men. So that in the first place, I put for a general inclination of all mankind, a perpetual and restless desire of power after power that ceases only in death. The cause of this is not always that a man hopes for a more intensive delight than he has already attained, or that he cannot be content with moderate power. Rather, it is because a man cannot assure the power and means to live well, which he might have at present, without the acquisition of more. That is why kings, whose power is the greatest, turn their endeavors to assuring it at home by laws and abroad by wars. When that is done, a new desire arises. In some it is the fame from new conquest. In others it is the desire of ease and sensual pleasure, and in others, it is a desire for admiration or being flattered for excellence in some art or other ability of the mind.

Love of contention from competition. Competition for riches, honor, command and other power inclines people to contention, enmity and war, because the way that one competitor has of attaining his desire is to kill, subdue, supplant or repel the other. In particular, competition for praise inclines people to a reverence for antiquity. Men contend with the living and not with the dead in order to obscure the glory of others and thus will be ascribed more praise than is their due.

Civil obedience from love of ease. From fear of death or wounds. Desire of ease and sensual delight disposes men to obey a common power. Due to these desires, a man abandons the protection that he might hope for from his own industry and labor. Fear of death and wounds disposes men also to obey a common power, and for the same reason. But on the contrary, needy and hardy men and those ambitious of military command who are not contented with their present condition are inclined to stir up the cause of war and to stir up trouble and sedition. There is no military honor but from war, nor do they have any such hope of mending an ill game, but by causing a new shuffle.

And from love of the arts. The desire for knowledge and the arts of peace inclines men to obey a common power. These desires contain a desire for leisure, and consequently, the protection from some other power than their own.

FOCUS QUESTIONS

1. According to Hobbes, what is good and evil?
2. What is man's natural inclination, and why?

Excerpts from *Leviathan*—Chapter 13, "Of the Natural Condition of Mankind"

Nature hath made men so equal in the faculties of the body and mind, as that, though there be found one man sometimes manifestly stronger in body or of quicker mind than another, yet when all is reckoned together the difference between man and man is not so considerable as that one man can thereupon claim to himself any benefit to which another may not pretend as well as he.

...From this equality of ability arises equality of hope in the attaining of our ends. And therefore, if any two men desire the same thing which nevertheless they cannot both enjoy, they become enemies—and, in the way to their end, which is principally their own conservation and sometimes their delectation only, endeavor to destroy or subdue one another. And from hence it comes to pass that, where an invader hath no more to fear than another man's single power, if one plant, sow, build, or possess, a convenient seat others may probably be expected to come prepared with forces united to dispossess and deprive him not only of the fruit of his labor but also of his life or liberty. And the invader again is in the like danger of another.

And from the diffidence of one another there is no way for any man to secure himself so reasonable as anticipation, that is, by force or wiles to master the persons of all men he can so long till he see no other power great enough to endanger him; and this is no more than his own conservation requires and is generally allowed. Also, because there be some that, taking pleasure in contemplating their own power in the acts of conquest, which they pursue farther than their security requires, if others, that otherwise would be glad to be at ease within the modest bounds, should not by invasion increase their power, they would not be able for a long time, by standing only on their defence, to subsist. And by consequence, such augmentation of dominion over men being necessary to a man's conservation, it ought to be allowed him.

Again, men have no pleasure, but on the contrary a great deal of grief, in keeping company where there is no power able to overawe them all. For every man looks that his companion should value him at the same rate he sets upon himself, and, upon all signs of contempt or undervaluing, naturally endeavors as far as he dares (which amongst them that have no common power to keep them in quiet, is far enough to make them destroy each other) to extort a greater value from his condemners by damage, and from others by the example.

So that in the nature of man we find three principal causes of quarrel. First, competition; secondly, diffidence; thirdly, glory.

The first makes man invade for gain; the second, for safety; and the third, for reputation. The first use violence, to make themselves masters of other men's persons, wives, children, and cattle; the second, to defend them; the third, for trifles, as a word, a smile, a different opinion, and any other sign of undervalue, either direct in their persons or by reflection in their kindred, their friends, their nation, their profession, or their name.

Hereby it is manifest that, during the time men live without a common power to keep them all in awe, they are in that condition which is called war, and such a war as is of every man against every man. For "war" consists not in battle only or the act of fighting, but in a tract of time wherein the will to contend by battle is sufficiently known, and therefore the notion of "time" is to be considered in the nature of war, as it is in the nature of weather. For as the nature of foul weather lies not in a shower or two of rain but in an inclination thereto of many days together, so the nature of war consists not in actual fighting but in the known disposition thereto during all the time there is no assurance to the contrary. All other time is "peace."

Whatsoever therefore is consequent to a time of war where every man is enemy to every man, the same is consequent to the time wherein men live without other security than what their own strength and their own invention shall furnish them withal. In such condition there is no place for industry, because the fruit thereof is uncertain, and consequently no culture of the earth, no navigation nor use of the commodities that may be imported by sea, no commodious building, no instruments of moving and removing such things as require much force, no knowledge of the face of the earth; no account of time, no arts, no letters, no society, and, which is worst of all, continual fear and danger of violent death, and the life of man solitary, poor, nasty, brutish, and short.

...The desires and other passions of man are in themselves no sin. No more are the actions that proceed from those passions, till they know a law that forbids them; which, till laws be made, they cannot know, nor can any law be made till they have agreed upon the person that shall make it.

To this war of every man against every man this also is consequent, that nothing can be unjust. The notions of right and wrong, justice and injustice, have there no place. Where there is no common power, there is no law; where no law, no injustice. Force and fraud are in war the two cardinal virtues. Justice and injustice are none of the faculties neither of the body nor mind. If they were, they might be in a man that were alone in the world, as well as his senses and passions. They are qualities that relate to men in society, not in solitude. It is consequent also to the same condition that there be no propriety, no dominion, no "mine" and "thine" distinct, but only that to be every man's that he can get, and for so long as he can keep it. And thus much for the ill condition which may by mere nature is actually placed in, though with a possibility to come out of it, consisting partly in the passions, partly in his reason.

The passions that incline men to peace are fear of death, desire of such things as are necessary to commodious living, and a hope by their industry to obtain them. And reason suggests convenient articles of peace, upon which men may be drawn to agreement. These articles are they which otherwise are called the Laws of Nature, whereof I shall speak more particularly in the two following chapters.

Excerpts from *Leviathan*—Chapter 14, "Of the First and Second Natural Laws, and of Contracts"

"The right of Nature," which writers commonly call *jus naturale*, is the liberty each man hath to use his own power as he will himself for the preservation of his own nature, that is to say, of his own life; and consequently of doing anything which in his own judgment and reason he shall conceive to be the aptest means thereunto.

By "liberty" is understood, according to the proper signification of the word, the absence of external impediments, which impediments may oft take away part of a man's power to do what he would, but cannot hinder him from using the power left him according as his judgment and reason shall dictate to him.

A "law of Nature," *lex naturalis*, is a precept or general rule found out by reason by which a man is forbidden to do that which is destructive of his life or takes away the means of preserving the same, and to omit that by which he thinks it may be best preserved. For, though they that speak of this subject use to confound *jus* and *lex*, "right" and "law," yet they ought to be distinguished; because "right" consists in liberty to do or to forbear, whereas "law" determines and binds to one of them; so that law and right differ as much as obligation and liberty; which in one and the same matter are inconsistent.

And because the condition of man, as hath been declared in the precedent chapter, is a condition of war of every one against every one, in which case every one is governed by his own reason, and there is nothing he can make use of that may not be a help to him in preserving his life against his enemies, it follows that in such a condition every man has a right to everything, even to one another's body. And therefore, as long this natural right of every man to everything endures, there can be no security to any man, how strong or wise soever he be, of living out the time which Nature ordinarily allows men to live. And consequently it is a precept or general rule of reason "that every man ought to endeavor peace as far as he has hope of obtaining it, and, when he cannot obtain it, that he may seek and use all helps and advantages of war." The first branch of which rule contains the first and fundamental law of Nature, which is, "to seek peace, and follow it." The second, the sum of the right of Nature, which is, "by all means we can, to defend ourselves."

From this fundamental law of Nature, by which men are commanded to endeavor peace, is derived this second law, "that a man be willing, when others are so too, as far-forth as for peace and defence of himself he shall think it necessary, to lay down this right to all things, and be contented with so much liberty against other men as he would allow other men against himself." For as long as every man holds this right of doing anything he likes, so long are all men in the condition of war. But if other men will not lay down their right as well as he, then there is no reason for any one to divest himself of his: for that were to expose himself to prey, which no man is bound to, rather than to dispose himself to peace. This is that law of the Gospel: "whatsoever you require that others should do to you, that do ye to them." And that law of all men, *quod tibi fieri non vis, alteri ne feceris*.

To "lay down" a man's "right" to anything is to "divest" himself of the "liberty," of hindering another of the benefit of his own right to the same. For he that renounces or passes away his right gives not to any other man a right which he had not before, because there is nothing to which every man had not right by Nature; but only stands out of his way that he may enjoy his own original right without hindrance from him, not without hindrance from another. So that the effect which redounds to one man, by another man's defect of right, is but so much diminution of impediments to the use of his own right original.

Right is laid aside either by simply renouncing it, or by transferring it to another. By "simply renouncing" when he cares not to whom the benefit thereof redounds. By "transferring," when he intends the benefit thereof to some certain person or persons. And, when a man hath in either manner abandoned or granted away his right, then is he said to be "obliged" or "bound" not to hinder those to whom such right is granted or abandoned from the benefit of it; and that he "ought," and it is his "duty," not to make void that voluntary act of his own; and that such hindrance is "injustice" and "injury" as being *sine jure*, the right being before renounced or transferred. So that "injury" or "injustice," in the controversies of the world, is somewhat like to that which in the disputations of scholars is called "absurdity." For, as it is there called an absurdity to contradict what one maintained in the beginning, so in the world it is called injustice and injury voluntarily to undo that from the beginning he had voluntarily done. The way by which a man either simply renounces or transfers his right is a declaration or signification, by some voluntary and sufficient sign or signs, that he doth so renounce or transfer, or hath so renounced or transferred, the same, to him that accepts it. And these signs are either words only or actions only, or, as it happens most often, both words and actions. And the same are the "bonds" by which men are bound and obliged: bonds that have their strength not from their own nature, for nothing is more easily broken than a man's word, but from fear of some evil consequence upon the rupture.

Whensoever a man transfers his right or renounces it, it is either in consideration of some right reciprocally transferred to himself, or for some other good he hopes for thereby. For it is a voluntary act: and of the voluntary acts of every man the object is some good "to himself." And therefore there be some rights which no man can be understood by any words or other signs to have abandoned or transferred. As first a man cannot lay down the right of resisting them that assault him by force to take away his life, because he cannot be understood to aim thereby at any good to himself. The same may be said of wounds, and chains, and imprisonment, both because there is no benefit consequent to such patience, as there is to the patience of suffering another to be wounded or imprisoned, as also because a man cannot tell when he sees men proceed against him by violence whether they intend his death or not. And lastly the motive and end for which this renouncing and transferring of right is introduced is nothing else but the security of a man's person in his life and in the means of so preserving life as not to be weary of it. And therefore if a man by words or other signs seem to despoil himself of the end for which those signs were intended, he is not to be understood as if he meant it or that it was his will, but that he was ignorant of how such words and actions were to be interpreted. The mutual transferring of right is that which men call "contract."

FOCUS QUESTIONS

1. What are the three principal causes of conflict? Explain each one briefly.
2. What does Hobbes describe as the natural condition of man (without government)?
3. What is the difference between "the right of Nature" and "the law of Nature"?
4. What does the law of Nature command man to do?
5. What right cannot be abandoned or transferred?

John Rawls

John Rawls is Emeritus Professor of Philosophy at Harvard University. The following selections come from his work, *A Theory of Justice: Revised Edition*, published in 1999.

Excerpts from *A Theory of Justice: Revised Edition*—Chapter 3, "The Main Idea of the Theory of Justice"

...Rather, the guiding idea is that the principles of justice for the basic structure of society are the object of the original agreement. They are the principles that free and rational persons concerned to further their own interests would accept in an initial position of equality as defining the fundamental terms of their association. These principles are to regulate all further agreements; they specify the kinds of social cooperation that can be entered into and the forms of government that can be established. This way of regarding the principles of justice I shall call justice as fairness.

Thus we are to imagine that those who engage in social cooperation choose together, in one joint act, the principles which are to assign basic rights and duties and to determine the division of social benefits. Men are to decide in advance how they are to regulate their claims against one another and what is to be the foundation charter of their society. Just as each person must decide by rational reflection what constitutes his good, that is, the system of ends which it is rational for him to pursue, so a group of persons must decide once and for all what is to count among them as just and unjust. The choice which rational men would make in this hypothetical situation of equal liberty, assuming for the present that this choice problem has a solution, determines the principles of justice.

In justice as fairness the original position of equality corresponds to the state of nature in the traditional theory of the social contract. This original position is not, of course, thought of as an actual historical state of affairs, much less as a primitive condition of culture. It is understood as a purely hypothetical situation characterized so as to lead to a certain conception of justice. Among the essential features of this situation is that no one knows his place in society, his class position or social status, nor does any one know his fortune in the distribution of natural assets and abilities, his intelligence, strength, and the like. I shall even assume that the parties do not know their conceptions of the good or their special psychological propensities. The principles of justice are chosen behind a veil of ignorance. This ensures that no one is advantaged or disadvantaged in the choice of principles by the outcome of natural chance or the contingency of social circumstances. Since all are similarly situated and no one is able to design principles to favor his particular condition, the principles of justice are the result of a fair agreement or bargain. For given the circumstances of the original position, the symmetry of everyone's relations to each other, this initial situation is fair between individuals as moral persons, that is, as rational beings with their own ends and capable, I shall assume, of a sense of justice. The original position is, one might say, the appropriate initial status quo, and thus the fundamental agreements reached in it are fair. This explains the propriety of the name "justice as fairness"; it conveys the idea that the principles of justice are agreed to in an initial situation that is fair. The name does not mean that the concepts of justice and fairness are the same...

One feature of justice as fairness is to think of the parties in the initial situation as rational and mutually disinterested. This does not mean that the parties are egoists, that is, individuals with only certain kinds of interests, say in wealth, prestige, and domination. But they are conceived as not taking an interest in one another's interests. They are to presume that even their spiritual aims may be opposed, in the way that the aims of those of different religions may be opposed.

I shall maintain instead that the persons in the initial situation would choose two rather different principles: the first requires equality in the assignment of basic rights and duties, while the second holds that social and economic inequalities, for example inequalities of wealth and authority, are just only if they result in compensating benefits for everyone, and in particular for the least advantaged members of society. These principles rule out justifying institutions on the grounds that the hardships of some are offset by a greater good in the aggregate. It may be expedient but it is not just that some should have less in order that others may prosper. But there is no injustice in the greater benefits earned by a few provided that the situation of persons not so fortunate is thereby improved. The intuitive idea is that since everyone's well-being depends upon a scheme of cooperation without which no one could have a satisfactory life, the division of advantages should be such as to draw forth the willing cooperation of everyone taking part in it, including those less well situated. Yet this can be expected only if reasonable terms are proposed. The two principles mentioned seem to be a fair agreement on the basis of which those better endowed, or more fortunate in their social position, neither of which we can be said to deserve, could expect the willing cooperation of others when some workable scheme is a necessary condition of the welfare of all. Once we decide to look for a conception of justice that nullifies the accidents of natural endowment and the contingencies of social circumstance as counters in quest for political and economic advantage, we are led to these principles. They express the result of leaving aside those aspects of the social world that seem arbitrary from a moral point of view.

FOCUS QUESTIONS

1. What principles is Rawls concerned with discovering in his theory?
2. What is the original position of equality from which he believes we must begin?
3. What are the two principles people in the original position would choose, and why?

Excerpts from *A Theory of Justice: Revised Edition*—Chapter 4, "The Original Position and Justification"

We shall want to say that certain principles of justice are justified because they would be agreed to in an initial situation of equality. I have emphasized that this original position is purely hypothetical. It is natural to ask why, if this agreement is never actually entered into, we should take any interest in these principles, moral or otherwise. The answer is that the conditions embodied in the description of the original position are ones that we do in fact accept. Or if we do not, then perhaps we can be persuaded to do so by philosophical reflection. Each aspect of the contractual situation can be given supporting grounds. Thus what we shall do is collect together into one conception a number of conditions on principles that we are ready upon due consideration to recognize as reasonable. These constraints express what we are prepared to regard as limits on fair terms of social cooperation.

Excerpts from *A Theory of Justice: Revised Edition*—Chapter 5, "Classical Utilitarianism"

The first statement of the two principles reads as follows.

First: each person is to have an equal right to the most extensive scheme of equal basic liberties compatible with a similar scheme of liberties for others.

Second: social and economic inequalities are to be arranged so that they are both (a) reasonably expected to be to everyone's advantage, and (b) attached to positions and offices open to all...

FOCUS QUESTIONS

Explain Rawls' two principles of justice in your own words.

5

Principles of Discussion and Debate

CONTENTS

> *"If a man will begin with certainties, he shall end in doubts; but if he will be content to begin with doubts, he shall end in certainties."*
>
> **—FRANCIS BACON (1561–1626)**

As we learned in Chapter 1, our upbringing and past experiences have a lot to do with what we think and believe. We already have opinions about a lot of ethical issues, often without really knowing why we hold those opinions. We might believe that something is right or wrong based on the opinion of someone else whom we respect or based on a single personal experience, which may or may not be relevant to the issue. When asked why we hold that opinion, we may be tempted to justify it by explaining why we believe it. While such explanations might be interesting from a psychological point of view—as in coming to understand ourselves better—they are usually too weak in themselves to convince anyone else, and sooner or later they even fail to convince us. Or we may invent justifications which will make our belief—and ourselves—look good, but are not the real reason for our belief. These, too, will not only fail to convince others, but will also fail to convince us, over time.

Ethical arguments must begin with critical thinking and end with an opinion, not the other way around. They attempt to explain why someone *should* believe something, rather than justifying why someone *does* believe it. To do this, we must begin with questions, not answers, then examine the facts and form logical conclusions to finally arrive at a considered opinion. This is what Bacon means when he says that if we begin with certainties (an opinion) we will in the end doubt or question it; but if we begin with doubts, or questions, and work our way toward a logical conclusion, we will end with certainty—with an opinion we can hold and defend with confidence.

APPLYING LOGICAL REASONING TO ETHICAL DEBATE

The first step in a debate is to begin with a question. The key word at this stage is *clarity*. In forming the question, it is crucial to state exactly what you mean, defining your terms and perhaps giving examples to illustrate your meaning. In an ethical debate, the question is usually concerned with whether something is right or wrong, or good or bad. Be aware that right and wrong are absolute judgments; a thing is either one or the other. Good and bad, however, are relative terms; something can be judged good, better or best, without implying that the opposite is bad. It may only be less good, or second best. Something may be bad, but not be the worst choice available. In other words, while right and wrong clearly indicate a moral imperative, good and bad give more leeway for making morally acceptable choices. Other terms that need to be explained are *should, ought* and *permissible*. When we say someone should or ought to do something, we are expressing a moral, but not a legal, obligation. *Must* implies a legal as well as moral obligation. When we say someone should not or ought not to do something, we are expressing a moral prohibition. When we say that something is morally permissible, we mean that it is acceptable, but neither morally required nor morally prohibited. There is a wide range of morally permissible behaviour, from behaviour that is admirable, but not obligatory, to behaviour that is selfish but not prohibited.

If a question is not clearly stated, you will find yourself arguing over misinterpretations of the question, rather than the issue itself. We might form a question such as, is violence in entertainment justified? This question is very vague. Are we referring to boxing, sports injuries, dog fighting, violent movies or videogames? In what way is it justified—as art, as an unavoidable byproduct of other activities, as entertainment in itself? The term violence also needs to be defined. Does it refer to deliberate physical assault? Does it include viewing accidental injuries in sports such as boxing and football? Cartoon or animal violence? A better phrasing of the question might be, is showing excessive physical violence between human beings in TV shows morally justified? "Excessive violence" will have to be defined with examples, but the question is now clear enough to direct the arguments toward the intended issue.

The next step is gathering information on the issue. Information refers to empirical (objective, sensory observations) and statistical facts. This step involves research and critical thinking. The key words at this stage are *accuracy, precision* and *relevance*. Accuracy can be determined by asking questions such as, is the information true? Was it gathered correctly? Is the source reliable? Precision means making sure the information is specific and detailed. Relevance means that the information is directly related to the question.

Critical thinking and logic are tools we use to reach reliable conclusions or judgments about a question or an issue. The judgments can be descriptive or normative in nature. As discussed in Chapter 4, "descriptive" refers to factual information that can be observed or measured, and "normative" refers to norms or standards used for moral evaluations. Therefore, a descriptive judgment is a conclusion about facts, while a normative judgment is a moral evaluation based on facts and logical arguments. Ethics is concerned with ultimately making normative judgments, although descriptive judgments are a part of the process of evaluating the facts. For example, research might include a study that demonstrated people were much less likely to show concern or to help a stranger immediately after viewing a violent TV show, and more likely to respond aggressively when pushed by a passerby. We would use critical thinking skills to analyze the study in order to determine if it was from a reliable source, conducted in a scientifically valid way, scientifically accurate in demonstrating what it claimed to demonstrate, and relevant to our question. Next we would make a descriptive judgment of the facts, such as: viewing violent TV shows desensitizes people to others' distress, decreases their willingness to help others and increases their aggressiveness.

The third step is forming logical arguments. The descriptive argument just given could be used to support the response that violence is not morally justified, but one argument is not enough. The key words at this stage are *depth*, *breadth* and *relevance*. Depth refers to examining the complexities of an issue. What makes this a difficult issue to resolve? Breadth refers to the variety of perspectives that need to be considered. What are the arguments on both sides of the issue, and what arguments can be given to counter them? Relevance is important again here, because the arguments must directly relate to, or prove, one or the other side of the issue.

The types of arguments used in this step come from the ethical theories studied in Chapters 2, 3 and 4. Is there a divine command concerning this issue in the religion that is relevant to you? What virtues of character apply to the issue? What principles and rights apply to it? A list of ethical principles and basic human rights appears later in this chapter, to refer to when making ethical arguments. What consequences could occur that could be used to argue one or the other side of the issue, and what logical or empirical evidence can be used to prove that those consequences are likely to happen? How can one or the other side of the issue be shown to be in the reader's best interests? While empirical and skeptical/critical thinking was required in the previous step, logical and reflective thinking are required in this step.

PERSUASIVE ARGUMENTS

Logic is the science of correct reasoning. Logical or well-reasoned arguments are formed by first making a statement or premise that everyone will agree with. Additional premises, which may be statements of fact or value statements that rely on the first premise, are added until they lead to a logical conclusion. The conclusion is logical and sound if the premises are accurate and the conclusion follows directly from them. There are two main forms of reasoning: inductive reasoning and deductive reasoning.

Inductive reasoning is used to draw a general conclusion from specific statements. An example is: (1) Tom likes sports; (2) John likes sports; (3) Mohamed likes sports; (4) Sunan likes sports; (5) therefore boys in general like sports. In order for the conclusion to logically follow from the premises, the specific statements must provide a sufficiently large and representative sample of the general group and the conclusion should be stated as a general rather than a universal truth. This type of reasoning is used in scientific experiments. It can involve statistics rather than individuals. For example: two-thirds of the people who viewed the violent TV show did not help the stranger and responded aggressively to the passerby, as compared to one third of those who did not view the TV show; therefore viewing violence in TV shows desensitizes people to others' distress, decreases their willingness to help others and increases their aggressiveness.

Deductive reasoning moves from a general premise to a particular premise and then to a particular conclusion. A simple example is: (1) all boys like sports (general statement); (2) John is a boy (specific statement); (3) therefore, John likes sports (specific conclusion). The first and second premises may need to be proved, or may be accepted as self-evident truths by everyone involved in the argument. If the first two premises are correct, and logically lead to the conclusion, as they do in this example, then the conclusion is correct. Here is an example where the premises do not logically lead to the conclusion: (1) all boys like sports (general statement); (2) Joan likes sports (specific statement); (3) therefore, Joan is a boy (specific conclusion). Because premise 1 does not say that all people who like sports are boys, the fact that Joan likes sports does not prove that she is a boy. Deductive reasoning cannot go from specific statements to prove a general conclusion. Here is an example: (1) John is a boy (specific statement); (2) John likes sports (specific statement); (3) all boys like sports (general conclusion). Because John is a boy who likes sports does not logically prove that all boys like sports.

Deductive arguments are arguments that build a series of premises which lead to a conclusion or moral judgment. If each premise is accepted or proved true, and each one leads logically to the conclusion, then the conclusion must be true. Here is another example of a deductive argument:

- ■ Premise 1 (general): Violence and physical assault of one person by another person is bad.
- ■ Premise 2 (depends on acceptance of first premise): Anything that increases violence and physical assaults is bad.
- ■ Premise 3 (depends on acceptance of second premise, must be supported by empirical evidence): viewing violent TV shows desensitizes people to others' distress, decreases their willingness to help others and increases their aggressiveness.
- ■ Premise 4 (may need supporting empirical evidence): desensitized, aggressive people are more likely to become violent or commit assault.
- ■ Conclusion (descriptive judgment, follows logically from the previous premises): viewing violent TV shows increases violence and physical assaults.
- ■ Conclusion (normative judgment, follows logically from the previous premises): violence in TV shows is bad.

Ethical arguments are normative and persuasive, rather than descriptive. Therefore the fourth and final step is evaluating the empirical evidence and the logical arguments and coming to an evaluative conclusion. In the example above, the final bullet point evaluates (places a moral value on) the logical, descriptive conclusion, and draws a normative conclusion: violence in TV shows is bad. One argument does not prove a moral conclusion any more than one battle wins a war, however. When ethical issues are concerned, there are usually good arguments on both sides of the issue. In order to make an informed decision on any ethical issue, it is important to research, reflect on, and evaluate all of the arguments on both sides of the issue. There may be one good argument against showing violence in TV shows, but five other good arguments which justify it.

LOGICAL AND EMOTIONAL FALLACIES IN THINKING

In order to debate ethical issues effectively and convincingly—or even to accurately evaluate the alternatives in our own minds—it is necessary to understand the basics of logical argument. This can best be explained by describing where reasoning can go wrong. When an argument fails, it is usually because of either a logical or an emotional fallacy. "Fallacy" comes from the word false; therefore, a logical fallacy is an argument that is "logically false" or not logical. This usually occurs when a premise does not lead directly to the conclusion, or significant facts have been omitted, exaggerated or oversimplified. Emotional fallacies usually appear as an attempt to exploit or manipulate the other person's emotions, rather than presenting a legitimate appeal to emotion. The following list includes the most common logical and emotional fallacies:

- *Non-sequitur.* This is an argument that suggests a logical connection (such as cause and effect) that does not logically follow from the evidence. Fact A does not necessarily lead to fact B. Example: I worked hard on this paper so I deserve an "A."
- *Post-hoc fallacy.* This occurs when one event follows another and we draw the conclusion that the first event caused the second, when in fact, the two events are not related. It is similar to a non-sequitur in that both fallacies involve a false assumption of cause and effect. The difference is that in the post-hoc fallacy, the assumed relationship is based on the fact that there is a temporal sequence to the two events (one occurred after the other), whereas in the non-sequitur, there is no basis for relating the two facts. A temporal sequence, however, is not proof of cause and effect. Example: I dropped a mirror and broke it just before my test. Then I failed the test. Therefore the broken mirror brought me bad luck in the test.
- *Begging the question.* This occurs when an argument is based on an assumption that is not necessarily accurate. Statements that begin with "obviously" or "everyone knows" and then state a "fact" that has not been proved are begging the question. If the proof has been given before the statement, then it is not a logical fallacy, but a conclusion. However, an argument cannot start with some facts concluded unless both debaters agree on them. Example: It's obvious that ethics of care is more compassionate than utilitarianism.
- *Circular reasoning.* This is similar to begging the question in that it avoids proving a point. A statement that simply repeats the original point, using different words, is circular reasoning. Example: Consequences are important because they are the result of an action.
- *Red herring.* This occurs when an irrelevant fact is brought up to distract from or side-step the main issue. The fact may seem to be relevant but is actually not proof of anything. Example: Mill suffered mid-life depression, so following utilitarianism doesn't increase people's happiness.
- *Either/or.* An either/or fallacy occurs when an issue is presented as having only two choices when in fact there may be more. It can include an emotional fallacy (manipulation) as well. Example: You're either with me or against me!
- *False analogy.* An analogy is a comparison between two things that are similar. A false analogy is when two things that are not similar are

compared as though they are, and the difference between them is ignored. Example: Pigs are only interested in activities that increase their pleasure and reduce their pain; therefore, people who pursue activities that increase their pleasure and reduce their pain are just like pigs. The important difference that has been ignored is that the things that give pigs pain and pleasure are different from the things that give people pleasure and pain.

- *Bandwagon.* This emotional fallacy attempts to manipulate people through their desire to belong or join in. To "jump on the bandwagon" means to do something because others are doing it. A bandwagon argument is one that endorses something simply because it is popular. Example: Everyone says morals are all relative, so they must be.

- *Two wrongs make a right.* This is similar to the bandwagon argument. Example: It's okay to paraphrase someone else's ideas in my paper as though they were my own ideas because other students are doing it.

- *Hasty generalization.* This occurs when a person makes a broad statement or jumps to a conclusion based on little or no evidence. The conclusion can be reached by stereotyping, generalizing from too few samples or by treating inferences or unverified information as fact. Example: "Two of my friends took this course and disliked it, so I'm not taking it." If the other twenty-eight students in the course enjoyed it, the speaker has probably made a hasty decision.

- *Slippery slope.* A slippery slope argument claims that certain generalized (usually negative) consequences will result if a particular course of action is taken. If there is clear and reasonable evidence to support that likelihood, the argument may be sound. If, however, the cause-effect relationship is oversimplified, the result is claimed to be inevitable (no future occurrence is inevitable), and there is little or no evidence to support the claim, then it is a fallacy. Example: If cloning is made legal, soon we will all be growing duplicate people to harvest their organs and keeping them in cages until we need them.

- *Improper use of authority.* This occurs when a supposed authority is quoted as proof of an argument, but the person cited is not really an expert in that field. Example: A college professor is a credible authority on the subject she teaches, but does not necessarily know more than anyone else about some other subject.

- *Dogmatism.* This is basically an opinion statement. It is the assertion that something that a person believes is true, without giving any supporting evidence. There is often a strong emotional element to dogmatism. Example: It is our moral duty to vote for the Green party.

- *Scare tactics.* This involves an emotional appeal rather than a logical one. Usually the potential danger is exaggerated or made out to be more certain to occur than it actually is. Example: Following 9/11 and prior to his second election, President Bush repeatedly put the United States on "yellow alert" due to terrorist threats. Because these threats were unsubstantiated and never materialized, they were merely scare tactics.

In order to present believable and persuasive arguments it is important to avoid these logical and emotional fallacies. It is also important to watch for them in the arguments or writing of others. The following exercise will give practice identifying errors in the writings of others. The next step is to be able to find logical errors in your own arguments.

EXERCISE 5.1

Analyzing Arguments

Examine the two opposing arguments on raising the minimum wage in Ontario at the end of this chapter, or another article provided by your teacher. What types of logical and ethical arguments are used (give examples)? Are they used correctly? List any examples of faulty reasoning and explain why they are faulty. Which article do you find more convincing? Why?

IMPORTANT PRINCIPLES TO CONSIDER

One way of arguing for or against an issue is to identify a basic principle of ethical behaviour and show how your position upholds that principle, while the opposite of your position undermines or violates the principle. This is effective when your readers are willing to accept the principle as a valid standard of behaviour (they agree that it is inherently good or right) and when you are able to prove that it is genuinely at risk of being violated by this issue. There is no definitive list of principles that we can use as a reference, but the following are some examples of important principles that should be considered when engaging in an ethical debate, and which most people recognize as valuable principles of conduct.

■ *The principle of equality.* This principle maintains that all people are equal. This does not mean that we are all the same; but that we are of equal worth and all have an equal right to participate in the benefits of Canadian society. Our right to equal treatment is protected in the Canadian Charter of Rights and Freedoms.

■ *The principle of equal consideration of interests (ECI).* This principle was described by Peter Singer in his book *Practical Ethics* (1979). According to this principle, "you should make judgments, decisions and act in ways that treat the interests and well-being of others as no less important than your own." It involves being fair and impartial when weighing your best interests against those of others. Consider the example of a supervisor who takes on all the best assignments. Under the principle of ECI, she should consider her subordinates' interests as equal to her own and divide the interesting and routine assignments equally between her staff and herself. Or she could assign projects on some other basis, such as who is the most experienced and qualified person to accomplish each project, or who needs to gain more experience in this area. As long as the best interests of everyone, including the supervisor, are being taken into account equally, the principle of ECI would be upheld.

■ *The principle of non-maleficence.* This principle involves avoiding actions that will cause harm to others or to their property. It is written into the Hippocratic oath for medical professionals, but is equally relevant to all fields. Intent is a factor in this principle. An example of this is: if John were to help his friend move apartments, he might unhook the washing machine from its pipeline. If that water pipe began to leak after they left for the new apartment, and caused water damage, John is not responsible because his intent was to help his friend and he could not have foreseen that the damage would occur. However, if John was a plumber, and he unhooked the washing machine in a way that was likely to cause damage, he would not be able to claim non-maleficence, because he should have been able to predict the problem and taken steps to avoid it. If he had been hired to do the job, he could be held accountable under professional malpractice (failure to maintain the standards of the profession) for the harm to his client.

■ *The principle of beneficence.* This principle goes beyond not doing harm. It requires actions that benefit others by preventing harm, stopping it when it is being inflicted and/or bringing about positive good. In the workplace, this means that we have a moral (and often legal) obligation to prevent harm by reporting unethical or incompetent practices of co-workers. We also have an obligation to act for the benefit of customers, patients or clients by doing work or giving advice that, to the best of our knowledge, will have beneficial results. An example of this principle is the obligation to report child abuse. If Celine volunteered at an after-school program for children and became aware that a child in the program showed signs of abuse, she would be required to report it. Even when beneficence isn't legally required, it is recognized as a good principle to live by.

■ *The principle of fidelity.* This principle involves fulfilling our commitments and obligations, whether they are verbal or in a written and signed contract. An example of this is a carpenter who agrees to do a small interior renovation for a private home and is then offered a large contract by a developer. Even though the second contract is more lucrative, and honouring both contracts will put the carpenter under severe time constraints, he is obligated to complete the job in the private home, which he had already agreed to. Fidelity can also refer to being loyal and supportive of those people who have a right to expect fidelity from us, such as family, friends, co-workers and employers.

■ *The principle of confidentiality.* This principle is about respecting the privacy of others and not divulging information we are privy to that might harm or embarrass people if made public. In some situations, confidentiality is limited by the potential for serious harm. For example, a psychologist, psychiatrist, or any medical professional must report a patient's threat of serious harm to himself or to another person, even though disclosing the threat violates the patient's confidence. Priests and lawyers, on the other hand, are obligated not to break confidentiality by reporting threats or confessions made by a client or made in the confessional. As individuals, if we withhold information told to us about a crime, we could be found guilty of being an accomplice. We are seldom, in our personal lives, given confidences of a criminal nature, but there are often times when we must decide whether or not we should keep secret something a friend or relative has told us.

■ *The principle of conservatism.* This principle protects the continuation of an accepted practice (generally medical practices). Professionals who wish to change an existing practice must prove valid reasons (including costs and benefits) for doing so. Those who wish to continue the practice are not obligated to prove its worth because it has already "passed the test of time." For example, women had to prove they should be given the right to own property and vote. Because these rights were historically reserved for men, men did not have to prove that women should not have those rights; the obligation of proof was on those who wished to change law and custom, not those who wanted to maintain the status quo.

HUMAN RIGHTS ISSUES

Closely related to the concept of principles is the concept of rights. In Canada we are guaranteed certain rights by the Canadian Charter of Rights and Freedoms as well as by provincial legal codes such as the Ontario Human Rights Code. Many of these are patterned after the United Nations Universal Declaration of Human Rights. They are all based on the fundamental ethical principles of equality, justice and freedom.

The Canadian Charter of Rights and Freedoms

The Canadian Charter of Rights and Freedoms is used to determine the validity of all other Canadian laws, so it is important to understand what is contained in it. First, the Introduction and Section 1 set out the authority and parameters of our rights. The introduction states that "Canada is founded upon principles that recognize the supremacy of God and the rule of law." Section 1 indicates that the rights and freedoms in the charter are not absolute; they are subject to reasonable limits that can be legally justified in a democratic society.

Section 2 lists the fundamental freedoms guaranteed to everyone: freedom of conscience and religion; freedom of thought, belief, opinion and expression, which includes freedom of the press and other communication media; freedom of peaceful assembly; and freedom of association. Sections 3–5 guarantee Canadians' democratic rights, such as the right to vote and the terms of office of elected representatives. Section 6 guarantees Canadians freedom of movement within Canada, freedom to relocate and find employment in other provinces and the freedom to leave Canada and to return. Sections 7–14 guarantee legal rights, including the right to life, liberty and security of person. These sections protect citizens against unreasonable search, seizure, detention and imprisonment. They guarantee the right to be informed of any charges made against us, the right to counsel, to be tried within a reasonable time, and to be presumed innocent until proven guilty in a fair and public hearing by an impartial tribunal. They further guarantee trial by jury, not being tried for the same offence twice, protection against cruel and unusual punishment, and they provide witnesses with protection against self-incrimination except where perjury is concerned.

Section 15 concerns equality. It guarantees Canadians protection from discrimination based on race, national or ethnic origin, colour, religion, sex, age or mental or physical disability. Everyone is equal under the law, and provision is made for laws and programs intended to benefit disadvantaged individuals or groups. Sections 16–23 protect the right to use either of Canada's two official languages and include the right to be educated in either language. The rest of the Charter, Sections 24–34, deals with Aboriginal rights and freedoms and the enforcement and application of the Charter. (Department of Justice, Canadian Charter of Rights and Freedoms, 1982)

Justice and Basic Human Rights

Not all rights are protected by law. Moral rights are justified by ethical reasoning and principles, but may or may not be defensible in a courtroom. For example, we have a moral right to do as we wish with our possessions. To a certain extent, it is also a legal right. Officials may not enter our home without a search warrant. However, animals are possessions, yet our right to do as we wish with them will not hold up in court if we are found to be treating them cruelly. Most of the time when we refer to rights, we are talking about something guaranteed to us, which would be upheld in a court of law. Our sense of justice is closely linked to ethical considerations, so it is worth examining these rights in a little more detail.

- *The right to be informed.* We have a right to be given information that is in our best interests to know. This is particularly true when we need the information to make a decision, such as a decision concerning our own health care (so that we can give informed consent), or a legal or financial decision. If we consult a professional, she has the related duty of full disclosure.

- *The right to autonomy.* The term autonomy comes from the Greek words *autos* (self) and *nomos* (rule). This means the right to make decisions for ourselves when these decisions involve our own well-being. An example of this is the right to spend the money we earn as we please, within legal limits, whether it be on cigarettes, gambling, investments, causes or charities. This right is closely related to the right to be informed, because without complete information our right to autonomy is compromised. The right to autonomy includes making decisions in every area of our lives, including health care, finances and marriage.

- *The right to privacy.* This is the other side of the principle of confidentiality. The right to privacy is the right to control the disclosure of information about ourselves. The fact that we may share information about ourselves or our work with a professional or an employer does not give him the right to pass this information on. Similarly, we have the right to privacy in our personal lives and the right to protect that privacy by excluding others from trespassing on our personal property. Anyone who invades our privacy repeatedly can be charged with stalking.

- *The right to freedom of expression.* This is the right to express our opinions without fear of reprisal. It is limited, however, by laws against discrimination, slander (verbal statements that are false and damaging to others), libel (written statements that are false and damaging to others) and harassment. The principle of not doing harm comes into play here. The Charter of Rights and Freedoms grants Canadians the right to state their opinions, unless those statements malign another person or group of persons, are unsubstantiated and are intended to or do result in significant harm to someone.

- *The right to a safe and healthy workplace.* Employees have a right to expect their employer to provide and maintain a safe and healthy workplace, within reasonable limits. This includes posting warnings about hazardous materials or dangerous conditions, and offering safety training for employees. Students and parents of underage students also have a right to demand safe and secure conditions in educational facilities.

- *The right to pursue our own best interests.* In Canada we have the right to pursue our own best interests as long as we do not break any laws, fail to live up to the standards of our profession or infringe upon the rights of others. In fact it has been proven by the test of time that it is in a society's best interests that its members take care of themselves within these guidelines. If the members of a society do not take care of themselves, they are not able to care for others or contribute to the general well-being and improvement of their society. The principle of equal consideration of interests (ECI) should be taken into account when pursuing our own interests.

- *The right to due process.* This is the right to appeal a decision made by others, whether it is a court decision, the decision of an employer to promote one employee over another for the wrong reasons (e.g., discrimination), or the decision to fail a student. It is essentially the right to question the arbitrary use of power and force those with authority to prove that they are not abusing their power over others. Without this legal right, none of our rights would be protected.

■ *The right to state our case before an impartial and unbiased adjudicator.* This right implies that we have an adversary—the person we believe we have a case against, or who has a case against us. Therefore, coupled with the right to state our case is the right to disclosure—our right to hear our adversary's case against us. Other judicial rights are linked to these two, such as the right to hear reasons for a decision and the right to appeal a decision.

■ *The right to justice.* Justice is society's legal expression of the value of fairness to everyone and the principle of ECI. This is also sometimes referred to as the "Duty of Fairness." Justice requires not only that the righteous be rewarded and the unrighteous punished, but also that the rewards and punishments fit the deeds. The concept of justice can be understood by considering four different types or categories of justice: procedural, distributive, compensatory and retributive.

Procedural justice has to do with due process. It requires that the same procedures apply to all members of society. In the court system, this means that everyone has the same opportunity to receive a fair hearing. The constitutional basis for procedural justice is section 7 of the Canadian Charter of Rights and Freedoms, which states, "Everyone has the right to life, liberty and security of the person and the right not to be deprived thereof except in accordance with the principles of fundamental justice." This guarantees us the right to state our case and ensures that the case will be judged impartially in a court of law before any authority or governing body can make a decision affecting our life, liberty or security.

Certain cases, however, set precedents for future judgments on similar cases, and social prohibitions change, so although due process may remain intact, the outcomes of trials vary. Does this make previous judgments unfair? Consider the case of Angelique Lavallee.

Angelique Lavallee Case for Debate

Angelique Lavallee was in an abusive common-law relationship with Kevin Rust in Winnipeg in the late 1980s. During a fight between them, Rust apparently told Lavallee, "either you kill me or I'll get you." He turned around. Lavallee pulled out a gun and shot him in the back of the head. At trial, she argued self-defence. A psychiatrist testified to the effects on her mental state of years of repeated abuse, and that in the state she was in she believed she was going to be killed and had no alternative but to shoot Rust. In 1990, Judge Bertha Wilson and the Supreme Court of Canada unanimously ruled to acquit her in a landmark case that recognized battered woman's syndrome. Following this case, other battered women successfully defended themselves using this defence. In 1993, the National Action Committee on the Status of Women demanded the immediate release of women in prison for killing their abusive partners, on the grounds that the defence of battered women syndrome had not been available to them before Lavallee's acquittal. (Toronto *Star*, October 10, 1993.)

Distributive justice is concerned with the fair distribution of goods, or benefits and burdens in a society. One example of this concept is the fair collection of tax dollars; another is the fair allocation of these tax dollars across the needs in our society—health care, social work, education, law enforcement, research, encouragement of the arts, assistance for low-income families, etc. In politics, the concept of distributive justice is debated between socialists, who believe that the goods produced within a society should be equally shared among all its members, and capitalists, who believe that although everyone has an equal right to compete in the marketplace, people's financial gains may differ according to their success. Canada's health care system, which makes the same care and procedures available to everyone regardless of wealth or social status (or lack of both), is an example of distributive justice. However, even with this system, decisions must be made about how to give people equal access to limited resources.

EXERCISE 5.2

Just Distribution of a Nation's Benefits and Resources

The following questions show the different perspectives on the issue of fair distribution of benefits and resources in a nation:

1. Should everyone receive an equal share of Canada's resources?
2. Should distribution be determined by people's needs?
3. Should individual effort determine distribution?
4. Should distribution be based on a judgment of people's merit or worthiness?
5. Should people receive according to their contribution to society?

Which of these five perspectives do you think is morally preferable? Why?

_____

_____

_____

_____

Which of these five perspectives (or a combination of which ones) do you think is closest to the actual distribution of wealth and resources in Canada? Why do you think so?

_____

_____

_____

_____

Can you think of other countries where resources are distributed according to different criteria than they are here? Which countries? What are their criteria?

_____

_____

_____

_____

Compensatory justice (also known as restorative justice) involves compensating members of society for wrongs that have been done to them, whether intentionally or accidentally. Victims of automobile accidents, of negative outcomes to a medical procedure, of wrongful dismissal at work, of slander or of wrongful conviction may all appeal to the courts for compensation, which usually takes the form of monetary compensation. Canadian Stephen Truscott's case to restore his name and be compensated for the years he spent in jail is an example of compensatory justice.

Retributive justice refers to the punishment accorded to wrongdoers. In order to be just, the punishment must be appropriate to the crime and uniform for anyone committing a similar crime. This is the most controversial aspect of the Canadian justice system. Obviously there is a fair amount of subjectivity involved in determining what constitutes a fitting punishment for a particular crime. Should the punishment for armed theft, with the threat of mortal violence, be more severe than the punishment for rape, which incurs actual but not necessarily fatal violence? To what extent should circumstances be taken into account in situations such as a statutory rape where the young woman is willing but underage and lied about her age, or a robbery where the thief is armed with a realistic toy gun? In order to answer these questions, we must first decide whether imprisonment is intended to punish the criminal, rehabilitate the criminal or protect society by removing the criminal.

According to the Criminal Code of Canada, retribution is only one aspect of a just and appropriate sentence. Other factors listed in the Code (C-46, s. 718) include:

a. denouncing unlawful conduct
b. deterring the offender and other persons from committing further crimes
c. separating offenders from society, where necessary
d. assisting in rehabilitating offenders
e. providing reparations for harm done to victims or to the community
f. promoting a sense of responsibility in offenders and acknowledgement of the harm done to victims and to the community.

EXERCISE 5.3

Determining the Purpose of Retributive Justice

Read the article titled "Jail Time = Less Crime" at the end of this chapter. In small groups, consider the purposes of retributive justice: punishment, deterrence, reparation and rehabilitation. Each group should decide which purpose is most important and prepare arguments supporting that choice. Your group should include as many of the following types of arguments as you can come up with:

- an argument using deductive reasoning
- an argument using inductive reasoning
- an argument that uses analogy correctly
- an argument that uses slippery slope correctly
- an argument applying one of the principles listed in this chapter
- an argument applying one of the rights listed in this chapter

Exchange your arguments with those of another group. Examine the other group's arguments, looking for incorrect or faulty use of logic. When your arguments have been returned to your group, make any corrections necessary. When all groups have done this, each group should share their arguments with the class.

EXERCISE 5.4

Classroom Debates

Divide the class into eight or twelve groups of three to five participants. Half of the class (four or six of the groups) should research capital punishment, and the other half should research the issue of young offenders, or some other aspect of our justice system. Be sure to bring in Canadian cases as examples, such as Stephen Truscott. For each issue, half of the groups should argue for the issue and the other half should argue against it. For example, a class divided into eight groups will have four groups debating capital punishment while the rest of the class listens, and four groups debating young offenders while the first half of the class listens. Of the four groups debating each issue, two groups will be debating for it (i.e., capital punishment should be reinstated in Canada) and two groups will be debating against it (i.e., capital punishment should not be reinstated in Canada). Each debate should have a moderator and a timer.

During the debate, each group speaks in turn. The first pro group (for the issue) begins. They should incorporate the following into their arguments:

State what the ethical issue is in clear, concrete terms.

_____

_____

_____

Who could be affected by this issue?

_____

_____

_____

_____

State any laws concerning this issue and what effect they have on it. In Canada:

_____

_____

_____

(Continued)

(Continued)

Elsewhere:

_____

_____

_____

Clearly state your position on the ethical issue.

_____

_____

_____

Give two or three arguments supporting your position.

_____

_____

_____

_____

_____

_____

_____

_____

Is your position that of an absolutist or a relativist? Explain why.

_____

_____

_____

The first opposing team should now be given the opportunity to do the same for their side of the argument. After they have spoken, the second pro team has the opportunity to criticize the opposing team's arguments or give counter-arguments to refute them. They should also identify any logical or emotional fallacies in the opposing team's arguments. They may also give one or two additional arguments based on the elements of logical reasoning to support their side of the debate. After they have spoken, the second opposing team has the opportunity to criticize both of the pro teams' arguments or give counter-arguments to refute them. They should also identify any logical or emotional fallacies in the two pro teams' arguments. They may also give one or two additional arguments based on the elements of logical reasoning to support their side of the debate. If there are four groups for each issue, the debate is now over; if there are six groups, the third pro team and the third opposing team now have an opportunity to criticize and build on the second team's arguments, in the same way the second teams did for the first teams.

Following the debate, open the issue to class discussion. The moderator should prepare several questions to put to the class in order to keep the discussion going, if necessary.

"A law... must have a moral basis, so that there is an inner, compelling force for every citizen to obey."

—CHAIM WEIDMAN (1874–1952)

Article 1: "Jail Time = Less Crime"

(Chad Skelton, Vancouver *Sun*, May 27, 2006)

Does prison work? With the introduction of several tough sentencing measures, the Conservative government reopened a fierce debate about whether putting more people in jail—and keeping them there for longer periods of time—has any meaningful impact on crime. In 2006, then minister of justice Vic Toews introduced proposals that would eliminate the option of house arrest (versus time served in a correctional facility) for several serious offences and impose minimum prison terms for many gun crimes that previously carried no such minimum. Toews felt confident that these measures would help lower the crime rate.

Many critics, including defence lawyers and criminologists, say longer prison sentences have little impact on crime, with many pointing to the situation in the United States as a cautionary tale. Over the past 20 years, the incarceration rate in the United States has more than tripled, caused in large part by the introduction in the 1980s of mandatory sentences (guidelines that impose the minimum prison sentence for specified crimes, and that require judges to hand out fixed sentences). During that same period, Canada's incarceration rate has stayed about the same. There are now an estimated two million people behind bars in the United States—per capita, that's six times as many as in Canada.

But did that explosion in the prison population bring down the crime rate? In short, yes. During the 1990s, the United States saw a dramatic drop in crime. The burglary rate fell by almost half, robberies went down by a third and the chance of having a car stolen—compared to the late 1980s—dropped considerably. Canada saw a drop in crime during that period, too.

Historically, one of the biggest challenges in assessing the impact of prison on crime has been that the two are so interrelated—a surge in crime will naturally lead to more people being sent to prison. In the mid-1990s, Steven Levitt, a prominent economist at the University of Chicago, found a way to solve this puzzle. With U.S. prison populations on the rise, human rights groups had filed lawsuits against several states, arguing that prison overcrowding violated offenders' rights—in some cases leading judges to order those states to reduce the number of people sent to jail. Levitt found those states that were forced to send fewer people to prison had more crime.

Crunching the numbers, he found that, on average, having one more criminal behind bars resulted in 15 fewer serious crimes a year. Based on those results, Levitt argued, the huge increase in the American prison population in the 1990s was responsible for a 12-percent reduction in violent crime and an eight-percent drop in property crime—about one-third of the total decline. Levitt argued the rest of the drop was due to the hiring of more police officers, the waning of the crack epidemic and—most controversially—the legalization of abortion 20 years earlier, which led to fewer unwanted children.

So how does having more people in prison cause the crime rate to go down? One possibility—that it turns criminals into better people—seems unlikely. In 1999, researchers at the University of New Brunswick examined 50 studies on recidivism that covered more than 300,000 offenders. Considering other factors—such as an inmate's criminal background and age—they found that the longer someone spent in jail, the more likely they were to commit another crime when they got out. The researchers found the impact was most significant for low-risk offenders—suggesting prison may indeed be a "school of crime" that makes people worse, not better.

Some argue that longer prison sentences send a message—deterring others from committing crimes. Most experts agree that for certain economic crimes, such as growing marijuana or committing fraud, the prospect of tougher penalties can make offenders think twice. The problem, experts claim, is that many of the most serious crimes (such as murder or assault) are crimes of passion, for which offenders rarely weigh the pros and cons of their actions. And drug-addicted offenders who commit property crimes out of desperation are not likely to be deterred by the prospect of serious jail time.

"If offenders were rational, sober, drug-free individuals, it would be easier to control crime," says Julian Roberts, a criminologist at the University of Oxford in England. "But unfortunately, that's not the case."

One strong argument that deterrence can work is made by a 1999 study by Levitt and Daniel Kessler of Stanford University, of California's Proposition 8 legislation—which imposed draconian, decades-long prison terms on repeat offenders. What made California such a good research subject is that it already had mandatory sentences for most serious crimes—the Proposition 8 penalties were just added on top. So, in the short term after the law had passed, no additional people were put behind bars in California; any drop in crime was likely the result of criminals being scared off by the new, tough sentences. Using other states as a comparison, researchers concluded that, in the three years after it was passed, the Proposition 8 law led to an eight-percent drop in crime.

The really interesting thing, though, is what happened next. Seven years after the law passed—when the first wave of offenders started serving their additional time—the drop in crime more than doubled, to 20 percent.

Why? It turns out the main reason prison works is also the most simple: It's not reform, it's not deterrence. Prison brings down crime because it takes criminals out of commission for the duration of their sentence. Referred to by criminologists as "incapacitation," prison works by giving criminals a time-out.

Some experts dismiss the idea of incapacitation as a factor in lowering crime rates because few crimes ever reach the courts. "Only about four or five percent of offences are actually sentenced," Roberts says. "Some offenders aren't caught. Some aren't convicted. So there's a limit to what the sentencing process can do to achieve large changes in the crime rate."

However, says Darryl Plecas, a professor of criminology at University College of the Fraser Valley in Abbotsford, B.C., that argument ignores the fact that most criminals commit offences on a regular basis. If you steal 20 cars a year, for example, the odds are probably going to catch up with you sooner rather than later. As for the worst repeat offenders, putting them away—even for a year or two—can prevent a lot of crime. "I don't think the average Canadian understands just how prolific some of these people are," Plecas says.

In the debate over sentencing reforms, one might think the Conservatives could take comfort in the fact that research backs up their argument that prison works. But the same research also suggests that—if the goal is reducing crime—these reforms focus on the wrong criminals. If the primary benefit of prison is "incapacitating" criminals for the duration of their sentence, it stands to reason that the best way to reduce crime is to ensure those you put behind bars are the busiest criminals.

For certain offences, Plecas says, as few as five percent of offenders commit a disproportionate amount of crime. For these "super-prolific offenders"—most of them drug-addicted property criminals—crime is simply a way of life. Plecas's research on sentencing has found that judges in British Columbia often give such repeat offenders only modest jail terms. "It's laughable," he says. "People with 80 prior convictions have been getting three-month sentences."

But the Conservatives' reforms contain no increased penalties for repeat offenders, except for gun crimes. Thus, judges have the power to give lenient sentences to burglars or robbers with horrendous records—as long as those offenders are careful not to use a gun in their crimes. But someone with no criminal record who is caught with a loaded handgun will go to prison for five years (and seven years for subsequent gun crimes); judges won't even have the option of giving a first-time offender a conditional sentence.

Plecas says he'd like to see the government bring in a mandatory five-year prison term for any criminal with at least ten prior convictions—a number research shows is a good sign someone is a chronic offender. "Let's not rinky-dink around with the one-off offender," he says. "Let's go after the people who are recidivistic—that's what's going to make a difference."

While Plecas's proposal may seem harsh, he argues that sentencing repeat offenders to several years of federal time is probably the only way to deal with them. As it stands now, Plecas says, many chronic offenders go through the justice system like a revolving door. "To me, it seems immoral to allow a person to go through 15 or 20 years of their life committing crime," he says. "Maybe it's better to say, 'Damn it, you're not going to court 30 times. You're going to court once and you're doing five years.'"

TWO OPPOSING COMMENTARIES: RAISING THE MINIMUM WAGE IN ONTARIO

Article 2: "Minimum wage should rise to $10"

(Toronto *Star*, September 20, 2006)

In 1995, the new Ontario Conservative premier Mike Harris froze the legal minimum wage in the province at $6.85 an hour. The freeze remained in place for eight years. That move affected thousands of Ontario's lowest-paid workers, many of them in unskilled and non-unionized jobs.

During the 2003 provincial election campaign, Liberal leader Dalton McGuinty pledged to right that injustice. Once he became premier, McGuinty took the first steps toward fulfilling that promise by lifting the freeze and committing his government to increasing the minimum wage in stages over four years. The base now stands at $7.75 an hour. Next February, it is scheduled to jump to $8 an hour.

But while McGuinty deserves praise for moving on his promise, he needs to do much more—and soon. Specifically, he should raise the minimum wage to $10 an hour, not $8 an hour, effective Feb. 1, when the next increase is due to come into force. And he and opposition parties should pledge to boost rates in future years at least in line with inflation.

For Canada's second-richest province, this would be a quick, responsible and fair way to help its poorest and most vulnerable workers who have failed to share, even to a limited degree, in the gains of a growing economy.

Since the beginning of 1995, the average hourly wage for employees in Ontario rose by more than 30 percent. Had minimum-wage workers kept pace with the average Ontario worker over that period, they would be paid more than $9 an hour today. Instead, workers earning the minimum wage saw no increase from 1995 to 2004, a period when they lost 20 per cent of their purchasing power to inflation.

While a $10-an-hour minimum wage, which is advocated by many anti-poverty groups, would certainly help, it would lift only some, not all, of Ontario's working poor out of poverty.

Take the example of Maheswary Puvàneswaran, the mother of two featured Saturday in the *Star* as part of a series on the working poor. Working as much as she can in two low-wage cleaning jobs, she earns just over $1,000 a month. She would need to earn a minimum of $15 an hour working full-time to bring her family up to the generally accepted poverty line.

To some, raising the minimum wage to $10 from $7.75 an hour in one step might seem excessive. When McGuinty raised the rate in previous years, a number of business leaders complained, saying Ontario's economy would be hurt because it is already suffering from higher energy prices and more competition from lower wage countries, such as China.

While there might be some job losses because of raising the minimum wage to $10 an hour, such an increase is fully justified because the minimum wage needs to be more reflective of the real levels of income needed by Ontario's working poor to enjoy a decent standard of living.

So why aren't we calling for McGuinty to raise the minimum wage even higher, to a level that would truly be considered "a decent living wage"?

Such a wage would be at least $15 an hour, and possibly even higher in cities such as Toronto where the cost of living is high. This is particularly true for families with just a single wage earner. Unfortunately, rather than pay such a high minimum wage, many employers would opt to contract out the work, in effect replacing full- or part-time employees with self-employed contractors, who are not covered by minimum wage laws.

This growing trend toward contracting out work, which is being pursued more and more even by governments, worries anti-poverty activists, who fear the poor or those who are in low-wage occupations will lose their jobs. They say the best tool for increasing the incomes of all working poor, not just those earning the minimum wage, would be a new government-funded earned-income supplement. Among the many groups supporting the idea of such a supplement is the Daily Bread Food Bank in Toronto.

Ideally, both an income supplement and a hike in the basic minimum wage would occur at the same time. Together, they could go a long way in eradicating the term "working poor" from our vocabulary. Such a combination, moreover, would mean taxpayers would not have to bear the full burden of ensuring all working Canadians a decent income. With a higher minimum wage, employers would also have to foot part of the bill.

However, it is unlikely that both programs could be implemented together in a timely fashion because Ottawa would be responsible for the earned-income supplement and Queen's Park for raising the minimum wage. It is rare when the two governments act in unison.

That's why it is important for McGuinty to take the first step by acting now to raise the minimum wage to $10 an hour. The working poor should not have to wait until Ottawa gets on board with an income supplement. They need help now. They have waited long enough.

Article 3: "The Injustice of the Minimum Wage"

(Andrew Coyne, *National Post*, January 10, 2007, p. A16)

You have to admit the timing was awful. Two weeks after legislating a 25% pay increase for themselves, to more than $110,000 apiece, members of the Ontario legislature approved a 3.2% increase in the province's statutory minimum wage: from $7.75 an hour to $8.00.

The Toronto *Star* was properly appalled. Granted, it was the fourth increase in the minimum wage in as many years, and true, the paper was not actually opposed to the politicians' pay hike, and no, the paper had not seen fit to raise its own workers' pay by 25% the last time they negotiated—they got roughly 8% over three years—but still: the optics. Eight measly bucks. When *everybody knows* the minimum wage should really be $10 an hour.

The paper has been campaigning for months for a $10 minimum wage, echoing an NDP private member's bill. Why $10? Why not $9, or $11? No one pretends that $10 an hour marks the difference between misery and happiness: even at 40 hours a week, that's still only $20,000 a year, and besides, hardly anyone works full-time for the minimum wage. (Indeed, hardly anyone works for the minimum wage at all: less than 5% of the province's workforce.) So what's so special about a $10 minimum?

If "because 10 is a nice round number" is the answer, why not $20? Or—an even rounder number—why not $100 an hour? If your answer to *that* is "because that would throw a lot of people out of work," then why should you not expect a $10 minimum wage to throw *some* people out of work? Or if an increase in wages has no effect on the demand for labour, then why stop at $10? Why not really do something for the working poor?

The whole point of a minimum wage is that the market wage for some workers—the wage that would just balance the supply of and demand for unskilled, transient, or young workers in highly unstable service industries—is deemed to be too low. If, accordingly, it is fixed by law above the market level, it must be at a point where the supply exceeds the demand. Economists have a technical term for that gap. It's called "unemployment."

Advocates of minimum wages either reject that elementary logic, or they don't care. The NDP is an example of the first: MPP Cheri DiNovo, the sponsor of that private member's bill, refers dismissively to "all those spurious arguments that this is somehow going to destroy the economy." But the *Star*, intriguingly, is in the second camp.

"While there might be some job losses because of raising the minimum wage to $10 an hour," the paper opined in a recent editorial, "such an increase is fully justified" by the need to make the minimum wage "more reflective of the real levels of income needed by Ontario's working poor to enjoy a decent standard of living."

Leave aside that the working poor will still not be enjoying anything like a decent standard of living, even at $10 an hour. What principle of social justice would suggest it was okay to toss some of the most vulnerable members of society on the scrap heap, forcing them out of their jobs altogether so that their still-employed co-workers could snag a raise?

The most influential philosopher of contemporary liberalism in fact prescribes the opposite. In *A Theory of Justice*, John Rawls argues we should measure our commitment to justice against how well the very worst off in society are faring, on broadly "there but for the grace of God" grounds. The aim of a just society should be to *maximize the minimum*—to improve the lot of those worst off, first off. That would suggest putting the interests of the unemployed ahead of those who already have jobs, rather than, in effect, locking the jobless out of the market.

The point is not that those struggling to get by on very low wages should be left to their own devices. The point is that wages, properly considered, are neither the instrument nor the objective of a just society. When we say their wages are "too low," we mean in terms of what society believes is decent. But that's not what wages are for. The point of a wage, like any other price, is to ensure every seller finds a willing buyer and vice versa, without giving rise to shortages or surpluses—not to attempt to reflect broader social notions of what is appropriate. That's especially true when employers can always sidestep any attempt to impose a "just" wage simply by hiring fewer workers.

Social goals should be socially financed. When we think about it, it's not a minimum wage we're really aiming for: it's a minimum income. If so, then the proper approach is to supplement the incomes of the working poor, through the tax-and-transfer system—not fix their wages and hope for the best.

6

Social Issues in Canada

CONTENTS

> *"I happen to feel that the degree of a person's intelligence is directly reflected by the number of conflicting attitudes she can bring to bear on the same topic."*
>
> —LISA ALTHER (1975)

Most of us have already thought about or discussed with friends many of the issues in this chapter. We may have formed our own opinions on some of them, and still be considering where we stand on others. We may even feel so strongly about one or another of these issues that it is hard to understand how others could see the issue differently, and easy to dismiss their point of view as "wrong" or "immoral" or even "stupid."

It's not a bad thing to feel strongly about important issues. But it's not a good thing to be so entrenched in our own opinions that we can't acknowledge the reasoning behind different points of view. This chapter is intended to offer an opportunity to explore different attitudes concerning familiar, and perhaps some unfamiliar, moral issues. The arguments presented may, in the end, confirm your original opinion, or change some of your opinions; but that is not what is important. What is important is that your opinions will be based on more information and a deeper understanding of the complexity of the issue and, hopefully, will be more respectful of different opinions. As Lisa Alther implies in the opening quote, the more we are able to understand and consider conflicting attitudes, the more worthy of respect our own opinion will be.

A brief summary of the laws pertaining to each issue will be given before the ethical arguments are presented. The relationship between ethics and the law will be further examined in Chapter 8; for now, we should remember that the law is only a reference point, not a moral argument. Because something is legal does not necessarily make it ethical. It is legal to smoke at home around small children, but is it ethical to damage their lungs with second-hand smoke? On the other hand, just because something is unethical does not mean that it should be made illegal. It may be unethical to waste our talents, but do we want a law that requires us to enter a certain profession because we have a natural talent for it? According to Hobbes, we should only agree to those restrictions on our freedom that are necessary to enable us to live together in peace and equality. Laws enable us to live with each other—ethics is what enables us to live with ourselves. Therefore, our purpose here is to examine these issues in order to understand the moral arguments on all sides and to evaluate them as much as possible without personal bias, before forming our own carefully considered opinion.

ABORTION

An abortion occurs when a developing fetus is expelled from the womb before it is able to survive on its own. Spontaneous abortions, also referred to as miscarriages, can occur naturally, but when one occurs as the result of deliberate human intervention, it is called an induced abortion. Abortions are legal in 54 countries around the world and illegal in 97 countries. Approximately 39 percent of the world's population lives in countries where it is illegal. According to recent abortion statistics, "There are approximately 46 million abortions conducted each year ... (and) ... 20 million of them (are) obtained illegally." (www.womensissues.about.com/cs/abortionststs.htm) In Canada, 110,331 abortions were performed in 1998, according to Statistics Canada. (Mallick, 2003)

Abortion is one of the most contentious moral issues in our society. People tend to have very strong feelings one way or the other, and those feelings often erupt into action. Usually the action takes the form of protests and verbal or written communications ranging from serious debate to emotional outbursts to open threats. But three Canadian doctors have been shot because they performed legal abortions: Dr. Garson Romalis in Vancouver, Dr. Hugh Short in Ancaster and Dr. Jack Fairman in Winnipeg. None of them died of their wounds, unlike some American doctors who have been killed.

Why is abortion such a volatile issue? For one thing, it is a life and death issue. For another, it is tied to one of our deepest instincts as a species: the protection of our young. For many, it is a religious issue, and even for the non-religious the question of abortion is connected to questions about the meaning and nature of life itself. Finally, abortion is a gender issue; it encompasses concerns about fairness and equality for both sexes. For all these reasons, many people have adopted an extreme position on the question of abortion. Even the language with which abortion is often discussed is emotionally charged: "pro-life" implies that opponents are pro-death; "pro-choice" implies that opponents are out to destroy all personal autonomy. In order to fairly examine the various moral arguments and points of view on this issue, we must avoid using labels and language steeped in emotional biases.

Applicable Canadian Laws

Until 1969, abortion was illegal in Canada and the maximum penalty for performing one was life imprisonment. In 1969, therapeutic abortions became legal, if four conditions were met:

■ the abortion was approved by a hospital committee
■ it was performed in a hospital
■ it was performed by a doctor
■ it was required to protect the life or health of the pregnant woman

A major problem with the therapeutic abortion law was that it was administered unfairly across Canada. Protecting a woman's health is open to interpretation and could include anything from preventing her death or invalidism to sparing her temporary physical limitations and/or emotional distress. Therefore, women who lived in communities where the hospital committees were receptive to abortion had no difficulty getting an abortion, while women who lived in communities where the committees were opposed to abortion were denied any access to safe, legal abortions. In 1988, the therapeutic abortion law was declared unconstitutional by the Supreme Court of Canada and abortion has been legal in Canada since then.

Under Canadian law, a fetus is not a person and has no legal rights. This means that anything done to a fetus prior to birth—even immediately prior to birth—cannot be brought as a charge against the person who did it. The fetus becomes a legally recognized person only at birth.

Ethical Arguments

Before we begin to discuss the various moral arguments surrounding abortion, what is your personal opinion about abortion?

_____

_____

After you have written it down, imagine that you can leave your opinion here on this piece of paper, separate from you, for now. Try to read this section as though you have no opinion at all on abortion, but are simply trying to understand the ways other people think about it.

Arguments for and against abortion fall into two main categories. There are deontological, or principle-based arguments, which present the issue as a conflict of rights. Then there are teleological, or consequence-based arguments, which consider the issue as a conflict between desirable and undesirable consequences.

Deontological Arguments

When deontological arguments are used, the main stakeholders—those most affected, whose rights are in conflict or at risk—are the pregnant woman, the father and the fetus. Others might become involved, such as friends, grandparents and lobby groups, but however strongly they may feel about the situation, their basic human rights are not at risk. To understand deontological arguments, we must determine the rights of each stakeholder and examine how those rights are threatened.

There are two rights which are at risk for the pregnant woman. The first is a person's right to pursue her own best interests, as long as no laws are broken or the rights of others are not infringed upon. Since abortion is not illegal, if a fetus is not a person with rights that can be infringed upon, then a pregnant woman should have the right to decide whether carrying the fetus to term is in her own best interests. Weighing those interests to make her decision involves a consideration of the consequences of the different options available.

The second right that is at risk for the pregnant woman is her right to autonomy, which is the right to make decisions which involve her own person. Those who make this argument claim that a woman has an absolute right to decide what will happen to her own body. A Kantian might phrase this position as "a woman must be treated as an end in herself, not as a means of incubating a fetus." While the right to pursue her best interests depends on the assumption that a fetus is not a person with rights, the right to autonomy does not. Even if a fetus is a person with rights, that does not necessarily mean that a woman is obligated to provide the fetus with the means of sustaining its life. Consider a similar example: if, by donating a kidney, you could save a person's life without endangering your own, are you obligated to do so? What about saving another person's life by donating blood or bone marrow? While both of these actions would be considered morally good, we do not consider them to be morally required.

In other words, we have the moral right to give or to refuse others permission to use parts of our body, even when their lives are at risk. But what if we did give permission? Would we have the moral right later to revoke that permission? If a woman intentionally became pregnant, it could be assumed that she gave permission to the fetus to use her body. In that case she may well be morally obligated not to withdraw a permission she willingly gave. One can assume that that is not the case when rape or incest are involved, but does unprotected sex imply consent for a fetus to use her body?

Although the father of an unborn child does not have immediate personal rights—i.e., neither autonomy over his body nor his own life are being threatened—arguments have been made that the father's genetic contribution and emotional involvement should give him some rights in determining the fate of his offspring. Counter-arguments claiming that a man does not have any rights over the body of a sexual partner generally carry more weight.

Before discussing the moral rights of a fetus, we must determine whether a fetus has moral rights. People have moral rights, so the question is, is a fetus a human being? More specifically, at what point should a fetus be considered a human being with moral rights? Before answering this, we have to consider the significant stages of fetal development and the approximate time each stage occurs.

■ Day 1: The ovum is fertilized by a sperm. Some people argue that a human being exists from the moment of conception, because it has its complete genetic makeup at this point. If there is no significant event to change its course of development (such as an X-ray or substances taken by the mother) then the next nine months are only a matter of growth. Do we consider a toddler less human than a teenager because he has not grown yet? Under this hypothesis, the "morning after" pill would qualify as abortion. Critics of this position argue that the bare genetic blueprint is not a human being. Consider the case where a fertilized egg splits to become identical twins. They may look alike, but they are not the same person, and differ from each other in many ways, even though they have the same genetic blueprint. The fertilized egg is therefore not the complete individual.

- Weeks 1–2: The fertilized ovum has reached the uterus and is now called a blastocyst. It is a ball of cells not much larger than a grain of sand. The cells are still undifferentiated, which means they have the ability to become any human part: organs, skin, bone, etc. At approximately the end of week 2 they begin to develop into specific body parts. When this happens, we call the blastocyst a fetus.

- Weeks 6–8: Brain waves can be detected in the fetus. Those who believe that a fetus has moral status at this point argue that since medically we use the termination of brain function (brain death) to indicate death, it is only reasonable to consider the beginning of brain function to be the beginning of life. Furthermore, what makes us uniquely human is our consciousness, language and thinking skills—the higher activity of our brain. Critics argue that the brain, like the rest of the fetus, develops slowly. There may not be a precise beginning, and even when brain waves are detected, much growth must occur before complex brain functions such as human thought and consciousness are possible.

- Weeks 12–16: "Quickening" (when fetal movements can be felt by the mother) occurs. Proponents for this stage say that quickening is indicative of self-initiated movement of the part of the fetus. Opponents argue that plants and animals also display self-initiated movement, but we do not grant them the moral rights of people.

- Weeks 20–28: "Viability" (fetal ability to live apart from the womb) occurs. Proponents for the fetus having moral rights at this stage argue that it is now potentially a separate being. If the fetus is removed from the womb at this point it is capable of living; therefore, to terminate the pregnancy, the fetus must not only be aborted, but also be destroyed or neglected (or not given the life support measures it needs and which we could supply). Proponents also claim that all of the development necessary to make a complete individual has now occurred. Opponents argue that viability is a relative term. Not only do different fetuses achieve it at different times, making it hard to determine when a particular fetus is viable, but also a fetus is only relatively capable of independent existence at this stage. No fetus would survive if it were delivered at this stage and not given life support. However, is it reasonable to tie moral rights to independence? How independent is a one-month-old? For that matter, we are all dependent to some extent on others. If moral rights were determined by independence, we would have to grant greater moral rights to Mennonites and farmers, and perhaps none at all to hospitalized patients.

- Weeks 28–40: Birth occurs. This is legally the beginning of human rights, and many people maintain it is also the correct point to grant moral rights. However, nature is inconsistent. Between premature births and overdue births, there can be two or even three months' difference in a baby's stage of development at the time of natural birth.

Determining when moral rights should be granted is crucial to the clash-of-rights arguments on abortion. If a fetus does not have moral rights until birth, then the mother's rights, and possibly the father's, are the only ones that need to be considered. If a fetus has moral rights as a person before birth, those rights must be taken into consideration at whatever stage they are granted. Extremists and moderates may still disagree on how much consideration should be given to the conflicting rights, however.

Extreme pro-abortionists claim that women have an absolute right over their own bodies, for the reasons previously argued. Extreme anti-abortionists use the sanctity-of-life argument, which claims that all human life is sacred, including that of a fetus, and must be protected from harm. They see abortion, even in the case of rape, as intentionally taking the life of an innocent person. The principles of non-maleficence (avoiding actions that will cause harm to others), beneficence (performing actions that benefit others) and equal consideration of interests (giving the interests of others the same moral importance that we give our own interests) all come into play here. Both of these positions are absolutist: abortion is either morally permissible or it is not, regardless of the situation or extenuating circumstances.

A relativist approach would be that sometimes abortion is morally permissible and sometimes it is not. One such argument would be that it is not morally permissible to have an abortion after a woman has given intentional (or implied) voluntary consent for the fetus to use her body, but it is permissible to have one if she did not give her permission. However, how do we define "giving permission"?

A more common relativist approach is that both the mother and the fetus have moral rights, but those rights must be weighed against each other. Each situation is different, and this gets us into consequence-based arguments. Before we go there, let's examine two other principle-based arguments: divine command theory and virtue ethics.

Divine command theory includes any arguments that appeal to a religious command regarding abortion. For example, interpreting the commandment "thou shalt not kill" as an indictment from God against abortion, as many anti-abortionists do, is a divine command argument. The strength of this argument, of course, lies in whether or not the recipient believes in a God, or in the same God, or interprets the religious quote in the same way. One could say, for example, that that command refers only to adult men, since women and children had no legal or moral rights when most of the major world religions were formed. It is important to note that there are both pro-abortionists and anti-abortionists who follow a religion, because religious precepts are interpreted differently by different people.

Virtue ethics would first of all say that a person who had virtuous habits would not find herself in the position of having to make such a decision, because virtuous habits (which does not necessarily mean sexual abstinence) do not lead to an unwanted pregnancy. Rape, of course, is the single exception to this position. However, supposing a follower of virtue ethics nevertheless found herself in this position, virtue ethics would require following the median way. A common moderate approach is that both the mother and the fetus have rights that must be considered. This argument usually grants a fetus evolving or increasing rights as it develops. In the first trimester, the rights of the fetus are given much less weight than those of the mother; in the second trimester, the weighting shifts so that only a very serious reason could justify terminating the pregnancy; in the final trimester, the rights of the mother and the fetus are nearly equal, so that abortion is only justified if the mother's own life is threatened.

Teleological Arguments

These are arguments that present the decision whether to have an abortion as a conflict of positive and negative consequences. When teleological arguments are used, all of the stakeholders must be considered: the pregnant woman, the father, the fetus, anyone else who will be affected by the decision and society as a whole. Consequence-based arguments can be used by those who take a relativist approach or those who take an absolutist approach.

Act-utilitarianism requires that each situation be considered independently, so that the happiness and harm for everyone involved in either course of action—continuing the pregnancy or ending it—can be weighed. Consequences of continuing the pregnancy for the mother could include loss of a job, financial problems, interrupted education, health considerations, the burden of caring for a child and other issues depending on the mother's situation. Good consequences should be considered also, such as the love and happiness a child could bring into her life. These must be weighed against the consequences of ending the pregnancy, which could include feelings of guilt or depression. The consequences for the fetus must also be weighed. An abortion would deny it life, but might also spare it from the burdens of poverty, being unwanted or having serious health issues (if it has a genetic illness or the mother is a substance abuser). Adoption, on the other hand, might resolve some of these issues. The consequences of either course of action for the father, grandparents and any others who will be affected by the decision must also be considered and weighed in the equation. Whichever course of action will cause the most happiness and least suffering to all concerned is the morally right choice; in some cases that will be abortion, and in others it will be carrying the child to term.

Rule-utilitarianism is more concerned with the long-term harms and benefits of abortion to society, and therefore takes a more absolutist approach. If the overall benefits to society of permitting abortions outweighs the harm done to society, then abortion is morally permissible; if the harms outweigh the benefits, it is not. For example, abortion robs society of the future contributions of those fetuses, while refusing abortions possibly robs society of contributions the mother might have made if she had to leave school. Legal abortions might also prevent the burden on society of caring for unwed mothers or seriously damaged infants or the horror of illegal backstreet abortions. The psychological effects on the society and its members of permitting versus abolishing abortion must also be considered. Arguments concerning the overall benefits and harms to society are very shaky, however, because of the obvious difficulty of getting any sound evidence to support them. Rule-utilitarianism involves the same considerations as enlightened self-interest, or social contract theory, in terms of determining what is in our collective best interest and is most likely to enable us to live together in peace.

EXERCISE 6.1

Evaluating Ethical Arguments

Consider the arguments for and against abortion. Without considering which position you agree with, simply examine the arguments themselves. List those from each side of the issue which you think are good, well-reasoned arguments.

1. _____
_____

2. _____
_____

3. _____
_____

4. _____
_____

For each one you chose, try to state clearly why you thought it was a good argument.

1. _____
_____

2. _____
_____

3. _____
_____

4. _____
_____

Now list some arguments from both sides which you did not find valid or convincing.

1. _____
_____

2. _____
_____

3. _____
_____

4. _____
_____

Why did you not think they were good arguments?

1. _____

_____

2. _____

_____

3. _____

_____

4. _____

_____

After you have written your answers, form small groups and discuss what you have written. Try to discuss the arguments and your opinions of them without choosing whether you are for or against abortion, or at least without letting the others in your group know your position on it. Concentrate only on the arguments themselves.

When the discussion time is over, review what you wrote previously on your own. Have you changed your mind about any of the arguments?

_____

_____

Now that you have carefully considered and discussed all of the moral arguments on abortion, what is your position on abortion?

_____

_____

Look at what you wrote at the beginning of this topic, before reading any of the ethical arguments. Has your position changed? _____
Why or why not?

_____

_____

If it has changed, how has it changed?

_____

_____

_____

Dr. Henry Morgentaler Case for Debate

Dr. Henry Morgentaler was instrumental in the fight against the therapeutic abortion law in Canada. Dr. Morgentaler, a Holocaust survivor, immigrated to Canada in 1950, and practiced family medicine in Montreal. In 1969, he gave up his family practice and began performing illegal abortions. For the next 19 years, "he endured several trials, numerous arrests, eight raids on his clinics, a firebombing and 10 months in jail. His legal battles have cost an estimated $2 million, mostly paid by supporters, except for $300,000 he covered himself." (Mallick, 2003) No jury has ever convicted Dr. Morgentaler; his jail sentence was the verdict of the Quebec Court of Appeal, in which five Roman Catholic judges overturned a jury's acquittal. When the Supreme Court struck down the therapeutic abortion law in 1988, Morgentaler says, "It was a vindication of everything I believed in. For the first time, it gave women the status of full human beings able to make decisions about their own lives." (Mallick, 2003) The prosecutor for the Supreme Court case, Alan Cooper, said, "I knew 90 per cent of Canada was against me. Dr. Morgentaler was like a national hero. Even devout Catholics were coming up to me during the trial and saying, 'How can you prosecute him?' Even my parents said that to me once." (Mallick, 2003)

Dr. Morgentaler was named to the Order of Canada on Canada Day, 2008. The decision caused some controversy; two previous recipients, Rev. Lucien Larre and the Madonna House Apostate on behalf of its deceased founder, Catherine de Hoeck Doherty, both returned their Order of Canada medals in protest. (Padwell, 2008)

EMBRYONIC STEM CELL RESEARCH AND CLONING

In order to explore the ethical issues involved in genetic research, we must first understand what genetic material is involved and how it is acquired. Stem cell research is an important aspect of regenerative medicine. The hope is that stem cells can be used to heal or regrow parts of the body that have been damaged by illness or in accidents. Currently, we graft skin or bones from another area of a victim's body onto the area where they are needed, or transplant healthy, functioning organs from another person. What if, instead, we could transplant cells that would grow into new skin, bone, muscle, lungs, heart, or whatever was needed? To do this, we would need cells that had the ability to become different body parts.

Stem cells are human cells that have not yet developed into specific tissue, such as lung, heart, skin, muscle, or bone. There are two types of stem cells: *multipotent* and *pluripotent*. Multipotent cells are only partially differentiated; this means they have the potential to become many things. Pluripotent stem cells, on the other hand, are not differentiated at all and can become any part of the human body. To be "differentiated" means to have begun to become a particular type of tissue.

Multipotent stem cells can be found in umbilical cord blood and in different parts of the adult body, including bone marrow, blood and the brain. What they have the potential to become depends on where they are found. Pluripotent stem cells can only be found in the blastocyst—the ball of cells that occurs five to ten days after an egg has been fertilized. Every cell in the inner mass of the blastocyst has the ability to become any part of a human body. After week two, the cells begin to differentiate—to become specifically lung tissue or bone tissue and so on, which is necessary for the blastocyst to develop into a human fetus. (The International Society for Stem Cell Research)

Cloning occurs when the nucleus of an unfertilized egg is removed and the nucleus of an adult cell is inserted in its place. The egg can then be stimulated into developing into an embryo because, unlike the unfertilized egg, the nucleus of an adult cell has a full chromosome count. The resulting blastocyst is genetically identical to the person (or animal) whose adult cell was used.

Applicable Canadian Laws

In October 2003 the Canadian House of Commons approved the Assisted Human Reproductive Law, which is based on the guidelines laid out by the Canadian Institute of Health Research (CIHR). This law permitted Canadian researchers to derive new cell lines from leftover, unwanted blastocysts from fertility clinics but not to clone embryos (perform nuclear transfers) for reproductive or research purposes, or to create chimeras (animals with human cells or organs). The CIHR has since produced the Updated Guidelines for Human Pluripotent Stem Cell Research (June 29, 2007). The guidelines follow six basic principles:

- research should have potential health benefits for Canadians
- free and informed voluntary consent must be given
- privacy and confidentiality must be respected
- no direct or indirect payments for tissues collected are permitted
- embryos may not be created for research purposes
- individual and community notions of human dignity and physical, spiritual and cultural integrity must be respected

The guidelines create a Stem Cell Oversight Committee to review all research proposals. Without the Committee's approval, no funding will be given. The guidelines also require all researchers to participate in a national registry of human embryonic stem cell lines generated in Canada and make them available to other researchers. This will reduce the number of cell lines needed for research purposes. The specific guidelines cover such things as requiring voluntary and informed consent and prohibiting commercial transactions or payments for the use of fetal tissue, amniotic fluid, umbilical cords and placentas, human somatic tissues or embryos originally created for reproductive purposes and no longer needed for that purpose. The guidelines also apply to Canadian research using lines developed outside of Canada.

Cloning research has been legal in Great Britain since 2001, but is not legal in Canada or the United States.

Ethical Arguments

Deontological Arguments

The main principle-based arguments against stem cell research are concerned with embryonic stem cells. Those who believe a fetus has moral rights as a human being from the moment of conception oppose the use of embryonic stem cells. This argument depends upon the legal and moral status of the blastocyst. If embryos have moral rights as people, then using them for research is treating them as means to our ends—medical knowledge and cures—rather than treating them as ends in themselves. This would be a Kantian argument against using embryonic stem cells, but it hangs on the premise that embryos are human beings. A second concern is how we acquire the fertilized embryos. Should we deliberately create fertilized embryos for research? Would we be creating a person for experimental purposes? Should we use aborted embryos? If we allow the use of aborted embryos, opponents offer a consequence-based concern: would that lead to encouraging or even paying women to abort?

Proponents of embryonic stem cell research argue that since the abortion of fetuses more developed than embryonic stem cells is legal, embryonic stem cell research should be allowed to proceed. Since the embryos and blastocysts which are used for research would be destroyed anyway, they are not being destroyed for research, but merely being used for a good purpose before they are destroyed. It is the same principle as using the organs of someone who is brain-dead, rather than letting them go to waste. A rights-based argument is that people have the right to donate their eggs or sperm, as they do their organs and bodies, for research or medical uses.

Divine command theory presents another argument: that in embryonic stem cell research and in reproductive cloning we run the risk of "playing God." This concern is motivated by religious convictions (only God has the right to create a human being), but it may also be motivated by human caution (we do not have the right or the wisdom to manipulate a human fetus and should not exert that kind of power over another human being).

A final argument against reproductive cloning is the fear that a cloned child could be exploited through being created for a specific purpose—either a social purpose (to meet a stated need for more soldiers, scientists, etc.) or a personal purpose. Already there have been cases where parents have selected a particular embryo from in vitro fertilization of their eggs and sperm because it was a genetic match for an ill child and could donate umbilical cord cells, blood or bone marrow to its sick older sibling. According to Kant, people must be treated as ends in themselves, not a means to other people's ends. Are cloned children ends in themselves or are they created as a means to someone else's end goal?

Teleological Arguments

The primary consequence-based argument in favour of stem cell research is that it will lead to new ways of relieving human suffering. By using stem cells to generate healthy tissue in place of diseased or malfunctioning tissues, stem cell research promises to find cures for illnesses such as Parkinson's disease, heart attacks, blood disorders and diabetes, as well as new ways to heal wounds, replace amputated limbs and heal spinal cord injuries. Stem cell cultures also allow researchers to observe the development of genetic diseases in order to learn how to arrest or reverse that development.

There are few ethical concerns with using adult stem cells or umbilical cord stem cells. These mostly involve getting voluntary, informed consent from the adult donor or the parents of the infant whose umbilical cord is being harvested. Adult stem cells have been successful in therapies for breast cancer, coronary artery diseases, leukemia and other blood disorders. Unfortunately, they are multipotent, which means their ability to produce different types of cells is limited. Umbilical cord stem cells have the same limitations, although these cells are less likely to be rejected by a recipient's body than adult cells from a foreign body. However, although there is a great supply of umbilical cords, the number of stem cells in each cord is limited, which increases the risk of rejection.

The same consequence-based argument applies to the use of embryonic stem cells. Embryonic stem cells from the blastocyst are the most versatile and vigorous stem cells, and therefore the most promising for regenerative medicine. Researchers hope to learn how to control their development in order to produce specific tissue, such as neurons to treat spinal cord injuries or insulin-producing pancreas cells. The main ethical issue in their use is the fact that they are taken from a fertilized embryo. If the embryo were placed in a womb, it would develop into a human being. Therefore, are we destroying a life as a consequence of using the stem cells from an embryo?

Currently, only embryos which have been created in fertility clinics and are not needed can be used for research in Canada. These embryos would be discarded in any case. However, will that always be the case? A consequence-based argument could be made against embryonic stem cell research along these lines. Will our research create a demand for embryonic stem cells, and where might that lead us? Would we encourage people to donate sperm and eggs for research or medical purposes? Would we encourage women to abort fetuses? Are we already starting down that path? From the point of view of act-utilitarianism one might argue that the happiness of all individuals cured of diseases or serious wounds would be greater than the unhappiness of the destroyed embryos—particularly if the embryos would have been destroyed in any case, or not created in the first case. If we consider rule-utilitarianism, would the potential long-term benefit to society of increased genetic knowledge and medical cures be greater than the potential harm of using human embryos?

Why or why not?

An argument for enlightened self-interest would be that it is in our own best interests to donate blastocysts for research to cure diseases we may someday suffer from. A similar, broader argument is that it is the responsibility of the government to act in the best interests of the people it governs, and it is in our best interests that stem cell research, including embryonic stem cells, is legal and supported with government funding.

Another ethical issue is the use of animals in human stem cell research. Before we use the results of our research to create tissues or organs on humans, we would need to test them on animals, which will result in the creation of chimeras. Is it ethical to produce human-animal hybrids? Presumably this could produce sentient sheep, for example, if human cells were permitted to become part of their brains. Moreover, if a chimera reproduced, and the human cells had invaded its sperm or eggs, a human being could be born.

Human cloning has its own set of ethical issues. Cloning can be done for therapeutic or for reproductive purposes. Therapeutic cloning would solve the problem of immunological rejection by a patient's body. The regenerative tissues created by stem cell research could be "personalized" by inserting a nucleus from one of the patient's own cells into the stem cell before stimulating it to become a certain type of tissue that the patient needs. It would then not be rejected as foreign tissue by his body. Another advantage of patient-specific stem cells is that researchers could observe the progress of a disease from its early stages to learn more about why and how the tissues malfunction. The ethical arguments for and against therapeutic cloning are the same as those for embryonic stem cell research—that an embryo has moral rights. In this case, we are not only using a fertilized egg which would otherwise have been discarded, we are actually creating one in order to use it. Even for medical purposes, this is morally questionable to many people.

Reproductive cloning produces genetically identical individuals through the transfer of the nucleus of one adult cell into an egg and allowing that egg to develop. Identical twins are natural genetic clones. Numerous animals have been cloned in the past two decades, and they have also been allowed to reproduce naturally. Many of the cloned creatures have suffered abnormalities and early deaths, however. Advocates for reproductive cloning claim that it is similar to accepted reproductive technologies such as in vitro fertilization and artificial insemination. They also claim that we already defy or alter the natural course of human life and genetics by curing illnesses and with other scientific advances, so cloning is just another method of doing so. Opponents claim that cloning may cause damage to the child as it has to cloned animals, and that cloning is an unnatural and "asexual" (non-sexual) method of reproduction.

Long-term consequence-based arguments claim that we do not know where cloning could lead us, both socially and genetically. This concern is met with the response that humans, like all life forms, are always changing and adapting. We have already undergone social and genetic changes which adapt us to live in the current technological era.

EXERCISE 6.2

Evaluating Ethical Arguments

Research into stem cells and cloning has an enormous potential to improve and extend human lives; it also presents some very serious ethical concerns, now and in the future. Do you think the benefits are worth the risks for the following research?

Stem cell research on adult and umbilical cord cells?

_____

Why or why not?

_____

_____

_____

Embryonic stem cell research?

_____

Why or why not?

_____

_____

_____

_____

Therapeutic cloning?

_____

Why or why not?

_____

_____

_____

_____

Reproductive cloning?

_____

Why or why not?

_____

_____

_____

_____

After you have written your answers, form small groups and discuss your answers together.

When the discussion time is over, review what you wrote previously on your own. Have you changed your mind about any of the arguments?

_____

_____

_____

_____

EUTHANASIA AND PHYSICIAN-ASSISTED SUICIDE

Euthanasia comes from the Greek roots *eu*, meaning good or happy, and *thanatos*, meaning death. What would you consider to be a "good death"?

You probably listed such things as painless, easy, quick, and perhaps expected (a death that came after you had time to prepare yourself, to say your good-byes and settle your affairs) or sudden (if you would prefer not to know in advance). Ideally, euthanasia is intended to be painless, easy, quick and expected—all elements of a good death. And yet the controversy around euthanasia goes all the way back to the dawn of medicine, in the Hippocratic Oath, which states, "I will give no deadly medicine to any one if asked, nor suggest any such counsel." Why is there so much disagreement about euthanasia? Before we answer that, we must be clear about what euthanasia is.

Euthanasia is the deliberate killing of another, dependent person by an action or by the omission of an action, for that person's alleged benefit. The four significant concepts here are:

- deliberate
- killing
- by action or omission
- for the person's benefit

These concepts will be described in reverse order.

First, euthanasia must be intended to benefit the person who dies. The purpose of euthanasia is to relieve that person's suffering, and the suffering should be sufficiently serious to warrant it. This is why it is called a good death, and not simply murder. Many of the ethical arguments for and against euthanasia, which we will discuss later, are related to this concept of beneficial intent and the difficulty of deciding what is in a person's best interest.

Second, a death is only considered euthanasia if it is directly caused by an action or an omitted action by someone else. *Active euthanasia*, also referred to as mercy killing or assisted suicide, occurs when some death-causing means are used. Giving someone a lethal injection or suffocating her are examples of mercy killing; providing someone with the means of killing himself, such as a "peace pill" which will cause his death, but letting him take it himself, is assisted suicide. In both cases, the action directly causes the death. The difference between mercy killing and assisted suicide is sometimes blurred. In September, 2004, a Montreal woman, Marielle Houle, helped her son, who was in the early stages of multiple sclerosis, to commit suicide. After he took a cocktail of drugs he found on the Internet, she put a plastic bag over his head and asphyxiated him. Her action merely assisted him in his goal of suicide, but it also was a direct cause of his death. In January, 2006, Houle was convicted of assisting in suicide but only sentenced to three years of probation. (Toronto *Star*, Jan. 27, 2006)

Passive euthanasia occurs when some treatment or assistance necessary to maintain the person's life, such as a respirator or a feeding tube, is withheld or removed. The patient dies because he cannot breathe, or cannot feed himself; the omission or withdrawal of assistance is at most an indirect cause of death. Passive euthanasia is often referred to as euthanasia by omission or "letting nature take its course."

Third, euthanasia only occurs when a person who was alive dies as the result of the action or omission. Removing a person who has been declared dead from artificial life support is not euthanasia because the person is already dead. The question that arises here is how and when we define death. At one time breathing was thought to indicate life, so people would hold a mirror to the person's mouth to see if he was still breathing and thus still alive. The temperature of the body remains warm until rigor mortis sets in, so people would feel the body to see if it was still warm. Now we have machines which can perform many functions for patients, either short-term while they recover or indefinitely; so the question of whether a person is alive or dead is more difficult. The current criterion is that a person is legally dead if she has permanently lost all detectable brain function. However, people in a coma or in a persistent vegetative state (PVS) are not brain dead. People in a coma are alive but unconscious, and can remain in that state for months or even years. In both a prolonged coma and in PVS, the cerebral cortex no longer functions but the brain stem continues to function. Respiratory and heart rate functions, facial reflexes and swallowing are all brain stem activities and can continue for years, even though the cerebral cortex is dead and the person will never regain consciousness. If we use the criterion of whole brain death, then such people are still alive; often the only intervention they need is a feeding tube. Because they are alive, removing the feeding tube is an act of passive euthanasia.

Fourth, the person's death must be the desired outcome for an action to be considered euthanasia. Not commencing treatment because it is believed that the treatment will not benefit a person or withdrawing treatment because it appears to be ineffective or too much of a burden to the patient are not euthanasia, even if the patient dies afterwards, because they were not done for the deliberate purpose of causing the death. Nor is administering high doses of painkiller, if the dosage is warranted, even if the physician knows the patient may die from the high dose, and the patient does in fact do so. This is referred to as the *double effect principle*. The intended effect of the painkiller is to relieve the patient's pain. The second, unintended effect is that the patient dies. If the desired effect of an action (or of the omission of an action) is sound medical practice (such as providing pain relief) and the action is necessary (a lower amount will not relieve the patient's pain) and the benefit outweighs the harm (relieving the pain of a terminal patient could be argued to be a greater benefit than the harm to the patient of dying earlier due to the painkiller) then it is not euthanasia. Of course, if a full recovery was expected and the patient was eager to live, then the benefit of relieving the pain completely would not outweigh the harm of causing death. The issue here is, how can we know what the real intention of another person is? Although the physician must be able to prove that the action or omission was medically justified, in an article in *Maclean's* magazine hospital staff acknowledged that euthanasia was being practiced in Canadian hospitals through the use of high doses of narcotic analgesics such as morphine. These are given to alleviate pain in terminal patients, but with the full knowledge that they will also cause the patient to die sooner. (Hawaleshka, 2005)

Euthanasia can be voluntary or non-voluntary. *Voluntary euthanasia* occurs when a mentally competent adult knowingly and freely asks to be helped to die. The patient makes the choice for himself. *Non-voluntary euthanasia* occurs when the person did not ask or consent to euthanasia. This does not mean that it was done against his will, only that others had to make the choice for him. Assisted suicide is necessarily voluntary because only the means of accomplishing it are provided; the patient must press the button or take the pill herself. Mercy killing and letting nature take its course may or may not be done with the voluntary consent of the patient. The difference between voluntary and involuntary euthanasia sounds quite clear, and often it is; but there are many situations where it is less clear. Someone who is in a coma or a persistent vegetative state cannot give her consent, even though euthanasia may be what she would want if she could. Nor can children or those who are mentally incompetent, as was the case with Tracy Latimer, whom we discussed earlier in this textbook.

People who think they may not be able to give consent when it is needed may choose to give consent in advance. A living will or advance directive is a written statement that indicates what a person wants done for her in certain medical circumstances. It must be composed while the person is mentally competent and able to communicate her wishes, and although it is not binding when the time comes, it is the equivalent of given consent. Terminally ill patients are often asked to make a statement to this effect when they enter a hospital, in case the need for extraordinary measures arises. They may also request a "do not resuscitate" (DNR) order on their charts, which will inform caretakers to let the person die if, for example, he stops breathing or his heart stops beating.

These directives will not result in mercy killing or assisted suicide, but may result in a natural death or in preventing the use of "extraordinary" or "heroic" measures. Extraordinary measures are medical interventions which are likely to be ineffective, are considered too burdensome for the patient, or in which the burden is disproportionately higher than the benefits. An ordinary intervention, on the other hand, is some act or treatment which has a good chance of benefiting the patient or resolving a life-threatening condition, so that its benefits outweigh any burdens it imposes on a patient. The same treatment may be considered heroic or extraordinary in one situation, say in being used to revive a terminally ill patient who will suffer more than she will benefit by the treatment—but could be considered ordinary in another situation, as in being used to revive a 26-year-old who was injured in an accident but is likely to recover if resuscitated. It is the situation, not the treatment, which determines whether the action is ordinary or extraordinary.

This, of course, poses the problem of evaluating the situation and determining the benefits and burdens of a procedure for another person. Not only can we not be sure what another person would consider too great a burden or too little a benefit, but we can not always know the precise result of a treatment. A blood transfusion may be effective in treating one person and less effective on another, for no known or predictable reason, and long-term benefits are even more difficult to predict. Furthermore, drugs and medical technologies are all experimental or extraordinary in the beginning, and become ordinary practices with use over time.

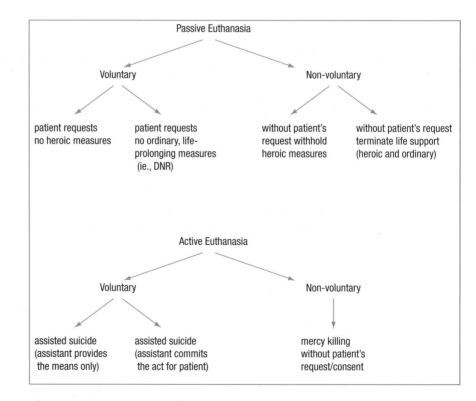

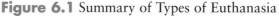

Figure 6.1 Summary of Types of Euthanasia

Applicable Canadian Laws

Suicide was decriminalized in Canada in 1972. Actively and intentionally assisting someone in suicide, however, is still illegal. Euthanasia is also illegal in Canada, despite the fact that a majority of Canadians believe that in some situations it is not morally wrong. In a 1999 Gallup Poll, Canadians were asked, "When a person has an incurable disease that is immediately life-threatening and causes the person to experience great suffering, do you or do you not think that competent doctors should be allowed by law to end the patient's life through mercy killing, if the patient has made a formal request in writing?" Seventy-seven percent of respondents considered mercy killing morally acceptable in this situation, and fifty-seven percent still considered it acceptable if the disease was incurable but not immediately life-threatening.

(Edwards and Mazzuca, 1999)

Three sections of the criminal code are relevant to the legal status of euthanasia:

Section 14. No person is entitled to consent to have death inflicted on him, and such consent does not affect the criminal responsibility of any person by whom death may be inflicted on the person by whom consent is given.

Section 241. Everyone who (a) counsels a person to commit suicide or (b) aids or abets a person to commit suicide, whether suicide ensues or not, is guilty of an indictable offence and liable to imprisonment for a term not exceeding fourteen years.

Section 215. Everyone is under a legal duty ... (c) to provide necessaries of life to a person under his charge if that person is unable, by reason of detention, age, illness, mental disorder or other cause, to withdraw himself from that charge and is unable to provide himself with the necessaries of life.

(Department of Justice Canada)

Under sections 14 and 241, all forms of mercy killing and active euthanasia, voluntary and involuntary, are illegal and a criminal offense. Under section 215, passive euthanasia, including withholding or withdrawing life-sustaining measures, is illegal, and doctors who do so could be charged with abandoning their patient. They are also under a legal obligation to prevent patients from harming themselves, which includes committing suicide.

On the other hand, Canadians have the right, under the Charter of Rights and Freedoms, to security of person, or autonomy. Under health care informed consent laws, Canadians can refuse medical care or decide which medical treatments they will accept or reject. This is where DNR and advance directive statements concerning heroic measures or specific treatments come in: any patient who is judged competent can refuse, or withdraw prior consent for, any treatment, either ordinary or extraordinary.

Ethical Arguments

Euthanasia, like abortion, is an issue many people have strong feelings about. Before we begin to discuss the various moral arguments surrounding euthanasia, what is your personal opinion about euthanasia?

Just as you did for abortion, imagine that you can leave your initial opinion about euthanasia here on this piece of paper, separate from you, for now. Try to read this section as though you have no opinion at all on euthanasia, but are simply trying to understand the ways other people think about it.

Deontological Arguments

Principle-based arguments for euthanasia usually focus on people's right to autonomy. If a person knows what he is doing (is mentally and emotionally competent) and his action is not harming anyone else, then he should have the right to decide for himself on matters that affect his life. This is similar to the argument for abortion—that we have an absolute right over our own bodies. A related argument is that our human rights guarantee us the right to freedom, which includes the freedom to choose whether to live or die. Another phrase sometimes used is the right to "die with dignity," implying that euthanasia and mercy killing are more dignified than a slow death in which the patient lingers for days or weeks in pain or in a morphine-induced "drugged state."

The argument against autonomy in cases of euthanasia is that in the situation of having to make such a decision, a person's mental and emotional competence is compromised by several factors. She may be experiencing extreme pain and fear, she may not completely understand her condition, and she doesn't know how the disease will progress in her particular case because no doctor can predict that with certainty. A decision made out of fear or without full knowledge is not an expression of autonomy. As we discussed under Socrates' theory of the healthy soul, we are not in control of ourselves (autonomy) when our emotional or physical elements override our reason. For example, people may ask for assisted suicide at a low point in their lives when they really mean it as a cry for help or an attempt to learn whether others still value them. When someone says his life is worthless, agreeing with him is not compassionate. A compassionate response would be to assure him that his life is important and to provide assistance and counselling and positive solutions to improve his situation.

Even if a patient's request to die is sincere, suicidal wishes are more often than not temporary. "Of those who attempt suicide but are stopped, less than four percent go on to kill themselves in the next five years; less than eleven percent will commit suicide over the next 35 years." (Suicide Factsheets, NRLC Dept. of Medical Ethics)

Another argument made against the right-to-autonomy claim is that euthanasia is not about the right to die; we already have that. Suicide is not illegal in Canada. It is the person who is performing euthanasia who will be granted a new right if euthanasia is legalized. Euthanasia is about the right to kill someone else. Whether the intent is altruistic or selfish, and regardless of having or not having the consent of the victim, the right to kill is very different from the right to die. Involuntary euthanasia, even for the best of reasons, is the opposite of autonomy; it is the height of medical paternalism.

Kant's famous phrase, "an *ought* implies a *can*," expresses the concept that we cannot be ethical (do what we ought to do) without having freedom to choose (we *can* act however we want). In other words, if there is a particular way we ought to behave (tell the truth), there must be other ways we can behave (we can choose to lie). Making moral choices requires the ability to make choices. This has been used as an argument for giving patients the choice of euthanasia. However, Kant's categorical imperative is not contradicted either way: if everyone could always choose euthanasia for themselves, the purpose of allowing euthanasia is not contradicted or nullified, because everyone in the world would not immediately ask to be euthanized. On the other hand, if no one could ever choose euthanasia, the purpose of refusing it is also not contradicted. This puts euthanasia in the realm of a morally permissible act, rather than a morally required or morally prohibited act. Kant, however, with his strict code of duty, did not consider an act based on self-gratification to have any moral worth. As we discussed when examining Kantian ethics, even helping others is not a moral act if it gives the person pleasure to do it; only acts done strictly out of duty are moral acts. Therefore, suicide or euthanasia are only ethical if they are done with right intent, out of a sense of duty. What is the argument for duty? The physician, friend or family member who performs euthanasia by assisting another person's suicide is morally justified, according to Kantian ethics, only if she is acting out of a duty to care for the other, and not for any personal reason, such as her own relief at not having to watch the other person suffer.

How do you think this argument affects the case of Tracy Latimer, which we discussed earlier?

_____

_____

_____

To decide this, we would have to know Robert Latimer's will, or intent, in killing his daughter. Did he do it because he believed it was his duty as a parent to spare his child from suffering, or to spare himself from watching her suffer? Often we act out of several intertwined motives, so that it is hard to know our own primary motive, let alone someone else's.

Following the same Kantian argument, a person is not morally justified in requesting euthanasia for merely personal reasons, such as relief from mental or physical suffering or a prideful desire not to be dependent on others. He is only morally justified if he does it out of a will to do his duty. The argument for the duty to die applies to situations in which continuing to live will place significant burdens on others, or on society. These burdens may be emotional (forcing loved-ones and caregivers to watch him suffer), physical (when extensive care-giving is required or others must sacrifice their time or their life plans), or financial. According to bioethicist John Hardwig, "A duty to die becomes greater as you grow older. As we age we will be giving up less by giving up our lives ... to have reached the age of say, seventy-five or eighty years without being ready to die is itself a moral failing, the sign of a life out of touch with life's basic realities." Another bioethicist, Margaret Pabst Battin, claimed that those living in rich countries have a moral obligation to "conserve health care resources by forgoing treatment or directly ending (their) life" in order to promote world equality. (Discovery Institute, Bioethics)

The argument given against the duty to die, at the individual level, is that, in fact, we have a duty to *not* commit suicide, because suicide has a devastating effect on those left behind and offers a bad example of how to cope with problems, particularly for young people. A social argument against the duty-to-die principle is that in a society which accepts this principle, instead of having to justify suicide and euthanasia as we do now, people will be forced to justify continuing to live, especially if they are dependent on others. These are both consequence-based arguments and will be discussed later, but they arise from the principle of a duty to die.

Divine command theory arguments are generally opposed to euthanasia. Every major religion has an injunction against committing suicide and killing others. This is based on the concept that God gave us life and it is up to Him, not us, to end it. The sanctity of life argument is also often brought up under divine command theory. This argument states that human life is sacred, or holy, and we should treat it with reverence. Those who hold this view claim that euthanasia devalues human life. Because human life is sacred, every life is worth living, regardless of a person's physical or mental condition; no one can decide that his or another person's life is not worth living.

Similar to the argument for the sanctity of life is the argument that a person's life has intrinsic value: it is good and worthwhile for its own sake. This view can be a part of divine command theory, or it can be held separately by those who do not follow a religion but nevertheless believe in the intrinsic value of human life. According to this point of view, arguments for euthanasia based on a poor quality of life incorrectly imply that human life is only valuable because of the things it allows us to do; when we cannot do those external things, life is no longer worthwhile. If, for example, a paraplegic is justified in wanting to die because the quality of his life is unacceptable, are we to assume that walking is what makes human life valuable? If mental impairment, either from birth or as the result of an accident, justifies a desire for euthanasia, is IQ what makes life valuable? If so, what level of IQ is necessary? Was Mother Teresa's life less worthwhile than Einstein's because she was less brilliant intellectually? Thousands of people whose lives she improved would not agree with that.

Virtue ethics requires that a life be based on virtuous habits, so the question here is, is it virtuous to commit suicide? Not is it morally acceptable or a basic human right, but is it a virtuous characteristic? If patience and endurance and courage are virtuous habits, it is hard to include suicide as a means of avoiding a difficult or painful situation as being equally virtuous. The arguments for a duty to die might have more weight in virtue ethics, but there would be no virtue in imposing a duty to die on someone else. Encouraging someone else to die, or helping him to do so, because you thought it was his duty is not a virtuous act. There may be some virtue in self-sacrifice, but there is no virtue in sacrificing someone else for your beliefs. That leads us to the second question that arises from this issue: is it virtuous to ask someone to help you do something illegal and emotionally difficult? Here, virtue ethics would have to respond that euthanasia is wrong because it is unfair and unethical to ask someone else to kill you. Virtue ethics also looks for a median way. An argument could be made that the median way between too much compassion (mercy killing or non-voluntary euthanasia) and too little (heroic life-support or repeated resuscitations when there is no hope) would be allowing a natural death (passive euthanasia) for terminal diseases. This is not to say it is the only virtuous decision in such a case; heroic measures could buy a person two or more years of life if a terminal disease goes into temporary remission as a result, and that, too, would be virtuous. Another median way might be the double effect, where enough pain relief to be effective is given despite the fact that the patient may die sooner because of it.

Teleological Arguments

Consequence-based arguments for euthanasia and mercy killing are concerned with increasing happiness by relieving physical and/or emotional pain and suffering, and providing an alternative when someone believes his quality of life is no longer acceptable. According to act-utilitarianism, keeping a suffering person alive merely prolongs her agony, and the suffering of those who love her, and is therefore neither compassionate nor ethical. If death is the best outcome in a particular situation, the means to that outcome are not important, unless the method made a difference to those involved. In other words, if the unhappiness caused by watching a loved one die could only be alleviated by the person's death, then whether the death comes about by lethal injection (active euthanasia) or removing the patient from life support (passive euthanasia), and whether it is voluntary or non-voluntary makes little difference, unless the method itself caused further unhappiness. For example, if active euthanasia caused the person who did it to suffer punishment, or non-voluntary euthanasia caused feelings of guilt, then the overall happiness would be greater only if passive, voluntary euthanasia were used. Sometimes a person's last days provide a time for understanding and reconciliation with loved ones and for spiritual and emotional growth. Having this time would increase the happiness of the patient and those left behind. In these examples, euthanasia would be wrong because a quick and early death would not be the outcome that would produce the most happiness.

The argument against using act-utilitarianism in general to resolve this issue is the difficulty of restricting a moral choice to a specific situation. When a decision is made in one situation, it tends to set a precedent, or an example of what should be done in similar situations. Sidney Callahan, an outspoken feminist, compares legalizing euthanasia to the legalization of abortion: "It is instructive also to look at the way abortion moved from being approved of as a tragic choice in exceptional cases to becoming a routinized necessity with only the most perfunctory of counseling or alternatives offered to women. Individual choices have a way of quickly becoming routine procedures in the larger institutions of society." (Callahan, 1999)

Rule-utilitarianism is concerned with making policies that will increase the overall happiness of a society. Therefore it is not concerned about individual situations but about setting rules and the effects those rules will have on everyone involved. Would legalizing euthanasia produce more happiness for more people in a society than prohibiting it would? In order to decide this, we must examine the potential outcomes of legalizing euthanasia and mercy killing.

One argument for euthanasia is that it frees up funds to help more people. It is a strain on our health care system to have dying patients taking up hospital beds, needing the time and care of doctors and nurses and requiring expensive medications and equipment. If a patient wants to die, the argument goes, why are we expending valuable resources keeping him alive against his will? It will produce more happiness for more people to spend our health care dollars on vaccinations, health centres, early diagnostic equipment and treatments for illnesses and injuries that can be cured instead of spending money on palliative care and treatment for hopeless cases.

Rule-utilitarian arguments against euthanasia claim that legalizing it may lead to abuse, exploitation and erosion of care for the most vulnerable members of our society. This is sometimes called a "slippery slope argument," because it says if we allow this, we will start to slide down a slippery slope toward allowing more and more things which we don't want at all. The slippery slope argument only works if it can be proved that the first step (allowing euthanasia) will actually lead to the others (abuse, exploitation and erosion of care). The three allegations will be examined in turn.

Abuse. Euthanasia is usually advocated for competent adults who can give informed consent and who are terminally ill and suffering great pain. However, once legalized, these requirements are often abused or ignored. Restricting euthanasia to competent adults 18 or older has been argued as being discriminatory on the basis of age. In Holland, where euthanasia is legal, a child of 16 can legally request assisted suicide and a child as young as 12 can request it with parental consent. The requirement of a terminal illness, which usually applies to someone with a life expectancy of six months (although doctors cannot accurately predict when a person might die) is often stretched to include an incurable illness, physical or mental deterioration, a meaningless or worthless life or a quality of life that is no longer acceptable, which may be stretched to include anyone who is suicidal. The problem with changing "terminal" to "incurable" is that it does not take into account the possibility of new cures or unexpected remissions, and either of these could happen in time to save even a terminally ill patient, let alone a disabled or suffering patient who is not immediately in danger of dying. The problem with including physical or mental deterioration is that it is an imprecise term, since we all deteriorate with age. As for including a life that is worthless or of an unacceptable quality, by what criteria do we judge that? Most physically and mentally handicapped people think their life is worth living, and those who don't may simply need time to adjust to their condition. No one wants to force another person to endure severe pain, but since physical and emotional pain are both treatable, granting euthanasia rather than treating the pain can be considered an abusive act.

Furthermore, voluntary euthanasia is argued to lead to involuntary euthanasia. Euthanasia could become a means of lowering health care costs. Will hospital staff begin encouraging patients to accept euthanasia, if it is available, to save money and resources for the hospital? Hospital stays are being shortened in Canada, but home care and hospice care for the sick and elderly has not been proportionately increased. If euthanasia is legalized, the concern is that pressure will be put on some patients to take that route. Euthanasia would predominantly affect the old, the poor and unemployed, the mentally or physically disabled, and the mentally or physically infirm. These are not the people who are lobbying for the right to it. The result could be involuntary euthanasia, and a stretching of the requirements for euthanasia. This is already happening in some countries where euthanasia is legal.

A national study undertaken by the Dutch government in September 1991 found that 9.1 percent of annual deaths were physician-induced. Some 2,300 of those were voluntary euthanasia, 400 were assisted suicide and 1,040 were non-voluntary euthanasia. The majority of the deaths were not officially reported as euthanasia. A second study done five years later showed similar results. As a result, the Dutch parliament legalized euthanasia and assisted suicide in 2001. Within a week of the law passing, the Health Minister requested that Parliament approve a "suicide pill" for healthy people who wish to die and for the elderly if they are tired of life. In 2004, a report commissioned by the Royal Dutch Medical Association argued that euthanasia should be provided for anyone who wanted it. Three months later, the University Medical Center Groningen admitted that it was euthanizing infants who had spina bifida and other disabilities. (International Task Force on Euthanasia and Assisted Suicide, prepared for the World Medical Association) "The fundamental question about euthanasia: whether it is a libertarian movement for human freedom and the right of choice, or an aggressive drive to exterminate the weak, the old, and the different. This question can now be answered. It is both." Richard Fenigsen, Dutch cardiologist. (Quotations on Euthanasia)

Exploitation. If euthanasia becomes acceptable, many will be made to feel guilty for not taking it. Depressed, sick, elderly and dependent people are all very susceptible to emotional, psychological and financial pressures, and their susceptibility can be exploited to coerce them into agreeing to euthanasia even if they do not want it. Dependency is particularly hard on women, many of whom spend their lives caring for others and see themselves now as a burden to those they have always cared for. (Euthanasia and Women, June 2003) In Oregon, where euthanasia is legal, the third annual report on deaths under the Oregon assisted suicide law showed that "in 63% of the deaths reported, fear of being a burden was expressed as a reason for requesting assisted suicide." As was mentioned previously, in a society which accepts euthanasia, people will feel they have to justify continuing to live, and those who are dependent on others and are not able to contribute to society for whatever reason may have trouble doing so.

The State of Alaska's argument against assisted suicide directly confronts the concern about exploitation. It states: "The terminally ill are a class of persons who need protection from family, social, and economic pressures, and who are often particularly vulnerable to such pressures because of chronic pain, depression, and the effects of medication." (Sampson et al. v State of Alaska, 09/21/2001)

Erosion of care. Physician-assisted suicide, even if it is voluntary, directly defies the "first, do no harm" principle of medical care. The physician is doing something that will cause a patient's death. This will result in a lack of patient trust in their doctors. Furthermore, if a physician withholds extraordinary measures from a patient she considers hopeless, she may withhold them from someone who could have been saved. We don't know a case is hopeless until we have tried everything and it has all failed.

Euthanasia is not necessary because there are alternatives, opponents argue. Pain medication can control the suffering, and hospice or palliative care can provide a natural death with dignity. This type of care focuses on providing comfort, relief from pain and emotional support rather than curing a patient. We need to improve our standards of care, but legalizing euthanasia will do the opposite because it will make an easier alternative available.

In Holland, little effort has been put into improving treatments for pain and other symptoms. This suggests that legalizing euthanasia might weaken society's commitment to expand services and resources for caring for the elderly and the terminally ill, or to finance research into geriatrics and fatal illnesses.

In response to these possible negative consequences of legalizing euthanasia, the question to be asked is, would we slide down that slope? Are there basic differences between Canada and Holland that would protect us from these outcomes? An opposing argument to the slippery-slope argument would be that legal protections can be put in place to prevent the negative consequences that would follow from legalizing euthanasia.

What protections or limitations do you think should be put into place if euthanasia were legalized in Canada?

_____

_____

_____

How likely do you think it is that those limitations would remain in force in Canada?

_____

_____

In rule-utilitarianism, all of the possible outcomes of legalizing euthanasia must be weighed against the possible outcomes of continuing to prohibit it, in order to determine which course would produce the most happiness for the most people in our society.

Enlightened self-interest could put forth arguments for either side of the question. On one hand, it might be in our own best interests to have the freedom to make the decision to live or die, and to seek the help of a physician to do either, without intending any harm to those who are ill, disabled and susceptible to coercion. On the other hand, it might be in our best interests to be protected against non-voluntary euthanasia by prohibiting it, even if some people are denied voluntary euthanasia because of it.

Which do you think is in your best interests?

_____

_____

Why?

_____

_____

_____

Sue Rodrigues Case for Debate

Sue Rodrigues was a Canadian woman in Victoria, B.C., who was diagnosed with Amyotrophic Lateral Sclerosis (ALS) or Lou Gehrig's disease in 1991. ALS affects the nerves, causing a progressive paralysis which shuts down all body functions until death occurs. Rodrigues did not want to suffer through the last stages of the disease, or put her family through caring for her at the end, but she also did not want to end her life before she reached that stage. However, by that time, she knew she would be unable to commit the act herself. She argued in court for the right to a physician-assisted suicide. Her case went all the way to the Supreme Court of Canada, where it was denied in a 5–4 ruling in September 1993. The Court explained its decision as a concern for "the young, the innocent, the mentally incompetent and the depressed." (Wood, 1994) In February, 1994, Sue Rodrigues died in her home with the help of a physician who, at her request, was never named.

EXERCISE 6.3

Evaluating Ethical Arguments

Consider the arguments for and against euthanasia. Without considering which position you agree with, simply examine the arguments themselves. List those from each side of the issue which you think are good, well-reasoned arguments.

1. _____

   _____

2. _____

   _____

3. _____

   _____

4. _____

   _____

For each one you chose, try to state clearly why you thought it was a good argument.

1. _____

   _____

2. _____

   _____

3. _____

   _____

4. _____

   _____

Now list some arguments from both sides which you did not find valid or convincing.

1. _____

   _____

2. _____

   _____

3. _____

   _____

(Continued)

(Continued)

  4. _____

_____

Why did you not think they were good arguments?

  1. _____

_____

  2. _____

_____

  3. _____

_____

  4. _____

_____

Discuss your answers with other students. After you have considered and discussed all of the moral arguments on euthanasia, what is your position?

_____

_____

_____

_____

Look at what you wrote at the beginning of this topic before reading any of the ethical arguments. Has your position changed? _____
Why or why not?

_____

_____

_____

If it has changed, how has it changed?

_____

_____

_____

Self-reflection

What would you say to a person who was considering euthanasia or assisted suicide if the person:

1. Was terminally ill and in constant pain?

_____

_____

2. Was seriously but not terminally ill or in pain, yet decided her life was not worth living?

_____

_____

3. Was 85 years old and tired of living but not ill?

_____

_____

4. Was 35 years old and tired of living but not ill?

_____

_____

5. Was 18 years old and physically healthy but did not want to live?

_____

_____

_____

6. Was 18 years old and severely physically disabled but not in pain or terminally ill?

_____

_____

7. Was married and had young children and suffered from depression?

_____

_____

8. Lived alone with no dependents or close family and was depressed?

_____

_____

Do you think that assisted suicide should be allowed in some, all or none of these situations?

_____

Why or why not?

1. _____
   _____
   _____

2. _____
   _____
   _____

3. _____
   _____
   _____

4. _____
   _____
   _____

5. _____
   _____
   _____

6. _____
   _____
   _____

7. _____
   _____
   _____

8. _____
   _____
   _____

MULTICULTRALISM, DISCRIMINATION, RACISM AND MINORITY RIGHTS

Canada is a multicultural country. Multiculturalism is not only a reference to our two official cultures, English Protestant and French Roman Catholic, or to Aboriginal languages and culture, but to all of the cultural heritages brought into our country by immigrants. Multiculturalism is an attitude as much as it is a federal policy. The United States, for example, has the same variety of immigrants, but it is considered a "melting pot" while we are a "mosaic." In the U.S., many different heritages are expected to enter the melting pot and emerge American. The U.S. may be made up of different peoples, but its intent is to be a one-culture nation: American culture. In Canada, immigrants are not expected to "melt away" their cultural heritage, but to add it to the mosaic of cultures that make up Canada, enriching our nation by the addition. Because our intent is to be multicultural, discrimination and racism are not only offenses against the groups they target; they are also an attack on what we stand for as a nation.

Discrimination is the result of prejudice and stereotypical thinking. Prejudice means pre-judging a person or event, based on opinions that are held before meeting the person or hearing the facts about the event. Usually, when we say someone is prejudiced, we mean he has already formed an opinion based on faulty reasoning such as stereotypical thinking.

A stereotype is a false, exaggerated or misleading opinion about a specific group of people, such as women, teenagers, homeless people, blacks, Muslims, etc. It is called a stereotype because it views all the members of that group as being a certain "type" of people. Generally, stereotypes focus on negative characteristics, maintaining that members of that group are intellectually or physically inferior, morally weak, cowardly, etc, as compared to members of one's own group. At best, stereotypes are "affectionately" patronizing (the helpless female who needs to be taken care of); at worst, they are hateful and dangerous (the job-stealing, man-hating "feminists" who need to be eliminated).

Stereotypical thinking, or thinking based on stereotypes, is foolish because it results in false conclusions. People are individuals, each with a unique set of characteristics, regardless of their social group. Deciding that all blacks are less intelligent than whites, or that all teenagers are troublemakers or all Muslims are terrorists is simply wrong and makes the person who thinks so look foolish. Stereotyping is harmful in a multicultural nation like Canada because it divides people into separate groups and discourages empathy between people who belong to different groups. Empathy is the ability to identify emotionally with the feelings of another person. People who cannot emotionally identify with others are more likely to discriminate against them and are capable of doing harm to them without suffering feelings of guilt.

Racism is the result of stereotyping, which is based on another person's racial background. But what do we mean by the term "race"? We could be referring to geographical location, genetic makeup, appearances or cultural differences. The problem with using geographical location is that it does not take mobility into account. That includes both modern mobility (immigration) and the fact that if we go back far enough, there are scientific reasons to believe all peoples originated in Africa and migrated around the world. Genetic make-up confirms this theory. The Human Genome Project, a massive international mapping of the entire human genome completed in 2000, found that humans as a species are 99.9% genetically identical. Although the final 0.1% may include racial differences, it is hardly significant enough in itself to be the basis of racism.

Appearance seems to be the most obvious factor in racism, but that says more about our reliance on visual information than any valid criteria. Only peoples who have remained geographically isolated have avoided at least some degree of visual assimilation through mixed marriages, and some of the most violent racism occurs between tribes such as the Tutsis and the Hutus in Rwanda, where there are no visible differences. Cultural differences, then, would seem to be a key element of racism. And, like each of the previous three criteria (geographical location, genetic makeup and appearances), in some cases it is. However, when immigration occurs, second- and third-generation Canadians are more in tune with Canadian culture than with the culture of their ancestral homeland. Religion can be considered a part of culture, and many "racist" clashes, such as between the Muslims and Hindus in India, are actually examples of religious intolerance rather than of racism.

Rather than having a legitimate source, racism is built on stereotyping and prejudice. Unlike stereotyping and prejudice, however, racism not only divides people into groups and makes false judgments about them, it also makes a value judgment about their worth. Racism justifies treating people badly because they are judged as being less valuable or less human than the racist's group. Sexism is similar to racism, except that the differentiation is made on the basis of gender rather than race. Despite their shaky foundations, racism and sexism are all too common, and often lead to acts of discrimination or hate crimes, such as destroying temples or beating and even killing individual members of another group on the basis of their race or sex.

In a democratic society, where the rule of the majority determines laws and public policy, it is important that the rights of minority groups are not over-looked. The term "minority rights" refers to laws that protect the rights of minorities, or small groups of people. The rights of minorities are protected in Canada by our laws against discrimination.

Applicable Canadian Laws

The Constitution Act of 1982 (section 27) validates Canada's stand on multiculturalism.

"27. This Charter shall be interpreted in a manner consistent with the preservation and enhancement of the multicultural heritage of Canadians."

The "Charter" refers to the Charter of Rights and Freedoms in the Constitution.

The Canadian Human Rights Act (CHRA) guarantees all Canadians the right to work and live without being hindered by discriminatory practices. According to the Act, discrimination means treating people "differently, negatively or adversely" because of what it refers to as "a prohibited ground of discrimination." There are eleven prohibited grounds of discrimination:

- Race
- Colour
- National or ethnic origin
- Gender
- Age
- Religion
- Marital status
- Family status
- Mental or physical disability
- Pardoned conviction
- Sexual orientation
  (Department of Justice, 2004)

It is up to the individual to prove that one of these grounds was a factor in the discrimination against him or her. In other words, if someone was not hired or not promoted, that person must prove that discrimination was one of the factors involved. It may not have been the only factor: perhaps the person was asked to write a sample business letter and his spelling was quite weak. However, if the person who was hired was also a poor speller, then obviously some other factor was involved in the hiring decision. In order to prove that discrimination was not involved, the employer must prove that the decision was made on other, valid grounds. There may be situations when some of those grounds are acceptable reasons to turn down a job candidate. If a job is physically demanding, such as loading trucks or working in a rock quarry, then it would be acceptable to turn someone down if he or she were disabled or too old to do the job. In a case like this, it isn't prejudice but realistic job requirements that are the deciding factor.

Systemic discrimination is involved if the problem is not so much prejudice as a job expectation or policy which may appear neutral but is, in fact, discriminatory. An organization or business which holds optional meetings, training sessions or even social events on Saturday mornings, and only on Saturday mornings, is an example of systemic discrimination. Any members or employees whose holy day is on a Saturday are going to miss out. There may be no intentional prejudice involved—the owners of the company might have thought they were simply offering some extra social or work-related benefits to their employees outside of work hours. Nevertheless, the result is discriminatory against certain groups of people.

Another area of discrimination is not being given the same service other people receive. A car salesman who ignores single women who walk into his dealership but rushes over to greet men or couples; a waitress who gives poorer service to Aboriginal people; a lawyer who takes one look at a poorly dressed teenager in the waiting room and suddenly can't take on any new cases; the bank manager who won't give a married woman a loan without her husband co-signing; the dance organizer who won't sell tickets to certain people; the social club whose membership is only open to Caucasians; the hockey team that doesn't accept girl players—these are all examples of discrimination and are against the law in Canada. Every Canadian has the right to participate equally in our society.

Discrimination also includes the issue of equal pay for work of equal value. This means that a job which is usually done by women cannot be paid less than a job of equal value which is usually held by men. In a health care environment, the job of nursing assistants is considered of equal value to the job of electricians, and must be compensated equally. In business or office settings, the jobs of secretaries and maintenance staff are considered equal. Exceptions to this rule occur when a difference in pay is justified by one of the following conditions:

- different performance ratings
- seniority
- labour shortages or surpluses which make a position easier or more difficult to fill
- "red-circling" an employee—which occurs when an employee agrees to take a position that is normally paid at a lower rate than he or she is currently receiving
- training and rehabilitation assignments, which usually occur when an employee has become disabled through illness or an accident, and cannot continue to do his or her previous job

(Department of Justice, 2004)

Although the CHRA only covers businesses, industries and agencies under federal jurisdiction, every province and territory has similar legislation which prohibits discrimination in their jurisdiction.

Discrimination can also take the form of written "hate messages" directed at specific persons or groups. This is one way of spreading racism and sexism. If the negative comments are based on any of the eleven prohibited grounds, they are subject to section 13-1 of the 1977 Canadian Human Rights Act, which deals with anti-hate speech. Hate speech is "telecommunication" of any material "that is likely to expose a person or persons to hatred or contempt." (Department of Justice, 2004) Some people consider this section to be in conflict with the Canadian Charter of Rights and Freedoms, specifically section 2(b), which guarantees Canadians "freedom of thought, belief, opinions and expression, including freedom of the press and other media of communications" as one of our fundamental freedoms.

The Criminal Code of Canada also has hate provisions in sections 318 and 319. Section 318 makes advocating genocide a criminal act, either by supporting or arguing for the killing of members of an "identifiable group" distinguished by their colour, race, religion or ethnic origin. Section 319(1) deals with "publicly inciting hatred." To be convicted of this, a person must:

- communicate statements
- in a public place that
- incite hatred against an identifiable group,
- in such a way that there will likely be a breach of the peace.

Section 319(2) adds the offence of "communicating statements, other than in private conversation, that willfully promote hatred against an identifiable group." Section 319 (3) describes when these sections do not apply, such as the statements made being established as true, or being made "in good faith": in other words, not with the intention or motivation of committing a crime or of spreading hate. (Criminal Code of Canada Hate Provisions—Summary)

Ethical Arguments

Multiculturalism promotes respect, understanding and acceptance for differences between people. Nations are generally founded on idealistic concepts, and the concept of a mosaic of cultures living together in peace is certainly an admirable ideal. But is it a practical basis for a nation? Does multiculturalism enrich us as a nation, or weaken us as a nation? In theory it should unite us, but in practice, does it actually divide us into many small subcultures?

_____

_____

Should we be asking immigrants to leave their culture behind when they come to Canada? Culture is a large part of a person's identity and is often bound up with his or her religion. Do we have the right to demand all that be left behind?

_____

_____

If we do not, do we have the right to demand that immigrants leave racial animosities behind? How can we maintain the image of a mosaic if Croatian Canadians retain their hatred for Serbian Canadians, Israeli Canadians for Arab Canadians, etc.?

What about the examples in our own history where respect has not been given to minority cultures? We earlier discussed the deliberate attempt to eradicate Native language and culture in residential schools. Another example is the forced move into internment camps of Japanese Canadians during World War II. These people lost their homes and businesses, and were deprived of their freedom and basic human rights. Both of these are shameful reminders of the failure of our national ideal. But are they also proof that multiculturalism as a national policy does not work?

Unfortunately, these are far from being the only examples of prejudice, racism and the abuse of minority rights in Canada. Whether we see ourselves as a multicultural nation or not, prejudice, racism and minority rights are moral issues that must be dealt with.

Deontological Arguments

Principle-based arguments on the issues of discrimination and minority rights focus on the principle of equality. According to this principle, all people are equal, and it is wrong, or unjust, to deny some of them significant social benefits, such as an equal opportunity to participate in the social and economic life of society, unless it can be proved that the different treatment is based on a proven difference in them. For example, if a job or a social activity requires a certain height restriction to be performed effectively or safely, then height is a legitimate difference, even if it will bar members of certain groups more than other groups. The difference must be relevant to the activity, however; if height is not necessary for another position in the company (or for another activity in the social club) then the restriction cannot apply generally, but only when it is relevant. As this example shows, the principle of equality deals more effectively with the treatment of groups than with the treatment of individuals. It is easier to identify and prohibit situations when groups are being discriminated against (such as an exclusive golf club not open to members of certain races, or an all-male workplace that won't hire women) than situations when individuals are being discriminated against in more subtle ways (such as when individuals just don't qualify for certain advanced positions for a number of reasons that might include their race or sex.) Nevertheless, requiring that people be treated as individuals, not as members of a group, discourages discrimination on the basis of belonging to a particular group.

Kant's moral imperative to treat people as ends, not as means, is applicable here. Each individual is equally worthy in his or her own right, and should not be considered merely an example of a particular group or treated as a means of showing one's dislike for the group he or she belongs to. Furthermore, if discrimination were made into a universal law (everyone should always discriminate against other groups), the purpose of discrimination (to undermine or eliminate a particular group) would be negated, because every group would have to be undermined or eliminated.

One problem with the principle of equality is that there are often real and relevant group differences. A particular difference, such as height (men are generally taller than women), strength and endurance (young adults are stronger than seniors) or ability to work on Saturdays may apply to most or all of the people in a group. This argument could be stated as, "All people are of equal worth, but they are also different and have different capabilities, and some of those differences are common to the entire group." It is important to ensure that this argument is not being used merely as a justification for discrimination, and that the differences and their commonality to the group are accurate, objective and can be proven.

Following the principle of equality sometimes requires responding to past inequalities. Affirmative action, also referred to as employment equity or preferential treatment programs, is one method of doing this. These programs, often established by the government, require employers to hire, promote or equalize the salaries of members of historically disadvantaged groups. There are two arguments used to justify affirmative action—past harm and special needs. The argument that affirmative action is necessary to right past harm is based on compensatory justice. Japanese Canadians who were placed in internment camps received a public apology in 1988 by then Prime Minister Brian Mulroney and $21,000, tax-free, as compensation for their losses. While it would be unrealistic to ask companies to compensate those who were not hired or were not promoted or were not equally paid because they belonged to a particular group, ensuring that members of that group are now in those positions is seen as a way of compensating for past harm. The argument against this reasoning is that compensatory justice should be applied to individuals rather than to groups. Not every member of a group was necessarily harmed by the past practice, and practicing affirmative action for people currently entering or in the workplace does not compensate those individuals who were harmed by discriminatory practices in the past. Compensatory justice, opponents of the past harm argument say, should be applied only to those who were personally wronged.

The argument that affirmative action is justified by special needs is based on the fact that in Canada we require that persons with physical or developmental disabilities be given special assistance. For example, schools, public buildings and workplaces must be made accessible to those with physical disabilities, and we have special, publicly funded programs for people with disabilities. Members of groups that were discriminated against in the past have a social disability—they are disadvantaged because of social conditions. Prejudice and stereotypical thinking placed them at a disadvantage just as much as any physical disability would have, and they need help in overcoming that disability. The argument against this is that compensation is given to individuals with disabilities; if they have offspring who are not disabled, those children do not receive special assistance. Therefore, unless it can be proved that there is still a lingering social disability attached to particular groups, that members of those groups currently experience, then present assistance in the form of affirmative action is not warranted. Of course, if it can be proved that the social disadvantage is still actively present, then members of the affected groups may well need and deserve assistance overcoming it.

There are a number of ways to administer affirmative action programs aimed at increasing the numbers of a particular group in the organization. The four main ones are as follows:

1. *Active search.* The pool of applicants is broadened by the organization actively seeking and encouraging members of the targeted group to apply.
2. *Tie-breaking.* The choice between equally qualified applicants is made by giving preference to a member of the targeted group.
3. *Extra qualification.* Being a member of the targeted group is made one of the additional qualifications, so that even if an applicant is slightly less qualified in other areas, his membership in the group grants him extra points.
4. *Setting quotas.* Creating a policy whereby a certain number or percentage of new hires or promotions must be from the targeted group, or the number or percentage must be achieved by a certain date. Achieving this generally requires giving preferences.

Opponents of affirmative action argue that these programs are morally wrong because they undermine the principle of equality. In fact, they are just as discriminatory as the behaviour they are meant to compensate for, but now they are discriminating against people who are not members of the targeted groups. This is referred to as reverse discrimination.

Divine command theory presents arguments on both sides of this issue. Since most of the major religions' holy books were written when women and children were not considered equal to men, discrimination on the basis of sex and age is endorsed in their scriptures. The resulting behaviour ranges from complete subjugation to the point of life-and-death power over women by men, as practiced by extremist Muslims or some modern religious cults, to a benevolent male paternalism where the husband makes all final decisions, to followers who practice complete gender equality. Originally, nearly all religions were also confined to a particular race or culture, and battling and enslaving members of other races or cultures was acceptable practice. Racism in the name of religion was certainly a part of the abuse that occurred at residential schools for Aboriginal Canadians, and religion-inspired racism and holy wars are still practiced by many followers of the major religions. But all major religions also include scripture that promotes peace, equality, compassion and respect for others. For example, "do unto others as you would have them do unto you" is a command that is common, in one form or another, across religions, and it is a clear injunction against discrimination of any kind. As we learned when discussing divine command theory in Chapter 2, religious writings require our interpretation, and therefore there will be differences in practice among their followers.

Virtue ethics takes the position that fairness to everyone is the middle way between indulgence or favouritism on one hand and intolerance or hostility on the other. A person of virtuous character would make decisions based on rational, objective and accurate information, rather than emotional prejudices.

Teleological Arguments

Consequence-based arguments are not concerned with equality but with the effects of discrimination. Do the benefits of discrimination, for those practicing it, outweigh the harm done to those who suffer from it? Does it promote happiness or unhappiness in the majority of individuals, and to society in general? According to act-utilitarianism, each situation must be considered separately.

Let us consider the example from Canadian history which we have already mentioned. In the case of Japanese Canadians during World War II, financial, social and emotional harm was done to all Japanese Canadians. Those who were not Japanese were either indifferent, saddened, or in a few cases, made happier because they benefited by buying the Japanese property and belongings cheaply. The happiness of those who benefited would also be lessened by the guilt that would accompany it; usually we are happier with gains we earn honestly than with those that come at someone else's expense. If Japanese Canadians were actually a threat to Canadian security, the harm prevented to all Canadians by putting them in internment camps would have to be calculated into the equation also, but this is now acknowledged to have been a false concern.

But are there any instances when discrimination is acceptable? In Canada, we do not allow anyone under 16 to drive a car, anyone under 18 to vote, or anyone under 19 to drink alcohol in public or buy cigarettes. This is discrimination based on age, and individual characteristics are not taken into consideration. Some 15-year-olds, undoubtedly, would be more competent drivers or more informed voters than some 20-year-olds. The justification for these requirements is that the harm done is minimal—a 15-year-old need only wait a year to drive, for example—and then must pass a test like everyone of any age to get a driver's license. Creating individual guidelines, or tests, for voting, on the other hand, would be so difficult, expensive and open to abuse, that age is the only fair requirement—and again, it causes little harm as a person only has to wait to turn 18. These are consequentialist arguments used to counter arguments that the principle of equality is not being upheld when members of certain age groups are being discriminated against in this way.

Rule-utilitarianism is more concerned with the overall effects on society of a general practice. Certainly, discrimination, racism and sexism create unhappiness in those who are victims, but they are minority groups. However, if we add the numbers of all members of minority groups in a multicultural country like Canada, and then include all females because we are also dealing with gender discrimination, then the practice of discrimination in Canada would harm more people than it would benefit. And does discrimination actually cause happiness? Do these attitudes make those who hold them happy, and is their happiness sufficient to counter the unhappiness they cause? It would be difficult to answer that for someone else, but hate is generally not considered an emotion that leads to happiness. It can be argued that living in a society where discrimination, racism and sexism were condoned and legally practiced would harm not only its victims, but also those who were seen to benefit from such acts in material ways, because it would harm them all psychologically. Legalizing acts of prejudice would encourage negative emotions and faulty reasoning in those who practiced them, as well as feelings of being threatened by their victims. Racism usually goes both ways. There is always the possibility that those who are being discriminated against will overthrow the group in power and will subject them to discrimination. In fact, over and over again, this has happened whenever one group is subjugated by another group.

An argument from enlightened self-interest would be agreeing to voluntarily give up the freedom to harm or discriminate against others in order to obtain the same agreement from them. A nation in which everyone was free to indulge in racist and sexist behaviour against everyone else would be similar to the natural chaos that Hobbes described. Under enlightened self-interest we are *not* free to satisfy our own needs if it means deliberately and intentionally harming others and if the harm to them is greater than the benefits. Furthermore, it is in our own self-interest to have laws against discrimination because they are our insurance that we will not be discriminated against.

Affirmative action is more controversial than discrimination. Consequentialist arguments for these programs claim that they benefit our society by breaking a vicious cycle of haves and have-nots. It is important to have minority groups as well as both men and women represented in positions such as lawyers, doctors, teachers, and in management positions in business and banking to ensure that members of those groups will not be discriminated against even in subtle, unintentional ways. These people also act as role models that encourage children from those groups to aspire to such positions. Some stereotypes are so deeply entrenched, at an almost subconscious level, that only by such programs can they be overcome. If this must at first be accomplished by affirmative action, then the benefits outweigh the harms, proponents argue. We all benefit when young people model themselves after successful, positive role models who are productive members of society.

Opponents counter these arguments by saying that affirmative action only serves to strengthen the belief that members of these groups are less capable. If they were equally qualified, they wouldn't need preferential treatment or special assistance. The programs stigmatize successful minority candidates; they are believed to have only been hired or promoted because they are from a minority group. Even those candidates who were hired solely for their qualifications are now suspect and have an even more difficult time proving themselves to their co-workers because of the existence of affirmative action initiatives. Finally, opponents claim that affirmative action programs actually increase racism and sexism because they build up resentment against the minority groups that are getting preferential treatment.

In order to morally justify affirmative action programs, it would be necessary to prove that the benefits outweigh the harm. Do these programs help the individuals they assist (do they continue to be successful?) in the long run, or harm them (by labelling them as not having earned their success)? Are they effective as role models for young people? Do they reduce the economic gap between minority and majority groups in the work force substantially? Are there other, perhaps better ways to accomplish this? Do they reduce racial and cultural tensions or escalate them? These are not easy questions to answer, but it is irresponsible to continue with affirmative action programs unless we have some idea as to whether they are likely to be successful.

Maclean's Case for Debate

There is much disagreement over Canada's anti-hate speech laws, which many people consider censorship. The Canadian Human Rights Commission (CHRC), as well as Human Rights Commissions in each province, investigate complaints about hate speech, including statements made over the Internet on professional and personal websites as well as personal blogs. This is a very controversial issue, as it can be seen to infringe upon our right to freedom of speech. One of the most notable recent cases is that brought against *Maclean's* magazine for an article entitled, "The Future belongs to Islam." The complaint was brought against the online version which appeared on *Maclean's* website, and it was brought to the Ontario Human Rights Commission, the British Columbia Human Rights tribunal and the Federal CHRC at the same time. The goal of the complainants was to force *Maclean's* to print a "mutually acceptable" rebuttal. However, *Maclean's* maintained that the article was "a worthy piece of commentary on important geopolitical issues, entirely within the bounds of normal journalistic practice." (Brean, 2008) As of July 2008, the Ontario Commission and the Federal CHRC both dismissed the complaints. The Federal CHRC found there was not enough evidence to support the complaint that the article was "likely to expose" Muslims to hatred or contempt. Despite being exonerated in the first two cases (the decision of the B.C. tribunal is still pending), *Maclean's* has paid a heavy price in legal defence, not in one court but in three, all for the same charge.

As a result of the controversy around this case, the CHRC launched an independent review of how it deals with Internet hate messages. Section 13–1 was last reviewed by the Supreme Court in 1990, following a case concerning telephone hate messages. At that time it was judged to place a "reasonable limit" on Canadians' right to freedom of expression; however, critics of the anti-hate speech law argue that the "legal test of 'likely to expose' is too loose because truth (believing your negative statement is accurate) is not a valid defence, and intent—whether malicious, journalistic or even scholarly—is irrelevant." (Brean, 2008) Recommendations following the review may include changing Section 13–1 or providing formal guidelines for the CHRC concerning hate messages on the Internet.

Should the CHRC, or any body, monitor the internet for racist or sexist comments?

_____

_____

Should they only be allowed to monitor certain types of sites on the internet? If so, which sites should be exempt?

_____

_____

What is the current status of the CHRC and it's involvement in comments on the internet?

EXERCISE 6.4

Evaluating Ethical Arguments

Consider the ethical arguments about discrimination, racism and the anti-hate speech laws. Without considering which position you agree with, simply examine the arguments themselves. List those from each side of the issues which you think are good, well-reasoned arguments.

1. _____

_____

2. _____

3. _____

_____

4. _____

_____

For each one you chose, try to state clearly why you thought it was a good argument.

1. _____

_____

2. _____

_____

3. _____

_____

4. _____

_____

Now list some arguments from both sides of the issues which you did not find valid or convincing.

1. _____

_____

2. _____

_____

3. _____

_____

4. _____

_____

Why did you think they were weak or bad arguments?

1. _____

_____

2. _____

_____

3. _____

_____

(Continued)

(Continued)

4. _____

   _____

Is multiculturalism a concept that should be maintained?

_____

Why or why not?

_____

_____

After you have written your answers, form small groups and discuss what you have written. Concentrate only on the arguments themselves.

When the discussion time is over, review what you wrote previously on your own. Have you changed your mind about any of the arguments?

_____

_____

_____

Now that you have considered and discussed all of the moral arguments on discrimination, racism and the anti-hate speech law, what is your position on these issues?

_____

_____

_____

Two Opposing Commentaries on Cultural Relations (Hérouxville, Quebec)

Article 1: "Hérouxville's dangerous notions"

Globe and Mail editorial, October 27, 2007

The good people of Hérouxville, Que., are feeling triumphant, and why shouldn't they? What their town council started last winter with its provocative code of conduct for minorities—no stoning or burning of women—helped reshape provincial politics in Quebec. Party leaders in Ottawa, one of whom is the Prime Minister of Canada, have pandered to them.

Intolerance is in the air. For the two nationalist parties in Quebec, no defence of the francophone identity can be too extreme. At special hearings on the "reasonable accommodation" of minorities in Quebec, members of the public have vented about the Muslims and the Jews. In Ottawa, the issue of Muslim women wearing face veils when they vote made it into the Throne Speech. Yesterday, the Harper government introduced a bill to force such women to show their faces at the polls.

The intolerance needs to be answered. Canada is not a country of them and us. It has a strong record of integration and social peace. Hérouxville is not defending Canadian traditions but attacking them.

A commission set up by Premier Jean Charest during the last election—to protect him from the passions set swirling by Hérouxville—is now travelling the province. Unavoidably, it has given a platform to intolerance. One speaker this week suggested Muslims be forced to live in outlying regions rather than be permitted to "take possession" of Montreal neighbourhoods. Hérouxville councillor André Drouin warned that immigrants were about to flood into Quebec because of global warming. He predicted that women will be stoned unless Quebec acts.

Be like us and we will accept you as our equals. That is the tenor of Hérouxville's 14-page written submission to the commission. While the authors claim that being like them is to "interiorize" religious observance, they have no problem with the Christian cross at the heart of the Quebec flag or with public celebrations of Christmas; those are part of the province's "patrimony." But little from other religions is similarly protected. No employee is entitled to a leave of absence for religious reasons; the implication is that non-Christian holidays can't be taken as a day off. Even vegetarianism is against the code. This is the bullying of the insular and narrow.

Being like us means asking for no religious accommodations. The paper says Christians were allowed by God to work on their Sabbath and make other compromises; and so, presumably, should non-Christians. "After many years of observance of God's order to fast during Lent, we had to give up this religious practice to have sufficient energy to work and study hard. Then again, by the grace of God and his sense of accommodations, we were able to avoid the promise of roasting in Hell after death." These are the strange verities that political leaders now wish to exploit.

Not every accommodation makes sense for Canada. The vulnerable need to be protected. Sikh children should not be exempted from bicycle helmet laws so they can wear turbans. Genital mutilation is always criminally wrong. Ontario was right to reject the creation of more publicly funded faith-based schools and the use of sharia law in family arbitration hearings. Government policy should not accentuate differences. An increasingly diverse Canada needs common rallying points.

But at its core, Canada is accommodating. An office building without a wheelchair ramp by its nature bars the disabled. The law forces it to build the ramp as an accommodation. Women until recently could not protect their jobs when they went off to have babies; the law now forces employers to make that accommodation. Those who practise religions whose Sabbath is not on Sunday are now entitled to a day off on their Sabbath, if taking it is not an undue hardship for their employer. All these accommodations have the same purpose: to make room for all to participate fully in society.

In any event, the debate has gone beyond accommodation to basic rights. The Quebec Council on the Status of Women wants individuals barred from wearing religious symbols in the workplace. Does a Sikh man wearing a turban somehow violate the rights of others? This is an insult to the country's pluralistic tradition, itself rooted in the accommodation made between English and French at the nation's founding.

Hérouxville is old Quebec, old Canada. The town of 1,300 people is almost entirely homogeneous. It has no mosque, no synagogue. When Mario Dumont, leader of the Action Démocratique du Québec, gave a cheer for Hérouxville, his party leapt from five seats to 41. The Parti Québécois, led at the time by the urbane André Boisclair, fell to third place. Now urbane is gone; the village is all. The PQ under Pauline Marois made a breathtaking attempt last week to steal back the identity issue from the ADQ. It proposed a citizenship bill that would take away political rights from anyone who comes to Quebec from outside the province, or from abroad, and who doesn't speak French well. In Ottawa, when the Chief Electoral Officer declared that the federal voting law did not require women to take off their veils during three recent by-elections in Quebec, he was attacked by the four major federal party leaders, who willfully distorted the Elections Act. Shamefully, they fed the dangerous notion of them and us.

Hérouxville's intolerance, if it were to spread, would lead Canada to the very problem that the town fears—the ghetto-like suburbs and riots of France. Canada may never change Hérouxville, but Hérouxville must not be permitted to change Canada.

Article 2: "In defence of Hérouxville"

(Jonathon Kay, National Post.com, Posted October 29, 2007.)

Nativism is supposed to be a right-wing creed. So why is Quebec, the most socially liberal province in the country, the only place where Canadians are candidly discussing how far we should go to "accommodate" immigrants? Why are Canadian cartoonists putting KKK costumes on the hotheads of Hérouxville instead of, say, Calgary or Red Deer? And why is it the PQ—not some cowboy-hat party out on the prairies—that's proposing a two-tier citizenship system?

It's not because Quebec is swinging right. It's because mono-culturalism is swinging left. Having decisively vanquished traditional Christians in the culture wars, feminists, gay activists and other progressives are no longer willing to risk their winnings by pledging multicultural solidarity with traditional Muslims, Hasidic Jews and other socially conservative immigrant groups.

This is a new phenomenon in Canada, but it's been going on for years in Europe. The old face of nativism used to be Jean-Marie Le Pen, a right-wing Gaullist and old-school bigot who complains crankily about Jews and Blacks. Le Pen is still around. (His National Front party got 10% of the vote in this year's French presidential election.) But today's young voters are drawn more to those cast in the mold of Dutch politician Pim Fortuyn.

When Fortuyn was assassinated in 2002, he was described in the Western media as a "right-wing" politician because of his scathing remarks about Muslims. But the label never fit: Fortuyn was a lusty, openly gay populist who championed euthanasia, liberal drug policies and same-sex marriage. He opposed traditional Muslim culture precisely because it conflicted with The Netherlands' anything-goes ethos.

In other words, muscular mono-culturalism is no longer the purview of the right. Having been liberated from the odour of racism, it's becoming a mainstream ideology, even a fashionable one, on the left.

With his infamous 1995 comments about "money and the ethnic vote," Jacques Parizeau came off as a sort of *Québécois* Le Pen (as do many of today's separatists, which is why the PQ's two-tier citizenship gambit will ultimately backfire). Mario Dumont and Hérouxville's counsellors, on the other hand, sound more like followers of Fortuyn. In this regard, I would urge all those outraged Canadian pundits who are taking Hérouxville as a byword for bigotry to actually read the town's 14-page submission to Quebec's commission on reasonable accommodation, in which the authors approvingly cite Turkey's militantly secularist founder, Mustafa Kemal Ataturk; celebrate Quebec's rejection of the Catholic "theocracy" of the Duplessis era; champion the rights of women and gays; and openly mock Christian fundamentalism ("Recently, the National Assembly allowed the opening of retail stores on Sundays. [God] accommodated us once again, sparing Hell to the faithful").

In other words, these people are claiming Quebec in the name of state-of-the-art European-style secular liberalism. The idea that "Hérouxville is old Quebec, old Canada"—which appeared in a *Globe and Mail* editorial last week—is not only wrong: It is the exact opposite of the truth.

Left-wing political trends aside, there are other reasons to have expected that Quebec would be the first part of Canada to decisively challenge multiculturalism, a doctrine that tends to thrive in wealthy nations beset by weak identities and postcolonial guilt. Compared to Anglo Canada, Quebec has a relatively strong sense of collective self. And for obvious historical reasons, Quebecers are more inclined to see themselves as history's victims rather than exploiters.

That's why multiculturalism has been a tough sell in Quebec from the get go. The doctrine became official Canadian government policy largely because Pierre Trudeau was looking to downplay the unique status of French culture by pretending it was just one of many filaments in a rich national tapestry. Even before the word *Burka* entered the popular parlance, many Quebecers rightly saw it as a scam.

But what starts in Quebec won't end here. The debate will spread, and we should be glad of that. For all the rhetorical stock Canadians have put in multiculturalism over the years, the fact remains that it is fundamentally incoherent: How do you intellectually defend a doctrine that preaches "tolerance" toward imported cultures that, themselves, are fundamentally intolerant toward women, gays, heretics and infidels?

Giggle all you like at the bumpkins of Hérouxville. At least, they're smart enough to know this question can't be answered. Maybe when the rest of us Anglos get over our own guilty Western hang-ups, we'll come to the same realization.

QUESTIONS FOR DISCUSSION:

1. Is the Hérouxville "code of conduct" an example of discrimination, racism or undermining minority rights? If so, which is it? Why do you think so?
2. If you do not think it is any of these, why isn't it? Is it a multicultural issue? If so, what does it say about multiculturalism in Canada?

ANIMAL RIGHTS

Consider all the ways that birds, fish and animals contribute to human existence. They are, first of all, our primary source of food (meat, fish, fowl, eggs, milk, cheese) and clothing (wool, fur and leather). Throughout human history they have been worshipped as gods (cows are sacred in India, cats were sacred in ancient Egypt) and trained to serve us (guarding our homes, herding sheep, being our eyes and sniffing out trails or illegal substances). Horses, donkeys and camels provided us with transportation; oxen, elephants and dogs worked and hunted alongside us; and pigeons carried messages for us. Many types of animals worldwide have been our pets and companions, while others have amused and entertained us in circuses, marinas, aquariums, aviaries, zoos and on race tracks. In modern times they have and are contributing as experimental subjects to our scientific and medical understanding and our ability to treat diseases. In all this parade of usefulness, we are only recently beginning to question whether this longstanding exchange of benefits has been a little one-sided in our favour.

Do animals have moral rights? Do humans have the unlimited right to use the other creatures on this planet as we wish? Or do we have a duty to limit the extent of our exploitation of them and of their habitats? What terms should be set for an ethical relationship between humans and animals? Animal rights activists have made this a controversial subject, and they are often perceived as extremists. However, what we regard as extremist often turns out only to be ahead of the times. Slavery abolitionists and suffragettes were also considered extremists in their day. Perhaps future generations will look back and wonder how we could justify our current behaviour toward other species that share our world, just as we wonder how people could own slaves or consider women unfit to vote.

Why are we asking questions about animal rights? We do not talk about plant rights, for example. Environmentalists talk about having a moral duty to preserve the environment, including natural vegetation, and we could also say we have a moral duty to preserve animal, bird and fish species or to care for creatures in our custody. This is like saying slave-owners had a moral duty to provide the necessities of life for their slaves and to treat them humanely. It is not the same as saying that blacks have moral rights equal to whites. Even if we don't go so far as to say that animals' moral rights are equal to humans' moral rights, saying that animals have moral rights is very different from talking about our duty toward them. If animals have moral rights, they have their own moral status, or moral worth, independent of us.

A right is usually defined as a strong and legitimate claim. As a human being, you have a moral right not to be physically abused, for example. Your right does not depend on whether or not other people believe they have a moral duty not to abuse you. Your moral right not to be abused is absolute. Even if someone, say a parent or a spouse or a criminal-minded stranger, believed he had a right or a duty to abuse you, or denied that she had a duty not to abuse you, their belief does not alter the fact of your right not to be abused. To give an example of a moral duty, if you borrow your parent's car, you have a moral duty not to smash it up, but that does not mean that the car has a moral right not to be smashed up. The duty in this case is to your parent, who owns the car, and to yourself, to live up to your own moral standards, not to the car. In the same way, to say that it is bad to make animals suffer, that we have a duty not to do so, is very different from saying that animals have a moral right not to be made to suffer.

Rights and duties are related, however. If you have a right not to be abused, others automatically have a duty not to abuse you. Their duty is based on your right, not on what they think or would like their duty toward you to be. If a child has a right to food, then those caring for the child have a duty to provide it. The duty is based on their relationship as caregivers to the child. Some rights are legal rights, protected by law, while others are moral rights, as we discussed in Chapter 5. In either case, there must be some grounds, legal or moral, on which the right is based.

The use of animals in research is an ethical issue for many people. It has been going on since before Aristotle dissected animals to learn about their inner workings, and has always been a part of human scientific advances. But are we justified in using animals this way? One concern is whether it is necessary to use animals at all. Could we get the same information through monitoring human patients, medical imaging and other noninvasive tests, population studies, autopsies and by using tissue and cell cultures? Another concern is whether the information gained is necessary. Some animal testing involves cosmetics, dyes, food additives, toiletries and other non-essential products. Are these things really worth the animal suffering that goes into testing them?

According to Partners in Research, the following facts about using animals in research should be considered:

- Number of additional years humans now live thanks to animal research: 23
- Number of illnesses animals and humans share in common: 200+
- Over 97% of the animals used by humans are used in the food chain. Fewer than 0.3% of the animals used by humans are used for biomedical research, teaching and testing.
- Currently, over 94% of the animals used in research are fish, rodents and birds. These animals breed rapidly and are inexpensive to feed and house. Only 1 to 1.5% of animals used in medical research are dogs or cats, and fewer than 0.5% are primates.
- There are very few animals used for cosmetic testing. Animals are only used in cosmetic testing when a new ingredient is developed.
- Without animal research, diseases like smallpox could not have been wiped out, and polio, whooping cough, tetanus, and measles would be much more common. Before the development of vaccines for these diseases, many babies died before even reaching their first birthday.
- Vaccine development is one of the great successes of animal research. Because of animal research, only 1 in 10,000,000 vaccinations fail. In Canada and most other countries, the law requires that every batch of vaccines be tested for safety and efficacy.

■ Over 135 million people in the world suffer from diabetes. Half of these people would die an agonizing death if it were not for insulin. With insulin these people lead relatively normal lives. Insulin also benefits many dogs which suffer from diabetes.

■ Computerized testing is currently an "adjunct" to animal testing. Computerized testing is not as effective or reliable as animal-based research because we do not know enough to predict how a new drug or chemical will work in our bodies. Good data must be available to feed into a computer.

———
(Partners in Research)

Many valuable discoveries have come from using animals in experiments, including Canadian physician Frederick Banting and his research team's discovery of insulin in 1921. Their research required ligating the pancreatic ducts of dogs—severing the connection between their pancreas and digestive system. (Bliss, 2008) Millions of diabetic humans and animals owe their lives to the suffering and deaths of Banting's test dogs. It is unlikely that insulin would have been discovered without the use of healthy test animals. If we considered animals as being equal in moral value to humans, would we still use them in such experiments? Would we use them to the extent that we do now?

Do we have a moral obligation concerning endangered animal, fish or bird species? If so, what is it based on? Do we have an obligation to them because we, in large part, are the cause of their extinction? We encroach on and destroy animal habitats, upset ecological balances by introducing non-native species, and have caused massive climate changes through global warming, to which they cannot adapt. Oil spills from our shipping and bycatch caught in fishing nets endanger waterbirds and marine species such as whales, dolphins and porpoises. Are we responsible for what we have caused? Where does enlightened self-interest come in? Is it in our own best interests to preserve species, both for the pleasure of observing them and because they may be of some yet unknown use to us? These concerns will be explored further under environmental issues.

If animals have rights, we must establish the grounds or basis of those rights. This is where ethical arguments arise. We will examine those arguments, but first, what does the law have to say about the treatment of animals in Canada?

Applicable Canadian Laws

The sections of the Criminal Code of Canada which deal with the treatment of birds and animals apply mainly to domesticated animals. Sections 444 and 445 make it an indictable offence to "kill, maim, wound, poison or injure" cattle, dogs, birds or any animals that "are kept for a lawful purpose." It is also an offence to place poison where animals may easily eat it. Under cruelty to animals, section 445.1, it is also an offence if a person:

(a) wilfully causes or, being the owner, wilfully permits to be caused unnecessary pain, suffering or injury to an animal or a bird;

(b) in any manner encourages, aids or assists at the fighting or baiting of animals or birds; (It is also illegal to have a cockpit on one's property or be present at a cockfight.)

(c) wilfully, without reasonable excuse, administers a poisonous or an injurious drug or substance to a domestic animal or bird or an animal or a bird wild by nature that is kept in captivity or, being the owner of such an animal or a bird, wilfully permits a poisonous or an injurious drug or substance to be administered to it;

(d) promotes, arranges, conducts, assists in, receives money for or takes part in any meeting, competition, exhibition, pastime, practice, display or event at or in the course of which captive birds are liberated by hand, trap, contrivance or any other means for the purpose of being shot when they are liberated; or

(e) being the owner, occupier or person in charge of any premises, permits the premises or any part thereof to be used for a purpose mentioned in paragraph (d).

The Code further includes wilful neglect, abandonment and failure to provide suitable and adequate food, water, shelter, care and supervision of an animal or bird, causing it pain, suffering or injury as indictable offences. The punishment for any of the above offences was increased in 2008 to imprisonment for a term of up to five years or a fine of up to $10,000. The court may also prohibit the person from owning, having custody or living in the same house as an animal or a bird for a minimum of five years, and paying the costs of care and treatment of the animal to relieve its suffering or injury after it has been confiscated. (Criminal Code of Canada, Department of Justice)

The Canadian Council on Animal Care (CCAC) was formed in 1968 to investigate the condition of animals used in research. The CCAC developed guidelines for the care and use of experimental animals and has also established assessment panels to oversee the use of animals in universities, government laboratories and commercial laboratories. As a result, according to the Canadian Federation of Humane Societies, the number of animals used for research decreased while the volume of research increased and the quality of care of animals used for research improved. "Current regulatory standards for medical research in Canada require that medical research be performed on animals. Although non-animal models can be used to reduce the number of animals required, they cannot replace animals altogether. By law, animals must be tested in basic medical research to determine how different treatments actually perform in a live body." Alberta, Ontario, Quebec, the Maritime provinces and Saskatchewan all have legislation specific to research animals. Saskatchewan and Alberta have incorporated the CCAC guidelines into the provincial animal protection acts. The Food and Drugs Act, Pesticides Products Control Act, Hazardous Products Act, and Canadian Environmental Protection Act also relate to animal testing. (Canadian Federation of Humane Societies)

There are no provisions in the Criminal Code for wild animals or endangered species, but there are federal laws such as the Federal Species At Risk Act (SARA) and The Health of Animals Act (1990), international laws such as the Migratory Bird Act, and provincial laws that do apply.

Ethical Arguments

We will examine the issue of animal rights from three perspectives, although there are many degrees of opinion between these perspectives.

1. Animals have as much moral worth as humans and we should consider their interests as equal to our own.
2. Humans have greater moral value than animals, but animals do have some rights and we have a moral duty to take those into consideration in our dealings with them.

3. Human beings alone have moral rights and the other creatures on Earth are here for our use.

Which of these three perspectives is closest to your own? Why do you hold that opinion?

_____

_____

_____

_____

Each of these positions will be considered in turn, along with the ethical arguments supporting and opposing each position.

1. Animals have as much moral worth as humans and we should consider their interests as equal to our own.

As stated previously, to determine whether animals have moral worth and rights, we must first establish the grounds on which those rights are based. Some people argue that in order to have rights, a being must be able to claim them as rights. The counter-argument to this is that infants and mentally challenged humans are not able to claim their rights, but they still have legal and moral rights. The two main grounds given for animal rights are that animals are sentient, and that they have conscious interests.

Sentience is defined as the ability to perceive or feel things. Animals have the same ability as humans to feel pleasure and pain; therefore, shouldn't they have the same moral right to increase pleasure and decrease pain as humans have? Jeremy Bentham, who developed the greatest happiness theory, which became utilitarianism, wrote, "The day may come when the rest of the animal kingdom may acquire those rights which never could have been withheld from them but by the hand of tyranny...The question is not, Can they reason? nor Can they talk? but, Can they suffer?" (Bentham, 1789) Those who support this viewpoint argue that there are humans who cannot talk, or cannot reason, but who still have rights. The only thing we all share, and on which our rights are based, is the capacity for happiness and pain. Since animals also have this capacity, they also have moral rights, such as the right not to suffer. Based on that right, humans have the same moral duty toward them as we do toward human beings with moral rights.

Many animals are also capable of other feelings, such as affection, loyalty, fear and anger, as well as pleasure and pain. Because of this, they have conscious interests, just as humans do, although of course those interests will be different. It is this ability to consciously want certain things that proves animals are beings who should have moral rights, some argue. Animals have an "inner life," just as humans do, and are the active agents in their own lives. For this reason, they have the same moral rights as humans.

Those who do not accept that animals have moral rights have been accused of speciesism. Peter Singer defines speciesism as a "prejudice or attitude of bias in favour of the interests of members of one's own species and against those of members of other species. It should be obvious that the fundamental objections to racism and sexism...apply equally to speciesism. If possessing a higher degree of intelligence does not entitle one human to use another for his or her own ends, how can it entitle humans to exploit nonhumans?" (Singer, 1975)

If animals have the same moral rights as humans, then some of the same principles of behaviour apply toward them as we use toward other humans. The most basic principle of equality should apply to humans and animals. How could one argue that humans and animals are equal? Obviously animals are not intellectually equal to human beings, or creative the way humans are, and it is just as obvious that humans are not physically equal to most animals. We cannot fly like birds, swim as well as fish, climb as well as squirrels or run as fast as just about any four-legged creature. However, if we look at equality that way, then human beings are not all equal, either. Some are smarter or more creative than others, some are kinder or more altruistic than others, some are physically taller, stronger or more athletic than others. Nevertheless, all moral philosophies are built on the premise that all people are equal, in the sense that they are of equal worth. According to Singer, "Equality is a moral idea, not an assertion of fact. There is no legally compelling reason for assuming that a factual difference in ability between two people justifies any difference in the amount of consideration we give to their needs and interests. The principle of the equality of human beings is not a description of an alleged actual equality among humans: it is a prescription of how we should treat human beings." This basic principle of equality must therefore "...be extended to all beings, black or white, masculine or feminine, human or non-human." (Singer, 1975)

Equality does not mean treating different beings the same; a parent would not treat an infant the same way she would treat a ten-year-old, but the two children are equally valuable to her. Equality doesn't require identical treatment; it means giving equal consideration. The principle of equal consideration of interests is how the principle of equality applies to animals, proponents of this viewpoint argue.

Although animals have different interests from ours, that doesn't mean their interests are less important than ours. A child has different needs and interests from an adult, a physically handicapped person has different interests from an Olympic athlete, men have different interests from women, and so on, but all their interests should be given equal consideration. The same is true for the interests of animals. Some of them may be different from human interests, but they have as much moral worth as our own interests have. It would be silly, for example, to give animals the right to vote, but taking their interests into consideration when we vote is equal consideration of interests. Other examples would be considering animal habitats and food sources as important as human developments and farmland, or remembering that wild animals value their freedom as much as we value ours.

The principle of non-maleficence also applies to animals the same way it applies to humans. This principle involves avoiding actions that will cause harm to animals. If we considered animals' rights to be equal to humans' rights, what kinds of actions toward animals would be required by non-maleficence?

_____

_____

_____

_____

The principle of beneficence requires actions that benefit animals by preventing harm, stopping it when it is being inflicted and/or bringing about positive good. What kinds of actions toward animals would be required by beneficence?

_____

_____

_____

_____

If species have rights as well as individual animals, what kinds of actions toward endangered species would be covered under non-maleficence and beneficence?

_____

_____

_____

_____

In summary of this position, if animals have equal moral rights to humans, anything we would not do to a human being, we should not do to an animal. That would have quite an effect on our eating habits and on the use of animals for experiments, not to mention all the industries supported by animal products.

2. Humans have greater moral value than animals, but animals do have some rights and we have a moral duty to take those into consideration in our dealings with them.

Those who take this middle position believe that a human life is worth more than an animal's life. Even though they may love their cat more than they care about a stranger's starving child, they would feel morally required to feed the hungry child before feeding their cat. Is this morally justified, or speciesism? On what grounds can we claim that animals have less moral value than humans? According to Bonnie Steinbock, the compelling difference between humans and animals, which justifies treating them differently, is that human beings can be held responsible for their actions. They can be motivated by moral reasons to treat others fairly. If your cat jumps onto the kitchen counter and eats the cheese sandwich you made for your lunch, you cannot hold him accountable for theft, or explain to him why his behaviour was unfair to you, because animals are not capable of acting from ethical motives. "If rats invade our houses, carrying disease and biting our children, we cannot reason with them, hoping to persuade them of the injustice they do us. We can only attempt to get rid of them. And it is this that makes it reasonable for us to accord them a separate and not equal moral status." (Steinbock, 1978)

The obvious next question is, how much more is a human life worth than an animal's? There may be some difference of opinion among those in this middle group concerning what rights animals do have and just how much more valuable human interests are than animal interests.

It is generally agreed that because animals are capable of physical suffering to the same extent as humans, they have the right not to be made to suffer, or to be treated cruelly. Cruelty is defined as the infliction of unnecessary pain or suffering. The Criminal Code covers behaviours on the part of animal owners or caretakers which are prohibited on grounds of cruelty, and the Canadian Council on Animal Care covers the humane treatment of experimental animals. Most people who hold this middle position would agree to those standards, such as keeping suffering and pain to a minimum and relying on methods other than tests using animals whenever possible in medical research. But what is necessary pain, and what is unnecessary? Theoretically, it is necessary to feel pain in order to know that we are wounded and to take steps to heal ourselves. Sometimes we decide it is necessary to risk pain or suffering to accomplish a greater good. We may do this for our own sake, as in getting a vaccine to avoid contacting hepatitis, or for someone else's sake, say in entering a burning house to rescue a child or donating blood at a blood bank so someone else might live. We sacrifice the lesser pain to achieve the more important good. This is just another way of saying that the benefits (happiness) must outweigh the harm (suffering).

If we make these decisions for ourselves, then isn't it morally acceptable to make similar decisions for animals? And if animals have less moral value than humans, sacrificing an animal to save humans is morally acceptable, according to this middle viewpoint. Therefore, animals should be used in research that will save human lives. An animal life for a human life is an easy thing to weigh; after that, it becomes more complex. How do we weigh other benefits to humans against the harm to animals? Are tear-free shampoo and rash-free cosmetics sufficient human benefits to justify animal suffering? Is our comfort worth more than an animal's life? We do not need fur coats or leather shoes and couches; we can use other materials to achieve the same warmth and comfort. Some people maintain that we do not need to eat meat, fish or fowl, while others maintain that we do, and that providing us with protein is a necessary sacrifice of animal lives.

What about using animals as entertainment? Are the benefits in human pleasure and education sufficient to justify the harm done to animals by keeping them in zoos, circuses, aquariums, etc.? Part of the answer to that question requires weighing the harm done to animals. Some animals appear to enjoy performing tricks for applause, while others obviously don't. Some species crave freedom while others seek out human companionship. Let's not get sentimental about life in the wild; it is, as Hobbes said, "nasty, brutish and short." Releasing a cow in the boreal forest is abandonment, not animal rights. If it is difficult to weigh happiness and harm for other people, it is even more difficult to weigh it for another species. All of this makes this middle position very complex, and subject to a lot of variance and disagreement among those who take it. That does not mean it isn't a valid ethical position; ethics is always a complex subject.

If we consider animals to have lesser rights than humans, what kinds of actions toward animals would be required by the principle of non-maleficence?

_____

_____

_____

_____

What kinds of actions toward animals, if any, would be required by the principle of beneficence?

_____

_____

_____

_____

3. Human beings alone have moral rights and the other creatures on the earth are here for our use.

Divine command theory generally puts forth this view, although not all followers agree with this position. The Old Testament of the Bible, which is common to Judaism, Islam and Christianity, states: "God said unto them [the first humans created] Be fruitful and multiply and replenish the earth and subdue it: and have dominion over the fish of the sea, and over the fowl of the air, and over every living thing that moveth upon the earth." (Genesis 2:28) The grounds on which humans claim they alone have moral rights are spiritual in this case. Only human beings have souls. Animals, as far as we can tell, do not worship a God or gods, or look forward to a future existence on a spiritual plane. If that is the basis of our moral worth, then it is reasonable to assume that animals do not have any, and have been put here for our use. It is important to note, however, that in some religions certain animals are sacred and have more moral value than humans. For example, cows are sacred to Hindus in India and cats were sacred in ancient Egypt.

Others who hold this viewpoint simply believe that animals are a lesser form of being than humans because they do not have our potential for reasoning and self-consciousness. They give similar arguments to those of Steinbock, only take the conclusion one step farther, to the point where animals have no moral rights. This does not mean we don't have a moral duty to treat other living creatures decently—but that duty is based on our virtue and our duty to obey the law, not on animals having rights.

Still another position that justifies this viewpoint is that of the law of nature. In the wild, animals kill and feed on one another; the survival of the strongest is nature's way. Human beings, because of our brains and our ability to use tools, have fought our way to the top of the food chain. We are the top predators, and every creature is our prey. We may choose to treat those beneath us humanely, to our credit, but they are nevertheless beneath us in nature's hierarchy.

This position does not mean that humans are justified in being cruel to animals, only that we are morally justified in using animals for human benefit without concern for the animals' benefit. There are still good reasons to treat animals well. One is that animals will serve us better in whatever capacity we are using them if they are healthy and well cared for. This position is one of enlightened self-interest. It is in our own best interest that the animals in our care are healthy and in peak working condition, just as we keep our car and other possessions in good condition. Another reason to treat animals well is for the psychological effect it has on us. Cruelty to animals can lead to acts of cruelty or abuse against people. Children exposed to the mistreatment of animals are believed to be negatively affected by the experience, and studies have shown that psychopaths often mistreated animals when they were children. Consequence-based arguments must take these effects into account. Therefore, because cruelty toward animals is bad for individuals and bad for society as a whole, our right to use animals for our own benefit should be limited by prohibitions against cruelty. However, for those who hold this third viewpoint, it is for our own sake that we should treat animals well, and not because they have any right to demand it of us.

EXERCISE 6.5

Developing Ethical Arguments

Work in small groups to write moral arguments for or against animal rights. Your arguments will depend on which of the three positions you take, so your group should decide that first.

State your position in clear, concrete terms.

_____

_____

_____

Argue for your position according to the following ethical approaches:

Principle-based or Kantian

_____

_____

_____

Consequence-based or utilitarian

_____

_____

_____

_____

Social contract

_____

_____

_____

_____

(Continued)

(Continued)

Virtue ethics theory

_____

_____

_____

_____

Divine command theory

_____

_____

_____

_____

Which of the previous arguments are absolutist and which are relativist? Explain why.

_____

_____

_____

_____

_____

SEXUAL RELATIONS, HOMOSEXUALITY, PORNOGRAPHY AND PROSTITUTION

Our most intimate relationships bring out the best and the worst in us. We can be moved to acts of loyalty, generosity and self-sacrifice or driven to acts of cruelty, deceit and selfishness in these relationships; their effect on us is far greater than that of more casual social or work-oriented acquaintanceships. Sexuality is usually an integral part of these relationships, and therefore how we behave as sexual beings is an important and deeply personal aspect of our moral character. The decisions we make about our sexual lives influence how we view ourselves and how we relate to other people, as well as how others view and relate to us.

There are a number of considerations involved in the debate over sexual relationships, including homosexuality and same-sex marriages. Premarital sex (which involves consenting adults who are both single) and extramarital sex (which involves consenting adults where one or both are married to someone else) raise very different concerns. Should sexual intercourse be accompanied by love and some type of commitment to a relationship? To what extent are principles of loyalty, honesty, fairness, promise-keeping and not using people for personal gratification involved? Is the consent of both parties fully informed and voluntary or is misunderstanding, deceit, physical (including alcohol) or emotional coercion or social pressure involved? Have harmful consequences such as pregnancy, sexually transmitted diseases (STDs) and physical or emotional harm to either participant or to others (friends, family, spouses, children) been carefully considered, as well as the pleasure and positive consequences? What are the psychological and physical effects of restraining sexual urges and abstinence? What are the psychological and physical effects of sexual intimacy if the relationship fails, or of promiscuity? How does religious belief affect sexual activity?

Another way of considering sexual morality involves determining the purpose of sexual intercourse. Once the purpose is determined, the practices that are most likely to achieve that purpose are right or good. They would be considered normal. Is there such a thing as "normal" human sexual practices, and what would they include or not include? If the purpose is human reproduction, then only sexual practices likely to achieve that end and support the raising of children are morally acceptable. If the purpose of sex is pleasure, or to form bonds and increase intimacy with another person, then sexual practices likely to increase pleasure or to strengthen the bonds between people would be morally acceptable. What moral behaviours would be acceptable to achieve each of these three purposes?

1. Reproduction:

_____

_____

2. Pleasure:

_____

_____

3. Bonding:

_____

_____

Specific issues around homosexuality and same-sex marriage involve religious beliefs and principles of discrimination, fairness, minority rights and, in the case of same-sex marriage, love and commitment. Marriage is also a social and legal institution, which affects kinship and family relations as well as inheritance and taxation laws; how do these issues affect moral arguments about same-sex marriage?

Pornography raises concerns about social harm in terms of gender stereotyping, dehumanizing sex, and encouraging what may be considered "unnatural" pleasures. Principles such as freedom of expression and censorship also apply to this issue. The slippery slope argument, implying that pornography leads to negative behaviours and attitudes, should also be considered. Child pornography raises a number of moral issues such as coercion, exploitation and the abuse of minors.

Prostitution raises specific concerns about coercion and the exploitation of others, as well as spreading STDs and HIV/AIDS. The main principles involved are autonomy (free choice over our bodies) versus traditional family values. There are some inconsistencies in the laws about this issue; although prostitution is not illegal, soliciting, advertising or profiting by it are illegal. Are these restrictions fair or morally justified?

Applicable Canadian Laws

Premarital, extramarital and homosexual sex between consenting adults are all legal in Canada, although extramarital sex will provide a spouse with legal grounds for divorce.

The Criminal Code of Canada, under sexual offences, sections 150–161, prohibits sexual relations between an adult and anyone under the age of 16 years, with or without the consent of the underage person, although it makes an exception if the underage person is 14 or 15 years old, the sexual partner is less than five years older, and the act is consensual. However, a person under 17 having sexual relations with a minor can be charged if he or she is in a position of trust or authority towards the minor, is in an exploitative relationship with the minor (i.e., wields control or strong influence over the young person) or if the minor is dependent on that person. These prohibitions include touching "directly or indirectly, with a part of the body or with an object, any part of the body of a person under the age of 16 years" or inviting the minor to touch them.

Lack of consent for sexual activity is defined in the Criminal Code as:

(a) the agreement is expressed by the words or conduct of a person other than the complainant;

(b) the complainant is incapable of consenting to the activity;

(c) the accused counsels or incites the complainant to engage in the activity by abusing a position of trust, power or authority;

(d) the complainant expresses, by words or conduct, a lack of agreement to engage in the activity; or

(e) the complainant, having consented to engage in sexual activity, expresses, by words or conduct, a lack of agreement to continue to engage in the activity. (Section 151 (3))

Anal sex is permitted between consenting adults 18 years of age or older, but incest and bestiality are prohibited under any circumstances. Rape (including date rape), the attempt to commit rape, an indecent assault on a female and an indecent assault on a male are prohibited under sections 144, 145, 149 and 156 respectively.

Pornography and prostitution, including the use of children for both, are prohibited under sections 163 to 213 of the Criminal Code. These sections deal with "offences tending to corrupt morals" and "procurement." Corrupting morals is described as making, printing, publishing, distributing, selling or possessing "any obscene written matter, picture, model, phonograph record or other thing whatever." This includes voyeuristic recordings, Internet postings and obscene theatrical productions. The Code further states, "Any publication a dominant characteristic of which is the undue exploitation of sex, or of sex and any one or more of the following subjects, namely, crime, horror, cruelty and violence, shall be deemed to be obscene."

While prostitution is not prohibited directly, keeping a "bawdy-house," transporting or directing someone else to one, living on the proceeds of a prostitute or soliciting clients are all illegal activities. Procuring, coercing, luring or even communicating with a child under 18 for sexual purposes, or knowingly permitting an underage person to engage in sexual activity in one's house, is an indictable offence. In fact, section 172(1) states: "Every one who, in the home of a child, participates in adultery or sexual immorality or indulges in habitual drunkenness or any other form of vice, and thereby endangers the morals of the child or renders the home an unfit place for the child to be in, is guilty of an indictable offence and liable to imprisonment for a term not exceeding two years."

(Criminal Code, Department of Justice)

Developing Ethical Arguments

EXERCISE 6.6

Developing Ethical Arguments

Divide the class into five groups. Each group will develop moral arguments for or against one of the following issues: premarital sex, extramarital sex, homosexuality and same-sex marriage, pornography or prostitution. After 30–40 minutes, the groups will present their arguments to the class.

State the ethical issue in clear, concrete terms.

_____

_____

_____

_____

Who could be affected by this issue?

_____

_____

_____

_____

How would the following ethical approaches we have studied view this issue:

Principle-based or deontological arguments. What principles or rights are involved in this issue? What argument(s) for the issue would support each principle or right? What argument(s) against the issue would support each principle or right?

_____

_____

_____

(Continued)

(Continued)

_____

_____

_____

How does Kant's maxim to treat other people as ends, never as means, apply to this issue? If it were made a universal law (everyone always did it or no one ever did it) would it defeat its own purpose? According to the universal law maxim, is this issue morally prohibited (if everyone always does it, it defeats its own purpose, therefore it cannot be a universal law and is morally wrong), morally required (if no one ever does it, it defeats its own purpose, therefore not doing it cannot be made a universal law and abstaining from it is wrong), or morally permissible (its purpose is not affected by being either universally practiced or universally abstained from)?

_____

_____

_____

_____

_____

Divine Command Theory. Historically, the primary influence on sexual morality has been religion, which places a high value on virginity and celibacy. Why do you think religions did this? Are those reasons still valid today? Are there divine commands concerning this issue? Are they open to interpretation? Do some members of religions interpret them differently from other members?

_____

_____

_____

_____

_____

Virtue Ethics Theory. Which virtuous habits apply to this issue? What is the median way between extremes in this issue?

_____

_____

_____

_____

_____

Consequence-based or teleological arguments. What general consequences should be considered when discussing this issue? What are the possible positive or negative consequences on each side of this issue? Which consequences are more likely and which are more significant?

_____

_____

_____

_____

_____

Act-Utilitarian. Who would be directly involved in situations involving a moral decision on this issue? What are the benefits and harms to those involved? What circumstances affect the decision on this issue? In which situations is this behaviour morally right, and why? When would it be morally wrong, and why?

_____

_____

_____

_____

_____

Rule-Utilitarian. What are the consequences to individuals and to society as a whole, particularly long-term consequences, which make this behaviour morally acceptable? What are the consequences that make this behaviour morally unacceptable? What moral rule should be made concerning this issue? What consequence-based arguments support this rule? What counter-arguments can be made?

_____

_____

_____

_____

_____

(Continued)

(Continued)

Social Contract Theory. Are there any restrictions on behaviour concerning this issue that might be necessary for everyone to agree to in order to enable people to live together in peace?

_____

_____

_____

_____

_____

Enlightened Self-Interest. Give an argument concerning this issue that supports pursuing your own best interests without intentionally harming someone else. How do the benefits of this course of action outweigh any harms?

_____

_____

_____

_____

Which of the previous arguments are absolutist and which are relativist? Explain why.

_____

_____

_____

_____

_____

SPORTS ISSUES: STEROID USE, PLAYERS' SALARIES, VIOLENCE IN TEAM SPORTS

Individually or in small groups, research one of the three topics previously listed in order to complete exercise 6.7. You should consider the following cases in Canadian sports history, along with others you may come across while doing your research.

Ben Johnson was a Canadian sprinter during the 1980s. He won three Olympic medals; the first two were Bronze, and the last one was Gold. He set consecutive 100m world records at the 1987 World Championships in Athletics and the 1988 Summer Olympics. Then he failed a drug test. At first he denied it, but later he admitted that he had been taking steroids since 1981. Johnson was suspended from competing and stripped of his titles and of the Olympic Gold medal. He attempted a comeback in 1991, but in 1993 was found to be taking testosterone and was banned from competing for life. He was called a "national disgrace" in news headlines. (CBC digital archives, retrieved 2008) On March 8, 2004, during an NHL hockey game between the Vancouver Canucks and the Colorado Avalanche, Canucks player Todd Bertuzzi grabbed Avalanche player Steve Moore from behind, punched him in the head and fell on top of him. Moore suffered three fractured vertebrae in his neck and will never play hockey again. Bertuzzi was charged with assault, and hit with a multimillion dollar lawsuit that is still ongoing. Canucks coach Marc Crawford has also been named in the suit, as he allegedly told Canucks players "to make (Moore) pay the price" for having hit Markus Naslund two weeks prior to the March 8 game. (Canadian Press, 2004)

Developing Ethical Arguments

EXERCISE 6.7

Developing Ethical Arguments

Working individually or in small groups, develop moral arguments for or against steroid use, players' salaries, or violence in team sports.

State the ethical issues in clear, concrete terms.

_____

_____

_____

_____

_____

Who could be affected by this issue?

_____

_____

_____

_____

_____

What Canadian laws are relevant to this issue?

_____

_____

_____

_____

(Continued)

(Continued)

How would the various ethical approaches we have studied view this issue?

Principle-based or Kantian

_____

_____

_____

_____

Divine command theory

_____

_____

_____

Virtue ethics theory

_____

_____

_____

_____

Consequence-based or utilitarian

_____

_____

_____

_____

Social contract

_____

_____

_____

Enlightened self-interest

_____

_____

_____

_____

Which of the previous arguments are absolutist and which are relativist? Explain why.

_____

_____

_____

_____

"Compassion is the basis of all morality."

—ARTHUR SCHOPENHAUER (1788–1860)

7

World Issues

CONTENTS

> *"I cannot teach anybody anything. I can only make them think."*
>
> —SOCRATES

Many of the ethical issues that we face as Canadians are also issues for other countries. Abortion, euthanasia, gay rights, cultural and sexual relations, violence and criminal behaviour are all concerns that each nation has to resolve for itself. The decisions one nation makes on how to deal with these and other internal issues may be of interest to other nations or even influence the way they deal with the issues. They do not, however, directly affect other nations. American attitudes on same-sex marriage do not affect gay Canadians, for example, except perhaps when they are visiting the U.S.

There are many issues, however, which have global implications. International war conventions and trade agreements and the policies of the World Bank are global concerns that affect all nations. Other issues which are decided internally by a country, such as harbouring terrorists or chopping down rainforests or other endangered environments, also have direct and serious repercussions for other countries. We must share the same world, and to a certain extent we are a global community. This chapter is concerned with some of those issues.

Do we have the right to force just war practices on other countries? Senator Romeo Dallaire's book, *Shake Hands With the Devil* (and the movie made from it), explores this issue through his experience in Rwanda. Do we have the right to insist that other nations protect their environment, because we are all affected by global warming? Perhaps we should look to our own "carbon footprint" first. What is our obligation to Third World countries in terms of assistance and foreign aid? These are extremely difficult questions. This textbook does not presume to have the answers; we all need to work on finding them together. It is a sufficient first step, as Socrates said, to make people think.

GLOBAL INEQUALITY AND FOREIGN AID

Global development, Third World poverty and foreign aid are each huge topics in themselves. The problems are complex and the solutions are neither simple nor easy to implement. Therefore, our purpose in this text is simply to begin the discussion with an overview of some of the concepts involved and some of the solutions that have been proposed.

We are all aware of Third World poverty. We are inundated with news releases and advertisements which show distant people suffering natural disasters, starvation and injustice. The gap between the economic status we enjoy in North America and that of members of a Third World country is enormous, and it is increasing rather than diminishing. In 2005, the World Bank estimated that 1.1 billion people in the world lived on less than $1 US a day, and were "chronically hungry, unable to get health care, lack safe drinking water and sanitation, cannot afford education for their children and perhaps lack rudimentary shelter... and clothing" (Sachs, 2005). Third World countries are generally more prone to natural disasters and less able to assist their people to deal with them. Because of poor nutrition, little health education and lack of accessible medical care, their people are more susceptible to diseases such as AIDS/HIV and malaria. The lack of a reliable, accountable infrastructure prevents them from getting the education, resources and technological access necessary for productive work. Finally, those who live in a more volatile political climate are often the victims of human violence and political uprisings.

The fact that we live in a country where we can take all these things for granted is simply a matter of having been lucky in what Rawls called the "natural l ottery." Consider your own situation.

What are some social and economic realities in your life that you take for granted?

The ability to

_____

_____

Access to

_____

_____

What are some future expectations that you believe you will be able to achieve?

_____

_____

You might have listed things such as owning a car and a house, making a good income, supporting a family, travelling, or early retirement. You probably didn't think to list clean drinking water or eating at least one meal a day or not going blind or having your children survive their infancy or living past the age of 45. While we do not all live in ideal situations, most of us don't have to worry about these most basic needs, and do not expect to face them in our future.

Do we have an obligation, as members of a developed nation, to respond to the suffering of people in undeveloped countries?

_____

_____

If so, how far do you think that obligation extends?

_____

_____

How can we respond most effectively?

_____

_____

These are not easy questions. Before discussing our responsibility—or alternatively, lack of responsibility—to developing nations, we should examine some of the causes of economic disparity. You have probably heard the expression, "the haves and the have-nots." We usually interpret that as meaning those who have or do not have wealth, measured in material possessions. Of course, there are many important elements of life that Third World countries have in equal or sometimes greater quantity than First World countries, such as a strong, supportive sense of community, close extended families, etc. But our focus here is on the issues of poverty and foreign aid, so here we are concerned with economic wealth. As an individual, one can inherit wealth or earn it through some learned skill or knowledge. When we are talking about countries, we must look a little deeper.

What is it that wealthy nations have, which makes them wealthy?

_____

_____

What is it that poor nations do not have, which makes them poor?

_____

_____

The Causes of Third World Poverty

Good, fertile land for growing crops, a temperate climate, natural resources like oil, diamonds or gold and clean drinking water could all be considered the natural inheritance of a country. Certainly countries with poor soil or too little arable land, with a climate prone to drought, hurricanes and other natural disasters, without enough water and neither oil nor precious minerals to mine are at a serious disadvantage. But there are nations that have many of these natural inheritances and are still poor, like Zimbabwe, and there are countries which have few of these but are nevertheless wealthy, like Japan. So although these are all contributing factors, there are also other factors which affect the economic development of a country. Internal influences include a nation's history and culture, education and health care systems, population density, physical infrastructure, political stability and accountability, and the amount of civil freedom and equality its people are given. External influences include colonialism and the trade practices of Western nations.

There is some debate as to how much influence the cultural and political climate of a nation affects its economic development. The debate usually centres around whether civil rights or foreign aid should be first on the agenda for a developing nation. Countries with a history and current culture which does not allow gender equality, freedom of speech and information, innovative thought and accountable government are stifling the political and economic contributions of many, if not a majority, of their citizens. Gender inequity denies a nation the skills and intellect of half its citizens. Restrictions on freedom of speech and information include restrictions on the translation of books and information and the sharing of ideas between nations. This severely limits a nation's productivity and its ability to compete internationally. Discouraging innovative thought forces a nation further and further behind in the global marketplace. All of these usually go hand-in-hand with an ineffective education system and an inadequate health care system. There is no debate that these affect a nation's development. Illiteracy and illness are a drain on any nation's economy, not only in decreased productivity, but also in increasing the number of people who need the support or care of others.

The last two factors, political instability and corruption, are perhaps the most important internal influence on a nation's economic development because they affect all the others. Political instability and civil wars redirect a nation's resources from development goals to military ones. A geographical nation doesn't necessarily constitute a national identity among citizens—internal cultural rivalries are a major source of conflict and a barrier to development. Even when the political climate is stable again, the aftermath of war, like that of natural disasters, means that rather than progressing, a nation must focus on rebuilding.

Corruption and mismanagement of a country's resources not only prevent funds from going to education, health care and the exchange of information, but also make wealthy nations hesitant to invest foreign aid in a country, since those who need it will likely never see the money. However, it should be noted that some countries with a high level of internal corruption, like Bangladesh, Indonesia and Pakistan, have achieved strong economic growth. (Sachs, 2005)

There are also external factors which affect or have affected the development of Third World countries. Historically, colonialism is one factor. There are two sides to the debate about colonialism, however. One side maintains that Western nations plundered the natural resources of their colonies, increasing their own wealth while impoverishing the colonized. There is no doubt that colonizing countries made money on Brazil's rubber, India's tea and Peru's gold.

But colonization is not a prerequisite of theft. In the past, for example, oil and diamonds have been taken from Africa and gold from the Yukon. Moreover, there have been many empires in human history, such as the Persian empire, the Egyptian empire and the Roman empire, and all of them have stolen wealth from their colonies. In turn, the other side argues, all of these empires have also left positive legacies, such as roads, bridges and buildings, and an education and communication infrastructure. This side also argues that the Western countries developed the natural resources of their colonies, and left that development process in the hands of the colonies when they were ejected.

Historical wrongs are not the only negative external influences on developing countries. Subsidies, trade agreements and global competition all affect the economic development of poor nations. According to an article in *The New York Times*, "the world's wealthiest nations give more than $300 billion of subsidies to their farmers every year" (*The New York Times*, Sept. 8, 2003). Poor farmers in developing nations cannot compete with exported goods from heavily subsidized farm operations in Western countries. Trade barriers, including agricultural trade agreements, also have a negative effect on developing countries. Kofi Annan, the seventh secretary-general of the United Nations, wrote the following:

> For wealthy nations to preach the virtues of open markets to developing countries is mere hypocrisy if they do not open their own markets to those countries' products or stem the flooding of the world market with subsidized food exports that make it impossible for farmers in developing countries to compete. Nor can they expect developing countries to protect the global environment, unless they are ready to alter their own irresponsible patterns of production and consumption. (Annan, 2001)

Global institutions such as the International Monetary Fund (IMF) and the World Bank also have a strong effect on developing nations. The IMF and the World Bank were created in 1944. Their role was to maintain international financial stability, but many of the policies that do that are hard on poor nations. Liberalization policies in trade and capital markets limit poorer countries' ability to compete either in exporting products or in maintaining local banks. Their high interest rates are also economically devastating to developing nations. Much of the financial aid given to poor countries cannot actually help their people because it must go to relieve debt caused by the World Bank's high-interest loans. Furthermore, the IMF and the World Bank often attach strings to their loans, such as requiring that the developing country not subsidize export products, while developed countries continue to subsidize their products. All of these practices contribute to the difficulties undeveloped countries face in entering the global marketplace.

EXERCISE 7.1

Ethical Considerations for First World Nations

There are a number of ethical considerations behind the question, do we have a moral obligation to help people in poorer countries? Individually or in small groups, think of some ethical arguments for or against assisting the world's poor.

Divine command theory:

_____

_____

_____

Virtue ethics theory:

_____

_____

_____

Enlightened self-interest theory:

_____

_____

_____

Consequence-based theory:

_____

_____

_____

Principle-based theory:

_____

_____

_____

Share and discuss your answers with the class.
Considering these arguments, what is your moral obligation?

_____

Has your position changed?

_____

_____

Ethical Issues Concerning Foreign Aid

For most people, the question of whether we should assist the poor in Third World countries is less difficult than the questions, how much assistance are we obligated to offer, and should it come from individuals or from the government?

Peter Singer, in his article, "Famine, Affluence and Morality," addressed the following question: How much are we obligated to give? He begins his argument with two assumptions: that we all agree that Third World poverty is a documented and acknowledged fact and that we also agree that "suffering and death from lack of food, shelter and medical care are bad." Singer then makes a principle-based point that "if it is in our power to prevent something bad from happening, without thereby sacrificing anything of comparable moral importance, we ought, morally, to do it."

Singer's article focuses on individual financial donations to help people in dire need, such as is caused by drought, earthquakes and other natural and man-made disasters. His two statements quoted above transform the virtue of generosity into the Kantian concept of a moral obligation or duty. In other words, giving to alleviate others' suffering is not just morally acceptable or morally good; it is a moral requirement or law. In order to be ethical persons, we must do this.

Singer introduces some consequence-based reasoning when he includes the specification, "without sacrificing anything of comparable moral importance." Here he is saying that the moral good must outweigh the potential harm. For example, if all Canadians, or if our government, gave all of our money to poor countries to relieve their suffering, Canada would become a Third World country, and we would cause ourselves to suffer. Since our suffering is of comparable moral importance to other people's suffering, we should not go to this extreme. However, new clothes, expensive vacations and other luxury items are not of comparable moral significance to starvation or death and therefore we are, according to Singer, morally required to use our money for the prevention of death rather than for the acquisition of luxuries. (Singer, 1972)

In light of this argument, let us look at what is actually being done to reduce Third World poverty. In September, 2000, the Millennium Development Goals were adopted by the U.N. and agreed to by all member countries. The eight Millennium Goals are as follows:

1. *Eradicate extreme poverty and hunger*, by halving the proportion of people who suffer from hunger and whose income is less than $1 US per day, between 1990 and 2015.
2. *Achieve universal primary education*, by ensuring that children everywhere, boys and girls, are able to complete a full course of primary education by 2015.
3. *Promote gender equality and empower women*, by eliminating gender disparity in primary and secondary education by 2005, and in all levels of education by 2015.
4. *Reduce child mortality*, by reducing the under-five mortality rate by two-thirds between 1990 and 2015.
5. *Improve maternal health*, by reducing the maternal mortality rate by three-quarters between 1990 and 2015.
6. *Combat HIV/AIDS, malaria and other diseases*, by having halted and reversed the spread of HIV/AIDS and the incidence of malaria and other diseases by 2015.
7. *Ensure environmental sustainability*, by integrating the principles of sustainable development into national policies, reversing the loss of environmental resources, halving the proportion of people without access to safe drinking water by 2015 and significantly improving the lives of at least 100 million slum dwellers by 2020.
8. *Develop a global partnership for development*, by including governments, international organizations and the private sector in assisting Third World development.

The progress of these goals can be reviewed at www.un.org/millenniumgoals/pdf/mdg2007.pdf.

In order to accomplish these goals, the U.N. set a target for each country to donate 0.7% of its gross national income (GNI) by 2015. In 2005, Canada's foreign aid level was at about .28% of the gross domestic product (GDP). (CTV News April 19, 2005) The 2005 federal budget committed to increasing Canada's aid budget by 8% per year up to 2010. This will increase Canadian aid to an estimated .33% of our GNI by 2010. This figure falls far short of our .7% commitment, and much of it is bilateral debt forgiveness for Iraq and Cameroon, rather than money which will go directly into development. (CCIC, 2005) How much we give is one issue; the other issue is, do we give our foreign aid effectively? A recent article in *National Post* lists four potential problems in how foreign aid is distributed. These are as follows:

1. *Fragmentation* (when aid budgets are divided into too many tiny, ineffective pieces)
2. *Poor selectivity* (when aid is given to corrupt and/or relatively wealthy regimes)
3. *High overhead* (excessive administrative and payroll costs)
4. *Use of ineffective aid channels* (such as food aid, that harms recipient economies and local farmers; and tied aid, that comes with strings attached that harm the recipient country)
(*National Post*, 2008)

The chief agency in Canada for foreign aid is the Canadian International Development Agency (CIDA). According to the *National Post* article quoted previously, CIDA ranked worst among bilateral aid agencies for fragmentation, ineffective aid channels and administrative and payroll costs (15% as compared to 7% for the United Kingdom, 4% for Australia and 3% for Japan).

Although our government may not be doing as well as it could, that does not negate our responsibility as individuals. Singer's argument, in fact, concerned individuals rather than governments. Before we condemn our government, we must consider whether its values are in accordance with our own. How do we measure up to Singer's proposal?

Can you list five items you purchased in the past month which were of equal moral importance to relieving hunger and suffering?

_____

_____

_____

Can you list five items you purchased in the past month which were of less moral importance than relieving poverty and hunger?

_____

_____

_____

Do you think Singer's conclusion that we are morally obligated to give as much of our money as we can, without causing suffering to ourselves and our dependents, is reasonable? Why or why not?

_____

_____

_____

_____

JUST WAR THEORY

Think about the term "just war theory" for a moment. Assume that by "just," we mean morally defensible. Why do we specifically identify "just" wars, as opposed to warfare in general?

_____

_____

Just war theory implies a certain attitude toward war—that it is essentially unethical and only under certain identifiable circumstances can we justify going to war. If warfare was morally acceptable to us, we would have an "unjust war theory" instead, which would describe the particular situations in which war was *not* acceptable. Just war theory, therefore, begins with the attitude that war in general is unethical, that non-violent resolutions are morally preferable to violent ones. Yet it also recognizes that it may, at times, be necessary and morally justifiable to resort to violence.

Militarism and Pacifism

From the viewpoint of virtue ethics, just war theory could be considered the median, or middle way, between pacifism and militarism. Militarism is the belief that military force is noble and just. Proponents claim that it brings out the virtues of heroism, self-sacrifice and loyalty, and that it is a natural aspect of human nature. This is in keeping with Hobbes "state of nature theory," although the intent of Hobbes's social contract is to restrict violence.

Would you consider the argument that the use of force is part of human nature to be a descriptive or a normative approach?

_____

Pacifism is the belief that the use of lethal force against another person or nation can never be justified. Both principle-based and consequence-based arguments can be used to support this position.

Can you think of two arguments for pacifism?

Principle-based:

_____

Consequence-based:

_____

Considering the violent history of Western civilization, it may seem that just war theory is a modern concept. The idea that a war must be morally justified, however, goes back to Cicero (106–43 BC). Later, Saint Augustine, Bishop of Hippo (354–430 AD), wrote about the ethical conflict between upholding the traditional Christian teachings of non-violence and loving one's enemies, and the necessity of defending the Roman Empire against invaders. He considered just war in the moral context of defence (of self or of innocent victims) against an aggressor. (Tucker, 1960) Saint Thomas Aquinas (1225–1274 AD) in his *Summa Theologicae* discussed, not only the conditions which made a war just, but also what behaviours were ethically acceptable during war. His ideas were expanded upon by later writers to form the model for current just war theory. More recently, the Geneva and Hague Conventions (1901) list specific rules aimed at limiting certain kinds of warfare. (*The Internet Encyclopedia of Philosophy*, Just War Theory)

There are three stages to any war, and each stage has its own ethical considerations and decisions. These stages are: the decision to enter into warfare, decisions concerning combat behaviour during a war, and decisions about how to end hostilities. Just war theory includes all three, although its primary focus is on the first two. There is a special Latin term for each stage. *Jus Ad Bellum* establishes the criteria for deciding when entering into war is morally justified. *Jus In Bello* determines what behaviours are morally acceptable during a war. *Jus Post Bellum*, which has been added more recently, covers morally acceptable peace agreements, reparation and reconstruction, and the prosecution of war criminals.

The Principles of Just War

Jus Ad Bellum

There are six principles which must be considered when a nation is deciding whether to declare war on another nation. These principles are: just cause, legitimate authority, right intention, probability of success, last resort and proportionality. All six must be satisfied in order for a war to be morally justified.

The principle of just cause demands that there must be a serious and ethical reason for going to war. The theory does not specify what causes are morally acceptable, but most theorists agree on several conditions.

Before reading further, describe some conditions under which you would consider Canada justified in going to war:

_____

_____

_____

_____

The first condition generally agreed upon as being a just cause is self-defence: when another nation initiates acts of aggression against a country, that country has the right to defend itself. However, what do we consider an act of aggression? Is it a violation of territory, an insult to national honour, a trade embargo (which could be considered an economic act of aggression)? Some of the above? All of the above? Most just war theorists agree that self-defence against physical aggression is a just cause for war, and some maintain that it is the only just cause.

This raises two questions. The first concerns preventive and preemptive strikes. These are defensive strikes against anticipated acts of aggression. An example of a preventive strike would be one nation destroying another nation's nuclear reactor because it could have been used to create nuclear weapons. Preemptive strikes have to do with timing. If a nation is blatantly arming and preparing itself for war, is it necessary for the intended victim to wait for the aggressive nation to actually cross its borders before declaring war? Is a preemptive strike part of an ethical self-defence? This is a difficult issue, because what happens if the strike turns out to be unwarranted, as in the case where the U.S. entered Iraq in 2002 preemptively to find and destroy hidden weapons of mass destruction, only to find that there never were any weapons of mass destruction in Iraq.

The second question concerns the issue of interventionism. If self-defence is the only justification for war, what happens when an aggressor is much more powerful than the country under attack, and it is unable to defend itself? Is it ethical for other nations to stand by and watch the slaughter of the smaller country? The U.S. Catholic Conference (1993) stated that "Force may be used only to correct a grave, public evil, i.e., aggression or massive violation of the basic human rights of whole populations." This quote does not limit the use of force to self-defence. However, once again, this requires an interpretation: What is meant by a "violation of basic human rights?" Is democracy a basic human right, or just one form of government among many? What about protecting the global environment, or the world's oil supply? Where does self-defence become self-interest? In the case of genocide or "ethnic cleansing," it is generally agreed that intervention by another nation is ethically justified. But what about the treatment of women by the Taliban? Is this just cause for other nations to intervene? How is forcing women to wear burkas different from Nazi Germany forcing Jews to wear Star of David armbands? What is the tipping point between cultural differences and basic human rights?

Although it may be difficult to assess or interpret just cause, it is still the first requirement of a just war. Because some interpretation is required, we must be all the more careful to ensure that "just cause" is not stretched to include reasons that are not serious and sufficient to warrant going to war.

The second principle, the principle of legitimate authority, states that only the duly constituted authority or head of a nation can declare war. Rigidly interpreted, this would mean that rebellion against a government is unethical, no matter what the circumstances. If a government is just and has the support of the majority of its citizens, it is reasonable to give it the sole power of declaring war. However, if a government is corrupt, ineffective or not accountable to its people, they may be justified in declaring war to defend themselves against it or against a foreign power which it may be in league with. The French revolution is an example of the first instance; the Vichy regime, a puppet government set up by the Nazis to govern France after the Germans invaded in 1940, is an example of the second instance. Therefore, although the principle of legitimate authority having sole right to declare a nation at war is required in just war theory, it is also necessary to consider the relationship between that government and its people, in order to determine whether the head of state's authority is legitimate.

Many just war theorists hold that the United Nations must sanction a war in order for it to be just. Others maintain that since the goal of the U.N. is to promote peace, it may have a conflict of interest against sanctioning war even when there is just cause. Also, given that the U.N. is not accountable to any body of citizens, its right to direct those citizens into war is questionable. On the other hand, because the U.N. is not allied to any one nation, its determination of just cause would be more objective.

What do you think?

The principle of right intention means that the intention or goal of the war must always and only be to resolve the just cause, with the eventual goal of peace. Correcting a suffered wrong, such as the invasion of one's country, is right intention; in this case, the just cause would be self-defence. Going to war to indulge a cultural or racial hatred, or for revenge, or to acquire material gains, are not right intentions. A war cannot be considered just if other intentions are hidden behind an alleged just cause. For example, if nation A intervenes in an uprising against the government of nation B, while actually wanting to secure oil rights within nation B, then nation A is acting not out of right intention to correct or prevent a wrong, but out of self-interest. According to Kant, good intent is the only condition of moral behaviour, since we cannot control or even reliably predict consequences. One of the criticisms of Kant, which applies to just war theory, is the difficulty of separating good intent from self-interest. What if, in the previous example, nation A's intent is to prevent the massacre of the uprising, a just cause, but the consequences will still include oil rights?

The principle of probability of success means we must consider the outcome of going to war. Where there is little or no likelihood of successfully achieving the just cause, war cannot be justified. In other words, the costs and likely benefits of even a just war must be weighed against each other. This raises some serious moral questions. Should we refuse to intervene in cases of aggression or genocide if the cost will be too high and there is little likelihood that intervention will be successful? But how can we be sure that war against a larger force will not be successful? Historically, smaller nations have often successfully repelled a stronger aggressor. One example is Cuba's successful resistance of an American-sponsored invasion in 1961; another less dramatic example is the War of 1812, when Canada resisted an attempted American take-over. Even without the possibility of success, however, a smaller nation's intent to fight could make the larger power reconsider whether the cost was worth it. The principle of probability of success must be considered because we should not throw away human lives in a hopeless cause. Nor should we squander a nation's resources, impoverishing the people, when there is no chance of success. In such cases there may be other ways to address the issue, such as civil disobedience.

The principle of last resort requires that military force should only be used after all peaceful alternatives have been tried and all other alternatives are proved to be impractical or unrealistic. This includes negotiation, mediation by a nation that is not involved in the dispute or by the United Nations, or the use of threats and boycotts. The area open to interpretation here is, when have these measures been exhausted? The principle of last resort is intended to emphasize that military interventions cause great suffering, loss of life, and other destruction. War should be avoided if at all possible, even when the probability of successfully achieving a just goal through military intervention is very high.

The principle of proportionality involves weighing the benefits of waging war against the harm it will cause, and making sure that the benefits are proportionally greater than the harm. "Proportionally greater" means that there is not only more good than harm to be achieved by war, but that the good is more significant than the harm. In other words, we must weigh their relative values. In the case of a nation intervening to prevent an ethnic massacre, the good done by intervening (lives saved) must not only be greater than the harm (lives lost during the intervention) but must be proportionally or significantly greater, in order to justify the intervention. Human lives, historical treasures, ecological resources and national economics are all costs which must be weighed in determining the good versus the harm of military force. This also includes considering the benefits and harm of choosing an alternative other than war or of doing nothing. This last consideration is similar to act-utilitarianism, and requires a similar process of evaluation. It is also complicated by the same problems as act-utilitarianism: How do we evaluate the worth of different things, not only for ourselves but for other people? Freedom, archeological treasures, protection of the environment, economic security, even life itself all hold different values within different cultures and for different people within those cultures. Nevertheless, the good to be gained must be deemed to be proportionally greater than the harm expected before a war can be justified. Think of this as the "Was it really worth it?" principle applied in advance.

The six principles of *Jus Ad Bellum* are aimed as much at preventing unnecessary wars as they are at justifying necessary ones. Although they pose many problems in interpretation due to being vague and sometimes mutually inconsistent, they offer a valid starting point for examining the ethical considerations of initiating military action. Even more important, they provide an essential focus or spotlight on ethics within the sphere of war.

EXERCISE 7.2

Determining Just Reasons for Initiating War

In groups of four or five, summarize each of the six principles of *Jus Ad Bellum*. Everyone in the group must agree that the summary accurately explains the principle.

Just cause:

_____

_____

_____

Legitimate authority:

_____

_____

_____

Right intention:

_____

_____

_____

Probability of success:

_____

_____

_____

Last resort:

_____

_____

_____

Proportionality:

_____

_____

_____

Now read the two articles following this section on Canada's involvement in Afghanistan (beginning on page 240). You might also be asked to do additional research into this subject by your instructor. Apply the six principles, using the information in the articles (and any additional research) to determine whether Canada's decision to send forces to Afghanistan was just. Your arguments for or against this decision must directly refer to the six principles of *Jus Ad Bellum*. No other arguments should be used.

Jus in Bello

This aspect of just war theory deals with conduct in war. Historically, when people see themselves as very different, whether because of race, colour, religion or culture, they do not adhere to war conventions. It is only when people recognize that they will be doing business with their present enemy after the war is over that they are willing to avoid military tactics or weapons which would result in lasting bitterness. This can be considered enlightened self-interest, or can be argued from a utilitarian viewpoint. The long-term benefits of ethical war conventions are that they prevent animosities from escalating and, therefore, make it easier to create a lasting peace afterwards. Principle-based arguments state that atrocious, murderous and humiliating acts are not an acceptable part of war, and those who employ them should be held accountable for their behaviour. Either way, ethical conduct during war should be applied to all wars, so that just war theory is universal.

There are two main principles to *Jus In Bello*: proportionality and distinction (sometimes referred to as discrimination). Other related principles are military necessity and responsibility.

The principle of proportionality answers the questions, what kind of force and how much force is morally permissible in war? Military initiatives should use no more force than is needed to achieve an objective and the methods used should be proportionate to the importance of the objective. In other words, if destroying a bridge was a military objective, only as much force as is necessary to destroy the bridge should be used. If a great number of lives, both military and civilian, would be lost trying to destroy the bridge, and the bridge is of little overall significance in winning the war, then the cost of destroying it is not proportional to the benefit of destroying it. On the other hand, if many lives will be lost, but the bridge is key to winning the war because it is the enemy's main supply line, and winning the war quickly will prevent future casualties, then the cost is proportional to the benefit to be gained. This principle also comes into effect when considering disproportionate force against an enemy. If one enemy is armed with submachine guns and the other with knives and pitchforks, it is unreasonable to assume that every knife-carrying villager must be gunned down in order to subdue the village. The principle of proportionality does not allow massacres.

The principle of distinction answers the questions, who and what are legitimate targets in war? Non-military targets, such as schools, hospitals and residential areas, are not considered justifiable targets. This distinction becomes less clear when considering targets such as bridges or railways which support the enemy effort even though they may not be direct military bases or armaments. Not all roads and bridges support the military effort, or support it in a significant way, and only those that do can be considered military targets.

It is generally also agreed that non-combatants are not legitimate targets. While there are civilian casualties in a war, their deaths should not be intentional or excessive. Since killing any human being is essentially unethical, just war theory has to provide reasons that justify killing combatants. In war it is sometimes difficult to determine who is a combatant and who is a non-combatant, so we will examine that distinction at the same time. The first reason given is that combatants are armed and trained and, therefore, pose a threat. This ties in with the self-defence justification. A wounded or disarmed soldier no longer poses a threat and, therefore, should no longer be a target.

A second reason given to justify killing combatants is that by joining an army, combatants voluntarily give up their right not to be targeted in war. This reason applies not only to soldiers, but also to civilians aiding the war effort in significant and deliberate ways. Civilians assisting the army by building weapons, acting as interpreters, transporting soldiers or weapons and engaging in guerrilla or resistance activities can all be considered combatants who have voluntarily given up their right not to be targeted. Farmers who produce food that feeds soldiers, on the other hand, cannot be considered combatants because their work is not specifically directed toward the military effort.

The final reason given to justify killing combatants is that those who join an army come to terms with being a target, and, therefore, are prepared to die. This is often considered a weak argument because non-combatants living in a war zone can also come to terms with their own deaths, but that does not justify targeting them.

The principles of proportionality and distinction are intended to limit the violence and range of war. Other considerations sometimes included in *Jus In Bello* are military necessity and the issue of responsibility.

The principle of military necessity states that any military action must be deemed necessary to achieve the goal. This principle would be used to justify destroying non-military sites or assets to defeat an enemy. An example would be destroying food sources in order to starve an advancing enemy army. A consequence-based argument for this would be that a "no-holds-barred" approach to war will produce a successful outcome with a minimum of expense and time. A principle-based argument might be that having a just cause is sufficient reason to use whatever means may be necessary to achieve it.

Certain military tactics are considered unethical regardless of how effective they might be in achieving the goal, because of their far-reaching effects. Weapons of mass destruction fall into this category. Nuclear bombs, land mines and biological and chemical weapons cannot be limited to combatants and military targets, nor can their effects be confined to the duration of the war. Therefore, they offend the principles of proportionality and distinction and cannot be justified under military necessity.

The final aspect of ethical conduct in war is that combatants be held responsible for their conduct. Being held accountable requires combatants to abide by ethical rules during war just as they would during peace. The main issues in this area have to do with obeying orders, particularly when those orders are morally questionable, and the status of ignorance, when soldiers may not know the effects of their actions.

EXERCISE 7.3

Analyzing Examples of *Jus In Bello*

View one of the following movies: "Shake Hands With the Devil," "Charlie Wilson's War" or "Bridge on the River Kwai." Identify several characters who uphold the principles of *Jus In Bello* and others who violate them, and explain how they do so. What motivates them to act as they do? What principles are they upholding or violating and what are the likely short and long-term consequences of their actions?

Jus Post Bellum. The term *Jus Post Bellum* has recently been added to just war theory. It covers the ethical issues around ending a war. The three main considerations are termination of hostilities, peace agreements and terms of surrender, and the prosecution of war criminals.

Termination of hostilities begins with a just cause for termination. A nation may end a war for any of three reasons. The first is if the just cause for going to war has been resolved. If the rights that were violated in the first place (either aggressive force against a nation or violation of human rights requiring intervention by another nation) have been put right (the aggressor is repudiated or the human rights violations are ended) then the war has achieved its goal and should be terminated. Further hostilities in this case would be acts of revenge or self-interest. The second just cause, which may occur in conjunction with the first, is if the aggressor is willing to negotiate terms of surrender. The third just cause would be if it became clear that achieving the just goal is impossible or is going to cost too much in terms of human lives and/or a nation's assets. These considerations are the principles of proportionality and probability of success in *Jus Ad Bellum*. Often what is predicted at the beginning of a war turns out to be different in reality as the war progresses, so these two principles must be reevaluated as the war progresses.

Peace agreements and terms of surrender must be made by a legitimate authority and accepted by a legitimate authority. Legitimate authority has been discussed already and the same qualifications apply here. The agreements made must also be just and fair in order to avoid future wars. Terms of surrender usually include such things as a formal apology, compensation for harm done (occupied lands returned, fines imposed, etc.) and some form of assurance that the hostility will not be nurtured and the aggression not repeated. Prosecution of war criminals may also be part of these terms, which will be discussed later.

Proportionality is an important issue here. Any compensation or reparation included in the terms of surrender must be proportional to the rights that were violated. Peace treaties and terms of surrender cannot be used as an opportunity to get revenge or achieve self-interested goals. For example, restoring occupied land to the original nation is just; annexing additional lands from the aggressor is self-interest. Levying a reasonable fine for damages to an invaded nation is just; refusing to permit the nation at fault to participate in the world economy is revenge.

The final issue for just termination of war is the prosecution of war criminals. War crimes are often referred to as crimes against humanity, because they are actions which violate our basic human rights and dignity, and are wrong in any culture or time period. Genocide, torture, humiliation and the use of excessive force are all examples of war crimes. Right intent is an important criteria for trying war crimes. The same level of objectivity and justice must be applied to the trials of war criminals as to any other types of criminals. If a nation cannot proceed with that level of objectivity, another, impartial adjudicator must assist. While combatants legitimately can and should be held responsible for their behaviour before and during a war, non-combatants should not be made to suffer punitive measures simply for being citizens of a nation in which war crimes were committed. This relates to the earlier discussion on who should and should not be considered combatants in a war.

A number of declarations have been written and agreed to which support various aspects of just war theory, taking it out of the realm of theory and into the realm of treaties and agreements. The Geneva Conventions are a series of declarations written from 1864 to 1977 which cover the treatment of sick and wounded soldiers, the use of poison gas and biological weapons, and the treatment of prisoners and of non-combatants. The United Nations Convention Against Torture prohibits "cruel, inhuman, or degrading treatment."

EXERCISE 7.4

Identifying the Theoretical Base of Just War Theory

State one Kantian or deontological position regarding *Jus Ad Bellum*.

_____

_____

State one Kantian or deontological position regarding *Jus In Bello*.

_____

_____

State one Kantian or deontological position regarding *Jus Post Bello.*

_____

_____

State one consequentialist or teleological position regarding *Jus Ad Bellum.*

_____

_____

State one consequentialist or teleological position regarding *Jus In Bello.*

_____

_____

State one consequentialist or teleological position regarding *Jus Post Bello.*

_____

_____

State one virtue ethicist position regarding *Jus Ad Bellum.*

_____

_____

State one virtue ethicist position regarding *Jus In Bello.*

_____

_____

State one virtue ethicist position regarding *Jus Post Bello.*

_____

_____

State one Hobbesian or enlightened self-interest position regarding *Jus Ad Bellum.*

_____

_____

State one Hobbesian or enlightened self-interest position regarding *Jus In Bello.*

_____

_____

(Continued)

(Continued)

State one Hobbesian or enlightened self-interest position regarding *Jus Post Bello*.

_____

_____

State one contractarian position regarding *Jus Ad Bellum*.

_____

_____

State one contractarian position regarding *Jus In Bello*.

_____

_____

State one contractarian position regarding *Jus Post Bello*.

_____

_____

State one ethics of care position regarding *Jus Ad Bellum*.

_____

_____

State one ethics of care position regarding *Jus In Bello*.

_____

_____

State one ethics of care position regarding *Jus Post Bello*.

_____

_____

Current Controversy: Canada's Involvement in Afghanistan

Article 1: "Afghanistan needs Canada,"

(John Manley, *The Ottawa Citizen*, January 25, 2008)

With help we can achieve our humanitarian and security goals in that troubled country—and assist Afghans to stand on their own.

The opening lines of my independent panel's report make it clear that Afghanistan is at war and that Canada is a combatant. That's the situation today, but a close reading of our work says it doesn't have to be that way forever. I am encouraged that many others are ready to take our findings and begin a serious dialogue on what exactly Canada's role should be in the future.

Soon Canadians will have a choice to make and the members of the Independent Panel on Canada's Future Role in Afghanistan hope that our report will help. The essential questions are these: How to move from a military role to a civilian one? And how to achieve a shift in responsibility for Afghanistan's security from the international community to Afghans themselves?

If I learned one thing from this inquiry, it is that our presence in that distant land does matter—to Afghans, to our allies and to our interests as Canadians.

Canada's role in Afghanistan is fully justified on many fronts—from the point of view of international law, humanitarian needs and Canadian and global interests in security. At the same time, I realize many Canadians are uneasy about Canada's mission there. They wonder what it's all for, whether success is achievable and, in the end, whether the results will justify the human and other costs. I believe our report goes some way to answering those questions.

Whenever we asked Afghans what they thought Canada or other NATO forces should do, there was never any hesitation: "We want you to stay; we need you to stay." Without the presence of the international security forces, they said, chaos would surely ensue.

If we are not willing to lend our military resources when asked to do so by the United Nations, for a mission co-ordinated by NATO, in a country whose democratically elected government wants us and whose citizens desperately need us, then we wonder where and when Canada would do so.

We found no operational justification for the termination of Canada's military commitment by February of 2009. At the same time, we are not in favour of an indefinite commitment. We also recognize that the status quo is not good enough. The most glaring need at the moment is for additional troops from NATO and other allies to ensure a greater degree of security that will make reconstruction and better governance possible. These challenges are interlinked.

We also believe that a premature withdrawal by Canada would squander our investment and dishonour our sacrifice to date. But Canada cannot, by itself, guarantee success in Afghanistan. That is why we made a key conditional recommendation in the report presented this week to the prime minister. We believe that, at a minimum, a battle group of 1,000 soldiers is needed to support the existing Canadian effort, as well as improved equipment for our armed forces, if the Kandahar mission is to succeed. If this cannot be mustered over the next year, then Canada should signal its intent to transfer responsibility for security in Kandahar. This will be a necessary litmus test for NATO.

While much of the attention has focussed on the military side of our report, other matters must also be addressed in parallel. For instance, the prime minister must step up and make this mission a top priority with a cabinet committee to ensure better co-ordination of Canada's efforts. Even more important, he must personally lead our diplomatic initiative, making our voice heard to a degree commensurate with our contribution. Along with our key allies, he should urge that the international community get its act together both in Afghanistan and with other countries in the region. There is a genuine need for a more coherent international effort across the board.

The ultimate objective is to help the Afghans assume responsibility for security, reconstruction and governance in their country. Additional troops will enable us to train the Afghan army; a better co-ordinated international effort on reconstruction, led by a high level representative of the U.N. secretary-general, will drive a more effective approach both to reconstruction and governance. Canada has the capacity to make a tangible contribution to all three.

Our panel has no illusions about the complexity of the challenge nor about the severe deficiencies in Afghanistan today but we believe that, if our recommendations are implemented, Canada will be better able to improve the prospects for success.

I hope that our work sparks a better understanding of why we are there and why we need a continued presence on the ground, in the corridors of power, and in the communities of ordinary Afghans who simply seek better lives.

John Manley chaired the Independent Panel on Canada's Future Role in Afghanistan. He is a former deputy prime minister and minister of foreign affairs.

Article 2: "Troops will not win the hearts and minds of Afghans,"
(Mohamed Elmasry, *Toronto Star*, January 24, 2008)
National President, the Canadian Islamic Congress

I am among the 219 Canadian individuals and organizations who submitted their views to John Manley on Canada's future role in Afghanistan.

But after reading his report I am disappointed.

"Foreign invasion is not a solution for the disastrous situation of Afghanistan. As our history demonstrates, we don't want occupation," said Malalai Joya, 29, the youngest female member of Afghanistan's parliament, when interviewed in December 2007 by the Canadian Centre for Policy Alternatives.

"Six years of Western military occupation clearly show that these armies have not come to provide us with security. The U.S. and its allies, including Canada, are supporting the sworn enemies of our people. If they continue this wrong policy, one day they will be faced with the massive resistance of our people, as our history shows," Joya warned.

But Manley and his panel did not bother to interview Joya before writing their report. It seems that her views—the authoritative product of history, culture and immediate lived experience—were not the views Manley was looking for.

Instead of recommending that Canada's mission steer a new course toward an internationally supported political solution that could achieve peace and stability, and allow us to bring our troops home sooner, Manley's group wants Canadian forces to continue on without a set time limit, staying until the Afghan police and army are able (if ever) to take over their own security duties in southern Afghanistan.

What Manley did not tell Canadians up front is that such a recommendation is nothing more than an open-ended strategy that actually avoids commitment to concrete and practical objectives, such as peacefully resolving the conflict that is making progress in any other area impossible to achieve.

It has become painfully clear that NATO countries cannot trust the Afghan army and police with sophisticated equipment for fear it will fall into the hands of the Taliban, or that the local officers themselves will desert regular government forces and join the Taliban. This very real possibility makes any suggestion that the above objective is achievable a blatant falsehood.

A Rand Corporation study stated that NATO needs 20 soldiers per 1,000 inhabitants to wipe out the Taliban, which translates to a force of about 500,000. The NATO coalition currently has only 30,000 to 50,000—enough to kill civilians on a daily basis, but not enough to control even a small part of Afghanistan. Canada maintains more than 2,500 troops in the country, mainly in the dangerous southern province of Kandahar.

The recent death of 26-year-old Richard Renaud from the Quebec City area marks the 77th time a Canadian soldier has died in Afghanistan since the mission began in 2002. In addition, one diplomat—Glyn Berry—was killed, bringing the current death toll to 78.

Asking NATO to post 1,000 more soldiers in Kandahar to help our troops may reduce Canadian casualties, but will not bring anyone closer to solving the problem.

In November 2007, the Washington *Post* reported that American intelligence analysts acknowledge there have been some battlefield victories in Afghanistan, but they highlight the unchallenged Taliban expansion into new territory, an increase in opium poppy cultivation, and the weakness of President Hamid Karzai's government as signs that the war effort is deteriorating.

Manley did not mention in his report, even for the record, that repeated opinion polls have shown that the majority of Canadians do not support Canada's mission in Afghanistan. Forty-seven percent of Canadians want our troops brought back from Afghanistan as soon as possible, and in Quebec the number who want the mission to end immediately is even higher, at 57 percent. Polls show that only 17 percent of Canadians want our troops to continue in their current combat role, while 31 percent said that Canadians should remain in Kandahar, but turn combat responsibilities over to another NATO country.

The Manley report mentioned the suffering of the Afghan people, but only in passing. Yet in 2007 alone, more than 6,000 Afghan people were killed, according to reports by The Associated Press, bringing the number of Afghan deaths to about 40,000 since 2001.

The British-based international aid agency, Oxfam, has warned that urgent action is needed to avert a humanitarian disaster in Afghanistan where millions face "severe hardship comparable with sub-Saharan Africa." Oxfam further cautioned that aid spending on Afghanistan has been only a small fraction (about three percent) of the military expenditure, and that most aid money received is diverted into high salaries for officials and administrators.

This conflict cannot be resolved through blunt military force. Canada should bring its troops home by February 2009 and should call for an urgent U.N. peace conference on Afghanistan.

Our MPs have the moral and political responsibility of treating the lives of Canadian men and women serving in Afghanistan with the same value they place on the lives of their own families.

Instead of sending people with weapons and heavy artillery, Canada should send an army of peacemakers, teachers, engineers, doctors, and nurses. We should send mine-clearing equipment and have a plan in place to build the best training centres, universities, and hospitals.

Let's try to win the hearts and minds of the Afghan people. Anyone who knows the character of Afghans will know this is a win-win situation, one well worth taking the risk.

GUERRILLA WARFARE AND TERRORISM

When people do not believe that their government speaks for them, they may be tempted to declare war themselves. In the earlier example given of the Vichy government in occupied France, which was controlled by the German invaders, the French Resistance was made up of guerrilla fighters. Civilians acting as armed combatants will use either guerrilla tactics or terrorism, the main difference being whether their intent is to resist armed combatants or to terrorize an ideological enemy. If guerrilla warfare and terrorism are considered acts of war, as they claim to be, then many of the tenants of just war theory should apply to them. Therefore, we will examine them according to the principles of just war theory.

Before we do, in what ways do you think the principles of just war will be met or not be met by guerrilla warfare and terrorism?

Guerrilla warfare:

_____

_____

_____

Terrorism:

_____

_____

_____

Guerrilla warfare generally has not been legitimized by a head of state and its combatants constitute a much smaller force than their opponents, so their likelihood of success is slim. They employ evasive and covert tactics rather than direct confrontation. Because they are a smaller force, they usually do not have any secure base and cannot detain prisoners, so they generally have a ruthless approach to wounded or unarmed enemy combatants, which includes anyone who actively collaborates with the enemy. In other ways they often follow just war conventions. They claim to have a just cause (the French Resistance fought an invading aggressor) and the right intentions (their goal was to reclaim their own country) and they limit their attacks to combatants. They may well have the support of the general population. When the war is justly terminated, guerrillas cease hostilities and disband. Guerrilla warfare is essentially a type of warfare which evolves out of certain political circumstances and military necessity.

Terrorists also believe that they have a just cause, but that cause is often founded in some form of national or religious fanaticism, rather than in repelling an invading force or preserving basic human rights. Terrorism is not based on reparation but on emotion; therefore, the intent may be justice, but it is accompanied by the desire for revenge, cultural cleansing or religious dominance. Terrorists may base their just cause on an historic wrong that needs to be corrected. The Irish Republican Army (IRA) and the Front de Liberation du Quebec (FLQ) both claimed to have just cause in repelling an invader (the English), although in both cases many years of peaceful government had passed since the invasion, and the current occupants have been native-born for generations. Not only do terrorists not have current just cause or have legitimate authority for declaring war, but they rarely have the support of the general population.

Although there is a wide divergence between terrorism and just warfare in *Jus Ad Bellum*, the main differences occur in *Jus In Bello*. Terrorists achieve their goals by spreading terror; in order to do so, they target non-combatants going about their daily lives and non-military operations such as water supplies, fuel depots, business centers and computer systems. According to Jean Bethke Elshatain in *"Just War Against Terror"*:

> Terrorists are those who kill people they consider their "objective enemy," no matter what those people may or may not have done. *Terrorist* and *terrorism* entered ordinary language to designate a specific phenomenon: killing directed against all ideological enemies indiscriminately and outside the context of a war between combatants. According to the logic of terrorism, enemies can legitimately be killed no matter what they are doing, where they are, or how old they are. (Elshatain, 2003)

The goal of terrorists is to create fear through random acts of murder and violence. Their cause may be to liberate their country, to right a past wrong, to seek vengeance, to destroy everyone in a particular culture, race or religion, to assert their own worth or to serve the will of God. They lack any ability to empathize with their victims and cannot imagine themselves being wrong. For these reasons the principles of *Jus In Bello* (distinction and proportionality) are meaningless in the context of terrorism. Terrorists justify the indiscriminate targeting of civilians as being the most effective and efficient way to demoralize an enemy, and therefore, the most economic way to force a surrender. They also claim military necessity, since terrorists operate despite a huge technological and military disparity between them and their enemy. Finally, they claim, with some justification, that civilians are being killed by the enemy, also. The difference between being a target and being collateral damage is of questionable importance to the dead and wounded.

The justifications for terrorism generally fall into three categories: military necessity, as discussed previously; Divine Command Theory, as it is narrowly interpreted by religious terrorists; and consequence-based arguments, such as "the end justifies the means." However, if this is used as a justification of terrorism, it would be necessary to prove that the means actually did accomplish the end. In the case of the FLQ, the October 5, 1970, kidnapping of British Trade Commissioner James Cross, and the kidnapping and murder of Quebec Labour Minister Pierre Laporte five days later, have not resulted in liberating Quebec from Canada. In fact, as several referendums have shown, the majority of Quebecois do not wish to leave Canada. The IRA has also not been successful in removing the English from Ireland, and Al-Qaeda has not reinstated its harsh interpretation of Islam anywhere. It would seem the means are not successful in achieving any purpose other than the twisted goal of spreading fear.

A second consideration when using utilitarianism to justify terrorism is that the benefits gained must outweigh the harm done. It is hard to imagine anyone arguing that terrorism has increased human happiness to the extent that could justify the harm and suffering it has caused, either in the long or short term.

And yet terrorism continues to attract followers, and their recruitment is fuelled by our attempts to combat it. Section 83 of the Criminal Code deals with terrorism. Specifically, section 83.18 states:

(1) Every one who knowingly participates in or contributes to, directly or indirectly, any activity of a terrorist group for the purpose of enhancing the ability of any terrorist group to facilitate or carry out a terrorist activity is guilty of an indictable offence and liable to imprisonment for a term not exceeding ten years.

Meaning of participating or contributing

(3) Participating in or contributing to an activity of a terrorist group includes

(a) providing, receiving or recruiting a person to receive training;

(b) providing or offering to provide a skill or an expertise for the benefit of, at the direction of or in association with a terrorist group;

(c) recruiting a person in order to facilitate or commit

(i) a terrorism offence, or

(ii) an act or omission outside Canada that, if committed in Canada, would be a terrorism offence;

(d) entering or remaining in any country for the benefit of, at the direction of or in association with a terrorist group; and

(e) making oneself, in response to instructions from any of the persons who constitute a terrorist group, available to facilitate or commit

(i) a terrorism offence, or

(ii) an act or omission outside Canada that, if committed in Canada, would be a terrorism offence.

Not only do terrorists target civilians and children, but they also use them as combatants. This raises the moral problem of child soldiers. Using children under the age of 18 as soldiers is against international laws for warfare. The case of Omar Khadr highlights this issue.

Omar Khadr: Case for Discussion

The current case of Canadian Omar Khadr brings a number of issues to light.

Omar Khadr is a Canadian who was raised in a Muslim home with strong sympathies for Al-Qaeda. When he was ten he was put into the Al-Qaeda family training camps and when he was fourteen he accompanied his father to Afghanistan. In July, 2002, when Omar was 15 years old, he was caught in a skirmish between Al-Qaeda and American soldiers in Afghanistan. Approximately 40 to 50 American soldiers and Afghan translators surrounded a mud hut compound where members of Al-Qaeda were believed to be making IEDs (remote control detonators) for anti-tank bombs. The translators approached the compound and were shot instantly, after which the American soldiers opened fire. Those in the compound returned weapon fire and threw grenades over the wall. U.S. bombers dropped 500-pound bombs on the compound until there was no more returned fire. American soldiers then went in to examine the compound. When they got close enough, someone fired a pistol and threw a hand grenade over the compound wall, killing Christopher Spear, an American soldier. Omar Khadr was found alive in the compound with two large bullet holes in his back. He was treated by a medic, taken to Bagram Air Base in Afghanistan for interrogation, and then imprisoned in Guantanamo Bay. Initially, it was claimed that Khadr was the one who threw the grenade and fired on the troops, killing Spear. However, according to Lt. Commander William Kuebler, Khadr's U.S. military-appointed defence lawyer,

> ...there was at least one other adult combatant alive in the compound when U.S. forces stormed it. That that individual was actually fighting U.S. forces, unlike Omar who was, according to one key government witness, sort of sitting down facing away from the fight slumped over against a bush suffering from what we know to be fairly serious wounds to his eyes at that point when he was shot in the back at least twice. (Lt. Commander Kuebler, CBC Interview, 2008)

This case poses several ethical problems. First, the legality of Khadr's treatment is in question. Second, Omar Khadr's status as a child soldier requires accommodations that have not been met. Finally, it must be determined whether Canada has an obligation to intervene on Khadr's behalf.

Omar Khadr's interrogation at Bagram and his imprisonment at Guantanamo Bay for the past six years without trial do not conform to national or international laws on the treatment of prisoners. Both at Bagram and Guantanamo, Khadr endured what Lt. Commander Kuebler called cruel, inhuman and degrading treatment, a violation of the Geneva Convention: "Omar was 15 and he had two golf ball-sized ... bullet wounds in his chest and yet he was exposed to confinement techniques such as being chained with his arms above his head for extended periods of time.... He was left in Guantanamo Bay, chained to the floor for extended periods of time, not allowed to use the bathroom, forced to urinate on himself." (Lt. Commander Kuebler, CBC Interview, 2008) In addition, according to Kuebler, Khadr was not engaged in terrorism. He participated with "a militia group in armed conflict with U.S. forces in the course of a war in Afghanistan. He's not alleged to have attacked civilians ... [or] a civilian target. ...[T]hey were making explosive devices for use against military forces in an armed conflict. In our view that's not terrorism, that's not a war crime." (Lt. Commander Kuebler, CBC Interview, 2008)

The U.S. Supreme Court has found Guantanamo Bay and the use of military commissions to be illegal. The very fact that Omar Khadr has been imprisoned for six years without a fair, legal trial contravenes his basic human rights for due process. Amnesty International, along with other international human rights organizations, has condemned Guantanamo Bay for operating outside the rule of law, and claims that "Detainees should be released unless they are to be charged with recognizably criminal offenses and provided with a fair trial before an independent and impartial tribunal..." (Homes, 2008)

The second issue this case brings up is that of child soldiers. Children as young as eight or nine can aim a gun and kill. Does that place them in the same category as adult armed combatants? Are they appropriate war targets? There is a lot of discussion on this issue both in the justice system and in international war conventions. Children are easily manipulated by adults to do things adults might not do. Most suicide bombers, for instance, are young people. Because of this vulnerability to manipulation by adults, there are a number of international agreements forbidding the use of children in war.

The United Nations Committee on the Rights of the Child emphasizes that any person under the age of 18 must be treated under the rules of juvenile justice, which includes rehabilitation and reintegration, and they must be "detained for the shortest appropriate period of time." The Optional Protocol to the International Convention on the Rights of the Child condemns the use of any person under the age of 18 in armed conflict, either as combatants, as messengers, porters, cooks or in any capacity whatsoever. The Protocol requires that these children be demobilized and given assistance for their emotional and physical recovery and their reintegration into society. Under the Rome Statute of the International Criminal Court, recruiting and using children under age 15 is a war crime. The U.N. Security Council Resolutions also bans the use of child soldiers and supports their reintegration into society. The Paris Commitments concerning children associated with armed forces states that such children are to be considered victims of offences against international law and must be "treated in accordance with international law in a framework of restorative justice and social rehabilitation." (Homes, 2008)

The third issue to consider is Canada's obligation to Omar Khadr as a Canadian citizen. Canada ratified the Optional Protocol to the International Convention on the Rights of the Child in July, 2000. In 2007, Canada adopted the Paris Commitments. Canada also worked on the U.N. Security Council resolutions, hosted the first International Conference on War-Affected Children in Winnipeg in September, 2000, and has ratified the Rome Statute of the International Criminal Court. Currently, Canada is actively involved in encouraging and assisting other countries, such as Sierra Leone, Colombia, northern Uganda and Afghanistan, to reintegrate their child soldiers into society. Clearly, Canada has played a leadership role in the cause of child soldiers, and other nations are watching to see what Canada is or is not doing in this case. Omar Khadr was captured at age 15, making him indisputably a child soldier. Yet no efforts have been made to rehabilitate or reintegrate him into society. Furthermore, he is a Canadian citizen who has been held in an illegal capacity and has suffered treatment which violates the Geneva Convention.

On the other hand, Omar Khadr was working with Al-Qaeda, a group which is at war with Canada and with our ally, the United States. Omar Khadr's father died in the compound skirmish, but the rest of his family remain outspoken supporters of Al-Qaeda and of terrorist tactics. He is now 21, and could pose an even greater threat, especially if he is reintegrated back into his militant family.

What obligation, if any, does Canada have to Khadr as a Canadian citizen?

_____

_____

What obligation, if any, does Canada have to Khadr as a child soldier?

_____

_____

What obligation, if any, does Canada have to the international community of nations?

_____

_____

What obligation, if any, does Canada have to protect its citizens?

_____

_____

What obligation, if any, does Canada have to its ally, the U.S.?

_____

_____

What do you think Canada should do in this case? Why?

_____

_____

ENVIRONMENTAL ISSUES

By the late 1960s Lake Erie was dead. There was too much pollution in the water for any life to survive. Other freshwater lakes and rivers were also full of pollutants like phosphated detergents, factory smokestacks belched lethal wastes into the air and our soil was poisoned with DDT and other chemicals. Since then, we've improved a lot. Lake Erie supports life again and there are laws restricting the use of the worst toxins and pesticides. We've learned to reduce, recycle and reuse. But is it enough? Natural disasters such as tornadoes, floods, earthquakes, forest fires and tsunamis are increasing. Climate change is making the depletion of the ozone layer a visible reality for even the skeptics among us. People are beginning to realize that environmental issues may be the most important problem that faces us today.

Environmental ethics are complicated because of the many different perspectives involved. Sometimes it is hard to understand the arguments environmentalists make, and disagreements arise before the debate can even begin. In order to begin the discussion of environmental ethics, imagine the following scenario. It will take a bit of imagination, but will help each of us to determine our own perspective on the environment.

One thousand students from a college are on a cruise. During the cruise, a meteor shower destroys the rest of the civilized world. The cruise boat is damaged and sinks, but there is an island nearby and everyone boards the lifeboats and reaches the island safely. The island is a tropical paradise, with a complete ecosystem of plants, insects, birds, mammals, and fish in the surrounding ocean, as well as in a freshwater lake on the island. There are no other humans, however, and no rescue will be coming. The ship's captain is elected the leader. Several crew members have brought vegetable seeds and pesticides from the ship, and others have brought hunting and fishing equipment. There may be no other place on Earth where these plants and animals still exist, but many of them will be destroyed if all the people from the ship are to be fed and housed and allowed to reproduce. The captain must decide what the ethical thing to do in this situation is. He has several options:

1. Might makes right. People are at the head of the food chain; everything else is here for humans to use however they want. Too bad for the plants, insects and other animals if they don't survive. The captain should do whatever is necessary to save all the people.

2. Morality is only about people, but the captain should be careful not to deplete the resources on the island in case they're needed for many generations. The captain should limit how much of the island is cultivated, limit the use of pesticides and limit births so people don't overpopulate the island and cause later generations to starve.

3. Everything on the island has moral value: the animals, birds, fish, insects and plants are all as important as humans. The captain should take as much care of the island and all life on it as of the humans. He should get rid of the pesticides (carefully) and they should live as part of the island system. If that makes their life harder and some people don't survive, well, the same thing is happening to all the living things on the island.

4. There is no way over a thousand people can live on this island without damaging and maybe destroying its ecosystem. The island is perfect without humans, and people aren't part of its ecosystem. Rather than ruining what might be the last living, natural habitat on Earth, the captain should divide up the food and water from the ship and make everyone get back into the life rafts and leave. When they've used up the last of the supplies, they'll die, but they won't have destroyed the island and maybe it'll be the source of life beginning over again on Earth.

Which option should the captain choose?

Those who chose option 1 or 2 chose the *anthropocentric* perspective. This is the traditional, human-centred view of the environment. People who take this perspective may well believe that the environment should be cleaned up and further pollution avoided, that rainforests should be preserved along with other natural habitats and endangered species protected from becoming extinct—but they also believe that all of this should be done because it is in the best interests of human beings. Who knows what cures for diseases might be found in the rainforest in the future? Incidents of diseases like cancer and asthma increase dramatically with constant exposure to airborne and chemical pollutants. If we don't take care of the environment our health and perhaps our descendents' very existence may be threatened. Natural wild areas also give us aesthetic pleasure and should be preserved for our children to enjoy. Anthropocentrism argues that humans have a responsibility to future generations not to use up all the non-renewable resources such as fossil fuels. "We don't own the Earth; we hold it in trust for our children," is the kind of argument someone with this perspective would make.

Those who chose option 3 in the previous scenario chose the *biocentric* perspective. They believe that animals and plants have rights just as much as people do, for their own sake, not only because they are or might be useful or give us pleasure. All living things are as much a part of creation as people and we have no right to destroy them or their habitats indiscriminately. Albert Schweitzer, the famous Swiss humanitarian, proposed biocentricism this way in his book, *Out of My Life and Thought*:

> The great fault of all ethics hitherto has been that they believed themselves to have to deal only with the relations of man to man. In reality, however, the question is what is [man's] attitude to the world and all life that comes within his reach. A man is ethical only when life, as such, is sacred to him, and when he devotes himself helpfully to all life....

Those who chose option 4 chose the *ecocentric* perspective. Ecocentrism attaches value and rights to whole ecosystems, including even the non-living elements in them, such as rivers and soil. Rainforests, wetlands, savannas and tundra all have value in their own right and should be preserved for themselves. Humans have no right to destroy or disrupt any ecosystem just for our personal benefit or profit. Selective hunting or careful use of natural resources like selective thinning of a forest would be morally acceptable if it allowed the ecosystem to remain healthy and diverse. Aldo Leopold, an early 21st-century forester and writer, called it a "land ethic." He proposed this ethical position in his book, *A Sand County Almanac*:

> All ethics so far evolved rest upon a single premise: that the individual is a member of a community of interdependent parts... The land ethic simply enlarges the boundaries of the community to include soils, waters, plants and animals, or collectively: the land. ...A thing is right when it tends to preserve the integrity, stability and beauty of the biotic community. It is wrong when it tends otherwise.

Environmental Pragmatism

Obviously people have very different perspectives on environmental ethics. However, it is possible to put aside differing opinions about what our relationship with the Earth is, and why we have obligations to it, and simply agree that certain things should be done. Whether we are acting out of self-preservation, out of a sense of responsibility to our children and their children, or to all forms of life, or to the Earth itself, we can all agree that protecting the environment is important. This position is called environmental pragmatism. Environmental pragmatism maintains that we can reach a consensus of environmental values which determine the environmental policies we can all agree upon.

From this pragmatic perspective, protection of the environment includes conservation of natural resources; protection of wilderness areas and endangered species; prevention of soil contamination and erosion; prevention or cleanup of air and water pollution; prevention of agricultural use of pesticides and chemical fertilizers; halting global warming and the depletion of the ozone layer; dealing with nuclear waste; and limiting human overpopulation and urban sprawl. That might sound a bit overwhelming, but we can discuss them in three main categories: pollution, use of natural resources and land health.

Pollution. Pollution includes the emissions, byproducts and waste from our production, energy and farming facilities, which are harmful to humans and other living things when they are released into the air, water and soil. In other words, it is not only the pollutants themselves that are the problem, but also the way we dispose of them. Even products that we use intentionally, such as chemical fertilizers and pesticides, can be considered pollutants if the damage they do to the environment is as great or greater than their benefits to us. Often the solution is to strike a balance between the harms and benefits, or finding a less harmful product which can accomplish the same thing. Waste is another important consideration, both for individuals and for corporations. Recycling and finding new uses for the things we throw out is crucial to cutting down on pollution.

Use of Natural Resources. Ethical issues surrounding the use of natural resources include sustainability and non-renewable resources. Sustainability means that an activity can be sustained—i.e., continued indefinitely—without depleting the resources necessary for that activity. Current intensive farming methods are not sustainable because they deplete the land and erode soil faster than it can be replenished. Current energy policies and transportation methods are unsustainable because they rely largely on non-renewable resources like fossil fuels. Fossil fuels such as oil and coal are limited; once they have been used up, we will not have any more. Wind and sun and water, on the other hand, are renewable resources because they can't be used up. One of the issues with non-renewable resources concerns using up resources which future generations will need; they have a right to expect us to limit our use of the Earth's non-renewable resources so they, too, will have the benefits of those resources. Another issue concerns the overwhelming proportion of the Earth's resources that First World countries take for themselves. Third World countries have as much right as the First World to benefit from these resources.

Possible solutions to this problem include using these resources more efficiently (e.g., more fuel-efficient cars) and developing sustainable methods of achieving our ends (e.g., solar panels to help heat our houses). For businesses, that might mean cutting back and accepting smaller immediate profits due to the expense (at least initially) of implementing more environmentally friendly production methods. For individuals, it means such things as consuming less energy in our homes and using alternate methods of transportation. Sustainable farming methods, for example, involve caring for the long-term productivity of the soil and practising crop rotation so that the soil continues to be fertile. Sustainable energy and transportation require developing alternatives such as solar and wind power to avoid depleting the Earth's limited supply of fossil fuels. It also involves creating more mass transit and building affordable living communities that are close to shopping, school and work.

One current controversy around this issue concerns the use of biofuels. Initially, this appears to be an excellent solution to the concern about depleting fossil fuels. Biofuels are considered to be carbon neutral. This means that because they grow back, the carbon released when they are burned is re-absorbed by the next crop, whereas burning fossil fuels releases carbon that cannot be re-absorbed. With over 600 million cars (and growing) on the planet, and with airlines also considering a switch, there will be considerable demand for biofuels if we continue to develop in this direction. Canadian companies (e.g., Iogen) are developing fuel production systems to use switch grass, a weed that grows on the prairies, or to use waste material from the forestry industry. But the use of biofuel has its downside. Palm oil is an excellent source of biofuel, and Third World countries are clearing their rainforests to make way for palm oil plantations. Malaysia is particularly involved and has been increasing its plantations since 1917. Destroying a diverse natural habitat such as a rainforest, and replacing it with a monoculture (a single plant production) has tremendous implications for our biosphere, for the ozone layer, for endangered species (such as the orangutan) and for the diverse plant species found only in rainforests. Another questionable source of biofuel is corn. The issues here are twofold: It takes a lot of energy and land to grow corn, and corn is food. The world population is rising and a steady increase in droughts and other climate disasters have impinged upon arable land in recent years, putting millions at serious risk of starvation. Can we ethically justify putting food into our cars instead of into human mouths?

Land Health. Land health includes preserving wild areas and biological and ecological diversity. Parks Canada defines ecological integrity as "the condition of an ecosystem where the structure and function are unimpaired by human-caused stresses, and the biological diversity and supporting processes are likely to persist." (Parks Canada, 2000) This means limiting human use of the land, not only by not developing too much of it for human habitation or agriculture, but also in forgoing the opportunity to mine or take lumber from restricted areas. The question is, what is that limit? Some environmentalists say that we have already taken up too much of the earth for human uses. Non-environmentalists might disagree. But pragmatically, we can all agree on the need to preserve natural spaces for four purposes:

- Park space within urban areas provides us with spaces to play and relax in, as well as providing space for smaller wildlife such as birds, insects and squirrels.
- Unique landscapes or wilderness park areas such as the Rocky Mountains, the badlands of Alberta or Algonquin Park in Ontario enrich our lives as well as offering sanctuary to larger animals, birds and plants.
- Preserving a variety of ecosystems, large enough in size to be self-sustaining, protects endangered plants and wildlife as well as accommodating natural processes (for example, large wetlands minimize the threat of floods and act to purify inland water systems).
- Biological diversity in nature creates healthier ecosystems, makes plants and animals more resistant to disease and increases the likelihood of discovering new medicines.

List five things an individual can do to live a more environmentally ethical lifestyle:

1. _____

2. _____

3. _____

4. _____

5. _____

List five things an organization or a business can do to be more environmentally responsible:

1. _____

2. _____

3. _____

4. _____

5. _____

Business's Responsibility in Protecting the Environment

Business owners and managers make decisions all the time. When they make decisions that will affect the environment, those decisions affect us, our children, future generations and the Earth itself. Whether they run a factory that produces smog or chemical wastes, a lumber industry that harvests trees, a manufacturing company which uses non-biodegradable packaging for its products or a store that wastes energy through poor insulation, they have made decisions that in some measure affect us all.

While it is true that all of our actions have some effect on the environment, it is important that environmental ethics play a part in business decisions. People in business can take one of two attitudes: either the classical position that business's only responsibility is to make a profit within the law, or the position that business has a responsibility to make a profit through sustainable production practices.

The argument for the classical position is that competitive markets benefit us all. They result in offering consumers a variety of products to choose from, at competitive rates, and allow consumers the opportunity to make their own choices. Those choices show what they are willing to pay for. If people desire environmental goods, they will show that by being willing to pay to leave wilderness spaces intact instead of building resorts on them, or by buying fuel-efficient cars and appliances. The problem with this position is that it is impossible to put a market value on most social goods, because they are values rather than products. There is no market for ecological diversity, endangered species or wilderness spaces. They can be destroyed, but they aren't something consumers can buy instead of something else, so they cannot be safeguarded simply by the market law of supply and demand.

It has also been argued from the classical position that there are no finite resources: human ingenuity will always come up with alternatives when one resource becomes too costly or is depleted, and that's what will happen when non-renewable resources are used up. Even if this is true, and solves the issue for future generations, it doesn't answer the accusation that the current use of those resources is not being fairly distributed among the world's population. And unfortunately, the only way we will learn if this is true is through a market failure. A market failure occurs when a market becomes unsustainable. The idea is that we learn from the failure and take corrective action. But when the goods are irreplaceable, such as wilderness areas, public health and safety or non-renewable resources, we can't take corrective action later—one failure is all we get.

Another attitude that businesspeople may take is the position that business has a responsibility to use sustainable production practices to make a profit. This means that businesses should not use energy or resources faster than they can be replaced or use too much of those which cannot be replaced, and should not produce more waste than can safely be absorbed into the environment. The amount of natural resources we deplete can be reduced by using them more efficiently. Energy-saving light bulbs, windows, insulation and production methods are all examples of how energy requirements can be reduced while still meeting production targets. Waste can be reduced by finding uses for byproducts and by creating longer-lasting, recyclable products. Urban developers can create more environmentally friendly human habitats designed to reduce commuting by clustering housing, shopping and work together, instead of the current practice where shopping occurs in downtown areas, employment is clumped into huge industrial parks and housing is built in distant suburbs.

Government's Responsibility in Protecting the Environment

As citizens we can get legislators to pass laws that will regulate and restrict our choices as consumers. There is environmental legislation at both the federal and provincial levels. The Canadian Environmental Act (1999) sets federal standards to prevent pollution and protect the environment and human health, including sustainable development. Each province and territory has legislation as well. But legislation is always a poor substitute for ethics. First, it sets up only the minimum standards that must be adhered to. Minimum standards serve to limit damage rather than to improve current practices with new technologies and innovative, environmentally friendly products and production methods. And second, when we count on legislation rather than on high ethical standards in people, we are overlooking people's resistance to change, the high cost of producing new, more environmentally friendly products, and business's influence over public policy through aggressive lobbying. The government, at both the federal and provincial levels, can also support environmental initiatives through grants, subsidies and tax breaks. The tax refund for purchasing a fuel-efficient car is one example, and there are many more.

List five things the government can do to be more environmentally responsible:

1. _____

2. _____

3. _____

4. _____

5. _____

EXERCISE 7.5

Analyzing and Evaluating Environmental Issues

Read the article "It's Not So Cool" by Anne Kingston. In class, discuss the arguments presented against the use of bottled water. Do you agree with the author? Why or why not?

Individually or in small groups, research an environmental issue that interests you. Take a position on the issue and write a short, persuasive article promoting your position.

Use one of the following topics, or one of your own choosing: biodegradable packaging, preserving natural habitats, saving endangered species, recycling, use of pesticides and/or fertilizers, alternate forms of energy, environmentally friendly urban planning, the production and use of ethanol fuels.

Article 3: "It's So Not Cool,"
(Anne Kingston, *Maclean's*, May 14, 2007)
Chi-chi restaurants are now banning bottled water. How did the ubiquitous accessory become the latest environmental sin?

When Alice Waters opened Chez Panisse in Berkeley, Calif., in 1971, it was at the vanguard of a "think globally, eat locally" gastronomic uprising. Now, in banning bottled water, the restaurant is at the forefront of another insurgency. Finally cluing in to the fact that importing bottled water from Italy is a flagrant violation of its mantra, Chez Panisse stopped serving Fiuggi still water last summer. It now serves free, filtered tap water. When it gets a carbonator up and running in the next week that will add fizz to tap water, the restaurant will stop selling sparkling Acqua Minerale San Benedetto.

The culinary mecca joins a growing number of restaurants willing to forgo 300 percent-plus markups on bottled water in return for increased customer loyalty. Mike Kossa-Rienzi, Chez Panisse's general manager, says the ecological damage associated with bottling water spurred them to action. "It's something we wanted to do for a while," he says. "Finally I thought, 'This is silly: we have this great water that comes out of our tap.' This is something we really think we need to do. We feel it is the right thing to do."

Increasingly, it's the fashionable thing to do. For years, David Suzuki and his brethren have railed against the environmental evils of bottled water—the pollution generated and energy expended in its production and shipping, the recyclable plastic bottles that rarely get recycled. More recently, church groups, including the United Church of Canada, have advocated members boycott the product on the moral grounds that water is a basic human right, not a commodity to be sold for profit. The edict was met by the wider public with much eye-rolling. After all, bottled water is entrenched as an icon of vitality, health, mobility and safety. No amount of righteous talk was about to wean people away.

Recently, however, the return-to-the-tap crusade has acquired momentum from the gourmands who once extolled bottled water's "volcanic temperament" and "mouth feel." Even the French, who introduced portable Vittel water in plastic bottles in 1968, are saying "non" to Evian, with bottled water sales in decline since 2003.

The notion that a bottled-water backlash could gain velocity might seem absurd given worldwide consumption of 167.8 billion litres in 2005. Canadians spent $652.7 million on bottled water that year, consuming 1.9 billion litres, 60 litres per capita, with sales up 20 percent last year. Bottled water became a status signifier—Cameron Diaz favoured Penta, Madonna preferred Voss Artesian Water. Still, we've seen a prop made glamorous by movie stars losing cachet and acquiring stigma before—the cigarette, for one, the Hummer for another. If early indications of backlash are any sign, what was once a fashion accessory is becoming a fashion crime.

The obvious driving force is green's new vogue. Now that we're shopping to save The Planet, toting a natural resource that costs more than gasoline in a plastic bottle destined to clog a landfill for a thousand years doesn't exactly telegraph eco-cred. Once-stylish water bars with "water sommeliers," like the one at Epic in Toronto's Royal York Hotel offering 25 international brands, suddenly seem passé, out of touch. Earlier this year, *Times of London* food critic Giles Coren announced his new zero-tolerance toward bottled water on his blog. Drinking it, he wrote, signals a gauche lack of global awareness: "The vanity of it! While half the world dies of thirst or puts up with water you wouldn't piss in, or already have, we have invested years and years, and vast amounts of money, into an ingenuous system which cleanses water of all of the nasties that most other humans and animals have always had to put up with, and delivers it, dirt cheap, to our homes and workplaces in pipes, which we can access with a tap."

A tap-water snobbery is emerging. Even restaurateurs unwilling to forfeit bottled-water revenue boast of drinking from the tap at home. "On the domestic front I refuse to buy it," says Toronto chef Mark McEwan, who operates the popular North 44 and Bymark. "The waste factor with these plastic bottles just makes me crazy." Jamie Kennedy, who runs several Toronto hot spots including Jamie Kennedy Restaurant, says he sources locally bottled water in glass bottles. "Why are we bringing in water from Fiji in a nation that's got more water than any other nation in the world?" he asks. "It's air freight, it's contributing carbon dioxide to the atmosphere, it's all those things that if you're environmentally conscious in the year 2007 you totally question." He sells Gaia water bottled in Caledon, Ont. The company delivers and picks up the bottles for recycling, he says. "We're not creating any bottle waste, which is fantastic. And it's delicious." Yet Kennedy drinks unfiltered tap water. "I'm cool with it," he says. "It's pretty darn good."

Indeed, born-again tap-water aficionados argue it tastes better than many bottled offerings. Kossa-Rienzi says Chez Panisse explored serving locally produced bottled waters but found none more palatable than tap. Last year, officials in Cleveland took offence when Fiji Water crowed in ads that its product was free of pollutants and "purified by island trade winds" with the punchline: "The label says Fiji because it's not bottled in Cleveland." A local TV show conducted blind taste tests to find the subjects preferred local tap water. Even self-proclaimed "water connoisseurs" are extolling the virtues of tap water. The noted Boston-based food writer Corby Kummer, known for his appreciation of aquatic nuances (he has proclaimed a preference for "water from the volcanic region between Rome and Naples"), says "it's time to rediscover municipal water." Unless he wants sparkling water, Kummer always asks for tap in restaurants. "I've long made it a point of pride as a sort of a counter-snobbish order," he says. "Now I'm noticing other people coming to the same conclusion."

Tap-water filtration regimes are a new bragging point. Poggio in Sausalito, Calif., triple-filters its tap water with a system that cost US$12,000. Five-month-old Susanna Foo Gourmet Kitchen in Radnor, Pa., spent US$50,000 on its high-tech filtration device. Then there are the purists. At organic Restaurant Nora in Washington, they use salt, then carbon, then paper to excise impurities. In an arresting development signalling tap water's new value, the Beverly Hills restaurant Entoteca has started charging US$8 for a litre of flat or sparkling water that flows straight from the filtered spigot. Kummer hints at the next direction tap-water snootiness will take with talk of his goal to "build a memory bank of municipal water tastes from around the country and around the world." He admits the taste of tap water isn't always pleasing.

"Sometimes, because of the way it's treated, it will taste either neutral, slightly chlorinated, and chemically or flat and bitter." But he finds it superior to bottled water sourced from municipal supplies. "That's not just filtered tap water," he says, "it's filtered tap water that they add proprietary minerals to. It tastes completely artificial."

Filtered tap water accounts for more than one-quarter of bottled water consumed by Canadians, according to the Bottled Water Association of Canada, an industry trade group. Coca-Cola uses municipal water from Calgary and Brampton, Ont., for its Dasani brand. The company filters the water five times to remove chemicals, odours and bacteria, and adds minerals for water billed "pure as water can get." Pepsi trucks in municipal water from Vancouver or Mississauga, Ont., for its Aquafina, which is marketed as "the purest of waters." Such claims justify massive markups. A litre (33.8 ounces) of tap water in Canada costs taxpayers an average of less than one-tenth of a cent, according to Toronto's city government. The markup on a litre of bottled water selling for $2.50, then, is 3,000 times. Small wonder Donald Trump entered the market with his "no-sodium" Trump Ice. As has Sylvester Stallone, as an investor in a bottler that produces Sly Pure Glacier Water purportedly from a 10,000-year-old carbon glacier at Mount Rainier, Wash. The industry, always ripe for Evian-is-naive-spelled-backwards satire, provides continual fodder with K9, the "first flavoured, vitamin fortified water for dogs," and the 2006 launch of US$38 Bling H_2O, bottled in Tennessee and marketed as the "Cristal of bottled water" in "limited edition, corked, 750 ml recyclable frosted glass bottles, exquisitely handcrafted with Swarovski crystals." Equally preposterous are water's vaunted magical properties: Propel Fitness Water promises to pump up energy, eVamor to "restore equilibrium," and Jana Skinny Water to help shed excess pounds.

Rejection of the industry's grandiose promises—and high prices—has fuelled the return to the tap in France, the world's second largest consumer of bottled water after Italy. That has been attributed to the efficacy of advertising campaigns launched by municipal water companies that extol the benefits, lower cost and environmental virtues of tap water. (In Paris, tap water costs less than a third of a European cent per litre. Groupe Neptune's Cristaline, a popular brand, sells for 15 European cents a litre, while Danone's Evian costs about 60 European cents a litre.) Earlier this year, Groupe Neptune fought back with billboards featuring a photograph of a white toilet marked with a big red "X." "I don't drink the water I use to flush," the posters read. "I drink Cristaline."

Such gross-out imagery—abetted by reports of ecological contamination and corrupt filtration like that in Walkerton, Ont., that caused 2,300 to fall ill and seven to die in 2000—transformed bottle water from a luxury only the rich could afford to a perceived necessity the mass market couldn't afford not to buy. As a result, bottled water's chic is diminishing. No longer does it offer the comfort of belonging to a private club drinking from an exclusive water supply. Indeed, Edmonton-based Earth Water, a national bottler of spring and osmosis water, forges an explicit connection between bottled-water consumption in affluent nations and the fragility of water supply in developing nations: it donates net profits to the United Nations Refugee Agency, which runs water-aid programs.

The alleged health and beauty benefits that made bottled water the preferred constant-hydration libation of celebrities (who can forget that widely circulated photo of Princess Di exiting the gym with her Evian?) are under new scrutiny. The industry remains steadfast in its claims that bottled water is cleaner and more rigorously tested than tap water. Elizabeth Griswald, a spokesperson for the Canadian Bottled Water Association, says bottled water is subject to three tiers of regulation—Ottawa monitors it under the Food and Drug Act; the provinces approve the sourcing of water; the industry also regulates itself. Tap water, she points out, is regulated only as a utility by the provinces with no consistent national standards. Unlike tap water that can flow through antiquated pipes, bottled water is produced in clean facilities and packaged in sterile bottles, she says. Still, the manufacturing process itself can contaminate. In 2004, Coca-Cola Co. recalled its entire Dasani line of bottled water from the British market after levels of bromate, a potentially harmful chemical, were found to exceed legal standards. In March, the Canadian Food Inspection Agency warned the public not to consume imported Jermuk Classic brand Natural Sparkling Mineral Water because it contained excessive levels of arsenic.

Rick Smith, executive director of Toronto-based Environmental Defence, an agency that tracks the exposure of Canadians to pollutants, doesn't buy industry claims. "There's a misconception that bottled water is safer, which is complete nonsense," he says. "Toronto's tap water has to meet standards for 160 contaminants; bottled water has standards for less than a half-dozen. And 650 bacterial tests are done monthly of Toronto water. The extent to which bottled water is tested for bacteria is barely known."

Smith foresees a looming crisis. "Bottled water is a not only a complete disaster for the environment but potentially for human health," he says. His greatest criticism lies with the polyethylene terephthalate (PET) bottle, the industry's real product. "The production of one kilogram of PET requires 17.5 kilograms of water and results in air pollution emissions of over half a dozen significant pollutants," Smith says. "In other words, the water required to create one plastic water bottle is significantly more than that bottle will contain." Then there is the waste factor. An estimated 88 percent of water bottles are not recycled. According to the Environment and Plastics Industry Council, Canadians sent 65,000 tonnes of PET beverage containers, many of them water bottles, to landfill or incineration in 2002.

The volatility of PET bottles, which should never be refilled due to risks of leaching and bacterial growth, remains uncertain. Last year, William Shotyk, a Canadian scientist working at the University of Heidelberg, released a study of 132 brands of bottled water in PET bottles stored for six months, and found that significant levels of antimony, a toxic chemical used in the bottle's production, had leached into the water. Shotyk, who has vowed never to drink bottled water again, is now studying the bottles over a longer term, given the lag times that can occur between bottling, shipping, purchase and consumption. The Canadian Bottled Water Association counters that the levels don't pose a risk to humans. "Technically bottled water will not go bad if you properly store it," Griswald says, though she admits algae will build up if it's left in sunlight in high heat.

Smith predicts concern about internal pollution will increase as more people are tested for chemical contamination. "There's mounting evidence that these containers are leaching toxins into the beverages we're drinking and our children are drinking and there are easy substitutes available," he says. The Environmental Protection Agency in the U.S. commenced a massive study in 2000. This year, Statistics Canada begins testing 5,000 Canadians for a wide range of contaminants. Early data from the U.S. is troubling, Smith says. "There's empirical evidence that these plastic ingredients are now in the bodies of every citizen," he says. "I am quite sure that a few years from now we will look back at these toxins and shake our heads and wonder, 'What the heck were we thinking?'"

Litigation against plastic manufacturers will rival that against cigarette companies, Smith predicts. On March 12, a billion-dollar class action suit was filed in Los Angeles against five leading manufacturers of baby bottles containing Bisphenol-A, a toxin found in hard plastic and linked to early-onset puberty, declining sperm counts and the huge increase in breast and prostate cancer. It is the first such suit to be brought against the industry. "What we are witnessing is the beginning of a tobacco-style fight," says Smith.

Already signs point to water awareness becoming the next trendy topic. The recently published *Thirst: Fighting the Corporate Theft of our Water*, by Alan Snitow, Deborah Kaufman and Michael Fox, chronicles the upsurge of international grassroots protest against groundwater depletion and the privatization of water by multinational bottlers. The community of Wisconsin Dells, Wis., for instance, waged a successful battle against Swiss-based Nestlé after the conglomerate announced plans to set up a Perrier bottling plant in the area.

Thirst's authors see a bottled-water backlash as crucial to preserving a public water supply. The campaign to wean North America from the bottle to the tap has been "a driving force in shifting cultural attitudes," they write, noting widespread bottled-water consumption reinforces the perception that water is a grab-and-go consumer product and that the water supply is not safe or well managed: "Local critics are beginning to see the industry as a harbinger of wider threats, including the commodification of water, the export of water in bulk, and the end of the keystone idea of affordable water as a public trust and human right." Paying grossly inflated prices for the natural resource, they contend, paves the way: "If we as individuals get used to paying whatever price the market will bear for bottled water as a product, will we slowly give up the collective commitment to clean, affordable water as a public service that must be guaranteed by government?"

Already, though, there are signs government wants in on the trend. San Francisco Mayor Gavin Newsom has just announced plans to copy Chez Panisse and provide carbonated filtered tap water at City Hall. Chez Panisse's patrons are now asking where they can buy their own carbonators, says Kossa-Rienzi. "It's definitely sparked a new consciousness."

> *"Goodness is the only investment that never fails."*
>
> —HENRY DAVID THOREAU (1817–1862)

Answers

The argument that use of force is part of human nature takes a descriptive approach.

Two arguments for pacifism are:

Principle-based: To kill another person is wrong in itself. This is an absolutist position as it implies that murder is always wrong, in all circumstances and for all people. If based on a religious imperative, such as the biblical commandment "Thou shalt not kill," it is also an argument from divine command theory.

Consequence-based: Using non-violent methods to achieve a good end are preferable to using violent methods because they are more effective in the long run. Violence does more harm than good because it perpetuates a cycle of revenge, which non-violent resistance avoids.

Laws and Codes of Ethics

CONTENTS

> *"Good laws have their origins in bad morals."*
>
> —AMBROSIUS MACROBIUS

The law refers to the system of rules in force in a society at a given time. The purpose of the law is to keep all members of a society focused on behaviours that enable the society to sustain itself and that allow its members to live together in harmony.

If every member of a society had the same moral standards and abided by them unwaveringly, there would be no need for a written set of laws. If no one stole from others, mistreated animals, or harmed other people, we would not need to create and enforce laws against theft, cruelty to animals, or abuse. If, on the other hand, people did these things and a society had no laws or lawkeepers to protect their victims, we would have Hobbes' state of nature, and our lives would be "nasty, brutish and short." To prevent this, we make laws, or rather, allow our government to do so, since the law is a reflection of what the government decides are the best rules for the country at that time. The intent of the law is to make it possible for people with different moral standards to live together under an agreed-upon set of rules of behaviour. As such, the law is primarily concerned with prohibiting certain behaviours, or placing restrictions upon our freedom to act. This is why, as the above quote states, good laws are the result of bad morals.

State a Canadian law you agree with which restricts your (and others') freedom to act.

State a Canadian law you disagree with, which restricts your (and others') freedom to act.

_____

ETHICS AND THE LAW
Law, Religion and Social Customs

A country has a system of morality just as an individual does. This system is embedded in both its written laws and its social customs. At one time, these injunctions held religious as well as legal authority, and covered all areas of ethical living. Consider the Ten Commandments, presumably dictated by God to Moses. They are, in fact, a societal code of ethics embedded within a divine command theory, and handed to a nation of people as written law. Despite the differences between Jews, Christians and Muslims, they all share the Ten Commandments. Most religions similarly incorporate standards of behaviour for their followers. Buddhism presents its followers with the Eightfold Path to spiritual peace, and Hinduism encourages the practice of Raja Yoga, both of which include a code of ethical behaviours.

These standards of behaviour bear the force of spiritual laws, and in some societies secular law as well. Canada does not have a codified separation of church and state, but there has been a secularization process in our justice system, driven to some extent by Canada's multicultural make-up; our laws are not directly based on a specific set of religious imperatives. This is not always the case in other cultures, where punishments as well as crimes may be taken directly from religious scripture, such as stoning a woman to death for adultery.

Removing the religious authority behind a nation's laws is an essential step in permitting discussion, change and growth. If God is the lawmaker, questioning the laws is heresy and only God can change them. In some cultures, such as some Islamic ones, this stasis may be considered a good thing, directing people to stay "pure" and closely attached to their religion. On the other hand, this situation could be considered stultifying, forcing a nation to remain tied to earlier understandings of morality and human nature. For example, in most ancient religions, women had little say in government, and keeping slaves was considered the norm. However, laws permitting slavery or denying the vote to women are not acceptable in Canada today. These examples show that in Canada our concept of right and wrong has changed, and our laws have changed with it. Just as a professional code of ethics has to be regularly reviewed and revised, we as members of our society must be vigilant in ensuring that our laws and customs remain fair and relevant to us.

List other laws which were relevant in the past yet no longer reflect current social values.

_____

_____

What are some current laws that you think might one day become unacceptable?

_____

_____

Separating law and religion also allows a further separation between law and social obligations and conventions. Social conventions or expectations arise out of culture, whether that be a racial culture, a religious culture or a cultural period in history. Different races may share a religion but have different expectations of their members, and those expectations may change over time even within the same race or cultural group. The climate or culture of a nation exerts a strong influence over the behaviour of its citizens. In a multicultural country like Canada, there are many different cultures, each with behavioural expectations of their members which may or may not be in accordance with the law and which may cause conflicts with other cultures. This was explored in Chapter 6.

Because social conventions and attitudes are not written or recorded, they are more flexible than laws. When the attitudes of members of a society change, social conventions and expectations adapt to these changes. Laws, though slower to change, do eventually reflect the attitudes of the majority of the members of a nation. So, finally, laws are changed to reflect the new values. And these new laws, in turn, further change social attitudes. In other words, we change the law and the law changes us.

Our attitude toward homosexuality is one example of this. It is condemned in the Bible and many other religious books, and those who practised it were once punished by law. When the law became distinct from religious belief, homosexuals could no longer be disciplined by the law. However, until fairly recently social conventions opposed homosexuality and society continued to mete out a form of punishment through ridicule, ostracism and, occasionally, personal attacks. Although there is no doubt that these actions occurred (and in some places continue to occur), in most societies they are not condoned by the law, and perpetrators can be punished. Because our understanding of human psychology and sexual orientation has increased, in Canada today there is more social disapproval directed against homophobics than against homosexuals.

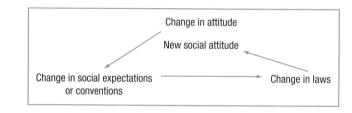

Figure 8.1

We can use unmarried cohabitation as an example that demonstrates this relationship.

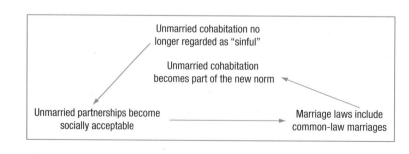

Figure 8.2

As discussed in Chapter 1, morality is to a large extent habitual. Consider the law requiring all car passengers to wear seat belts. When this law was first passed in Ontario in the 1970s, many people argued that it infringed upon their personal rights. Others countered this argument, saying that seatbelt use would benefit taxpayers by decreasing the effects of car accidents, therefore saving money on expensive medical treatment. Now, three decades after the law was passed, the debate has been forgotten. Most people don't think twice about buckling up. We are so used to making choices in accordance with our society's laws and values that we are often unaware of even doing so. Like the air we breathe, the laws and social conventions of our society are often taken for granted. Air is virtually indiscernible until it moves, and then we recognize it as a breeze, a wind, or a hurricane. In the same way, we rarely examine our ethical choices until something changes and they get shaken up a little. This can happen because of a personal experience or as a result of being exposed to ideas or attitudes that differ from ours. Consider the following examples:

■ Bob was opposed to physician-assisted suicide until he watched his mother suffer through an excruciatingly long and painful death. Now he lobbies and speaks out for a change in the law in favour of physician-assisted suicide.

■ Susan always held a conventional attitude toward marriage. When the issue of gay marriage surfaced she was opposed to the practice, almost by reflex. However, after reading several newspaper articles on the subject, seeing devoted gay couples being married on TV newscasts and discussing the issue with her friends, her attitude changed.

These examples show how habitual opinions on ethical issues can change through exposure to different attitudes or experiences. The more deeply held an opinion is, the more it will take to change it.

Ideally, our personal, societal and professional morality will be identical. Real life, however, is rarely ideal. Furthermore, laws are formed mostly according to the attitude of the majority, not by consensus. In a well-functioning democratic society, everyone is, to some extent, involved in critiquing and refining its ethics, as is reflected in its laws and social attitudes, customs and expectations. This is accomplished through voting, freedom of speech (in discussion and in print), lobbying, strikes, rallies and demonstrations, petitions, precedent-setting court cases, etc. The first step in this process is becoming more aware of social issues and learning to examine them critically. The following two exercises will provide an opportunity to do this.

EXERCISE 8.1

Examining a Current Social Issue

Find two articles that argue opposing sides of a current social issue. You can use two articles supplied by your instructor, or find two on your own. They can be opinion pieces, editorials, letters to the editor, or journal articles. You might want to select a subject related to your field of study. It is better not to choose a subject you already have strong opinions about. Write a paper about the topic, comparing the arguments in the two articles.

(Continued)

(Continued)

■ What is the ethical issue involved? (Describe it as clearly as you can.)

_____

_____

■ What is your own immediate reaction to this issue? Why?

_____

_____

■ Which arguments in either article might cause you to reconsider your initial reaction?

_____

_____

_____

_____

■ Which article is more convincing? Why? (Consider such things as factual evidence, logical reasoning, expert opinions, reliable source and broad base of arguments as discussed in Chapter 5.)

_____

_____

_____

_____

■ Is this an important social issue in Canada? Why or why not? What are its social implications?

_____

_____

_____

_____

■ What kinds of experiences might cause you to reconsider your opinion on this issue?

_____

_____

_____

_____

■ What are some things that could be done to promote a change in social attitude or in the law on this issue?

_____

_____

_____

_____

If all ethical decision-making were captured in the laws of our society, our lives would be very constricted. Many of our current rights and freedoms would be taken away. No one would consider cheating on a partner, lying to a friend, or being drunk in our own home to be examples of ethical behaviour. Yet we would not want these acts to be made illegal, because we value our freedom to choose for ourselves how we will behave. In fact, the law reflects society's minimum standards. Social convention, religion and personal ethics include standards of conduct that the law does not address. To put it in very simplistic terms, the law is concerned with what we *must* do; ethics is concerned with what we *should* do.

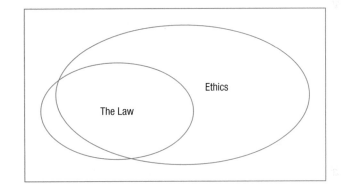

Figure 8.3

The relationship between ethics and the law is very complex. Ethical behaviour doesn't simply go beyond the law. As Figure 8.3 shows, there are large areas where the two subjects are in accord and overlap—consider all the laws that match your ethical beliefs—and areas where they do not overlap. The area where our ethics go beyond the laws of our country are areas of personal choice. For example, we may consider extramarital sex unethical even though it is not illegal, and refrain from it. The law neither requires this standard of behaviour from us, nor is it in conflict with it. The smaller area where the law is outside of our personal ethics is where the law and our ethics are in conflict. For example, although some Canadians believe that euthanasia or assisted suicide for terminal patients is ethical, the practice is illegal. If we tried to act on our ethical belief and help a loved one end his or her life, our action would be punishable by law.

A PERSONAL CODE OF ETHICS

We all want to live in a predictable world where we can trust and be trusted. As we discussed in Chapter 1, we must examine our lives and our behaviour to ensure that we are living up to the principles we believe in and are acting ethically. This examination is also important for us to feel confident and good about ourselves. Socrates said: "The unexamined life is not worth living." (Socrates, in Plato's *Apology*) However, it is also true that the endlessly examined life is unlivable. Examining our every word and action, every single day, is impossible. We have to get on with living.

Nor is it necessary to examine every choice we make. Many of the decisions we face are for recurring situations, and we need to choose how to respond to them only once. The opportunity to shoplift, for example, could occur frequently when we are in a store. We need to make the decision not to shoplift only once, and then to act on it consistently. The decision does not have to be made again every time we go shopping.

What is important is to make these decisions consciously. We must base our decisions on the values and principles we choose to live by rather than have them made for us by habit or external pressures. We behave as ethical beings when we make conscious, deliberate and fully considered ethical choices, not when we simply avoid behaving badly by doing what we have been told.

Why Have a Code of Ethics?

It is important not only to make conscious, considered choices about how we want to behave, but also to record our choices. This adds legitimacy and weight to our intentions and helps us to remember to uphold our choices. Since our values and beliefs can change with life experiences, having a record simplifies the task of regularly reviewing our ethical guidelines. This written record is called a code of ethics, sometimes referred to as a code of conduct. We are all familiar with the idea of professional codes of conduct. It is just as important to have a code to live by in our personal life as it is in our professional life.

Why is it important? What does a code of ethics really accomplish? To answer these questions, we should examine some codes of ethics.

EXERCISE 8.2

Reviewing Codes of Ethics

In small groups, find a code of ethics on the Internet, or use one supplied by your instructor. It can be related to your field of study or to a profession that interests you. Print off enough copies for the entire group. As a group, analyze the code of ethics, answering the following questions. Be prepared to share your observations with the rest of the class.

1. What types of behaviour are covered in the code of ethics?

_____

_____

2. What issues are particularly emphasized?

_____

_____

3. Why do you think these are important issues for this profession?

_____

_____

4. What issues are not covered or not emphasized?

_____

_____

5. Why do you think these are not important issues for this profession?

_____

_____

6. Are laws, company policies, or standards of practice referred to?

_____

_____

7. What surprised you about this code? Did it cover issues you weren't expecting to find, or omit issues you expected it to include?

_____

_____

8. Did it offer clear and specific direction or was it vague and general? Would employees understand exactly what was expected of them?

_____

_____

9. Did it include a process for seeking clarification or further direction?

_____

_____

10. Did it include a process for reporting breaches to the code?

_____

_____

11. If so, do you think it was a good process? Why or why not?

_____

_____

12. Were there clearly stated consequences for not following the code?

_____

_____

(Continued)

(Continued)

13. Do you think these consequences were strong enough to ensure compliance with the code?

_____

_____

An organizational or professional code of ethics holds all of its members to the same high standards of practice. It protects its members by clearly defining acceptable and unacceptable behaviours and stating the repercussions of failing to live up to its standards. It provides a benchmark for self-evaluation and continuing improvement. It describes its members' professional responsibilities to each other, to supervisors and underlings, to clients, patients or customers, to management, a board of directors and to shareholders. It describes procedures for its members to deal with ethical concerns. And it defines the organization or profession: this is who we are, what we do, and how we do it. A personal code of ethics does the same thing on an individual basis. It describes who we are, what type of behaviours we find acceptable, and how we want to live.

Many ethical decisions have already been made for us. Despite the potential benefits or temptations of a course of action, or the pressure put upon us by supervisors, peers, or others, we know what the right thing to do is. It is set out for us in the written standards of our profession, and/or dictated by provincial or federal laws. An example would be harassment. In Canada, there are laws against harassment, and there are clear and serious repercussions for breaking these laws.

However, there is a broad range of personal and professional activity that cannot be dictated by law, company policies, or professional standards of practice. And even those rules that are dictated require a personal interpretation and commitment to the specific behaviours that support them. For example, at what point does making a few jokes about someone become harassment? However carefully this point is defined, individual judgment is still required. Ethical behaviour throughout an organization or in a country can flourish only when each of us is personally committed to behaving ethically. Therefore, even though we are bound by the provincial and federal laws of Canada and by the ethical standards of our profession and the place we work, it is also important to consider creating a personal code of ethics. The process of doing this—of thinking through our beliefs, values and principles and converting them into actions and behaviours—makes us confident of and more committed to our ethical choices. It also increases our awareness of the ethical expectations of our country, our workplace and our profession because the process of creating a personal code of ethics includes researching and examining the laws, company policies and professional standards of practice that we are or will be expected to comply with. A personal code of ethics also provides the opportunity for self-reflection. It allows us to define ourselves in ethical terms and to act consistently and in accordance with our principles regardless of the suddenness or emotional grip of a particular situation.

WRITING A CODE OF ETHICS

In order to be useful, a code of ethics must relate to one's personal and professional needs by including direction on all the issues that one might face. If the code is not relevant to our daily life, we will not use it. Not only must our code be relevant to our work, school and personal life, it must also be based on our beliefs and values. After all, the purpose of a code of ethics is to ensure that we are acting in accordance with what we believe and the principles we value. In Chapter 1, we reflected on our beliefs and values, and whether our behaviour was in line with them. How do we go about writing a code that will accomplish this?

Whether it is written for an organization or an individual, there are four stages to writing a code of ethics:

1. Identifying the values and principles on which the code is to be based.
2. Transforming those values and principles into ethical behaviours.
3. Organizing and writing the document.
4. Reviewing and revising the code.

Identifying Important Values and Principles

A code of ethics must be based on values and principles shared or at least agreed upon by everyone who is to abide by it. So the first step in writing a code of ethics is to identify which values and principles are essential to the individual or group of people involved and reach reasonable agreement on these.

List the values you consider important personally and professionally.

_____

_____

_____

_____

Although the terms "values" and "principles" are often used interchangeably, they are slightly different. A value is something we consider important. For example, many people value honesty. A principle, however, is usually stated as an ethical rule that can be used to judge people's behaviour. If a supervisor takes the interesting assignments and gives her assistant the unpleasant ones, she violates the principle of equal consideration of interests. Chapter 5 included a discussion of some important principles that should be considered when writing a code of ethics. These are:

■ the principle of equal consideration of interests (ECI)
■ the principle of non-maleficence
■ the principle of beneficence
■ the principle of fidelity
■ the principle of confidentiality
■ the principle of conservatism

Other values and principles which are not listed here, particularly those that stem from religious beliefs, may also be used as the basis of an individual code of ethics, or of a group code if the members are cohesive in their beliefs. This would be the case with a religious school or a charitable group with religious or cultural affiliations. A list of values which could be used as the basis of a code of ethics is included at the end of this chapter.

Human rights, as discussed in Chapter 5, should also be considered as part of the basis for a code of ethics. These are:

- The right to state our case before an impartial and unbiased adjudicator
- The right to due process
- The right to justice (procedural, distributive, compensatory and retributive)
- The right to be informed
- The right to autonomy
- The right to privacy
- The right to freedom of expression
- The right to a safe and healthy workplace
- The right to pursue our own best interests

After determining which values, principles and human rights the code of ethics will be based on, the next step is to turn these into actions.

Transforming Values, Principles and Rights into Ethical Behaviours

A code of ethics is a record of ethical behaviours based on values and principles. Values and principles are broad, general statements about what matters. However, it is not always immediately obvious in a specific situation how a value or principle translates into action. Since the purpose of a code of ethics is to give clear direction about acceptable behaviours, the body of the code must be written in terms of actions and behaviours, not principles. It is not good enough to write down "Show respect for others." Ethics are action-oriented, and this statement does not offer enough clear direction as to what actions should be taken. A better statement that would support the principle of showing respect for others would be "Answer politely when I am spoken to." What other specific behaviours would be involved in showing respect for people?

1. Answer politely when I am spoken to or questions are asked of me.

2. _____

3. _____

4. _____

5. _____

6. _____

7. _____

8. _____

Every principle that is listed as the basis of a code of ethics must be carefully considered to determine the specific actions that will support or demonstrate it. These actions make up the code of ethics.

EXERCISE 8.3

Converting Principles into Ethical Behaviours

Break into small groups and list three values or principles which are important to you, and which you would want to include in your code of ethics.

1. _____

_____

2. _____

_____

3. _____

_____

As a group, convert each of the principles you listed into five ethical behaviours.

Principle:

_____

Ethical Behaviours:

1. _____

_____

2. _____

_____

3. _____

_____

4. _____

_____

5. _____

_____

Principle:

_____

(Continued)

(Continued)
Ethical Behaviours:

1. _____
   _____

2. _____
   _____

3. _____
   _____

4. _____
   _____

5. _____
   _____

Principle:

_____

Ethical Behaviours:

1. _____
   _____

2. _____
   _____

3. _____
   _____

4. _____
   _____

5. _____
   _____

Since ethics is concerned with the way one ought to behave toward others, it is necessary to consider personal and professional relationships while writing a code of ethics. Turning values and principles into actions is more complex when the element of relationship is involved. For example, the principle "Show respect for others" will have different supporting behaviours depending whether the "other" is a supervisor, a co-worker, a customer, a friend, a parent, a sibling, a teacher or a classmate. Some supporting actions may overlap in different relationships, such as showing respect by refraining from making negative comments to others about them. However, other supporting behaviours will change to reflect the nature of the relationship. For example, when dealing with a supervisor, respecting others will include respecting the supervisor's authority and completing the tasks she assigns. When dealing with a classmate, it will include respecting different lifestyles. When dealing with an assistant it will include assigning a fair work-load. When dealing with a friend it will include listening to his problems and helping him when he asks you.

The process of turning values and principles into ethical behaviours involves a balancing act between being specific enough to give clear direction and giving general guidelines to cover situations that cannot be foreseen. The statement, "Avoid situations involving a conflict of interest," does not give clear direction as to what constitutes a conflict of interest or how to avoid it. "Don't accept gifts from customers of over five dollars," is clearer and still leaves room for courteously accepting a small tip or a pen with the client's logo on it, items which it would be silly to refuse on the basis of conflict of interest. However, it would be impossible to cover every situation that might involve such a conflict. Focusing on specific behaviours alone could be misunderstood to mean that anything not mentioned is acceptable. The best course of action is to state the ethic in general terms and follow it with more specific directions and examples of situations.

Think of four values that you consider important in your personal relationships.

_____

_____

How would you turn those values into ethical behaviours in the important relationships in your life? Use the following chart to record your answers.

In Exercise 8.2 we examined codes of ethics for different professions and discussed issues they addressed and issues they omitted. A code of ethics should be based on the values and principles that are important to the group's members and also be relevant to their professional duties. Every organization and profession has particular areas of risk. These are defined as areas in which the members or employees of a particular organization are most likely to commit a breach of ethics, based on the nature of the business. A manufacturing company is more likely to face environmental issues than a job-finding agency; health professionals and lawyers are more likely to face confidentiality issues than automotive salespeople; financial institutions and consultants are more likely to face issues around misuse of clients' money than teachers. The content of a code and the thoroughness with which each area in it is covered will therefore differ for each organization and profession.

What are the high-risk areas in your chosen profession?

_____

_____

_____

Value	Parents	Siblings	Friends	Girlfriend/ Boyfriend/ Spouse

A code of ethics should be written in clear, straightforward language, and be as concise as possible. It should also be written in a positive tone (indicate what should be done, rather than what must not be done). It must give specific direction for behaviour without limiting its scope. It is impossible to imagine every situation in which a person might find himself. Therefore, some of the directions for behaviour should be broad, general directions, with examples to clarify their meaning. A general statement might read something like this: "I will be honest in all my dealings with my teachers." Examples of specific behaviours might be added to clarify the general statement, such as: "For example, I will always tell the truth about why I missed a class or why I handed an assignment in late."

A code of ethics should also refer to laws, professional standards of practice and company policies that the person or people writing it must uphold.

These need not be written out in full, as they are already recorded in other documents, but should be referred to in the code with directions as to where they can be located. A personal code might state: "When I'm spending volunteer time with my 'little brother' I will abide by the policies of the Big Brothers organization. These policies are stated in their document titled '—.'"

EXERCISE 8.4

Reviewing Organizational Policies

Working in small groups, review an organization's policies. Groups could use the policies of a volunteer organization, a student's workplace or a local company. If possible, request the policies relevant to the students' intended profession. Each group will report back to the class the results of their review. Groups should consider the following questions:

What areas are covered by the company policies?

_____

_____

_____

What are some areas that are not covered?

_____

_____

_____

Compare the company policies with the codes of ethics you reviewed in Exercise 8.2.

_____

_____

_____

_____

_____

_____

Organizing Ethics Statements within a Code

Standards of practice are usually very specific, but laws and company policies are often written in general terms, so these must be transformed into clear directions by considering the behaviours that would support them. This should be done in the same way that values and principles are transformed into ethical behaviours. When this has been done, the code of ethics is often quite lengthy. Therefore, it has to be logically organized so that when someone is faced with an ethical choice, she can easily find the section in the code that refers to that issue. There are several ways to organize a code of ethics. Three different methods are by values and principles, areas of responsibility, or personal and professional relationships.

Values and principles

When organizing a code by values and principles, the first thing to do is to group similar values and principles together. An office worker might group her ethical principles under the headings "professional attitude," "compliance with laws and office policies," and "maintaining good customer relations." Professional attitude would include such things as ethics relating to health and safety, dress code, using professional language, attendance, following supervisors' directions, and showing courtesy and respect to others in the workplace. Compliance with laws and policies might include confidentiality, conflicts of interest and use of company property. Good customer relations might include representing products or services honestly, dealing respectfully with complaints and considering the clients' best interests.

Areas of responsibility

Another way to organize a code of ethics is by areas of responsibility. A student might determine that his responsibilities include "gaining knowledge," "working with others," and "preparing for evaluation." Under gaining knowledge, he might include regular class attendance, taking good notes at lectures and completing assigned readings. Working with others might include behaviours when doing group projects, joining study groups and being helpful to other students. Preparing for evaluation might include personal guidelines for studying before tests and giving himself adequate time to complete assignments. Other areas of responsibility might include work and family responsibilities.

Personal and professional relationships

A code of ethics could also be organized according to the relationships in a person's life. Ethical behaviours could be divided into those required when dealing with parents, siblings, friends, co-workers, supervisors, customers (depending on one's job), teachers and fellow students. Since most values and principles involved in dealing with others apply whatever the relationship, there will be some overlap in the general guidelines. But the supporting behaviours will usually be different, as discussed earlier in this chapter. Even if there is some repetition, it is best to be as thorough as possible in outlining ethical behaviours for each relationship, if the code is organized this way.

Even if someone has a code of ethics, it will not be useful to her if it is not well-written and easily understood. Nor will she use it if it doesn't give clear directions and isn't organized in such a way that it makes finding the appropriate section easy.

EXERCISE 8.5

Writing a Code of Ethics

Follow the first three steps on page 271 to create a code of ethics that will guide your personal and professional conduct. Your code should begin by stating the values and principles that are important to you personally and to your present or future profession. The body of the code should convert these values and principles into ethical behaviours.

When writing your code of ethics, consider the following:

■ Give clear direction for specific behaviours as well as general guidelines.

■ Use brief, practical examples to make your general ethical statements clear.

■ Indicate where civil laws, company policies or standards of professional practice fit into your code.

■ Organize your code for easy reference.

Refer to the list on page 280 at the end of this chapter (Values to Consider in Writing a Code of Ethics) and to the earlier sections on principles and rights for some of the values, principles and human rights that might form a basis for your ethics.

After you have written your code of ethics, refer back to your personal reflections in Chapter 1. Compare your code of ethics to those reflections. How has your thinking about ethics and ethical issues changed during this course?

Revising the Code of Ethics

A code of ethics is never finished. Laws change. Business practices and expectations change; people take on new jobs, or advance in their profession, which creates new areas of responsibility and decision-making. Technological advances create new areas to consider. New relationships bring life changes such as marriage and parenthood. People have life experiences which change their beliefs or values, and they make choices, good and bad, which uncover areas of behaviour that need to be reviewed or added to the code. The code of ethics should be reviewed and revised at least every five to seven years. Revision is a two-fold process. First, consider the values and principles listed for the original code. Are they still current and relevant? Should others be added? Second, consider the changes in your work and/or professional practice. Are there any new laws, policies, standards of practice, technological changes or other kinds of changes in the way you do business? Do any of these open up new risk areas that should be dealt with in the code of ethics? Consider the relationships in your life. In what ways have they changed or been added to? All of these changes should be captured in the revisions to your code of ethics for it to continue to be a useful document for every area of your life.

> *"If you would convince a man that he does wrong, do right. But do not care to convince him. Men will believe what they see. Let them see."*
>
> —HENRY DAVID THOREAU (1817–1862)

Answers

SOME BEHAVIOURS REQUIRED OR INVOLVED IN SHOWING RESPECT FOR PEOPLE ARE:

1. Answer politely when they speak to me or ask questions of me.
2. Keep confidential information they share with me to myself.
3. Don't talk about them behind their backs.
4. Don't make jokes at their expense.
5. Keep any commitments I make to them.
6. Don't make comments that make me look good and make them look bad.
7. Recognize and thank people for their contribution to our work/study group/relationship.
8. Don't use sarcasm.

Some Values to Consider When Writing a Code of Ethics

- Compassion
- Courtesy
- Patience
- Fairness
- Generosity
- Faith/Spirituality
- Self-motivation
- Concern for the environment

- Unbiased attitude toward others
- Professional attitude and appearance
- High standards of work
- Honesty
- Loyalty

- Personal responsibility
- Maintaining confidences
- Promise-keeping
- Respect for others
- Reliability

Note: This is an incomplete list. Values are personal, and some of the values on this list will not be relevant to some people, while other people may have some values not mentioned here.

Making Ethical Decisions

> *"The self is not something ready-made, but something in continuous formation through choice of action."*
>
> —JOHN DEWEY (1859–1952)

Every day we make ethical decisions: whether to stick to the speed limit and arrive late or take the risk of speeding; whether to cheat on an exam or plagia-rize an essay; whether to report to work tired or slightly under the influence and compromise our performance, or turn down that extra shift; whether to lie to a friend or a parent, or face their displeasure; whether to report the unethical behaviour of a classmate or co-worker; whether to spread or keep to ourselves something we were told in confidence. The list of decisions with moral implications, large and small, which we face regularly in our personal and professional lives, is endless. These are ethical decisions because they require an action or a behaviour that will affect others as well as ourselves.

As Dewey's words imply in the above quote, every time we make an ethi-cal decision we are deciding what type of person we wish to be. It is therefore important to think our choices through very carefully before we act. It is much harder to change our character, and other people's opinion of us, than it is to continue to uphold our good character through making ethical choices when faced with a decision.

MAKING ETHICAL CHOICES IN COMPLEX SITUATIONS

Self-reflection can help us identify the morals and principles we wish to live by. Personal and professional codes of ethics can turn those morals and prin-ciples into ethical behaviours. But even the most comprehensive code of ethics cannot cover every situation in which we may find ourselves. There will be times when the ethically correct course of action is very difficult to follow, and it will sometimes even be difficult to determine what the ethical action is. This type of situation will cause us to feel ethical distress.

There are three basic types of situations that cause ethical distress. These situations present either *a locus of control issue, an ethical problem* or *an ethical dilemma*. When we are in ethical distress, the first priority is to determine which type of situation is involved. In order to do so, we must determine who the *moral agent* in the situation is. A moral agent is:

> (A)ny being who is capable of thinking, deciding and acting in accordance with moral standards and rules. A moral agent may not always fulfill the requirements of a moral standard or rule, that is, he need not be morally perfect. But he must have the capacity to judge himself on the basis of such a criterion and to use it as a guide to his choice and conduct. (Taylor, 1975)

The moral agent in a situation of ethical distress is the person who is responsible for resolving the situation and is in a position to do so. The moral agent must be capable of understanding the situation and be able to act voluntarily to resolve it.

Locus of Control Issues

A locus of control issue is a situation in which morals or principles that are important to you are being violated; however, you are not in control of the situation and you do not know what role, if any, you should take in resolving it. In other words, you are not the moral agent at the centre of this situation. The perfect resolution to a locus of control issue would be for the person or persons who are acting unethically to stop the behaviour, but you have no way of making them do so. It might not even be clear who does have authority in this situation. Consider the following example:

> Aaron has been working at McDonald's part-time for three years. His friend, Chris, has been working there for four years and has the most seniority of all the student employees. One day Chris tells Aaron that the manager, Mario, said that when the current assistant manager leaves, the position is Chris's if he wants it. Chris could really use the extra money to help with his college expenses, and Aaron is happy for his friend. Several months later, Mario brings his cousin, Anthony, in to work. Anthony has obviously never worked in a fast-food place before; his slowness annoys customers, and he makes a lot of mistakes. Aaron and Chris are constantly having to sort out his errors on customer orders. Two weeks later, Aaron hears that the assistant manager is leaving. He asks Chris if Mario gave him the job of assistant manager. "No," Chris says, "Mario gave it to Anthony." Aaron begins to notice that Chris is no longer working as fast, or as carefully. When errors occur, instead of correcting them, Chris just shrugs and refers the customer to Mario or Anthony. He understands why Chris is doing this, but it still doesn't seem right.

The way to solve a locus of control issue is to identify who the moral agent in this situation is. You are only the moral agent within your personal sphere of influence. Aaron must define the sphere within which he is capable of and responsible for acting, and ensure that all his behaviours and decisions within that area are ethical. The questions he must ask himself in order to accomplish this are:

- Who is behaving unethically?
- Who is responsible for supervising that person?
- Am I in a position to stop this behaviour? On what authority?
- Am I required to act unethically as a result of this behaviour?

- Who is being hurt by this behaviour? Am I ethically obligated to assist the injured parties? In what way?
- Can I live with this situation? If not, what options do I have?

As a result of considering these questions, it may become apparent that the problem needs to be redefined in a way that enables you to be the moral agent. In other words, what is the ethical issue that faces you because of this situation? Aaron, for example, might redefine his problem as being: "What must I do in order to remain personally and professionally ethical, given the situation in this workplace?" He is no longer trying to solve someone else's ethical issues, but has focused on what he should do within his sphere of influence. The answer may be to model ethical behaviour himself, even if others aren't, or perhaps to look for employment elsewhere.

Ethical Problems

An ethical problem is a situation which poses extremely difficult choices for living up to high ethical standards. For example, a moral or principle that is important to you is being challenged, but there is a barrier preventing you from doing what you know is right. Unlike a locus of control issue, in this case you are the moral agent (the person responsible for making the decision, also referred to as the decision-maker). The perfect resolution to an ethical problem would avoid compromising any personal and professional values, while still achieving a positive outcome for everyone concerned. Consider the following example:

> Arthur is the floor supervisor at a meat-packing plant. Although the plant is kept at a cool temperature, physical exertion causes the employees to work up a sweat. Jorge has been working here for almost three months. At first his co-workers accepted him, but during the last month Arthur has received numerous complaints that Jorge smells bad. People are beginning to refuse to work next to him. Arthur spoke to Jorge about this, but Jorge replied that he showers every morning before coming to work. The problem has even reached the manager, who advised Arthur to catch Jorge doing something wrong and let him go before his three-month trial period is up. This seems unfair to Arthur, since Jorge is a good worker, but how long can he keep forcing disgruntled employees to work beside him?

In order to resolve an ethical problem, the ethical agent must identify the barrier and overcome it. The principles of honesty and fairness will be violated if Arthur fires Jorge for a trumped-up reason. He knows it is not ethical to do so. But he is facing pressure from his manager and the workers he supervises and, quite frankly, talking to someone about body odour is not something he feels comfortable doing. Furthermore, he did approach Jorge and Jorge didn't take the hint, so Arthur is even more reluctant to bring it up again. In thinking it through, Arthur realizes that this is the real barrier for him, since the manager and the workers will be satisfied whichever way the problem is solved. When Arthur takes Jorge aside for a frank discussion about the problem, he learns that Jorge doesn't think he can afford to buy another pair of work clothes until he has a secure job, so he takes his work clothes home to be washed only on the weekend. Arthur tells Jorge of a cut-rate place to buy work clothes so he will have a spare pair and can wash them daily.

Ethical Dilemmas

An ethical dilemma is a situation in which morals and principles that are important to you are in conflict. You must choose between two or more courses of action, but there is no "right choice"; you must find the "most right" or "least wrong" alternative. The perfect solution to an ethical dilemma does not exist. Resolving it requires finding the option that upholds the most important principles and has the least negative outcome for everyone concerned. The following situation is an example of an ethical dilemma.

> Elizabeth's mother has three months to live. The oncologist has told Elizabeth this, but has also told her that her mother insisted, when she was first diagnosed, that if the disease progressed to the terminal stage she did not want to know. Now, a decision has to be made about whether to use heroic measures to prolong her life. The doctor has left it up to Elizabeth to either tell her mother the truth and let her make the decision, or lie to her about her condition and make the decision for her. Elizabeth must choose between honesty and respect for her mother's wishes. She must also choose between the principle of autonomy (allowing her mother the right to decide for herself whether life-prolonging measures should be used) and the principle of benevolence (doing what's best for her mother). If she chooses honesty and autonomy, she will not be respecting her mother's wishes, and will not be upholding the principle of benevolence. If she chooses respect and benevolence, she will be betraying the principles of honesty and autonomy. Elizabeth must also take the rest of the family into consideration. Should she tell them? Would she be putting them in the position of having to lie also? If she doesn't tell them, will they feel betrayed when they find out? Whose needs and rights are more important?

As Figure 9.1 demonstrates, the first step in resolving any of the three situations of ethical distress is identifying which cause is involved.

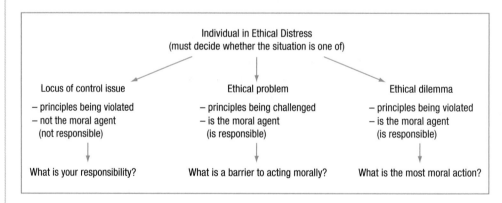

Figure 9.1

Determine which of the following is a locus of control issue (LOC), which is an ethical problem (EP) and which is an ethical dilemma (ED).

1. In a job interview you are asked if you are knowledgeable in the use of a software program that is essential for the position. You are going to take a course to learn the software, but it doesn't start for several months. The job starts next month. _____

2. You have just learned that your competitor won the academic award you were trying for. You know that he bought the major essay he handed in, in the one course where his grade was better than yours, while you wrote your own essay. _____

3. You're sent on an expensive training session at company cost with a co-worker who is also a friend. He is undergoing serious problems at home and you want to be supportive. On the second day he shows up drunk and makes some derogatory comments about your manager, then falls asleep in his chair. When you return home, you are both asked to train groups of employees on the new techniques. You know your friend won't be able to do this safely or effectively, since he missed half the session. _____

There are a number of methods that can be used to resolve an ethical dilemma. These techniques can also be useful in resolving ethical problems, since not all ethical problems are as straightforward as the example of Arthur and Jorge. Strategies for resolving an ethical dilemma fall into three classifications: *principle-based*, *reflection-based* and *procedure-based* methods.

Principle-based methods

A principle-based method is a way of organizing the principles we wish to live our lives by, so that when an ethical choice has to be made, some evaluation has already taken place. A code of ethics is principle-based. But a code of ethics alone doesn't help with ethical decision-making that involves conflicting principles, because it doesn't prioritize values or principles. A moral or priority compass can assist in identifying which morals or principles should take precedence in a situation that presents an ethical dilemma.

A moral compass is a personal evaluation of which morals and principles are most important to uphold. It tells us where "true north" lies when we need moral direction. If Elizabeth, in the previous ethical dilemma, had already created a moral compass for herself, it might look like this:

| **First** |
| Treat everyone with respect |

| **Second** | **Third** |
| Be compassionate | Be honest |

For Elizabeth, true north is respecting other people's opinions and values. She might think of this as "doing unto others what they would have you do unto them." Next is acting with compassion. Elizabeth believes "We are all responsible for helping each other," but this is subject to respecting others' wishes and beliefs. Finally, although Elizabeth believes in being honest with people, she has seen cruelty justified with the words "At least I'm honest," and she thinks that honesty should be subject to respect and compassion.

A moral compass is a reflection of our values; it is neither right nor wrong. Elizabeth could just as easily have the following moral compass:

| **First** |
| Always be honest |

| **Second** | **Third** |
| Treat everyone with respect | Be compassionate |

In this case, true north for Elizabeth is being honest. "Honesty is always the best policy in the long run," she might say. Next is being respectful of others. Elizabeth might consider this to be second because, in her opinion, being honest with people is her way of showing them respect. And finally, compassion for others is important to Elizabeth, but she does not consider it to be an excuse to avoid telling them the truth when necessary. A moral compass can also be created to deal with specific, recurring conflicts, such as demands or obligations at home and work. A person who is under pressure from many directions might write the following moral compass for himself:

| **First** |
| Meet the needs of my family |

| **Second** | **Third** |
| Act in the best interests of my career | Help out my friends |

It is important to note that a third priority is not a low priority. It is only subject to the first and second moral priorities when it is in conflict with them.

Reflection-based methods

A reflection-based method for resolving ethical problems and dilemmas is one that is based on personal reflection. This can take the form of answering a series of questions. The questions involved usually presuppose that a particular course of action is being considered, and the questions are intended to probe the ethical validity of that action. Reflection-based models are more helpful in resolving an ethical problem because the problem is not complicated by conflicting principles and the questions will not only examine the course of action being considered, but will also get at whether the barrier is ethically valid. If this method is being used to resolve an ethical dilemma, the questions should be posed for each possible course of action separately, and the results compared and evaluated to find the best solution.

The most common of these models is often referred to as the "ethics check questions." The three questions are:

- Is it legal? (Is the action being considered against the law? Does it violate any company policies or professional standards?)
- Is it balanced? (Is it fair to everyone who will be affected by it in the long term as well as the short term? Does it promote a win-win situation?)
- How will it make me feel about myself? (What is my "gut" feeling about the action? Will I be proud of myself afterward? Would I want my family, friends or neighbours to know it?)

Other models of this type usually include a more extensive list of questions that are intended to cause reflection on either the possible outcomes or the potential liabilities of the action.

Questions that direct attention to outcomes include: Which course of action will achieve my goal? Which will achieve the goal of my employer? Which will do the least harm to all concerned? Would I choose this option if I were in the position of the other people who will be affected by it? What are the likely long-term as well as short-term consequences? What are the wider implications of this action if my intention/message is understood? What are the implications if it is misunderstood?

Questions that direct attention to potential liabilities include: What is my real motive? What personal and professional obligations do I have in this situation? Could I defend this course of action before a legislative committee? What would my supervisor/CEO/board of directors or the legal counsel of my company say about it? What do my co-workers think of this option when I discuss the problem with them?

What other questions might be useful to reflect on before acting?

Procedure-based methods

A procedure-based method for resolving ethical dilemmas involves following a step-by-step process. This is more time-consuming than prioritizing ethical principles or reflecting on key questions, and is therefore usually reserved for more complex dilemmas where a number of people will be directly affected by whichever course of action is finally decided upon. Because it involves following a standardized procedure, however, the final decision is more objective, especially if more than one person is involved in the process. Furthermore, each step can be documented and held up for scrutiny afterwards. Therefore, this type of method for ethical decision-making is preferred when the outcomes may be serious and the decision-maker is likely to be held accountable for the consequences of his or her decision.

There are many procedure-based models, involving between six to ten steps, but all of them have similar components. The number of steps varies because in some models several components are grouped together into one step.

The individual components of a procedure-based model of ethical decision-making include:

- fact-finding
- issue identification
- identifying the stakeholders
- analyzing possible alternatives
- considering any practical constraints
- evaluating the alternatives
- implementing the chosen action
- monitoring the outcome

Each step involves a number of considerations.

The first three components—fact-finding, issue identification and identifying the stakeholders—should all be taken care of before any course of action is even considered. It is dangerous to make any decision without all the necessary information, and these three steps will give a clear picture of what must be taken into account in order to discover the most ethical resolution for the dilemma. The three steps are somewhat concurrent. Identifying the issues may uncover the need for more fact-finding; identifying the stakeholders may lead to discovering new ethical issues and, once again, require more fact-finding.

Fact-finding This involves a careful and thorough review of the facts and background context of the situation. Often an overlooked detail will resolve or alter the ethical issues. Consider this example:

> Dave and Gina are professors at Eastridge College. The college has very strict guidelines for preserving confidentiality when returning student papers. One day, Dave notices a cardboard box full of graded student papers sitting on the counter at the front of the room in which all the faculty office cubicles are located. Students arrive, sort through the papers, and leave throughout the day. Gina's name and class number are on the box. Dave is concerned that the students' privacy is not being respected, and this practice directly violates college policy. He isn't sure whether he should talk to Gina, to the students, or to the chair of the department.

The missing information here might be that Gina discussed this arrangement with her students and they agreed to receive their papers in this manner, rather than having to wait until their next class with her. Two students were not comfortable with this arrangement, and these students receive their papers directly from Gina in class. Knowing this would alleviate Dave's concerns.

Gathering all of the information will rarely completely resolve the dilemma, but it will help to clarify what ethical issues are involved and prevent mistakes that are embarrassing or worse. In recording the information gathered, factual neutrality is essential. "Gina is not respecting student confidentiality," is not a fact; it is a personal interpretation of the facts. The way the facts are stated can weight the issues before an ethical assessment has even begun.

Issue identification This step begins with a carefully considered statement of the ethical issue or issues involved. These may be personal, systemic and/or corporate. The personal or professional morals and principles that are in conflict should be clearly identified, as well as all relevant laws, company policies and procedures, and professional standards of practice that could apply to this situation. Next, identify which of those, if any, are being violated. Then reconsider whether this is a locus of control issue, an ethical problem or an ethical dilemma, and who the appropriate ethical agent in this situation is. Write down the ethical issue(s) involved.

In the previous example there are personal issues (Dave's personal values include respect and consideration for students) and corporate issues (Gina's procedure in returning marks appears to be against college policy). Two principles in conflict are loyalty to a colleague versus responsibility to students. A further issue is whether Dave is the appropriate moral agent in this situation. His responsibilities do not include monitoring colleagues. At this point, Dave might have reconsidered the three types of problems and decided that this was not an ethical dilemma but a locus of control issue.

Identifying the stakeholders A stakeholder is anyone who will be affected by the outcome of the action taken. If they will be affected, they can be considered to have a stake in the decision. This includes individuals as well as groups. It is important not to limit the list of stakeholders to those individuals who will be directly and immediately affected. Ethical decisions made by professionals will have an effect not only on colleagues in the same workplace, but also on other professionals in the same field, on current and future clients, and possibly on suppliers and people employed in related industries. Seeing the whole picture will often put concerns for the individual or individuals involved into perspective.

Considering the various individual stakeholders also means identifying their beliefs and values related to the situation and their issues. It is very difficult to determine what the outcome of a course of action will be for another person without knowing how she interprets the situation.

In the situation recounted earlier concerning Elizabeth and her dying mother, Elizabeth's decision will directly affect Elizabeth, her mother and all the members of her family. Elizabeth would be wrong to assume that her beliefs and values are shared by her mother and her family. While Elizabeth herself might wish to be told that her condition was terminal so she could prepare for death, her mother and family might prefer to retain hope to the very end. Elizabeth cannot determine the harm or benefits of telling or not telling her mother the truth without knowing her mother's beliefs and values concerning this issue and taking them into consideration.

Elizabeth's decision will also affect the doctors, nurses and other caretakers helping her mother, and may affect their treatment of other patients in the future. It may be a precedent-setting case for the hospital or for society. To a greater or lesser extent, all these people are stakeholders.

In a situation where the ethical agent is not closely related to the primary stakeholders, the divergence of values and beliefs is likely to be even greater, especially if different cultures or religious affiliations are involved. For example, a decision to hold monthly meetings with the sales staff on Saturday mornings could be seen to have the same outcome for everyone—one of their leisure days will be partially compromised, but they will all be paid overtime. However, a little fact-finding will show that the consequences are very different for different people:

> Tom has a part-time contract Saturday mornings that pays only two-thirds of what the overtime pay is and he is delighted to drop the contract in favour of the meetings. Mary has been able to arrange to take Wednesday afternoons off in lieu of Saturday mornings in order to volunteer at her daughters' school, which is something she has wanted to do for two years. She, too, is delighted to attend the meetings. Moshe and Abe are Jewish; working on Saturday violates their religious beliefs. They are so upset that they are planning to bring forward a grievance on grounds of discrimination.

Without this kind of fact-finding, it is impossible to accurately predict the consequences a decision will have on the other stakeholders.

Analyzing possible alternatives At this stage in the process, the ethical agent should list all the possible courses of action open to him. The alternatives should all be written out, but only those actions within the ethical agent's power can be considered. To go back to our earlier example, Dave cannot include in his alternatives "Gina could stop distributing student papers in this manner" because Dave cannot control Gina's behaviour, only his own. Instead he might write down "Talk to Gina tomorrow about student confidentiality and college policy and try to persuade her to stop distributing student papers in this manner." This he can do; however, he should accompany this with a follow-up course of action within an identified time frame, in case Gina refuses, or agrees but then doesn't change her behaviour.

Table 9.1 Analyzing Possible Alternatives

Principles and Consequences	Values and Principles Upheld: Explain how	Values and Principles Violated: Explain how	Probable Outcome and Short-term Impact: How likely?	Probable Outcome and Long-term Impact: How likely?	Laws, Policies, Standards Obeyed or Disobeyed
Alternative #1: Dave does nothing					
Stakeholder #1: Dave	Support and respect colleagues: Dave is respecting Gina	Students' confidentiality: Dave is enabling Gina to violate this	Dave is not comfortable with Gina and feels ethical distress	If a student complains Dave could be at fault for not reporting	College policy about reporting unethical practices
Stakeholder #2: Gina	Support and respect colleagues: Gina feels respected by peers	Students' confidentiality: Gina isn't made aware of problem	Gina will continue current practice	Sometime a student will complain: Gina gets in trouble	College policy about returning papers and grades
Stakeholder #3: Gina's students	None	Students' confidentiality is being violated by a professor	Students may be upset: their grades may suffer	If a student complains, he may be known as a troublemaker	College policy about students' rights
Alternative #2: Dave speaks to supervisor					
Stakeholder #1: Dave					
Stakeholder #2: Gina					
Stakeholder #3: Gina's students					

When all possible courses of action have been identified, they must be analyzed one by one. This means writing down, for each course of action, any law, company policy or professional standard that will be obeyed or disobeyed, the principles that will be upheld and those that will be violated for each stakeholder, the possible outcomes (long-term and short-term), and the likely impact (long-term and short-term) on each of the stakeholders. Since outcomes are to some extent unpredictable, the likelihood of each potential consequence and impact should also be stated. The impacts on various stakeholders must take into account the beliefs and values of the stakeholder as much as possible. It would be helpful to seek input from the people involved in order to determine this. Information in the analysis should be objective and descriptive.

There is a lot of information to analyze in this step. It would be helpful to use a graph to record it all. The next step, evaluating the alternatives, will be easier if the analysis is clearly written and easy to follow. The table on pages 301-302 at the end of this chapter (Analyzing Alternatives) could be helpful. An example of how to use the table appears on page 290, using Dave's dilemma over Gina's manner of returning papers. Practice analyzing alternatives by filling in the second alternative for the three stakeholders identified.

Considering any practical constraints Any practical constraints that could prevent a course of action from being implemented must also be considered. For example, if the budget for professional development is depleted for this fiscal year, then this is a practical constraint against asking the department chair to arrange a workshop for college professors on ethical evaluation and student feedback procedures.

Table 9.2 Analyzing Practical Constraints

Alternative #1	There are no practical constraints against Dave doing nothing.
Alternative #2	

Evaluating the alternatives Evaluating the alternatives is different from analyzing them. The analysis should have provided a comprehensive picture of each alternative in terms of principles, consequences, impacts and their likelihood. Now this information must be evaluated. The most ethical alternative is not necessarily the course of action that violates the fewest principles and has a negative impact on the fewest number of people. Not all principles are of equal weight, and not all stakeholders will be equally impacted.

How a principle is violated must be considered. A "little white lie," such as an insincere compliment to avoid hurting someone's feelings, is very different from a life-threatening deception, such as denying being HIV-positive to a sexual partner and not using a condom. Both these examples violate the principle of honesty, but no one would judge them to be of equal weight. The first example violates the principle in an insignificant way, the second example in a significant way. The difference in the significance of the violation has to do with both the intention of the person violating the principle and the potential consequences. In the case of the insincere compliment, the intention is benevolent and the potential consequences will not be harmful. In the second example, the intention is to gain personal gratification at another's expense, and the potential consequences are that the misinformed and unprotected sexual partner could contract AIDS and die.

When evaluating the alternatives, how a principle is upheld is as important as how it is violated. An ethical alternative should not only avoid violating important principles, but should uphold them in a significant way. For example, if his girlfriend doesn't ask certain questions, a man is not lying when he refrains from volunteering information. The principle of honesty is not being actively violated. However, it is not being actively upheld either. Giving his girlfriend important information that is in her best interest to know, even if she did not ask about it, is upholding the principle of honesty in a significant way.

Some of the outcomes and impacts listed in the alternatives table will be more likely to occur than others. The information gathered in the fact-finding stage and the stakeholder identification stage will help to determine this. For example, Elizabeth's sister believes strongly in respecting other people's wishes. Therefore, she is less likely to feel betrayed when she learns that Elizabeth withheld the seriousness of her mother's condition than their brother, who believes in honesty at any cost and is no great respecter of opinions that don't coincide with his.

The practical constraints listed for some alternatives will also indicate the likelihood that they will successfully achieve the intended outcome. In Dave's situation at Eastridge College, one possible alternative might be a staff meeting to discuss preserving confidentiality for students. If, however, in the practical constraint table Dave has written that Gina rarely attends staff meetings, then a staff meeting on the subject is unlikely to produce the desired outcome of changing Gina's practices because she is not likely to be there.

Ethical decisions must be based on principles and consequences, not on personal likes and dislikes, in order to make the decision as fair and impartial as possible. This is in line with the principle of Equal Consideration of Interests (ECI). ECI does not negate self-interest, but demands that the interests of the ethical agent making the decision should have the same weight as the interests of any other stakeholder.

However, evaluating the alternatives means making value judgments, and a value judgment is based on personal opinion. It involves prioritizing the principles and values in conflict; judging the significance of how each alternative upholds or violates these values; determining which long- and short-term impacts are more serious and which are less serious; indicating which outcomes are more likely than others and why; and deciding which laws, policies and professional standards must be upheld and which can be bent for a greater good. There are some situations when principles and consequences may be in conflict. Sometimes the best outcome may be achieved only by breaking a moral principle. In the case of Elizabeth and her dying mother, Elizabeth may know that her mother is prone to depression and that the likely outcome of telling her the true state of her health is that she will succumb to despair. If, on the other hand, Elizabeth lies to her mother and tells her that the doctor says her chances of recovery are good, her mother will continue to hope and will be much happier during her last few weeks. Elizabeth's intentions are benevolent and she believes that violating the principle of honesty in this case will lead to the best outcome for her mother.

Evaluating the alternatives also includes documenting decisions. The reasons for making the above value judgments must be stated in order to justify selecting one alternative and discarding the others. The ethical rationalization for a course of action should include the following considerations:

- Whether it supports the principle of ECI
- Which conflicting values and principles are more/most important and why
- Whether it upholds important values or principles in a significant way
- Whether other alternatives violate or fail to uphold important values or principles in a significant way
- Which outcomes and impacts are more/most important and why
- Which outcomes and impacts are more/most likely and why
- Why this course of action is more likely to have the best outcome
- Why this course of action is more likely to promote the most significant positive impacts and/or avoid the most significant negative impacts on all stakeholders

Implementing the chosen action Having chosen the best alternative, we now need to consider how it should be implemented in order to achieve the desired outcome. The method of implementing a decision will influence, to a greater or lesser extent depending on what the course of action is, how the decision is received, how it is interpreted and ultimately how successful it is in achieving the desired outcome. Potential negative impacts can be lessened and likely positive impacts can be increased by a well thought-out implementation plan. And if there is any question of future liability, it is just as important to document and be able to justify the process of implementing a decision as it is to document and be able to justify the decision itself. If possible, without breaching confidentiality, the decision should be shared with the other stakeholders before being implemented. If the course of action requires sharing information with someone, careful consideration should be given to what specific information should be shared, including what does not need to be shared, to whom the information should be given, when and where it should be given, and what format the communication should take. Is this something that should or should not be shared through an email, a telephone conversation, a face-to-face meeting? Should it be put in writing? Is there a way it can be divulged anonymously, and if so, are there reasons for taking this route?

Every implementation plan should include a time frame, a specific and detailed process which can be justified, and a method of monitoring the outcome.

Monitoring the outcome An important part of ethical decision-making is accepting responsibility for the outcome of our decisions. Consciously following this step-by-step process should make unforeseen results less likely, but no one can predict every outcome of a decision. The other people involved may respond in unexpected ways, and there are always missing facts. However thoroughly the first step of this process is carried out, no decision-maker can possibly know everything about a situation. Decision-makers should be concerned about missing information, but not unduly so. Otherwise the entire process would come to a dead halt at step one. While deliberately delaying action is sometimes an ethical choice, indefinitely postponing a decision is not.

The outcome should be monitored and evaluated to determine whether the goal was successfully met, whether the important principles were upheld and interpreted by everyone involved as having been upheld, and whether the impact on the various stakeholders was what had been anticipated. If any of these three aspects of the outcome are unsuccessful, the decision-maker will have to determine why, and what should be done to correct the problem.

The implementation process should also be evaluated. If the outcome was not as expected, it is possible that the process and not the decision itself was at fault. Even if all three aspects of the outcome turned out satisfactorily, the implementation plan should be evaluated. Determining what went well and what went badly in the process will provide valuable information for implementing future decisions.

EXERCISE 9.2

Using the Procedure-based Model

Participants should form groups of four to five members. Each group will be given one of the case studies at the end of this chapter. Your task is to resolve the ethical dilemma presented in the case study by working through the eight steps of the procedure-based model: fact-finding, issue identification, identifying the stakeholders, analyzing possible alternatives, considering any practical constraints, evaluating the alternatives, implementing the chosen action and monitoring the outcome. You may invent missing information, but it must be consistent with the rest of the dilemma. Use the chart titled "Analyzing Alternatives" on pages 301–302 at the end of this chapter and hand it in to your professor with your completed analysis and resolution of the case study.

After you have reached a resolution you all agree on, your group should discuss what it has learned about using the procedure-based model and resolving an ethical dilemma as a group.

Each group will present its case study and resolution to the rest of the class. In order to justify your resolution you must demonstrate in detail an appropriate and thorough application of each step, including a visual of the completed table analyzing the alternatives, and be prepared to answer questions at the end of your presentation. When all the groups have made their presentations, the entire class should discuss the benefits and disadvantages of resolving an ethical dilemma individually or as a group.

Creating a Personal Action Plan for Ethical Decision-Making

What is the best method of resolving ethical problems and dilemmas? What is the best way to live with locus of control issues that disturb us? Each person will answer these questions differently, and different situations will require different approaches. One of the drawbacks of procedure-based methods is that they are time-consuming. Not all decisions can wait, although if the consequences may be serious it is usually wise to take the time to work through the method. The descriptive analysis of the organization should be conducted separately from the process of setting normative standards for the organization.

Not all ethical problems, or even all ethical dilemmas, are complex enough to require the use of a procedure-based method. One or more of the steps may be unnecessary in a given situation, or it may be necessary to add another step that the decision-maker feels is important.

A personal action plan for ethical decision-making should include some reflection on how to cope with locus of control issues, and at least two methods of resolving ethical problems and ethical dilemmas. One method should be relatively straightforward and timely, such as a priority compass, and the other should be a procedure-based model for complex dilemmas with potentially serious consequences for one or more of the stakeholders.

Figure 9.2 shows the types of ethical distress and how an individual can resolve them.

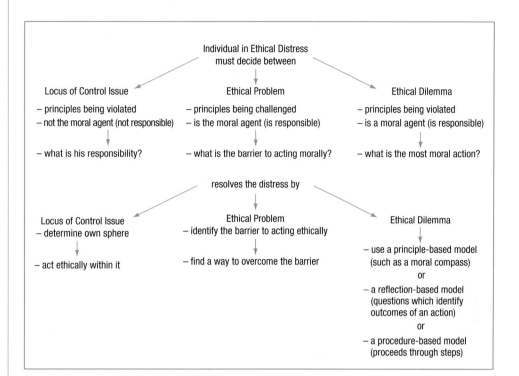

Figure 9.2

EXERCISE 9.3

Action Plan for Ethical Decision-making

How will you resolve ethical distress? Create your own action plan either by using some of the methods you have learned in this chapter or by creating your own methods. You must take into consideration both moral principles and consequences in your plan.

Locus of control issues:

_____

_____

_____

_____

_____

_____

(Continued)

(Continued)

_____

_____

_____

Straightforward or time-sensitive ethical problems and dilemmas:

_____

_____

_____

_____

_____

_____

_____

Procedure-based model for complex ethical dilemmas:

_____

_____

_____

_____

_____

_____

_____

_____

_____

_____

EXERCISE 9.4

Using Your Action Plan

Consider an ethical dilemma you or someone you know has faced or could be faced with. Write it out, including as many details as possible. Then, using your version of a procedure-based model (which could be the same as the one in this text or one adapted to suit you) resolve the dilemma step by step.

> *"Reputation is what other people know about you; honour is what you know about yourself."*
>
> —LOIS MCMASTER BUJOLD (1999)

Answers

EXERCISE 9.1:   1. EP   2. LOC   3. ED

EIGHT CASE STUDIES OF ETHICAL DILEMMAS FOR STUDENTS TO RESOLVE

These eight case studies can be used for class discussions or for Exercise 9.2. The following questions should be considered for each case study:

- What are the ethical issues involved?
- What are the relevant facts?
- Is there any missing information you should seek?
- What is your initial response?
- What is the best method of resolution?

Case Study #1

Your best friend has just told you that she's pregnant. She says she hasn't told her boyfriend because she knows he would want to keep the baby, and she just can't go through with it. They're too young to get married and she doesn't want to have to drop out of school. You and she have always been pro-lifers, but she says this has changed her opinion and she's going to have an abortion. She wants you to go with her and to back her up when she tells her boyfriend she's staying with you for a "girls' night." You still believe in pro-life, and besides, even though you've never been interested in dating her boyfriend, you've been friends with him a long time. In fact, you introduced them. What should you do?

Case Study #2

A close friend of yours was in a car accident and has just been told he will be paralyzed from the waist down. The next day, when you visit him in hospital, he asks if he can trust you with a secret. You tell him, "Of course," but then he tells you he'd rather die than spend the rest of his life in a wheelchair, and that he intends to die. He says it will be better for his parents, too, when he's dead, because otherwise they'll always have to take care of him or pay someone else to. You try to talk him out of it, but he says he's made up his mind, and he has a right to make decisions about his own life. Then he says, "This is just between us. You said I could trust you, or I wouldn't have told you." You leave, hoping that he just needed someone to listen to him and doesn't really mean it. If you betray his confidence, he'll be furious, and right now he really needs your friendship. What should you do?

Case Study #3

Ayesha, a fellow employee at the Tim Hortons on your campus, is your friend, but she repeatedly shows up late for work. You and others have covered for her in the past, but some of the other part-timers are beginning to resent her tardiness and several have made comments to her about it. Sometimes a student working there has been late for a class because he or she couldn't leave until Ayesha arrived. However, she has not responded to peer pressure to correct her behaviour.

One day, she missed a shift entirely. Someone told the manager, and now Ayesha has come to you and asked you to corroborate her story that she called in sick that evening. You were working that evening and you know she didn't call. In fact, the next morning in school she told you she'd been on a date with a good-looking guy in one of her classes. There aren't many jobs on campus, and you only got this job because Ayesha was already employed at Tim Hortons and she told the manager you were a good worker, so you feel you owe her for that. Besides, she's your friend, and shouldn't friends stand by each other? If you tell on Ayesha, you will lose a friend, and she might tell other students that you ratted on her. However, her behaviour is disrupting the morale at work and making things difficult for everyone.

Case Study #4

Your suite-mate, Marie, has been skipping classes for the past three weeks, apparently spending the whole time on her computer. She quit her job, makes excuses when you or her other friends ask her to go out with them, and has even started eating snacks in her room instead of going out for meals. You're afraid she might be gambling or gaming; whatever it is, it seems like it's taking over her life. She's losing weight and not sleeping and she looks terrible. When you asked her about it, she said she was "working on something" and wouldn't talk any more about it. Should you leave her alone, like she seems to want, or try to do something? And if so, what?

Case Study #5

You and four friends have rented a house to live in while you're at college. One evening, hanging with your house-mates and some other friends, someone suggests a midnight raid on the campus. It sounds like a harmless prank—removing some signs, leaving suggestive graffiti on classroom whiteboards and around the campus, "relocating" a school mascot, releasing crickets in the cafeteria and plugging all the keyboards into the wrong computers in the computer labs. Everyone agrees to meet at the west entrance of the main building at midnight. You're not really comfortable with the idea, but all your friends are in on it so you decide to go along. When you arrive at the west entrance, however, instead of eight people, there are at least fifteen, and one of them is a guy called "Mallo." You don't know whether that's a nickname or a short form of his real name, but he gives you the creeps, and you avoid him even though he's friends with one of your house-mates. Three other guys who hang with him are also there, and everyone seems pretty drunk. You're getting a bad feeling about this whole escapade. Pretty soon your fears are realized when Mallo and his gang start throwing furniture out the windows. Without calling attention to yourself, you slip out of the room and return home. Next morning the police are on campus. You learn that over a dozen computers were smashed, the mascot was destroyed and a security guard was beaten so badly that he's in the hospital. Police are asking anyone who knows anything about the raid to come forward. You talk to one of your house-mates at lunch and she says, "I was so drunk I don't remember very much after the four of us moved that mascot together. But if anyone talks, we're all in serious trouble." She doesn't remember you leaving and doesn't believe you when you say you did. What should you do?

Case Study #6

You work part-time at Northern Alternatives, a large clothing store. Although you are paid a salary and are not on commission, a key component of the over-all job evaluation at this site is the amount of sales you generate. Sales are tracked on an individual basis and are reported on the honour system. There are specific rules regarding what can and can't be counted as a sale. For example, if a customer comes in and buys the loss leader (an item advertised on sale to attract customers into the store) it does not count, but any additional items you sell that customer as accessories do. Also, if a customer brings in a gift coupon, you can count any sales above the amount on the card, but not the ones covered by the gift card.

One day another part-time worker confides to you that he is counting sales that don't qualify. He further informs you that management isn't checking the results for accuracy. This employee has recently been given an award of recognition for sales volume. A week later, you hear a rumour that the company is planning to downsize its sales force after Christmas, which is four months away. Competition for sales has increased noticeably. You wonder whether you should count sales that don't qualify, or perhaps report the employee who has been breaking the rules.

Case Study #7

There's a girl on campus whom nobody much likes, named Jasmine. She hangs around your group of friends because none of you are cruel enough to tell her outright to get lost, though there have been lots of hints, which she hasn't taken. She overhears talk about a house party you're all going to. When you arrive, the place is already packed with students. At one point you notice her there, sitting alone with a drink. Later in the night, you're surprised to see one of the guys in your group, Simon, talking and laughing with her. He spends quite a while with her, and brings her several drinks. You notice this because you like Simon, and you're a bit annoyed that his attention will just encourage her to hang around even more. You've heard him make fun of her when she's not around, so why is he doing this now? An hour later, when you go upstairs to pee, you hear someone crying in a bedroom. You open the door. Jasmine is lying on the bed with her skirt up, crying. Simon is pulling his pants up. He zips and brushes past you, saying, "Just ignore her, she's drunk. She wanted me to do it, anyway." You close the door again, telling yourself it's not your concern. Jasmine doesn't come near your group again; in fact, she starts skipping the class that you and Simon and she are in together. Should you do or say something about what you saw?

Case Study #8

A couple of friends ask you to go clubbing with them on Thursday. You tell them you have to work on the major essay for a course you're all in together. The paper is due Friday, and you wish you'd started earlier, like they must have. They laugh and tell you about a website where you can buy essays cheap, and mention the names of a couple of students who did it last semester with the same professor and never got caught. "Why do all that work if you don't have to?" says one of your friends. "If the prof can't catch us, that's her problem." You write your own essay anyway, but when they're handed back, you get a B while they both get A's. It doesn't seem fair, but what can you do? They're both popular with other students, and if you rat on them, they'll tell everyone to avoid you. Maybe you should just buy your next essay, too?

The following graph is a helpful tool to record the information needed to analyze alternatives.

ANALYZING ALTERNATIVES

Principles and Consequences	Values and Principles Upheld: Explain how	Values and Principles Violated: Explain how	Probable Outcome and Short-term Impact: How likely?	Probable Outcome and Long-term Impact: How likely?	Laws, Policies, Standards Obeyed/ Disobeyed
Alternative #1					
Stakeholder #1 (the moral agent)					
Stakeholder #2					
Stakeholder #3					
Stakeholder #4					
Alternative #2					
Stakeholder #1					
Stakeholder #2					
Stakeholder #3					
Stakeholder #4					

Principles and Consequences	Values and Principles Upheld: Explain how	Values and Principles Violated: Explain how	Probable Outcome and Short-term Impact: How likely?	Probable Outcome and Long-term Impact: How likely?	Laws, Policies, Standards Obeyed/ Disobeyed
Alternative #3					
Stakeholder #1					
Stakeholder #2					
Stakeholder #3					
Stakeholder #4					
Alternative #4					
Stakeholder #1					
Stakeholder #2					
Stakeholder #3					
Stakeholder #4					

REFERENCES

Abortion statistics. www.womensissues.about.com/cs/abortionststs.htm.

Annan, Kofi (2001). *Development Without Borders*. Harvard International Review, Summer, 2001.

Baird, F. E. & Kaufmann, W. (2003). *Ancient Philosophy*, 4th Ed. New Jersey: Prentice-Hall Inc.

Baird, F. E. & Kaufmann, W. (2003). *Modern Philosophy*, 4th Ed. New Jersey: Prentice-Hall Inc.

Baird, F. E. & Kaufmann, W. (2003). *Nineteenth-Century Philosophy*, 3rd Ed. New Jersey: Prentice-Hall Inc.

Becker, Elizabeth (2003, Sept. 9). Western Farmers Fear Third-World Challenge to Subsidies. *The New York Times*, p. A8.

Bertuzzi was ordered off ice before Moore hit, lawyer says. Canadian Press (2008, January 26). Kitchener *Record*, p. E1.

Bliss, Michael. Who Discovered Insulin. physiologyonline.physiology.org/cgi/reprint/1/1/31.pdf.

Brean, Joseph (2008). Hate Speech Complaint Dismissed. *National Post*, retrieved June 28, 2008 from www.nationalpost.com/related/topics/story.html.

Brean, Joseph (2008). Human rights body to review Internet role. *National Post*, retrieved June 18, 2008 from www.nationalpost.com/related/topics/story.html.

Cahn, S. M. & Markie, P. (2002). *Ethics: History, Theory and Contemporary Issues*, 2nd Ed. New York: Oxford University Press.

Callahan, S. A. (1999). Feminist Case Against Assisted Suicide and Euthanasia. *The American Feminist*, retrieved Summer, 1999 from www.feministsforlife.org/taf/1999/summer/conas&eu.htm.

Canada Is Mismanaging Its Foreign Aid (2008, June 25). *National Post*, retrieved June 28 from www.nationalpost.com/opinion/story.html?id=610991.

Canada, Department of Justice (1982). Canadian Charter of Rights and Freedoms. Ottawa, ON: Queen's Printer for Canada. http://laws.justice.gc.ca/en/.

Canada's Federal Budget and Foreign Aid. www.ccic.ca/e/docs/002_aid_2005_fed_budget_analysis.pdf.

Canada's Foreign Aid Levels. CTV News (2005, April 19), retrieved June 24 from www.ctv.ca/servlet/ArticleNews/story/CTVNews/111391582447.

Canadian Federation of Humane Societies. http://cfhs.ca/research/medical_testing.

Canadian Institute of Health Research (CIHR). www.cihr-irsc.gc.ca/e/34460.html.

Canadian International Development Agency (CIDA). www.acdi-cida.nsf/en/NIC-5313423.

Coach joins Bertuzzi in lawsuit. Canadian Press (2008, March 29). Kitchener *Record*, p. E3.

Criminal Code of Canada Hate Provisions: Summary. www.media-awareness.ca/english/resources/legislation/canadian_law/federal.

Cruse, Amy (1957). *The Book of Myths*. Toronto: Clarke, Irwin & Company Limited.

Dallaire, Senator General Romeo (2008). CBC Interview, retrieved June 17, 2008 from www.cbc.ca/national/blog/video/transcripts/senator_general_romeo_dallaire.

Discovery Institute, Bioethics. www.discovery.org/scripts/viewDB/index.php?command=view&program=DI%20.

Edwards and Mazzuca (1999, March 24). "Three-quarters of Canadians support doctor-assisted suicide." Princeton, NJ: The Gallop Organization, Gallop Poll Releases. www.gallup.com/poll/releases.

Elshatain, Jean Bethke (2003). *Just War Against Terror: The Burden of American Power in a Violent World*. New York: Basic Books, p. 115.

Euthanasia and Women (2003). Retrieved June 2008 from www.SPUC.org.UK.

Gilligan, C. (1982). *In a Different Voice: Psychological Theory and Women's Development*. Cambridge, MA: Harvard University Press.

Hawaleshka, Danylo (2005, September 5). "We Are Killing." *Maclean's*, p. 26.

Helped Son Kill Himself, Woman Gets Probation. Canadian Press (2006, Jan. 27). Toronto *Star*. Retrieved from www.thestar.com.

Homes, Mrs. Hilary (2008, May 12), addressing the Subcommittee on International Human Rights of the Standing Committee on Foreign Affairs and International Development. (Retrieved June 17, 2008 from http://cmte.parl.gc.ca/cmte/ CommitteePublication) http://archive.makepovertyhistory.ca/e/aim3.html?q=e/ aim3.html#aid.

International Society for Stem Cell Research, The. www.isscr.org/public.

International Task Force on Euthanasia and Assisted Suicide, prepared for the World Medical Association. www.internationaltaskforce.org/rpt2005_3.htm.

Internet Encyclopedia of Philosophy, The. Just War Theory. Retrieved June 4, 2008 from http://www.iep.utm.edu/j/justwar.htm.

Kuebler, Lt. Commander (2008). CBC Interview. Retrieved June 17, 2008 from www. cbc.ca/national/blog/video/transcripts/lt_commander_william_kuebler.html.

Kingston, A. (2007, May 14). It's So Not Cool. *Maclean's* Magazine, pp. 38–41.

Leopold, A. *Sand County Almanac*. New York: Oxford University Press, p. 262.

Mallick, Heather (2003, January 18). Why Doesn't This Man Have the Order of Canada? Toronto *Globe and Mail*. Retrieved June11, 2008 from www.theglobeandmail.com/ series/morgantaler.

MacKinnon, Barbara (2007). *Ethics: Theory and Contemporary Issues*, 5th Ed. Florence, KY: Thompson/Wadsworth.

Millennium Development Goals. www.un.org/millenniumgoals/pdf/mdg2007.pdf.

Padwell, Terry (2008, July 2). Morgentaler Named to Order of Canada. Kitchener *Record*, p. A3.

Panel on the Ecological Integrity of Canada's National Parks, Unimpaired for Future.

Parks Canada (2000). http://www.pc.gc.ca/docs/pc/rpts/ie-ei/report-rapport_1_e.asp.

Partners in Research. http://www.pirweb.org/pir03d_facts.htm.

Quotations on Euthanasia. www.euthanasia.com/quotationsoneuthanasia.html); also www.euthanasia.com/argumentsagainsteuthanasia.html.

Running Off Track: the Ben Johnson story. CBC Digital Archives. Sachs, Jeffrey (2005, March 14). The End of Poverty. *Time* Magazine, p. 46.

Sampson et al. v State of Alaska (2001, September 9). www.euthanasia.com/ quotationsoneuthanasia.html.

Schweitzer, A. (1949). *Out of My Life and Thought*. New York: Holt, Rinehart & Winston.

Singer, P. (1979). *Practical Ethics*. Cambridge, UK: Cambridge University Press.

Singer, Peter (1972, Spring). Famine, Affluence and Morality. *Philosophy and Public Affairs*, Vol.1, No. 3. Princeton, NJ: Princeton University Press, pp.229–243.

Singer, Peter (1975). *Animal Liberation: A New Ethic for Our Treatment of Animals*. New York: Random House.

Skelton, Chad (2006, May 27). Jail Time = Less Crime. The Vancouver *Sun*.

Steinbock, Bonnie (1978, April). Speciesism and the Idea of Equality. *Philosophy*, vol. 53, no. 204, pp. 247–256.

Suicide Factsheets, NRLC Dept. of Medical Ethics, Washington D.C. www.euthanasia. com/debate.html.

Tucker, Robert W. (1960). *The Just War*. Baltimore: Johns Hopkins University Press.

Wood, Chris (1994, Feb 28). The Legacy of Sue Rodrigues. *Maclean's*, p. 21.

INDEX